Praise for Amy S. Greenberg's

A Wicked War

"In her absorbing and valuable *A Wicked War,* Penn State's Amy S. Greenberg does a splendid job of vivifying this disgraceful episode in American history." —*Reason*

"The seldom-sung Mexican War emerges as one of America's most morally ambiguous and divisive conflicts in this illuminating history." —*Publishers Weekly*

"A provocative main idea in a freshly original narrative." —*Booklist*

"Amy Greenberg's original and moving narrative of the U.S. invasion of Mexico relates the gradual loss of enthusiasm for waging what began as a popular war of conquest. How peace ultimately prevailed is the most surprising part of her story." —Daniel Walker Howe, Pulitzer Prize–winning author of *What Hath God Wrought*

"No less a warrior than Ulysses S. Grant had good reason to decry the war with Mexico as 'wicked.' In Amy S. Greenberg's dramatic and deeply engaging political narrative, the reader gets the grit of the campaign and rich insight into the fascinating historical actors who stage-managed (or resisted) this all-important, under-studied war. In these fast-turning pages, we see clashes among political opportunists, moments of eloquence, and pathos—all under the rising sun of American power." —Andrew Burstein and Nancy Isenberg, authors of *Madison and Jefferson*

"*A Wicked War* gives the U.S.-Mexican War a personal dimension and immediacy that has been lacking until now. Amy Greenberg makes us live the war vicariously through the lives of the aging patriarch Henry Clay, who lost a son in Mexico; the husband-and-wife presidential team of James K. and Sarah Polk; the lanky and somewhat disheveled Abraham Lincoln, still learning about politics; and others. This is a rare melding of great storytelling and analysis of an era that shaped not only the United States but the entire North American continent."

—Andrés Reséndez, author of *A Land So Strange*

"*A Wicked War*, with its emphasis on politics rather than military history, does for the Mexican-American War what James McPherson did for the Civil War with *Battle Cry of Freedom*, greatly broadening our understanding of the war. Certainly Professor Greenberg's book will immediately become the standard account of the Mexican War, at last giving it an important place in the history of the United States. This book restores my faith in the merits of narrative history."   —Mark E. Neely, Jr.,
Pulitzer Prize–winning author of *The Fate of Liberty*

AMY S. GREENBERG

A Wicked War

Amy S. Greenberg is Edwin Erle Sparks Professor of History and Women's Studies at Penn State University. She is a leading scholar of Manifest Destiny and has held fellowships from the Guggenheim Foundation, the Huntington Library, the New-York Historical Society, and the American Philosophical Society. Her previous books include *Manifest Manhood and the Antebellum American Empire*, *Manifest Destiny and American Territorial Expansion*, and *Cause for Alarm: The Volunteer Fire Department in the Nineteenth-Century City*. She lives in State College, Pennsylvania, with her husband and two children.

A Wicked War

A Wicked War

Polk, Clay, Lincoln, and the 1846
U.S. Invasion of Mexico

AMY S. GREENBERG

VINTAGE BOOKS
A Division of Random House, Inc.
New York

FIRST VINTAGE BOOKS EDITION, AUGUST 2013

The Library of Congress has cataloged the Knopf edition as follows:
Greenberg, Amy S.
A wicked war : Polk, Clay, Lincoln, and the 1846 U.S. invasion of Mexico /
by Amy S. Greenberg.—1st ed.
p. cm.
Includes bibliographical references.
1. Mexican War, 1846–1848. 2. Mexican War, 1846–1848—Political
aspects—United States. 3. Mexican War, 1846–1848—Influence.
4. Polk, James K. (James Knox), 1795–1849. 5. Clay, Henry, 1777–1852.
6. Lincoln, Abraham, 1809–1865. I. Title.
E404.G79 2012
973.6'2—dc23 2012019887

Vintage ISBN: 978-0-307-47599-2

Maps by Mapping Specialists, Ltd.
Author photograph © Fred Weber
Book design by Maggie Hinders

www.vintagebooks.com

Printed in the United States of America
10 9 8 7

For Rich, Jackson, and Violet

I do not think there was ever a more wicked war than that waged by the United States on Mexico. I thought so at the time, when I was a youngster, only I had not moral courage enough to resign.

—ULYSSES S. GRANT, 1879

Contents

Maps and Images

Introduction

THIS IS THE STORY of five men, four years, and one foreign war. Henry Clay, James K. Polk, Abraham Lincoln, John J. Hardin, and Nicholas Trist were bound together in unexpected political and personal battle during the years 1844–48 as America's war against Mexico unfolded, then stumbled to an end. That conflict, which breached George Washington's injunction to avoid entanglements abroad, was an act of expansionist aggression against a neighboring country. It reshaped the United States into lord of the continent and announced the arrival of a new world power. The U.S.-Mexican conflict also tipped an internecine struggle over slavery into civil war. Though both its justification and its consequences are dim now, this, America's first war against another republic, decisively broke with the past, shaped the future, and to this day affects how the United States acts in the world.

This is also a story about politics, slavery, Manifest Destiny, Indian killing, and what it meant to prove one's manhood in the nineteenth century. It explores the meaning of moral courage in America, the importance of legacies passed between generations, and the imperatives that turn politicians into leaders. And it attempts to explain why the United States invaded a neighboring country and how it came to pass that a substantial number of Americans determined to stop the ensuing war.

This is not a comprehensive history of the U.S.-Mexican War. Military tactics, minor battles, and General Stephen Kearny's Army of the West receive limited coverage in these pages.[1] Nor does this volume fully explore the Mexican side of the conflict.[2] What this volume offers instead is a narrative history of the war that Ulysses S. Grant deemed America's most "wicked," as seen through the eyes of five men, their wives, and their children. Their views are in many cases radically different from our own, their justifications often impure, and the results of their actions sometimes at odds with their intentions. But all were forced to sacrifice what was dear to them in the name of something greater: justice, morality, and America's destiny. Their experiences help us understand how the war and its unintended consequences shaped the meanings of American identity, ethics, and patriotism.

Two of these characters will likely be unfamiliar. Colonel John J. Hardin was a congressman from Illinois and the first in his state to volunteer to fight Mexico. During his political career he was well known throughout Illinois and Washington, D.C., and an Illinois county seat was named in his honor. His obscurity today is largely the result of a tragic early death on a Mexican battlefield. Hardin has no published biography, and until now few historians have thought his life worth exploring.[3] But his martyrdom at the Battle of Buena Vista made him a national hero, and in the mid-1840s he was Abraham Lincoln's greatest political rival. His death removed a key obstacle from Lincoln's rise to power.

John J. Hardin commands attention not only for his military fame and relationship with Abraham Lincoln but also because he was, in many ways, typical of the men who volunteered to fight Mexico. A self-described patriot, Hardin was both a warrior and a member of the opposition Whig Party from a western state where James K. Polk's Democratic Party held the balance of power. Like thousands of other Whigs, he volunteered to fight despite distrusting both Polk and his objectives. He firmly believed that patriotism knew no party, and that it was the destiny of the United States to expand into Mexico. But like many other soldiers, Hardin lost his faith in America's Manifest Destiny during the course of his service. Although his name is now forgotten, this study will reveal the surprising legacy of Hardin's life and death, which lives on today.

Nicholas Trist is somewhat better known. His name appears in most studies of the 1846 war, although few people know much about the man who defied his president and his party to bring the war to a close. Trist has not commanded much historical attention, but he was one of the best-pedigreed Democrats in America in the 1840s, grandson-in-law to Thomas Jefferson and an intimate associate of Andrew Jackson's.[4] He was an unlikely rebel. As the only man to single-handedly bring an American war to a close, he deserves recognition for his achievement. But his radical actions also demand explanation. This volume attempts to place Trist's evolving perspective on the war in the context of both his experiences in Mexico and personal relationships that long predated his secret assignment to negotiate a treaty with that country.

The literature on Polk, Clay, and especially Lincoln, by contrast, is vast.

But the following pages offer a different portrait of each of these men than you are likely to find elsewhere. Relatively little has been written about the web of connections among the five main characters in this book. And with one exception, little has been said about the impact of the war on their lives and the lives of their families. That exception, of course, is President James K. Polk. The war was closely identified with the man who started it, so much so that at the time opponents called it "Mr. Polk's War." The war defined Polk as well. It was his great project, the culmination of his life's work, and his legacy to the United States.

James K. Polk tends to inspire strong reactions among his biographers, many of whom have difficulty remaining objective when considering his leadership style and actions. Even his supporters have had trouble justifying his tactics, and other biographers have concluded that familiarity does indeed breed contempt.[5] This study neither deifies nor demonizes him. Polk was a complex character, a deeply conservative man in a surprisingly modern marriage, determined to micromanage a war despite having virtually no military experience, and in many ways an anomaly among southern Democratic politicians. His success was in large part due to his dependence on his wife, Sarah, who was truly his political partner. The childless couple worked harder than anyone else in Washington to advance what they believed to be America's destiny. By placing Polk in the context of his most important relationships, above all his marriage, this study offers a different perspective on both a misunderstood president and a conflict that rightfully should have been known as "Mr. and Mrs. Polk's War."

Henry Clay's biographers have been almost unanimous in their admiration for the greatest American politician who never became president.[6] Clay was widely adored in his own time, and even admirers of his arch-foe Andrew Jackson have had difficulty remaining objective in the face of Clay's personal magnetism and remarkable accomplishments.[7] But most of the dramatic events in Clay's political career took place prior to his loss to Polk in the presidential race of 1844. This study takes 1844 as the starting point for considering Clay's accomplishments. Three years after his defeat by Polk, Henry Clay delivered what was perhaps the single most important speech opposing the war. It was an act of great bravery on his part, and an event that has rarely merited a single page in his biographies. Given the length of Clay's career, the oversight is understandable, but the 1847 Lexington address not only changed the course of Clay's career, it also had a dramatic impact on Lincoln, Polk, and the American nation.

Nor will you read much in other volumes about Lincoln and the war with

Mexico. Abraham Lincoln's "Spot Resolutions" opposing the U.S.-Mexican War were the signature position he took during his single congressional term. But scholars have never evinced much interest in Lincoln's early political career. There is exactly one full-length study of Lincoln in Congress, which concluded that his congressional term was a "failure."[8] Historians have debated whether opposing the war cost Lincoln his seat, and if the victory of a Democrat in the 1848 race "could only be interpreted as a repudiation of 'Spotty' Lincoln's views on the Mexican War."[9] They have also differed over why Lincoln adopted his antiwar position in the first place. But scholars have never considered the larger impact of the U.S.-Mexican War on Lincoln's life, or noted that events in Illinois, including his service in the Black Hawk War, may have galvanized him to join the national movement to end the war with Mexico. No one has previously documented how extensively Lincoln's antiwar statements were reported around the nation. The Spot Resolutions brought Lincoln his first taste of the national political acclaim that he deeply craved. And his stance on the war with Mexico ultimately shaped him as a politician and a leader.

This book is the tale not just of five men and their families but also of the rise of America's first national antiwar movement.[10] The fact that there was a national antiwar movement in the 1840s will come as a surprise to most readers. Histories of the U.S.-Mexican War have almost always focused on the conflict's dramatic battles rather than the home front. Although one of the very first histories of the war was written by an antiwar activist (William Jay, the son of *Federalist Papers* coauthor John Jay), much of the twentieth-century scholarship on the war followed the lead of Justin Smith, who won a Pulitzer Prize in 1920 for his two-volume *The War with Mexico*.[11] While meticulously researched, Smith's celebratory history of the war was suffused with racism and his desire to justify America's part in the war. For decades before Smith's publication, historians and the public had ignored the war, their ambivalence caused by their inability to fit a war for territory into the history of a freedom-loving people. Smith not only vindicated the war but also drew a lasting and unfair portrait of antiwar opponents as irrational radicals deeply out of step with their nation.

Those few volumes that have examined the home front in detail have focused on the widespread initial enthusiasm for the war and agreed with Smith that, outside New England, Americans were united in their support for the cause. The single monograph to consider the antiwar movement in detail concluded that it "had little effect on the war's duration, outcome, or final terms."[12] With a few exceptions, most scholars continue to agree that antiwar criticism was limited because even opponents of the war in some way "accepted" its inevitability. Mexico was weak, the United States was strong, and it was destiny that the American republic would take a continental form.[13]

This volume makes a very different argument. Looking closely at the writings of politicians, soldiers, embedded journalists, and average Americans watching events in Mexico from a distance, it contends that the war was actively contested from its beginning and that vibrant and widespread antiwar activism ultimately defused the movement to annex all of Mexico to the United States at the close of the war. This volume gives voice to the views of peace activists and credit to them for their successes, revealing how politically risky agitation by politicians—including freshman congressman Lincoln and three-time presidential loser Clay—both moved public opinion in the direction of peace and prevented President Polk from fulfilling his territorial goals in 1848.

Nor was antiwar sentiment limited to Polk's political opponents. A Wicked War reveals how frequently volunteer and regular soldiers, as well as their officers, expressed their own ambivalence toward the conflict. This was particularly true for those who witnessed the many atrocities against Mexican civilians committed by U.S. troops. America's men volunteered to fight in overwhelming numbers, but once they arrived in Mexico their enthusiasm flagged. America's war with Mexico had the highest desertion rate of any American war, over 8 percent. Some of those deserters chose to fight for the enemy, joining the San Patricio Battalion. Their ambivalence came to be shared by the American people, even in western towns such as Springfield, Illinois, where support for the war once had been overwhelming.[14]

The ultimate annexation of half of Mexico, lands that became California, Nevada, Utah, and parts of Arizona, Colorado, Kansas, New Mexico, Oklahoma, and Texas, seems inevitable only in retrospect. Indeed, in 1845, Polk's dream of taking California was so audacious he didn't dare share it with the public. The land came at a great price. The U.S.-Mexican War had one of the highest casualty rates of any American war. Over 16 percent of the seventy-nine thousand American men who served in the war died, most from disease. Mexican casualties are harder to estimate, but at least twenty-five thousand, most civilians, perished in the course of the war.[15]

The war against Mexico did not take place in a vacuum. The narrative that follows reveals just how crucial history, both personal and national, was to the events of the 1840s. A warrior tradition, forged in battle against Britain and the Indian inhabitants of North America, and honed through chattel slavery, set the stage for America's invasion of Mexico and provided the context through which these five characters understood their personal and national destiny. The war between the United States and Mexico was in many ways a predictable development, given the nearly uninterrupted series of wars against Indian peoples fought by the United States government from its earliest days. Widespread racism led many Americans to equate Mexicans with Indians and to conclude that the former were no more deserving of their own land than the latter.

But in another sense the war against Mexico marked a dramatic break in American history. America's president invoked a dubious excuse in order to invade a neighboring republic and pursued a war for territory over the objections of a significant portion of Americans. This was unprecedented. All the land taken from Mexico, historians now acknowledge, could have been acquired peacefully through diplomacy and deliberate negotiation of financial recompense.[16] It should hardly be surprising that Americans had deeply ambivalent feelings about a war they knew would change their country and their lives.

This is an intimate story of a few of those lives: supporters who died to make America great and opponents who sacrificed their careers in order to save America from what they believed to be ruin. The war took a distinct toll on each of the main characters in this story. By speaking against it, Clay willingly antagonized his political base: he effectively gave up any hope of becoming president. For his protests, Lincoln was spurned by his jingoistic constituency and retired from Congress after a single term, his career apparently over. Trist was ousted from the State Department, sank into poverty, and fell out of history. Hardin was needlessly killed leading a poorly timed charge at the Battle of Buena Vista. And Polk, as true a believer in American exceptionalism as any president, worked himself to death in the service of a conflict that left his reputation in tatters. Their experiences in the late 1840s reveal the nobility and often high cost of conviction. They also show the indelible signature of war on a nation's identity and purpose.

A note on names: While the people of Mexico and the United States have an equal right to be called Americans, in the pages that follow I reserve the

term for residents of the United States simply because there is no graceful alternative. Many Mexican place-names were spelled differently in the
1840s than they are today. I have left direct quotations in their original state
but otherwise have standardized the spelling of cities and towns, including
Veracruz, and Monterrey in Nuevo León, to conform to their current spelling. I do this, again, for purposes of clarity.

PART ONE

Polk's Dream,

1844–45

―――――――――――――

Poke & Texas, *that's the thing, it goes like wild-fire*
with the folks as kant rede, nor don't git no papers.

—A MISSISSIPPI WHIG, 1844

I

Valentine's Day

FEBRUARY 14, 1844, did not unfold as sixty-six-year-old Henry Clay planned. It was Valentine's Day, no longer a sleepy saint's day relegated to religious calendars, but fast becoming a national craze. Stationers had discovered profit in the increasingly sentimental culture of middle-class America by promoting a holiday dedicated to the novel practice of exchanging store-bought cards. Christmas presents were still considered suspect, even profane, by American Protestants in the 1840s, but among the urbane it had become a "national whim" to send engraved or printed tokens of love through the mail, more than thirty thousand in 1844 in New York City alone. Urban post offices around the country were "piled with mountains of little missives, perfumed, gilt, enameled, and folded with rare cunning . . . they overflow with the choicest flowers of love, poetry and sentiment."[1]

Most everything fashionable in 1840s America was imported from Europe, and this whim was no exception. Initially, almost all Valentine's Day cards were British-made. But perennially insecure Americans complained that the old empire was "defrauding" Uncle Sam "of a rightful increase in his revenue." U.S. firms rose to the challenge: they began producing and marketing their own sentimental cards, and advertising them in newspapers. Countless shops sold these valentines in towns and cities, and peddlers brought them into rural areas. Within just a few short years American-made valentines had become ubiquitous. Nothing better demonstrated the increasing complexity and sophistication of American commerce in the 1840s, or the rise of a female-centered culture of romance and sentimentality, than did the wholesale American embrace of a commercialized Valentine's Day. In 1844 it was being celebrated like never before. It had, according to some observers, achieved "epidemic" proportions.[2]

Valentine's Day could have been made for Henry Clay. During his nearly forty years in national politics, he had been both lauded and condemned for his attention, attachment, and deference to the ladies, so much so that the number of women he had kissed had become a running joke in Washington. The trappings of organized religion left him cold, but he was renowned for his sentimentality and deep emotion. He was easily moved to tears, and when Clay wept while delivering a speech in Congress, listeners on both sides of the aisle found themselves similarly moved. As the founder of the preeminent Whig Party, a political organization devoted to the growth of American business, Henry Clay was the public face of American commerce. It was Whig legislation, conceptualized by Clay, that enabled American card producers to compete with British imports, and that financed the roads and bridges over which the thousands of valentines traveled.

In early 1844 he could lay claim to being the "most popular man in America."[3] "Prince Hal," as his supporters warmly called him, was the nation's most distinguished statesman, renowned for his oratory, his brilliant legal mind, his legislative prowess, and for his decades of service to the nation. He led the charge to war against Britain in 1812 and helped negotiate the Treaty of Ghent, which ended the conflict in 1815. His Missouri Compromise of 1820 calmed a sectional firestorm by maintaining the balance of slave and free states while also limiting the future spread of slavery to south of the Mason-Dixon line. As secretary of state under John Quincy Adams in the 1820s, he was an avid supporter of hemispheric solidarity, embracing the newly independent nations of Latin America as republican kin to the United States. And he promoted a vision for the economic development of the nation, what came to be known as his "American System," that proved so compelling it became the platform for a new political party.

His personality was as dazzling as his résumé. There was no better conversationalist in Washington, no more charming man to meet at a party, no one more ingratiating when he wanted to be—which was always. He was a master at the fiddle and a brilliant teller of jokes. He never ceased to remind his listeners that he came from humble origins (Clay was the first national politician to refer to himself as a self-made man).[4] But by the time he entered politics he carried himself, and behaved, exactly like what he was: a southern gentleman who loved parties, gambling, whiskey, and women, who was open in his affections and undeniably magnetic. His wife,

Henry Clay, 1844. From a daguerreotype portrait by Anthony, Edwards and Co. Library of Congress Prints and Photographs Division.

Lucretia, conveniently remained home in Kentucky, where she faultlessly managed their large family and equally impressive estate, Ashland.

His excesses were in the past, youthful indiscretions that only his enemies would deign to dredge up. Now he was a mature politician, his appeal nationwide. He was the "Sage of Ashland." Although he carried himself like a southerner, his vision of an American economy based on commerce and manufacturing was warmly embraced in the North. Despite owning scores of slaves, he professed to hate slavery.

Clay's popularity was in no way the product of his outward appearance. His self-assurance frequently crossed into arrogance, but even Clay would admit that nature had not blessed him with beauty. The freckles, blue eyes, and white-blond hair of his youth alone would have placed him outside the era's manly ideal, but far worse were his facial features: a cavernous mouth rimmed with thin lips, and a receding cleft chin that emphasized his very prominent nose.

But Clay made the best of what he had. Tall and thin, with delicate hands, he was graceful in his demeanor and careful in his dress. The real draw was his sparkling wit and great desire to please. "No portrait ever did him justice"; neither painting nor daguerreotype could capture his easy and winning smile or his ability to connect almost instantly with a new acquaintance. "His appearance upon the whole was not at first prepossessing," one visitor to his house noted, "but when you heard him converse, you felt you were under the influence of a great and good man."[5]

His popularity among women was legendary. They flocked around him when he appeared in public, treasured mementos of his visits, and purchased reproductions of his likeness. They cheered his elections and promoted his causes. It was generally acknowledged that "if the Ladies . . . could vote, the election of Mr. Clay would be carried by acclamation!" They continued to find him irresistible well into his middle age, when his receding hairline did nothing to diminish his remarkable wit and courtesy. As his closest female friend, Alabama socialite Octavia LeVert, explained, Clay had "a heroism of heart, a chivalry of deportment, a deference of demeanor," all of which were "irresistible talismans over the mind of the gentler sex."[6]

Nor were women alone in succumbing to Clay's charms. There was a "winning fascination in his manners that will suffer none to be his enemies who associate with him," wrote one congressman. "When I look upon his manly and bold countenance, and meet his frank and eloquent eye, I feel an emotion little short of enthusiasm in his cause." Clay easily disarmed wary strangers; even lifelong opponents of his legislation found the legislator difficult to dislike in person. His political antagonist, South Carolina senator John C. Calhoun, believed Clay was "a bad man, an imposter, a creator of wicked schemes." But after decades of political battles between the two, Calhoun concluded, "I wouldn't speak to him, but, by God! I love him."[7]

Henry Clay was an American original, glamorous and magnetic to a fault, but far from perfect. He was spoiled by a lifetime of acclaim (he first entered the Senate at the tender and unconstitutional age of twenty-nine), and even his friends admitted he could be a prima donna. His wit could be biting, and he was easily bored. Impulsive and ardent, he too often spoke before thinking, made promises he couldn't keep, and later came to regret his decisions. His ambivalence about slavery led many voters on both sides of the question to discount him as opportunistic. As a young man he passionately argued that Kentucky should end slavery through a plan of gradual emancipation similar to those being adopted by the mid-Atlantic states. When that plan was rejected he devoted himself to the cause of colonization, believing it possible to end slavery by colonizing freed slaves in Africa.

But forty years later his wealth derived in large part from the unpaid labor of fifty men, women, and children whom he owned. His enemies called him a demagogue, but not to his face. Like other southern gentleman, Clay kept a set of dueling pistols and had put them to use more than once. But these excesses were also in the past, the dueling pistols now just for show.

By all measures February 14, 1844, should have been a blissful Valentine's Day for Henry Clay, "full of glorious recollections—and pregnant with never ending happiness," as it was for so many others. But this was not to be. In place of a scented, embossed, cherub-decorated paper heart, Henry Clay received intelligence that day that put a damper on his hopes and shook him to the bone.[8]

Clay was near the end of a two-month stay in his favorite city, New Orleans, when the local paper broke the news. He was lodging in the elegant and urbane home of Dr. William Mercer, on Carondelet Street, close to the hotels and business establishments where he spent his days winning over the wealthy men of the city with his brilliant economic plans, and evenings flattering their wives and sisters. The fun ended when he picked up the paper on February 14. Clay was flabbergasted, unwilling to believe the news, but also afraid it was true: reportedly President John Tyler had secretly negotiated a treaty to annex the Republic of Texas and was at that very moment lining up supporters for the bill in the Senate. Surely the great Henry Clay, who until two years before had been the senior senator from Kentucky and who was currently preparing for his third presidential run, should have known about a matter of such monumental importance both to the nation and to his status as a power broker in Washington. How could he be so out of the loop? "Address me instantly," he demanded of his friend and Senate successor, John Crittenden. "If it be true, I shall regret extremely that I have had no hint of it."[9]

True it was. In the winter of 1843–44, Secretary of State Abel P. Upshur had nearly drafted a treaty with the Lone Star Republic and had employed his masterly lobbying abilities to persuade a majority of U.S. senators to secretly pledge their support for it. By late January Upshur felt confident enough of the passage of the treaty to assure Texas leaders that forty of America's fifty-two senators were committed to Texas's annexation. With two-thirds of the Senate lined up, annexation was all but ensured.

This was a startling turn of events, both for Henry Clay and for the nation. Clay's insider status was legendary. America's first congressional power broker, Clay became the Speaker of the House of Representatives on his first day as a congressman in 1811, and made the speakership second only to the presidency in its power. As Speaker, Clay offered patronage, controlled legislation and desirable committee appointments, and even decided who became president in the contested election of 1824, favoring Adams over Andrew Jackson despite the fact that Old Hickory had received more electoral and popular votes. The following decades became known as the Age of Jackson, but they could just as surely be called the Age of Clay, for Clay was as much a force of nature in American politics as his archfoe. The difference, of course, was that Andrew Jackson had won two presidential elections, while Henry Clay had twice lost.

In 1844 Henry Clay was consumed with the notion that his time, at long last, had come. Dozens of important men had accrued debts to him over his many years in office, and Clay was ready to call in those debts in order to accede to the nation's highest office. Clay hadn't been officially nominated yet; the convention wasn't until May. But New Orleans was the launching pad for a lengthy tour of the Southeast designed to shore up his support in the region, and so far things had gone swimmingly. In public squares and in private drawing rooms, the good people of New Orleans proclaimed Henry Clay their undisputed choice for president. Nothing appeared to stand in his way—until he heard the news about Texas on Valentine's Day.

Texas had been brewing as a problem since 1835, when a band of slave-owning American settlers, attracted by Mexico's generous immigration policies and the ample land available for growing cotton, rose in rebellion in the Mexican state of Coahuila y Tejas. The Texians (as they called themselves) invoked the American Revolution to justify their actions, but their objections to Mexican rule extended beyond representation, taxes, and trade. In 1830 Mexico attempted to restrict immigration into Texas and to limit slaveholding. The laws were utterly unenforceable, and probably just as many in the region were as upset about Mexico's attempt to collect revenue and increase central authority as they were about the fate of their slaves. But the survival of the "peculiar institution" made for a perfect call to arms. The nation was, in the words of a Texas newspaper, attempting to "give liberty to our slaves, and to make slaves of ourselves."[10]

Most Americans viewed the Texas Revolution not as a war for slavery but as a race war between brown Mexicans and white Texians, and as a result supported the Texians wholeheartedly. Thousands of white American men from the South and West illegally crossed into Texas in order to join the fight against Mexico. Many fewer, primarily ministers and abolitionists, attacked the legitimacy of the rebellion. In Philadelphia, Quaker abolitionist Benjamin Lundy left no doubts about his views on the subject when he titled his 1836 pamphlet *The War in Texas; A Review of Facts and Circumstances, Showing That This Contest Is a Crusade Against Mexico, Set on Foot and Supported by Slaveholders, Land Speculators, &c, in Order to Re-establish, Extend, and Perpetuate the System of Slavery and the Slave Trade.* A second edition expanded on his arguments against "the grand deception" calling itself Texas independence.[11] But outside New England, where a significant minority supported the abolition of slavery, few Americans believed that Mexicans occupied the moral high ground in this conflict. Not even Quaker Pennsylvania was a safe place to protest the Texas Revolution: a Philadelphia mob destroyed Lundy's printing press and threatened his life a year after the second edition of *The War in Texas* appeared in print.

Marked by dramatic battles, the Texas Revolution was ripe for exploitation in America's vibrant and competitive penny press. There was no need to exaggerate or sensationalize. Mexican troops, driven by the battle cry "Exterminate to the Sabine" river, acted barbarously. First came the cruel slaughter of American Texians by Mexican general Antonio López de Santa Anna at the Alamo. Mexican forces piled up Texian corpses, soaked them in oil, and set them on fire. At Goliad, although his subordinate agreed to treat surrendering forces as prisoners of war, Santa Anna arbitrarily set aside the agreement, marched 340 Texians out of town, and had them all shot. Then came the astounding victory of the rebels under the command of a former Tennessee governor, Sam Houston, at the Battle of San Jacinto. Mexico sustained fourteen hundred casualties in eighteen minutes, while only seven of Houston's men died. Texians took their revenge, slaughtering defenseless Mexican soldiers who cried out, "Me no Alamo. Me no Goliad."[12]

It made for great headlines, and Americans followed the conflict with intense partisanship. But not every battle was deemed newsworthy: when Texas slaves attempted to seize their own freedom, the uprising was brutally quelled by white Texians. But since this story had no place in the newspapers' heroic narrative of white Texian freedom, it was relegated to a few abolitionist publications and to the Mexican press.[13]

Texians declared a republic in March 1836 and captured Santa Anna at the Battle of San Jacinto on April 21. In May they forced him to sign a treaty acknowledging Texas's independence and withdrawing his troops south of the Rio Grande. In a second secret treaty, Santa Anna promised to support boundary talks wherein Texas would have a boundary that would "not lie south" of the Rio Grande.[14] Mexico's government promptly repudiated Santa Anna and all his negotiations with Texas, but Texians and Americans rejoiced. Although Mexico steadfastly maintained that Texas was a rebel province and not an independent nation, President Andrew Jackson offered diplomatic recognition to the self-proclaimed republic. And then Texas turned to the United States for annexation.

In 1836 the United States could have annexed Texas, but only at the cost of war. Not only would Mexico have considered the annexation of its rebel province an act of aggression, but so would the rest of the world. As a result, three presidents and the majority of congressional representatives turned their backs on annexation, and for good reason. A state of intermittent warfare continued between Texas and Mexico.

Almost every American believed that the United States had a special destiny in the world. They took it for granted that the blessings of "republican liberty" enshrined in the Constitution "should expand over the earth, and spread their benign influence from pole to pole."[15] But few in the 1830s felt that territorial expansion should proceed at the cost of war with a neighboring republic. Not even Andrew Jackson—a mentor and personal friend of Sam Houston's and the man whose actions led the Five Civilized Indian Tribes to walk the Trail of Tears so that expansionists in what is today the American Southeast could take their land—was willing to propose the annexation of Texas.

Jackson had more than one possible war in mind when he sidestepped the question of the annexation of Texas. Few politicians wanted to disturb the delicate sectional balance between North and South. Men who believed with their whole hearts that all of North America would eventually become part of the United States, who lobbied even for the acquisition of Canada, objected to allowing Texas into the Union. For the enormous territory would enter as a slave-owning state, possibly as many as five slave states. And for those who believed (as did many northerners) that there was a "slave power conspiracy" at work in the government, the last thing they wanted to do was increase the power of the South, particularly in the Senate. Antislavery firebrand John Quincy Adams, a fixture in Congress since the end of his presidency in 1829, made exactly this point when he warned his colleagues in no uncertain terms that annexing Texas would "secure and rivet" the "undue ascendancy of the slave-holding power in the government."[16]

So although Americans felt a strong kinship with the white population of Texas, and most Texians, under siege by Mexico and falling into ever greater debt, were desperate to join the Union, year after year annexation remained unconsummated. Jackson's successor, the "little magician" from New York, Democrat Martin Van Buren, skillfully sidestepped the issue of Texas with his customary political adroitness. So too did the first Whig president, General William Henry Harrison, elected after Van Buren's magic proved insufficient to extricate the Democratic Party from a national financial panic that started under its watch in 1837 and lingered through the election of 1840.

It took a desperate man to upset the status quo and make the annexation of Texas a reality. John Tyler, a rogue Whig distrusted by both his own party and the opposition Democrats, had been William Henry Harrison's vice president, succeeding the aging former general when he died of pneumonia in 1841, just a month after his inauguration—thus forever branding him "His Accidency." However, Tyler's greatest ambition was to be elected to his own term. To achieve that, all he had to do was smoothly manage the remainder of Harrison's.

This proved to be beyond Tyler's abilities. He plowed his rough way forward for four years, a slaveholding Virginia aristocrat who had allied himself with Clay and his Whigs in the 1830s out of a shared distrust of Andrew Jackson's Democratic agenda. But his states'-rights ideology made him just as suspicious of the nationalist program of internal improvements and centralized banking that Clay's party attempted to push through after Harrison's election. In power for the first time, the Whigs understandably considered the presidencies of Harrison and Tyler their own.

But Tyler would not play along. He repeatedly vetoed legislation to centralize the banking system, infuriating Henry Clay, who had masterminded the legislation, and ultimately leading to the resignation of nearly the entire presidential cabinet. Clay formally read Tyler out of his party. Whig stalwarts in the cabinet, many of whom were indebted to Clay, were replaced by yes-men and cronies, including Abel Upshur, a close friend since Tyler's youth. Clay's supporters were dismissive of Tyler's men, but objective minds (and there were a few in Washington at the time) recognized that the new secretary of state was a man of substance. As navy secretary, Upshur had done a brilliant job modernizing and reorganizing the navy. One underestimated his capabilities at one's own risk.

Now a president without a party, Tyler made overtures to the Democrats, but they proved no more receptive to supporting the rogue president than had been their opponents. Desperate for an issue that might win him election, Tyler saw salvation in Texas.

Tyler reasoned that sentiment in favor of annexation was so high outside Washington that accomplishing it would keep him in office without the help of either major party. He pursued Texas with the conviction that the annexation of that republic, independent from Mexico for only seven years, was essential not only to the "salvation of the Union" but also to the salvation of his own political career.[17]

Tyler and Upshur threw themselves into the project beginning in 1842. Texians, concerned that overtures from the United States would mobilize Mexican forces against them, demanded a guarantee of military protection before commencing the courtship. Upshur offered a verbal promise, enough to start the proceedings, but Texas demanded something in writing before taking the relationship to the next level. The same day that Clay read in the paper that Tyler was on the verge of presenting an annexation treaty to the Senate, the Texians got their own valentine. On February 14, 1844, the American representative in Texas promised, in secret negotiations, that the moment Texas signed a treaty of annexation, "a sufficient naval force shall be placed in the Gulf of Mexico, convenient for the defense of Texas, in case of any invasion which may threaten her seaboard," and measures would be taken "to repel any invasion by land."[18] Signed, the document essentially committed U.S. troops to certain war with Mexico.

The U.S. Constitution specifies that Congress, and only Congress, has the power to declare war. Tyler blanched when he received a copy of the pledge several weeks later. He instantly recognized that the vow to provide military protection to Texas exceeded his powers as president and would infuriate Congress if, or rather when, it was made public. He countermanded the written pledge, but not before the courtship had advanced to the point of no return on Texas's part. Mexico began massing forces near the Texas border. Not long after Valentine's Day, annexation suddenly appeared inevitable.

None of this should have come as a surprise to Henry Clay. His Washington friends might not have told him explicitly about the treaty, but several of them had warned him of Tyler's intentions. Nor did one need inside information to figure out that the Texas issue was on the verge of exploding.

The tension had been building for months. Over the course of the fall of 1843, the legislatures of several southwestern states petitioned Congress for the admission of Texas. After the president spoke out in favor of annexation, his supporters unleashed a sophisticated propaganda campaign extolling the advantages of annexation and advancing specious claims that Texas rightfully "belonged" to the United States by virtue of the Louisiana Purchase. Rumors of British designs on Texas began appearing in Democratic newspapers. Americans both resented and feared their former colonizer, and threats of British encroachment were almost always effective at mobilizing the public. Now it appeared that if the United States didn't move fast, the British might annex Texas themselves, abolish slavery there, and threaten the peace and security of the United States.

In November the *North American,* one of the nation's leading papers, stated definitively that "the project of annexing Texas to the United States will be proposed and urged by the acting President and his Secretary of State," while that same month local newspapers from Charleston, South Carolina, to Bridgeport, Connecticut, proclaimed it "certain" that a treaty would soon come before Congress.[19]

Clay himself had been inundated with letters from supporters about the issue, most of which he ignored. To one friend he replied in early December, "I am surprised that Texas should occasion you so much uneasiness at the North. In the whole circle of my acquaintance in K.[entucky] I do not remember to have heard lately a solitary voice raised in favor of or against Annexation."[20]

This was balderdash. Few states had stronger ties to Texas than Kentucky. Many of the original settlers of Mexican Texas hailed from the Bluegrass State, the Texas secretary of war was a Kentuckian, and, as Clay well knew, his good friend John Crittenden's son George was currently serving in the Texas army. Texas annexation was hugely popular in Clay's state and growing more so by the day, as it was throughout the entire Southwest. In the last months of 1843 Whig voters in both the North and South began pestering their representatives with questions about Clay's views on annexation, and newspapers from Indiana, Kentucky, Boston, and New York openly debated how the Sage of Ashland might vote on an annexation bill.[21]

Clay ignored it all. He refused to accept that John Tyler, the very definition of an impotent politician, could negotiate a treaty of annexation with Texas, let alone convince two-thirds of the Senate to ratify it. It was too implausible to contemplate. "Let Mr. Tyler recommend" annexation, he told a friend, "if he please, and what of that? . . . Such a recommendation would be the last desperate move of a desperate traitor." When John Crittenden warned Clay in early December that Tyler had set his sights on Texas, Clay dismissed his concerns. Having already determined that annexation was impossible, Clay was sure that Tyler was introducing it "for no other than the wicked purpose of producing discord and distraction in the nation." This was nothing more than a cynical plot on the part of extremists to divide both the country and his party, and Clay did not "think it right to allow Mr. Tyler, for his own selfish purposes, to introduce an exciting topic to add to the other subjects of contention that exist in this country."[22]

Manifest Destiny aside, Henry Clay had his own destiny to consider. His five-month electioneering tour of the Southeast would return him to Washington for the opening of the Whig nominating convention in May 1844. He would not allow Texas to become a diversion, either from the economic issues that mattered to the country or from the forthcoming election that mattered to him. The same week that Clay arrived in New Orleans, a New York abolitionist paper expressed astonishment that anyone could still doubt that a bill to annex Texas would come before the present session of Congress. The following day the *Telegraph* of Houston reported that Texas's House of Representatives had passed a joint resolution in favor of annexation. Although the article was quickly reprinted in the papers of New Orleans as well as the rest of the United States, Henry Clay somehow missed the news.[23]

Clay's degree of denial in this matter was astounding but not really out of character. His critics had long condemned him for trying to be all things to all people. But Clay's unwillingness to engage with deeply divisive issues wasn't primarily the product of his personal ambition. It was a necessary survival mechanism for any presidential hopeful within the two-party political system of the era. Because the Whigs and the Democrats were national parties, a candidate who alienated the mass of his supporters in one or another region lost all hope of winning a national election. Appeasing both the North and the South was a delicate balancing act, and becoming more so by the day, but Clay had thus far demonstrated an excellent sense of balance. Surely it wouldn't fail him now.

Texas was no ordinary issue, however. It was proving to be exceptionally polarizing. Secretary of State Abel Upshur publicly maintained that annexation would be for the good of the entire nation, but he wrote privately to a friend in August 1843 that the South should "demand" the annexation of Texas regardless of the opinion of northerners. "The history of the world does not present an example of such insult, contempt, and multiplied wrongs and outrages from one nation to another as we have received and are daily receiving from our northern brethren!!" Upshur wrote. "It is a reproach to us that we bear it any longer."[24]

Nor were all southerners as circumspect as Upshur. Most saw no need to keep their feelings to themselves, and many northerners found the southern bluster difficult to stomach. As Texas heated up and Henry Clay remained cold, abolitionist papers increased their invective against politicians afraid to "exasperate the South" lest they "feel her talons." The country was full of men like Clay who refused to see that "the South has been anxiously watching and earnestly making its opportunity to strike a death-blow on the free labor of the North." This push for Texas was a prime example. Extremists on both sides agreed that more was at stake than merely winning an election. This debate was about manhood itself. "This is not the spirit of manly freedom," one paper declared in disgust. "When men at the North act like slaves, the South will treat them as such. When they are tame, she will domineer—when they whimper she will put on the lash—but when they face her with a look of manly decision, she will cringe, and be respectful to our honor and our rights."[25]

Henry Clay thought he could navigate these waters, but on Valentine's Day he received evidence that his sense of direction had failed him. This news should have raised a warning flag and made him question his political intuition, perhaps even reconsider the extent of his omniscience. But because of his towering faith in his own abilities, he instead considered this only a momentary lapse. It would take nearly a year before Henry Clay realized that this momentary lapse was something far greater, that his life and his country were on the verge of dramatic change.

On February 27, 1844, Secretary of State Upshur completed negotiations with Texas to bring the republic into the United States. He and President Tyler had done the impossible: Texas would be a state at last. All that was left was to sell it to the Senate.

The following day dawned bright and cloudless. Senators broke early from a lively debate over the future of the Oregon Country, jointly controlled by the United States and Britain, which was the object of increasing and passionate desire by northern expansionists. Thousands of American settlers had made the arduous trek by covered wagon to farm its fertile soils, and they were anxious to see British claims to the region extinguished. But Britain's navy was the most powerful in the world, and the country's claims to the region equally formidable. Plenty of senators had strong feelings about how to handle Britain, but this debate would have to wait.

The wealthy and powerful in Washington were off to a party. Senators, members of the cabinet, and assorted other luminaries lucky enough to receive one of the formal invitations on thick card stock gathered at Bradley's Wharf "precisely at 11 o'clock" for a cruise of the Potomac aboard the new steam frigate *Princeton*, the "pride of the navy."[26] Tyler and Upshur were there, with ample reason to celebrate. The afternoon promised both entertainment and relaxation. The guests would have the great good fortune to witness a demonstration of the world's largest naval gun, nicknamed "Peacemaker," and a lavish banquet belowdecks would cap the festivities.

Both the *Princeton* and its cannon represented the fulfillment of a personal crusade on Upshur's part to strengthen the U.S. Navy, which had been perennially underfunded and long the subject of mockery. The *Princeton* and "Peacemaker" offered evidence that the scientific and financial resources poured into the navy had paid off. These technological marvels surely offered proof that the U.S. Navy was more than prepared to face Mexico, or even England if need be, in battle. As the flag-festooned vessel steamed along at a brisk pace through abundant ice floes, the secretary of state must have felt a special pride.[27]

Spirits among the passengers were high, and the champagne flowed freely. When the captain fired off "Peacemaker," the cheers of the well-dressed crowd were universal and enthusiastic. They headed belowdecks for an elaborate feast, appetites stoked by the display of American militarism. As the sun began to set, the *Princeton* turned toward her anchorage. With Mount Vernon, George Washington's historic estate, in view, Thomas Gilmer, a rising political star who had been secretary of the navy for just ten days, called on the captain for one final cannon discharge in honor of the nation's first president.

Most of the guests were still belowdecks and felt little concern when they heard a loud explosion. But as billowing smoke filled the cabin, and shouts and screams echoed from above, it became obvious that something had gone terribly wrong. "Peacemaker" had exploded, instantly killing Upshur and eight other men, including Henry, the slave who dressed President Tyler each morning; Thomas Gilmer, the new secretary of the navy; and David Gardiner, a former state senator from New York. Dozens of others were injured, including one of the nation's leading expansionists, Senator Thomas Hart Benton of Missouri, whose right eardrum was shattered.

John J. Hardin, an up-and-coming thirty-four-year-old congressman from Illinois, was on deck when the gun burst. His wife, Sarah, the mother of three young children, was fortunately still in the cabin. "The horrors of that scene are still before me," he wrote to a friend a week later. "The ghastly countenances of the dead, the shattered limbs, the gashes in the wounded and their mournful moanings, can neither be described or imagined. Yet sadder and more piercing to the breast than this were the wailings and shrieks of agony of the wives of those who were killed."[28]

President Tyler survived. At the time of the explosion the widowed president was belowdecks flirting with Gardiner's twenty-four-year-old daughter Julia, a New York belle less than half his age. Tyler proved instrumental in helping Julia overcome the grief of losing her father, and Julia lessened the president's distress over the "awful and lamentable catastrophe" that was in fact the worst tragedy ever to befall a presidential cabinet.[29] Two months later the couple was engaged.

The explosion aboard the *Princeton* left Washington in shock and the fate of annexation in question. Supporters and foes alike recognized that without Upshur guiding matters, Tyler would have a difficult time bringing Texas into the Union before the 1844 nominating conventions in May. The president knew it too. Only days after the tragedy he admitted to one of his daughters that along with his closest servant, two friends, and the man who would have been his father-in-law, his hopes of reelection died that afternoon as well.[30]

Had he been in Washington, Henry Clay might well have been aboard the *Princeton*. Instead he spent that fateful evening at a "splendid ball" in Mobile, Alabama, held in his honor by his friend Octavia LeVert and her husband.[31] Clay had several months of strenuous campaigning ahead of him, but the disaster bought him time to consider his options regarding Texas. Upshur's replacement as secretary of state was John C. Calhoun, a brilliant proslavery ideologue from South Carolina. It would be his job to prepare the Texas treaty for ratification by the Senate.

While Calhoun got settled in his new office, Clay consulted with Whig colleagues about how best to turn the Texas issue to his political advantage. In the decades before the Civil War, the easiest way for a politician to reach a mass audience was to write a letter for publication and submit it to a friendly newspaper; within days he could expect to see it reprinted in local papers around the nation.

Having finally come to the realization that Texas was not going away, Henry Clay determined to publish just such a letter. He would clearly outline his reasons for opposing annexation, and explain to the public, his public, why Tyler's treaty was such a disaster. To a man, however, Clay's friends rejected this plan. They recognized what Clay did not: that Texas annexation was wildly popular across the South and West. Unless the candidate was willing to openly antagonize potential voters, he needed to hold his tongue.

But as he slowly traveled from Mobile back to Washington, Henry Clay grew increasingly dissatisfied with this course of action, or rather inaction, as he saw it. He was inundated by questions about Texas by audiences in Alabama, Georgia, and South Carolina. The good citizens of Charleston wanted to know if he was "for or against the annexation of Texas."[32] The New Orleans *Picayune* demanded that both Clay and Martin Van Buren, the presumptive Democratic nominee, "respond like men" and "declare categorically" their views on the subject, "for thousands are anxious to know what they think."[33]

Why shouldn't Clay respond like a man? Once a subject captured Henry Clay's attention, it wasn't in his nature to remain quiet. He was sure that he could provide an answer to the Texas question that would "reconcile all our friends, and many others to the views which I entertain." As he told his incredulous friend John Crittenden, "Of one thing you may be certain, that there is no such anxiety for the annexation here at the South as you might have been disposed to imagine."[34] Henry Clay might have accepted that a treaty was on the table, but he was still in denial that many Americans could possibly support it.

By the time Clay reached Raleigh, North Carolina, on his sixty-seventh birthday, he had determined to write the letter. With typical impetuosity, he turned right to it. Seated beneath a towering white oak on East North Street, Clay composed a missive that he would later come to regret. He outlined his many reasons for opposing annexation: the crippling Texas debt the United States would be forced to assume, the decided opposition of a large portion of Americans, the likely sectional discord, the evidence that the United States had relinquished all claim to Texas in an earlier treaty, and, most important, the fact that Mexico had never abandoned its claim to the region. Make no mistake, Clay warned readers: "annexation and war with Mexico are identical." Such a war, Clay argued, would be a catastrophe. "I regard all wars as great calamities . . . and honorable peace as the wisest and truest policy of this country."[35]

Clay mailed the letter to John Crittenden in Washington with instructions that it be published in the nation's leading Whig newspaper, the *National Intelligencer,* the following week. No doubt anticipating his friend's reaction upon reading such a definitive rejection of annexation, Clay assured Crittenden that the likely Democratic nominee, Martin Van Buren, would "occupy common ground" with him on the issue.[36] There would be no political repercussions. Clay was sure of it.

When Secretary of State John C. Calhoun submitted the completed treaty to the Senate on April 22 for closed debate, its fate looked promising. But events that week would conspire against the annexation of Texas. The first strike against it was the work of a shocked antislavery Democrat, Senator Benjamin Tappan of Ohio. Firmly believing that the treaty would "disgrace the nation," Tappan leaked it to the press. The administration had hoped to keep the details out of the public eye for as long as possible, but on Saturday, April 27, the treaty appeared in full along with supporting documents that revealed the covert nature of the proceedings and questionable promises made to Texas, including that Valentine's Day commitment to protection from Mexico. That same Saturday Henry Clay's Raleigh letter rejecting the annexation of Texas also appeared in print, as did a letter from Martin Van Buren on the same subject.[37]

Van Buren's language differed from Clay's, but he too rejected annexation. The canny New Yorker was considered by many to be the very epitome of the scheming politician, and Whigs were not alone in condemning "his selfishness, his duplicity, his want of manly frankness." Yet conscientious scruples led him to oppose immediate annexation, political ramifications aside. Given that every other nation would consider the annexation of Texas an unjustified act of aggression against Mexico, Van Buren suggested that annexation might "do us more real lasting injury as a nation than the acquisition of such a territory, valuable as it undoubtedly is, could possibly repair." He argued that "we have a character among the nations of the earth to maintain. . . . The lust of power, with fraud and violence in the train, has led other and differently constituted governments to aggression and conquest," but the United States was motivated by "reason and justice." If Van Buren had anything to say about it, the United States would not lose that reputation over Texas.[38]

Nor was that all the news on Saturday, April 27. A fourth astounding report could be found in the columns of the Washington daily press: a letter from John C. Calhoun to the British minister, Sir Richard Pakenham, stating that the annexation of Texas was essential to the security of the South and to the expansion of slavery, which Calhoun argued was a social ideal. Because slavery was "essential to the peace, safety, and prosperity of states in the union in which it exists," Texas must be annexed.[39]

This was not the spin the administration had hoped for from the secretary of state. Like Calhoun, Tyler and Upshur were slaveholders, but they had steadfastly maintained a public stance that annexation was an issue of national interest, unconnected to slavery. Upshur was confident that the initial "burst of repugnance at the North" toward the idea of annexation could be overcome once the North realized the economic advantages of the union. He had explained his reasoning to Calhoun back in August 1843: "I have never known the north to refuse to do what their interest required, and I think it will not be difficult to convince them that their interest requires the admission of Texas into the Union as a slaveholding state." Tyler and Upshur spent the winter of 1843–44 making exactly this argument.[40]

Calhoun refused to play along. The new secretary of state was a pro-slavery radical and an uncomfortable fit in a political system that divided Americans by party rather than section. Seemingly forgetting that in his role as secretary of state his allegiance belonged to the nation as a whole and not to his beloved South, Calhoun released his letter to Pakenham precisely because he wanted to force the Tyler administration to publicly embrace slavery. In the process he upended the Texas debate on the eve of ratification.

So it was that on the very day the public became aware of the annexation treaty in all its detail, both of the likely presidential candidates rejected the annexation of Texas in a manner that strongly suggested collusion, while the secretary of state willfully alienated northern support of the treaty by casting the issue in starkly sectional terms. Tyler's dream of annexing Texas, once so close, began to evaporate along with the promised north-ern support for the treaty. The Whig-controlled Senate Foreign Relations Committee sat on the treaty for three weeks and then sent it back to the Senate without comment on May 10. Senators of both parties called for a full investigation into the irregular manner in which the administration had conducted its negotiations, particularly the promises made to protect Texas. Even Democrat Thomas Hart Benton, one of the Senate's staunchest expansionists, alliteratively railed against the "insidious scheme of sudden and secret annexation" brought forth by "our hapless administration."[41]

None of this made the slightest difference at the 1844 Whig national conven-tion, which met in Baltimore less than a week after the treaty and the con-troversial letters appeared in the Washington daily press. Van Buren's letter left Whigs in "a perfect state of exultation."[42] Few of them doubted that Old Van, a northerner in the pro-expansion party, would be hurt far worse by his anti-annexation stance than would Clay, a southerner in a party that was ambivalent about expansion. Come November, Clay should have no prob-lem beating Van Buren in the general election.

Thousands of Whigs from around the country traveled to Baltimore to make Henry Clay's coronation official. On the second of May they paraded through Baltimore, a "great mass of noble, fine-looking fellows," for almost an hour and a half. The weather was cool, the skies overcast. It was a joyous and colorful procession, a "day of jubilee" with "each state under its proper banner, and each individual swelling out its numbers, with flags and patriotic devices, badges and the weapons of peace." According to sixty-three-year-old Philip Hone, a wealthy sophisticate and member of the New York delegation, it "presented a pageant more bright and brilliant than any I ever beheld." He delighted in the crowd. They were "cheered on by the bright eyes of the prettiest young women in the world . . . with handkerchiefs waving overhead and wreaths and bouquets thrown at their feet."[43]

The crowd was equally pleased by the loud, colorful, and festive proceedings. Congressman John J. Hardin of Illinois was dumbstruck. "The Grand procession . . . far exceeded anything which I imagined or could describe," he wrote his wife, now back home in Illinois with their children. "It was larger than ever was convened, or ever will be again convened in the United States in my lifetime. There were arches & flags & banners extended across the streets by scores; & banners & flags in the procession by hundreds. The procession was 4 or 5 miles long. . . . The city contains 130,000 inhabitants, & all the inhabitants, & all its citizens, with their tens of thousands from other states were on the streets through which the procession passed. Every window on the street was open & filled with human hands."[44] Hardin couldn't help but conclude that the American people loved and trusted his Whig Party.

Spectators noted the many live raccoons, symbols of the party ever since Harrison had been portrayed wearing a coonskin cap in the election of 1840, as well as highly polished and beribboned looms, spinning machines, and cotton presses, all of which spoke to the Whig faith in developing American industry. The parade also featured ballot boxes, stuffed eagles, bands of minstrel singers, and mechanics carrying the tools of their trades.

But far outnumbering these were flags and banners, many sewn and presented to the delegations by Clay's legions of female supporters, testifying to the party's frenzy for one man. "Harry, the Star of the West" was lauded as "the champion of American industry," "our brave chieftain," and "our country's hope." New Jersey Whigs professed their adoration for Clay because "he's honest, he is capable, for his patriotism and talents we honor him, for his virtues and worth we will elevate him." Baltimore Whigs coupled a portrait of Clay with the motto "History and fame will long proclaim our Harry's Deeds." New York City Whigs married an image of Clay to his famous statement that he would "rather be right than be president," but lest that sentiment seem out of place, the Alabama banner reminded viewers that "there's no such word as fail."[45] Perhaps the delegations from the Southwest offered fewer images of Clay than those in the Northeast, but the unity of the Whig Party was striking in its totality.

Clay's visage was even more ubiquitous at the assembly, which gathered in the Universalist Church on Calvert Street. "Clay badges hung conspicuously at all button holes. . . . Clay portraits, Clay banners, Clay ribands, Clay songs, Clay quick-steps, Clay marches, Clay caricatures, meet the eye in all directions." All of Baltimore seemed to be in a frenzy for Henry Clay, and leave it up to the Whigs to figure out a way to make money from the spectacle. Hat shops offered "Clay hats," and tailoring shops offered Clay coats.

The marketing of Henry Clay was in full bloom, and the Whigs were in absolute heaven. "Oh, the rushing, the stirring, the noise, the excitement! To see it and feel it all is glory enough for one day," gushed a reporter. The enthusiasm reached all the way to New York, where a barber publicly professed his change of heart. No longer would he support Van Buren, since, as he told one reporter, "all the world's going for Clay; and I, as barber, must go too."[46]

In proceedings that were "brief and to the purpose," Henry Clay was unanimously nominated his party's candidate for president, on a platform that said nothing about Texas. The resolution was "accompanied by such cheers and clappings of hands as the world never heard before." The hall vibrated with the applause. Philip Hone declared it "one of the most sublime moral spectacles ever exhibited" and wrote in his diary, "I shall always rejoice

ABOVE *Whig campaign ribbon, Baltimore National Convention, 1844. Silk ribbons featuring Henry Clay's likeness were produced by the thousands for the Whig National Convention in Baltimore and proudly worn by delegates. This particular design proclaims Clay "the fearless Friend of his Country's Rights" and offers a whitewashed image of Ashland, Clay's Kentucky estate, worked not by slaves but by a white farmer. Clay, and the Baltimore convention, carefully avoided discussion of the controversial issues of slavery and Texas.* Susan H. Douglas Political Americana Collection, #2214, Rare and Manuscript Collections, Cornell University Library.

that I was present." The following day an independent newspaper declared, "We never saw such a spirit of enthusiasm as now exists amongst the whigs in favor of Henry Clay," and predicted that if Clay were "not elected president," then the editors "don't know a hawk from a handsaw."[47]

As for Prince Hal, his bliss was complete. He felt "profound gratitude" for the unanimous nomination. It had taken ten weeks, but his valentine had arrived at last. The people loved him; the Texas treaty, mired in committee in the Senate, was in doubt; and as for the Democrats, "I do not think I ever witnessed such a state of utter disorder, confusion, and decomposition as that which the Democratic Party now presents," he crowed to a friend. Everything seemed to be going Henry Clay's way. Not that he ever had any doubt. He was "firmly convinced that my opinion on the Texas question will do me no prejudice at the South."[48]

He was right about the Democrats, at least. In the weeks before their own convention at the end of May, matters looked particularly bleak. The party of Andrew Jackson had been adrift since the economic panic of 1837 and subsequent shocking victory of William Henry Harrison in 1840. Recent developments did not augur well for a return to power in 1844. Van Buren's letter deeply unsettled party leaders in the South and West, and by mid-May it was widely reported that "gentlemen of the Mississippi Delegation, as well as from Alabama and Virginia, have openly declared that they will not go for any candidate that is not for the annexation of Texas."[49]

But without Van Buren, what chance did the party have against Henry Clay? The latter was not alone in assuming that Van Buren "is really the strongest man of their Party." Many Democrats doubted "whether anything can be done now—any candidate that may be proposed—or any measure that can be adopted—can stay the great and overwhelming tide that is urging the party that came into power with Gen. Jackson to utter dissolution."[50]

Old Jackson himself was hardly more positive. Terminally ill at his Tennessee estate, he admitted to a friend that he was "unmanned" by Van Buren's rejection of Texas, and "shed tears of regret" when he read it. Old Hickory had allowed diplomatic consideration to rule when he was president. He had kept Texas at arm's length despite believing in his heart that territorial expansion was America's destiny, despite a close personal relationship with Texas president Sam Houston, despite feeling as deeply as anyone that the Texians were kin who belonged back in the family.[51]

Now, at the close of his life, he felt the pull of Texas once more. Jackson was no longer the power broker of his party, but his opinion still counted. And he believed the time for annexation had come. Rousing himself from bed, he fired off a string of letters to friends and supporters, so many that they seemed to one concerned recipient to "manifest a mania" on the sub-ject.[52] Van Buren's position was wrong. The party would have to find a new candidate, one who favored the annexation of Texas. Jackson loved Van Buren but could no longer support him. He wrote directly to his for-mer vice president and warned him that his election in 1844 was impos-sible under these circumstances. Van Buren, shocked by the desertion of his mentor, destroyed the letter.

It wasn't easy for Jackson to reject Van Buren, but the interests of the party, *his* party, and of his nation came first. Old Hickory had a plan for the salvation of both. He put pen to paper once more, and summoned James K. Polk to his bedside.

2

———————

"Who Is James K. Polk?"

WHEN ANDREW JACKSON called, James Knox Polk answered. He had long been known as "Young Hickory," and his career was as much an offshoot of Jackson's as the nickname implied. Polk wasn't sure why the old man needed him, but the content of the communication made no difference to Polk's prompt response. It was sixty miles from Polk's home in Columbia to the Hermitage, outside Nashville. Polk started packing immediately after receiving his summons.

The Democratic Party had been created by Andrew Jackson in his own image. He was the first common-man president, or rather the first president who represented himself as a common man, since his plantation, slaves, and vast wealth were decidedly uncommon. His public persona was the back-woods general, a man who had risen from nothing, who had led a group of volunteers to an astounding victory over the British at the Battle of New Orleans, and whose interests were those of average people. It was the "virtuous yeomanry" who, Jackson maintained, "of their own mere will brought my name before the nation for the office of President of these U. States" and "sustained me against all the torrents of slander that corruption & wickedness could invent, circulated thro subsidized presses and every other way supported by the patronage of the government."[1] Jackson believed that his victory was the victory of the people over entrenched interests and corrupt politicians, including Henry Clay, who ruled Washington.

Jackson's election marked the death of a certain deferential politics that ruled during the era of Washington, Jefferson, and John Adams. Voters chose the first generation of American statesmen on the basis of their superior education and experience. But that began to change after 1815, when states eased their requirements for voting, enabling scores of white men to exercise the franchise for the first time. Jackson's inferior education and shocking inability to spell led the East Coast elite to snicker about his literacy, or lack thereof, but bothered "the people" not a bit. In 1824, 1828, and again in 1832 "the people" turned out for Andrew Jackson. His image would cast a long shadow over the Democratic Party, as countless politicians, including James Polk, attempted to emulate the hero of New Orleans.[2]

Jackson's Democratic Party both expressed and embraced this ideal of popular democracy, and posed the thesis that political outsiders made ideal politicians. Any candidate saddled with inherited wealth and a good education suddenly found them heavy weights to bear. Americans were looking for the common touch. If a man could connect with his constituency, deliver a heartfelt speech about opportunity and equality, and convince the voters that he felt their pain, that he was one of them, then no office in the land was out of reach. If said candidate had proven his martial valor on the battlefield against Native Americans or the British, all the better. A remarkable number of Democratic politicians in the 1830s, particularly in the South and West, rode Indian killing to elected office.

James K. Polk was just one member of the cadre of Tennessee politicians whose fortunes rose precipitously after Jackson's election. They were true believers in the principles of Jacksonian democracy, affirming territorial expansion, upholding the rights of the common man, and opposing the urban elite and their sources of power—their banks, factories, and social institutions. The young Tennessee Democrats, including Polk, Sam Houston, and David Crockett, hoped to turn the former liability of a backwoods southwestern upbringing to their advantage, and perhaps emulate Jackson's remarkable ascent.

David Crockett was an early adopter of the model. He was a natural showman, a brilliant stump speaker, and a prodigious teller of jokes. His marksmanship was legendary, and he fought ably under Jackson's command in the U.S. war against the powerful Creek tribe from 1811 to 1813. He made it to Congress, where he chose to fight against Jackson rather than with him. He broke with Old Hickory over the president's Indian removal policy. Crockett thought it wrong and believed that the Five Civilized Tribes deserved to keep their land. He joined the opposition, wrote a best-selling autobiography, and became one of the first American folk heroes, a character on the stage, and the hero of tall tales. Despite his fame, Tennessee voters still punished him for opposing Jackson. After losing reelection to Congress, he famously told his constituency to "go to hell," and that he would "go to Texas."[3] He kept his word, and in 1836 gained martyrdom when he died defending the Alamo.

Sam Houston was another natural at the game, and like Jackson made political hay out of his military service in the War of 1812. His ability to charm a room was equaled only by his astounding capacity for alcohol, and after two terms in Congress in the 1820s he became Tennessee's most charismatic governor. Houston also moved west to Texas. Some said the move came at the encouragement of President Jackson, who hoped Houston might turn his talent at causing trouble toward fomenting an uprising. Houston did just that but fared better than Crockett. He led Texas forces to victory at San Jacinto, and in 1836 he was elected the first president of the republic.

And then there was James Knox Polk. Of the three young Tennessee politicians, Jackson loved Polk best. Polk always came when Jackson called, and Polk never betrayed him. He was truly Young Hickory, though Jackson wouldn't live to see the full extent of Polk's devotion.

James K. Polk was born in western North Carolina in 1795 to wealthy, slave-owning parents, the eldest of ten children. His mother was a strict Presbyterian, his father's faith in the democratic ideals of Thomas Jefferson was equally absolute. James was never baptized; his father's refusal to acknowledge the existence of God derailed the ceremony. No doubt the event caused his mother pain and worry, but on the southern frontier a husband's authority over his family was close to absolute; and if a man wanted to keep his son from God's grace, there wasn't much a mother could do about it.

When James was ten, the family moved to Tennessee, where his father became a judge and one of the richest men in the county. James's faith in territorial expansion was grounded in his history. His parents and grandparents had prospered at the expense of Native Americans, following the frontier west as the federal government negotiated treaties displacing tribes from their land. Westward expansion was the source of the family's riches.

James was a small, sickly child. He was never able to compete with his brothers and friends at the physical contests so important to establishing dominance in the southern backcountry. But he showed a natural aptitude for both mathematics and Latin, a language that Henry Clay, to his life-long chagrin, never mastered. As a teenager he was crippled with pain from urinary bladder stones. His father found a doctor in Kentucky willing to try a highly experimental treatment, and at age seventeen James under-went a harrowing surgery without benefit of anesthesia. The stones were removed, but at a cost: James never fathered a child, as the surgery likely left him sterile.[4]

His recovery seemed miraculous. James threw himself into his scholar-ship, and his parents encouraged his talents. They sent him back to North Carolina for the best education in the region. He excelled at the Univer-sity of North Carolina, graduating first in his class. He took up law, but his passion was politics. By the early 1820s he had hitched his star to Jackson's.

Polk was no natural at the game of politics. To start, he had little mili-tary experience. Although he was promoted to colonel in the local mili-tia, he never aimed a rifle at an Indian or anyone else. Many of his college chums volunteered to fight the British in the War of 1812. Polk would have loved to be part of that epic struggle against America's nemesis. The young War Hawks of the day believed it was a second American Revolution. But his health hardly allowed it. Five foot eight and painfully skinny, Polk had excellent posture, but he was almost always sick or recovering from illness. He lacked charisma, couldn't tell a joke to save his life, and was an unin-spired public speaker. Where Houston and Crocket were warm, Polk was cool. He had chilly gray eyes and a stern mouth, and he wore his dark, unruly hair brushed straight back. Closemouthed, even sullen, formal in his words and calculating in his thought, he lacked a politician's deft touch. Polk was not a man that people liked.

But he overcame these liabilities, as he had so many others in life, through sheer will. He campaigned twice as hard as his opponents, worked twelve to fourteen hours a day, and, perhaps out of insecurity that he hadn't fought in a war himself, adopted a belligerent attitude toward other nations that played well with the folks back home. He would never be a great speaker; his supporters claimed that "his ambition was to distinguish himself by substantial merit, rather than by rhetorical display." John Quincy Adams noted that he had "no wit . . . no gracefulness of delivery, no elegance of language," but he taught himself how to deliver a speech laced with enter-taining anecdotes.[5] He forced himself to meet and greet, to mingle with the people, although it never came naturally to him. He perfected a public per-sona of direct honesty that stood in stark contrast to his private reticence. While not as good as Crockett's bonhomie, for the most part it did the trick.

James K. Polk, 1845. Lithograph by Charles Fenderich. Library of
Congress Prints and Photographs Division.

Polk also married well. Rumor has it that it was Jackson who encouraged
Polk, then a young state legislator, to court the teenage Sarah Childress. Polk
had gone to school with her brother and had met and admired the young
woman. He followed Jackson's advice in this as in everything else. The
couple married at her parents' plantation near Murfreesboro, Tennessee, in
1824, when Sarah was twenty and James twenty-eight.

Polk's bride hailed from a background like his own: the Childresses were
also slave-owning Presbyterians at the very pinnacle of Tennessee society.
Sarah's father was a wealthy land speculator who recognized and encouraged his eldest daughter's unusual intelligence. Like the Polk family, he
looked east to North Carolina for schools worthy of his bright progeny. Sarah
attended the exclusive Moravian Female Academy, the very best school
open to women in the region, and like her future husband she excelled aca-
demically. But her father's untimely death, when she was only fifteen, cut
her formal schooling short. Returning home to comfort her mother, in deep
mourning for her beloved father, Sarah found solace and direction in the
strictures and ritual of the Presbyterian Church. Throughout her life she

Sarah Polk, 1829. This portrait of Sarah Childress Polk was painted by Ralph E. W. Earl when she was twenty-six, had been married for five years, and was living in Washington, D.C., while James served in Congress. James was pleased with the portrait. "Mr. Earle has caught exactly the look of mischief that few people outside myself ever see," he reportedly remarked (Bumgarner, Sarah Childress Polk, *34).* Courtesy James K. Polk Memorial Association, Columbia, Tennessee.

had a weakness for beautiful clothes that stood somewhat at odds with her general solemnity and disdain for affectation. With her strong features and dark, deep-set eyes, Sarah was considered striking rather than beautiful by all but her closest admirers, but her reputation for intelligence, exemplary piety, and very fine wardrobe were beyond dispute.

Sarah was the perfect partner to James Polk, and as the years passed they forged a union of remarkable strength. She fulfilled all the normal expectations for political wives: she was social where he was not, and ever solicitous of his fragile health. She fought a valiant battle to get him to eat and sleep on a regular basis. But theirs was far from a typical nineteenth-century marriage. Childless in an era when the birth and upbringing of children defined a woman's married life, Sarah threw herself into her husband's work. And far from being threatened by her strong opinions and political acumen, James embraced his wife's capabilities. Early in their marriage, when she would lobby James to put out the lamp and come to bed, Polk instead put her to work. "Taking up a newspaper, he would quietly reply, 'Sarah, here is something I wish you to read.' And so he set me to work too," she remembered.[6]

Soon she was analyzing political debates for him. She became a regular companion on James's political excursions, one of the only wives who traveled with their politician husbands. "He always wished me to go," she recalled, "and he would say, 'Why should you stay at home? To take care of the house? Why, if the house burns down, we can live without it.' " Whether James's primary goal was preventing his wife from becoming lonely in their childless house or he needed her advice, Sarah Polk became James Polk's closest political advisor. This suited her fine. "Knowing much of political affairs she found pleasure in the society of gentlemen," one friend of hers remarked. Rather than socializing with other wives, Sarah could be found with the men. "She was always in the parlor with Mr. Polk."[7]

Sarah Childress Polk was every bit as much a Democratic stalwart as her husband, and of the two she was the more ambitious. James liked to joke that "had he remained the clerk of the legislature she would never have consented to marry him," but probably he wasn't far off the mark.[8] Before their wedding Sarah extracted a promise that he would run for Congress. Although she perpetually worried about her husband's fragile health, as well as his unbaptized soul, her trust in his political destiny was total.

For many years that trust seemed well placed: Polk was elected to seven straight terms in the House of Representatives and with President Jackson's support became Speaker of the House for two of them. Sarah was no small part of his success, fulfilling her responsibilities "with ease and dignity." She took extra rooms specifically for entertaining at the Washington boardinghouse where they lived, and successfully served as intermediary between her prickly husband and the rest of Washington.[9]

Sarah's behavior would not have been out of place in the first decades of the nineteenth century, when Dolley Madison and other canny political wives used social events to build political alliances. But a separation of public and private spheres in the early 1830s left Washington politics almost exclusively in the hands of men. Sarah's political maneuvering definitely stood out. Not long after he became Speaker, one of Polk's allies wrote that he was glad Sarah was "engaged in the amusement of politics, though from my heart I could wish that she had some more amusing amusement to amuse herself with—something more domestic for instance." But Sarah didn't need domestic concerns to amuse herself; James's career was fully consuming for both of them. They devoted all their energy to ensuring that Young Hickory was viewed as the legitimate political offspring of the also childless Jackson.[10]

Old Hickory had high hopes for his acolyte. He thought Polk might make a good vice presidential candidate when he got a bit older, eventually even president in his own right. When Jackson left the White House in early 1837, after two glorious terms in office, James and Sarah Polk were part of the party that accompanied him back to Tennessee. During one of those long carriage rides, Jackson turned to Sarah. Looking into the young woman's dark eyes, he told her that "the scepter shall come back to Tennessee before very long, and your own fair self shall be the queen."[11]

But that seemed like ancient history in 1843. The Panic of 1837 had hit Tennessee and the Democratic Party hard. Whigs argued that Democratic legislation had destroyed the economy and that it was time for new ideas. After eight years of Jackson in the White House, Democrats were in no position to persuasively argue otherwise. Polk made the selfless choice to return home and attempt to save the fortunes of the state party. Sarah successfully coordinated his campaign for governor of Tennessee in 1839, but he couldn't stop the party's slide. Tennessee voters seemed bewitched by the Whigs' program for economic development, which encompassed building good roads, stabilizing the banking system, and implementing protective tariffs to support fledgling industry. There may not have been many voters who replaced their framed portraits of local hero Andrew Jackson with those of his archrival, Henry Clay, but the state went for the Whigs in the 1840 presidential election. Tennessee appeared nearly beyond redemption for the Democrats.

Polk's fortunes fell just as hard. Twice in a row he lost bids for the Tennessee governorship to a charismatic Whig who was a far better speaker and had all the personal charm Polk lacked. In 1843, fresh off his second loss, both he and Sarah worried about his future. Polk wasn't wanted as governor; the people of Tennessee had made that clear. He might return to the House of Representatives, or perhaps Andrew Jackson might lobby his Washington supporters for a cabinet position for Polk once the Democrats returned to power. Old Hickory wouldn't want Young Hickory to fall into total disrepute.

But perhaps Polk was also beyond redemption. After the second gubernatorial defeat, Jackson stopped writing to Polk about his vice presidential prospects. He stopped writing about Polk's political future altogether. Even

Sarah Polk had to admit that Jackson's prophecy was taking on the air of a fairy tale.

All this was before the issue of Texas turned the presidential race upside down. Polk was an attorney by trade, but like his parents and grandparents he made his real money off westward expansion and slavery. He first began speculating in land in western Tennessee while a member of Congress, using slaves to clear and improve property that he then sold for a handsome profit. Polk appears to have paid more attention to his investments in land than to his investments in human flesh. Despite warnings from family members that one of his overseers treated Polk's slaves with disturbing brutality, Polk continued to employ the man.[12]

Polk also used slaves to grow cotton on a plantation in Mississippi. He spent most of April 1844 there, insulated from the chatter about Texas, but made it back to Tennessee before news broke of Van Buren's startling stand on annexation. Tennessee Democrats were outraged. Few were surprised by this kind of response from Henry Clay, but Martin Van Buren? They had expected better from the Democratic front-runner.

As for Polk, he had always supported annexation. Texas, he believed, was just a first step toward the realization of a far greater, God-given goal: that of a United States stretching from shore to shore, taking its place in the world as Europe's equal. He felt no hesitation in saying so. Well before Van Buren's betrayal became public, Polk announced that he favored the "immediate reannexation" of Texas, picking up on the fanciful idea, introduced by Mississippi senator Robert J. Walker, that Texas, as part of the Louisiana Purchase, had once belonged to the United States and was wrongly traded away by then Secretary of State John Quincy Adams in the 1819 Transcontinental Treaty. In fact, the United States had no legitimate prior claim on Texas.

"Reannexation," however nonsensical, was a brilliant rhetorical move on Walker's part. A Pennsylvanian who fully embraced both slavery and expansion when he moved to the South as a young man, Walker recognized that lobbying for the "reannexation" of Texas could serve several ends. It might ease the consciences of northerners who felt funny about taking land still claimed by Mexico, since America's claim supposedly predated Mexico's, indeed predated Mexico's independence from Spain. It also discredited John Quincy Adams for "giving away" Texas, and by extension discredited northerners and Whigs as hostile to the interests of the South.

In reality Adams was one of the foremost expansionists in the early republic; he had even attempted to purchase Texas from Mexico in 1827 when he was president. Since the end of his presidency, however, he had devoted himself to the "sublime and beautiful cause" of abolition and was now the leading voice against slavery in Congress. This made him an easy target for Democrats, and any opportunity to link Adams to more moderate Whigs such as Clay was not to be lost.[13]

Polk recognized the value of Walker's gambit and embraced it. "Let Texas be reannexed, and the authority and laws of the United States be established and maintained within her limits," Polk proclaimed. The United States needed to seize the present opportunity to be "re-united with a country from which the United States should never have been separated." He also called for the annexation of the whole of the Oregon Country, envisioning a United States that spread all the way to the Pacific, encompassing British Columbia and Vancouver Island. Polk was quick to perceive that "the Texas question . . . swallows up all others at present." As he wrote Cave Johnson, a fellow Tennessee politician, "It is impossible to arrest the current of the popular opinion and any man who attempts it will be crushed by it."[14]

Polk's views were published but not widely reprinted. Despite twenty-two years as a dedicated Democrat, he was still an obscure figure even within his own party, a nobody outside Tennessee. His statements in support of annexation did nothing to increase his profile among national Democratic power brokers. With Jackson's help he might still secure the number two slot on a Van Buren ticket. But more likely Polk would get some sort of position abroad in a Democratic administration. One newspaper suggested he might be named foreign minister to Vienna.[15] Even with concerns about the Texas issue on the rise, Democratic nominating conventions were predictable things in those days, and Van Buren was still the presumptive nominee.

It was just two short weeks before the Democratic convention when Andrew Jackson summoned Polk to the Hermitage to confer about Texas. Polk made the first fifty miles of his trip in two days, arriving in Nashville on a Sunday. He spent the night in a hotel, and the next morning he set out on horseback to see Jackson.

While riding from town to the estate, Polk met Jackson's nephew, Andrew Jackson Donelson, traveling in the opposite direction with a letter written by Old Hickory for publication. The letter called for the immediate annexation of Texas and openly rebuffed Van Buren, implying that he had dug his own grave on the issue. Jackson had been writing similar letters to members of his party for weeks but thus far had not publicly rebuked the man who Polk still assumed would be the party's nominee. How would it possibly help the chances of the Democratic Party for the general to issue a statement such as this?

Polk wasn't one to criticize Jackson, but he brought both Donelson and the letter back with him to the Hermitage. There he found the ex-president intensely agitated on the subject of Texas and speaking "with almost all his former energy." Jackson railed against Van Buren, suggested he should withdraw from the race since he couldn't possibly beat Clay in the general election, and then turned his attention to Polk. "The candidate for the first office should be an annexation man and from the Southwest," he told the younger man, and Polk himself was "the most available man."[16]

Polk was incredulous. "I have never aspired so high," he wrote to Cave Johnson afterward. He was only forty-eight, surely too young to be president, certainly too unknown. What madness! Polk concluded that it would be "utterly abortive" to put his name forward.[17]

But after he had slept on it, the plan didn't seem quite so far-fetched. Two days later Polk had entirely come around to Jackson's view. Perhaps he was the man for the moment. Statehood for Texas had long been his cause; the moment was right to expand freedom's territory in a great western push not just to Texas but to California and Oregon as well.

America needed it. Polk was smart enough to see the great opportunity before him, one that his country would embrace. As Polk surveyed America in 1844, he saw a young nation experiencing growing pains and at the same time desperate to claim its place among leading nations. Nearly everything was in transition, and there was no clarity about the future. Economic developments that heralded a "market revolution" were increasing class divisions between the newly and ostentatiously rich and poor people with little opportunity for upward mobility. Great waves of immigration from Europe were changing the country's ethnic profile, and xenophobia, then called "nativism," was on the rise. Women had begun demanding recognition and power, undermining male authority at home and in public. Religious revivals emerging out of the Second Great Awakening gave birth to reform movements that dared insist society radically change. Workingmen were forming trade unions. And there were the hotly contested issues of slavery and temperance, so divisive that few dared truly engage with them. No wonder, then, that a shifting electorate, one whose electoral participation had expanded dramatically in the 1820s and 1830s to encompass virtually all white men, regarded the values and assumptions that had once defined the two political parties as less and less meaningful.

In the midst of these shifts, Polk understood, one core belief remained that could both galvanize his party and unite the nation: Manifest Destiny. The push west could solve all of America's problems. It could provide the immigrant masses crowding American cities with land of their own to farm and a stake in society, as well as reinforce patriarchy by providing men with a means of supporting their families in an environment where strength and physical skill mattered. It would buttress American democracy by reducing the growing strength of manufacturing in the economy and the influence of the northeastern urban elite who profited from that system. And Alta California, on the far west coast, was home to harbors that might allow the United States to compete with Europe for control of trade with China. Expansion would make America strong. Expansionism was a winning political issue and the best policy for the country. But—and Polk believed this in his very soul—it was also *right*.

He saw clearly that the long years during which cool heads had prevailed on Texas were over. There had been a quick romance and Americans had fallen for Texas, even mythologizing the Alamo's dead. The American people were ready for annexation; indeed, they believed just what Polk did—that the United States was destined to expand and should take every opportunity to do so. Didn't everything in America's short history point to that conclusion, from the Puritan understanding of America as a city on a hill, a model to be replicated by others, to previous territorial acquisitions (the Louisiana Purchase of 1803, the purchase of Florida from Spain in 1819, the displacement of the Five Civilized Tribes in the 1830s), and finally the nation's incredible population growth (from four million to seventeen million people between 1790 and 1840)? The nation's very character made expansion inevitable. Americans had a go-ahead, get-ahead nature, with strains of ambition and individualism that led them to constantly push westward, to and beyond the frontier.[18]

Polk instinctively grasped all of this. Expansion was a winning political issue, at once a promise of national glory and a symbol of dynamic change. Still, he was not its standard-bearer merely to sway voters. He truly believed that Americans were exceptional, that his country was marked for greatness. Manifest Destiny was not a matter of if but merely one of how. And it justified almost any tactic. The issue was, for him, a perfect marriage of politics and conviction. Tyler had done him the enormous favor of bringing the statehood of Texas into the mainstream, and now he would do the rest.

Still, something else was at work in Polk's vision, something that held great appeal for the majority of southern Democrats. For he was a slave-holder. Ever wary of the growing power of the North and the agitations of

"Matty Meeting the Texas Question," 1844. This satire of the disorder in the Democratic ranks was most likely produced by a giddy Whig in the summer of 1844, not long after Polk's nomination. Andrew Jackson prods a very unwilling Martin Van Buren in the direction of Texas, represented here as a hideous hag propped up by Thomas Hart Benton and John C. Calhoun. Calhoun offers to "introduce you to the Texas Question, what do you say to her Ladyship?" Van Buren replies, "Take any other shape but that, and my firm nerves shall never tremble." In the background, Polk suggests to Dallas that although Texas might not be "the handsomest lady I ever saw," she was worth $25,000 a year (the amount of the president's salary) and a "little stretching of conscience." By representing Texas as a nonwhite, monstrous, knife- and chain-wielding woman, the printmaker clearly expressed his view that the Republic of Texas would make an undesirable addition to the United States, and anyone who felt otherwise was ignoring his "conscience." Library of Congress Prints and Photographs Division.

abolitionists, men such as Polk scorned an interfering central government and were desperate for new slave states to buttress the strength of their "peculiar" institution. They believed not only that territorial aggrandizement was the key to national vigor but also that slavery itself meshed well with democracy. Polk and his fellow southern Democrats did not believe that a nation of liberty was one in which all men were literally free. True independence instead consisted of a community of landholders thriving through ownership of their farms and self-determination of their rights.

He could be the instrument of Manifest Destiny. Polk put pen to paper and began offering a case for his nomination, not for the vice presidency but for the great prize itself. Polk would not attend the Democratic convention; it was considered unseemly for politicians to push forward their own candidacies. But if the opportunity arose, his supporters would be ready.

. . .

May 27, 1844. It had been a month since the Whig convention, and the Clay posters, coats, ribbons, and garlands were long gone when the Democrats gathered in Baltimore for their own convention. The weather had turned hot and spirits were low. On Monday morning a great crowd gathered outside the Odd Fellows Hall on North Gay Street. Democratic delegates had chosen the elegant Egyptian Saloon within the hall, the largest in Baltimore, for their meeting, but the space was clearly too small. Although "every possible arrangement had been made" for "the business of the convention," the animated crowd spilled out into the street.[19] Martin Van Buren clearly commanded a majority of delegates, but this was no unified assembly. The rifts among the Democrats were obvious to all.

At exactly noon, the hour set for the start of the convention, a minority group committed to the annexation of Texas, and led by "reannexation" promoter Robert J. Walker of Mississippi, seized the floor and changed the convention rules so that a winning nominee required two-thirds of all votes. In their haste to pull the rug out from under Old Van, his opponents had forgotten to bring a minister forward for the customary prayers offered up at meetings of this sort. After rectifying this oversight, which struck some delegates as a bad omen, the annexationists returned to the work of overthrowing Martin Van Buren.

Their favored candidate was Lewis Cass of Michigan, a stolid, serious man of tremendous girth with a pronounced sympathy for the South. Abolitionist William Lloyd Garrison called him "lick-spittle to southern power, and base panderer to slave traffickers." Van Buren's supporters were hardly more positive, deriding the Michigan senator's supporters as "Jack Casses." But Cass's expansionist credentials were above reproach. He had been instrumental in the Indian removal of the 1830s, arguing loudly and repeatedly that the "savage" Cherokee were undeserving of their lands, despite the tribe's wholesale acceptance of the norms of their southern neighbors. The Cherokee were literate Christians and profitable farmers, and some even owned slaves. The only thing that made them savage was their race, but that was enough.[20]

Cass's invective had only increased since then, along with his open disdain for virtually all residents of North America lacking his skin color and citizenship. His views could not be further from Van Buren's: he would annex Texas, just as he hoped to annex Canada, Cuba, and any other territory in the Western Hemisphere that might be available.

To the astonishment of Van Buren's many supporters in Odd Fellows Hall, Cass quickly began to gain on the front-runner. By the seventh ballot he was firmly in the lead. At that point, however, the Jack Casses were faced with the unpleasant reality that their man was no more likely than Van Buren to win the votes of two-thirds of the assembled delegates, particularly given that most of Van Buren's delegates would sooner vote for Clay than allow "the *damned rotten corrupt venal* Cass" the victory of the nomination. Tempers flared, and the Van Buren delegates threatened to return home. The convention deadlocked.[21]

Complicating matters for the Democrats was the fact that Tyler supporters had chosen to hold their own convention over on Calvert Street at the exact same time. Tyler no longer hoped to win the presidency; that dream had died with Abel Upshur and the *Princeton* explosion. That was fine with him; newly engaged, Tyler had a ravishing young bride to focus on. But he was desperate to save his Texas treaty, which had been drowning in a sea of criticism in the Senate for the previous three weeks. Tyler's presidential convention was designed to do one thing: blackmail the Democratic Party into embracing Texas.

There was no problem with crowding at Tyler's convention. Since being dismissed by the Whigs, "His Accidency" had surrounded himself with sycophants from the Democratic Party, many of whom were profiting handsomely from government contracts and other spoils of office. A select assortment of these officeholders and friends of the president gathered in Calvert Hall to nominate the president on his own ticket and a pro-annexation platform.

What they lacked in numbers they more than made up for in enthusiasm, as well as "large supplies of brandy and water, whiskey and gin." Tyler's sham convention may well have been as "contemptibly ridiculous" as critics claimed, but at least the proceedings moved quickly. "Tyler and Texas" were unanimously endorsed by the assembled delegates, who then drifted over to Odd Fellows Hall to see how matters stood with the Democrats. Face-to-face with gloating and inebriated Tyler supporters, Van Buren's distressed delegates had no choice but to acknowledge that Texas would be the leading question in the coming election.[22]

After "an anxious day of strife discord, intrigue, and factious cabal," the Democrats adjourned for the evening. Several thousand of the most enthusiastic—"men's men," as one account put it—headed off to smoky taverns and to Monument Square, where a pro-Democratic rally was set. Unfortunately Tyler's supporters had the same idea. The Democrats took up space in front of the courthouse, while Tyler supporters colonized the front stairs of P. T. Barnum's City Hotel. The two groups sized each other up and proceeded to hold dueling rallies within earshot, "with the most discordant voices, and with gesticulation violent and threatening."[23]

The Democrats themselves were far from a unified front. Some speakers proclaimed in favor of Cass, others for Van Buren. The crowd shifted between the two podiums, with one particularly inebriated Tyler supporter, "as gloriously happy as need be," drawing the lion's share of the crowd. The Democrats took offense, and "at one time the signs threatened a general row" complete with "bloody nose or a cracked skull. But the discord confined itself to words."[24]

Disgruntled Democrats eventually seized the space and forced the outnumbered Tyler supporters to retreat. But it wasn't much of a victory. The majority of delegates had arrived in Baltimore ready to support Van Buren, yet the majority had not ruled. One speaker summed up the crowd's sense of powerlessness when he pointed up to a window in Barnum's City Hotel and with the force of "one of the furies" asked that "these shouts could reach the ears of the conclave that is now assembled in a room above . . . who are now in concert endeavoring to concoct a scheme to cheat the people out of the nomination of their favorite, Martin Van Buren."[25] They might have intimidated Tyler's supporters, but the crowd recognized that the real power lay elsewhere that night.

About 1:00 a.m., the "men's men" headed back to their hotels and boardinghouses, hardly knowing what the next morning might bring, besides the expected headache. Their convention was wide open. Just as Andrew Jackson predicted, Old Van had been thrown over. Now the Democrats needed a compromise candidate. He would have to be acceptable to supporters of both Cass and Van Buren, and he would have to favor annexation. Ideally, he would also be able to charm John Tyler out of the race.

Jackson's plan was coming together perfectly.

The men's men in Monument Square were right: the important decisions were being made elsewhere that Monday night. Democratic operatives cloistered themselves in a nearby hotel room and hammered out a solution to the deadlock between Van Buren and Cass. By dawn they had settled on a candidate who had the power not only to unify the fractured and angry delegate pool but also perhaps to pull out a victory against Henry Clay in November. He wasn't particularly well known, he hadn't received a single vote on the first day of the convention, and his reputation was shaky even in his home state. But he had no enemies and was a true believer in annexation. James K. Polk had been anointed.

The delegates came around quickly. He was no one's first choice, but the following morning, on the ninth ballot, Polk was unanimously proclaimed the Democratic nominee for president in 1844, America's first dark-horse presidential candidate. The Whig platform said nothing about Texas, but the Democratic platform called for "the re-occupation of Oregon and the re-annexation of Texas at the earliest practicable period." Polk needed to appease the Van Burenites and to balance the ticket with a northerner. He offered the vice presidency to Van Buren's closest supporter, New Yorker Silas Wright. But Wright turned him down, telling friends that he "did not propose to ride behind on the black pony [slavery] at the funeral of his slaughtered friend" Van Buren.[26]

Polk turned next to Pennsylvania senator George M. Dallas, who was even more of a political nonentity than himself. Dallas was roused from bed at three in the morning by a group of inebriated supporters who didn't immediately blurt out the good news. Since Dallas had no idea he was a candidate for office, he answered the door in his slippers wholly believing that something horrible had happened to a loved one. But Dallas quickly warmed to the news and accepted the unexpected honor.[27]

Thanks to the wonders of Samuel Morse's newly invented telegraph, Washington received nearly instantaneous notice of Polk's nomination. But Young Hickory was so little known that listeners assumed the device had erred: "When the wonder working telegraph proclaimed the final nomination, it was heard by all the faithful with speechless amazement." "Who is James K. Polk?" reporters wondered. Not everyone was rendered speechless. Jackson protégé Thomas Hart Benton cursed the "damned fools" in Baltimore when he heard of Polk's promotion.[28]

Henry Clay was incredulous. "Are our Democratic friends serious?" he asked. This couldn't possibly be right. "What principles has Mr. Polk ever developed or upheld to entitle him to a Nation's confidence at the chief administrator in its affairs?" the *National Intelligencer* queried. "Recently weighed in the balance as Chief Magistrate of his own State, having been found wanting and discarded from its service, what probability is there that, with this known judgment against him at home, he can find favor with the People in other States who have no other knowledge of him than such as this?"[29]

Polk was "conspicuous for nothing but his blind, implicit and unhesitating submissiveness" to Andrew Jackson; he seemed to have no notable accomplishments. "As to Mr. Polk, what is he?" asked one critic. "A worthy enough, amiable enough person, individually, but, as a public man, utterly without abilities, without services, without reputation." New Yorker Philip

Hone marveled in his diary that the Democrats had chosen "General Jackson's chief cook and bottle washer." A Whig paper in Maryland, noting that "never before did such success follow upon so little effort," hypothesized that "after this, any man may set up for the nomination of President . . . and the more humble his abilities and the more obscure his position, the more certain may he rely upon success."[30]

The independent *New York Herald* agreed. "Of the nomination of Mr. Polk we hardly know how to speak seriously. A more ridiculous, contemptible and forlorn candidate, was never put forth by any party. He has neither the vigor, respectability nor the elements of any reputation, even half so much as Captain Tyler. . . . Mr. Polk is a sort of fourth or rather fortieth-rate lawyer and small politician in Tennessee, who by accident was once speaker of the House of Representatives. He was rejected even by his own state as governor—and now he comes forward as candidate of the great democracy of the United States."[31]

The irregular nature of the convention proceedings led some observers to wonder if the Democrats were attempting political suicide. "Disabled, by a cunning and successful stratagem, from the support of Mr. Van Buren, whom they really preferred, to whom they owed the honor of a nomination, and to whom a decided majority actually gave their votes . . . the Convention appears . . . rather than break up in utter confusion, to have unanimously thrown away its vote, and *let itself down* on Mr. Polk."[32] The Democrats "must be Polking fun at us!" one Whig paper punned.[33]

The *New York Herald* predicted that "the singular result of all these laughable doings of the democracy in Baltimore, will be the election of Henry Clay, by a larger majority than ever was received by Jackson or Harrison." Clay's path to the presidency was open. "With Polk and Tyler in the field to divide the democracy, who, were they rolled into one person, would hardly make a man, Mr. Clay must get the State of New York with perfect ease." The results would surely be the same in Pennsylvania and Virginia. The big states would easily fall into Clay's lap.[34]

Gleeful Whigs, in agreement that "this nomination may be considered as the dying gasp, the last breath of life, of the 'Democratic' party," were jubilant. It would hardly be a race at all. "Since our opponents have thought proper to put a nag upon the course which has neither speed nor bottom . . . , why, the western charger may take it easy, and gallop or walk over the course at his leisure."[35]

So confident was one group of Clay's supporters that they commissioned an enormous suite of solid rosewood bedroom furniture for his use in the

White House. They spared no expense in either materials or craftsmanship. The thirteen-foot bed, topped with a crimson cover and state pillows, cost more than a modest house, and was accompanied by six chairs, a dressing table, armoire, two marble-topped washstands, and a standing mirror. It was furniture fit for a prince, built on a princely scale. It would never fit into a normal home.[36]

Clay was just as sanguine. "We must beat them with ease if we do one half our duty," he wrote happily on June 7. The following day the Senate rejected Tyler's Texas treaty, with thirty-five senators opposed and sixteen in favor. Just as in Baltimore, the Democrats were divided, while the Whigs stood nearly unanimous against annexation and in favor of Henry Clay. As spring turned to summer, the future seemed clear. "The presidential election may be said to be decided as soon as it opens . . . Mr. Clay will have only to *walk over the course.*"[37]

3

_____

The Upset

NO POLITICIAN COULD devote as many evenings to poker and whiskey as
had Henry Clay and expect a decorous presidential campaign. Washington
was a tight community, and even those who had no personal memory of
Clay wagering a hotel in a game of cards, or gleefully smashing $120 worth
of crystal glasses and decanters at the close of a particularly wild party back
in the 1820s, knew his reputation for "fun and frolic" full well. His friends
rightly protested that the Sage of Ashland had mellowed in his old age. Harriet Martineau, a thirty-six-year-old British social critic renowned on both
sides of the Atlantic for her astute observations, asserted in 1838 that Clay's
"moderation is now his most striking characteristic; obtained, no doubt,
at the cost of prodigious self-denial on his own part." She marveled at his
"truly noble mastery" of his passions.[1]

That mastery went only so far. Clay still liked to drink, and that fact
alone was enough to raise questions about his self-control among the many
religious Americans who had sworn off intoxicating beverages in the previous decade. And Clay had a reputation to contend with. Stories circulated,
not all of them false, that when drunk Clay would lose his temper, slip into
self-pity, and display a range of behaviors that were decidedly unmanly and
unbecoming in a statesman of his stature. The stresses of presidential cam-
paigns brought out his worst. Not long before the 1840 convention Clay had
famously declared, "I would rather be right than be president," but when
told that the war hero Harrison had been chosen as the Whig nominee over

44

himself, he reportedly vented his rage in a drunken tirade that astounded observers. Screaming, cursing, shaking his fists, Clay proclaimed that "my friends are not worth the powder and shot it would take to kill them!"[2]

Four years later, no expense was spared in the attempt to kill Clay's candidacy. Polk's supporters lingered over Clay's heroic gambling, creative profanity, and drinking binges, and they greatly exaggerated his duels and Sabbath breaking. Democratic processions carried banners inscribed "No Gambler" and "No Duellist." One particularly creative pamphlet demonstrated how Clay had supposedly violated every one of the Ten Commandments.

Nor were the accusations limited to Clay's supposed debauchery. Southerners accused him of befriending abolitionists, while abolitionists pointed to Clay's slave owning to drum up support for a new third-party political organization, the Liberty Party, which directly attacked slavery and the mainstream parties that sustained it. Jackson renewed his old claims that Clay had cheated him out of the presidency in 1824 by making a "corrupt bargain" with John Quincy Adams. The character assaults were unrelenting, but Clay played it cool. "I laugh at the streights to which our opponents have been driven. They are to be pitied." He was used to scurrilous attacks; they did nothing to shake his confidence.[3]

Whigs would have slandered their opponent just as violently had they found anything to impugn. But Young Hickory's general obscurity masked a long career of aggressively wholesome habits. He had been happily married to the same woman for twenty years, and "his private life . . . has ever been upright and pure." Polk didn't gamble, drink, or fight duels. Although he professed no religion, he kept the Sabbath holy anyhow, a fact attributed to the "auspicious domestic influence" of his wife, "his guardian angel amid the perils and darkness of the way." Sarah Polk's insistence that her husband attend church with her each Sunday was well known. If he was "engaged in the company of men who, either from indifference or carelessness, forgot the Sabbath and its universal obligation," Sarah would enter the room "shawled and bonneted" and "ask her husband and his friends to go with her to church, saying that she did not wish to go alone." Indifferent men quickly came to realize that you didn't talk politics with James Polk on a Sunday unless you were willing to spend several hours in a Presbyterian church afterward.[4]

Sarah ensured that James conformed to her standards of religious observance, but he actually had stricter "ideas of propriety" than she did, and privately admonished her for not conforming to his "delicate conception of the fitness of things." If she ventured to make a joke about another person, he rebuked her: "Sarah, I wish you would not say that. I understand you, but others might not, and a wrong impression might be made." It was customary in the 1840s to view women as the keepers of moral virtue in society, but in this case Sarah attributed her own moral standards to the "strict" moral "school" run by her husband.[5]

His work ethic was just as faultless. Polk's campaign biography noted that "his course at college was marked by the same assiduity and studious application which have since characterized him. . . . [I]t is said that he never missed a recitation nor omitted the punctilious performance of any duty." Nor did he ever miss a vote in Congress, where he "always performed more than a full share of" his work. Since his youth, Democrats claimed, James K. Polk displayed a love of labor and degree of focus that clearly distinguished him from his Whig opponent. Polk's supporters noted that "habits of close application at college are apt to be despised by those who pride themselves on brilliancy of mind, as if they were incompatible." But this widespread disdain of hard work was "a melancholy mistake." What was "genius," they asked, other than hard work?[6]

Polk's virtues were many, but they didn't necessarily make for exciting verse. "Let us poke him in the chair say what they may, for in principles and honesty he excels Henry Clay," wrote the poet laureate at the University of Vermont.

> For morals and sobriety his character is upright,
> Nor in quarrels or wrangles does he ever delight;
> In gambling and dueling he never engages,
> And a war with his colleagues he never wages.[7]

Truth be told, Young Hickory was somewhat boring: a grind, perhaps, and very liable to charges of being a Jackson sycophant, but personally above reproach. The only dirt the Whigs could dig up was about Polk's iconoclastic father, who, they claimed, had been a Tory in the Revolution. But it was a feeble attack, and of little impact.

What Clay's supporters didn't quite realize was that a boring sycophant didn't make it to the top of the ticket without being exceptionally canny. Polk ran a very good campaign. One of his first moves was unifying his fractured party by promising to serve only one term in office. His rivals for the nomination had only to look forward four years for their own chance.

He also enlisted Old Hickory in the fight. The general was more than happy to resume his decades-old battle against his nemesis Henry Clay, whom he had long believed to be a "reckless demagogue, ambitious and regardless of truth when it comes in the way of his ambition." And although he was so weak as to be "scarcely able to wield my pen or to see what I write," he promised Sarah Polk that "I will put you in the White House you can so adorn if it costs me my life!" Jackson's greatest service was convincing John Tyler, recently returned from a lengthy honeymoon in New York, that it was time for him to retire. On August 20, Tyler formally withdrew from the presidential race and endorsed Polk. The Whigs could no longer count on the pro-annexation vote being split between two candidates. Polk also did an excellent job convincing immigrants, particularly Catholics, that the Whigs were xenophobic nativists, and that if awarded the presidency, Henry Clay would take away their schools, churches, and political rights, withhold the blessings of citizenship, and ensure that few of their brethren would ever join them in the United States.[8]

Until the end of the summer, Clay ran his 1844 campaign as if domestic issues were all that mattered. Politically, he offered his countrymen the same compelling program of industrialization, modernization, and market growth that his Whigs had successfully used to outmaneuver the Democrats in previous years. For Clay, annexation was a diversion, and war for Texas senseless. Why should the nation risk lives for land when its fate centered on tariffs and trade? Henry Clay promised to stabilize the banking system, institute a tariff for revenue, and support manufacturing. He would ensure governmental economy. He campaigned on the promise that technological progress and economic development would result not merely in riches for a few but a rising tide for all. He was the Whig candidate. What Whig voters wanted and expected from government was not territorial expansion but the construction of a nice macadam road to get them from their village to the city.

One person inspired by Clay's platform was an ambitious former state legislator in Illinois. The thirty-five-year-old lawyer Abraham Lincoln was a Whig on the rise. Lincoln had grown up worshipping Clay from afar. As a backwoods boy in Kentucky he had read Clay's biography over and over, as if memorizing the facts of the politician's life would allow him to emulate it. Although by 1844 he'd still never actually heard the man speak, he'd read and studied almost every important speech Clay had delivered. Clay, Lincoln said, was "my beau ideal of a statesman," and it was the older man's sweeping vision of economic progress that had first convinced him to become a Whig.[9]

While the politician from Illinois had no illusions that he was in his hero's league, he identified with him nonetheless. After all, both were self-made men, attorneys from western states; both had a political realist's bent, and both held the conviction that economic growth should be America's priority. Lincoln had no fears of a powerful central government, for he believed, along with other Whigs, that the purpose of government was "to do for a community of people, whatever they need to have done, but can not do, *at all* or can not, *so well do*, for themselves."[10] The fact that Clay was a slaveholder didn't bother Lincoln at all. In fact, the young Whig seemed generally unconcerned about slavery, viewing agitation to end it primarily as a nuisance that split his party. Illinois, and America, needed what the Whigs had to offer—good roads and bridges and access to credit—so that poor young men of promise, men such as himself, could overcome the humblest of circumstances and make a name for themselves.

Abraham Lincoln grew up poor—poor in a way that other self-proclaimed "common men" such as Clay and Polk could not dream of. With little formal education, he made his own way to the small town of New Salem, Illinois, in 1831, where his lively wit, physical strength (he was a superb wrestler), kindness, and striking intelligence won him friends and supporters. Less than a year after arriving, war broke out against the Sac and Fox Indians when they attempted to reclaim lands in Illinois that had been ceded to the United States in a treaty of dubious legitimacy. Just as war against the Creeks propelled a generation of Democrats in the Southwest to prominence, the Black Hawk War, as it was known, became a springboard for political advancement for young men on the Illinois frontier. Abraham Lincoln was elected captain of a volunteer militia unit in the conflict. In his three months in uniform, he never saw combat, which may have been just as well, since his company was woefully unprepared: when the men were mustered into service, thirty of them lacked firearms.

He may not have fired a shot, but Captain Lincoln witnessed shocking atrocities by Indian combatants that shaped his views of the rules of war, and proved an unexpected early test of his military leadership and character. Arriving at the scene of a recent massacre along the Fox River, Lincoln and his men gazed upon "scalps of old women & children." According to a volunteer in Lincoln's company, "The Indians Scalped an old Grand Mother—Scalped her—hung her scalp on a ram rod—that it might be seen & aggravate the whites—They cut one woman open—hung a child that they had murdered in the womans belly that they had gutted—strong men wept at this—cold hearted men Cried." Whether or not Lincoln was one of the "strong men" who wept, he refused to respond in kind, even when the passions of his men made restraint difficult. Several under his command testified that when an "old Indian" named Jack appeared in camp bearing a letter of support from Lewis Cass, the volunteers rushed at him. "We have come out to fight the Indians and by God we intend to do so," they told their captain. But Lincoln defended Jack, warning the volunteers, "Men this must not be done—he must not be shot and killed by us." Some in the unit considered Captain Lincoln "cowardly" for saving Jack's life. But he stood by his unpopular decision and refused to bow to the passions of the mob.[11]

This was Lincoln's first personal experience with the bloodlust of combat. Unlike many other veterans of Indian wars who justified the wanton destruction of enemy property and life as a reasonable response to the uncivilized action of a savage enemy, Lincoln emerged from the Black Hawk War seemingly committed both to the rules of war and to the sanctity of civilian life. In the face of a murderous enemy, an enemy seemingly inferior in both race and culture, Lincoln was highly unusual in upholding such a scrupulous moral standard. He was unlikely to forget what he saw during the Black Hawk War, or the conclusions he drew about the rights of civilians during wartime.

Immediately after returning to New Salem in 1832, at the age of only twenty-three, he ran for the State House of Representatives. At six foot four, in mismatched clothes too short in both the legs and the sleeves, his outfit topped off with an old straw hat that did nothing to flatter his sunburned face, Lincoln had neither pretension nor, as he put it, "wealthy or popular relatives or friends to recommend me." But thanks to his militia service he "was acquainted with everybody," had a good name in the county, and had friends to spare. He came in eighth in that race, but his simple speaking style and support for the Whig principles of a national bank, internal improvements, and a high protective tariff won him admirers. He told audiences that "if elected I shall be thankful; if not it will be all the same," and he clearly meant it. Failure did nothing to dampen his ardor for office. When he ran again for the statehouse in 1834, on a platform that reflected Henry Clay's principles, he won, and in 1836 he was not only reelected but chosen minority-party leader. Lincoln moved to the new capital of the state, Springfield, where he trained as a lawyer.[12]

Springfield was good to Abraham Lincoln. He made an advantageous marriage in 1842 to Mary Todd, a staunch Whig partisan who was the daughter of a prominent Kentucky Whig. She was described by her sister as "the most ambitious woman I ever knew."[13] The union brought Lincoln

social stature and much-needed funds: Mary's father, Robert Todd, visited the couple not long after their marriage and was so taken by his new
son-in-law that he promised them a generous yearly stipend. Abraham and
Mary Todd Lincoln, along with a new baby named after their benefactor,
applied some of the funds to the purchase of a modest one-story, five-room
wooden-frame structure on the corner of Eighth and Jackson in downtown
Springfield. The fifteen-hundred-dollar purchase price also bought them
several outbuildings and an eighth of an acre of land. The house wasn't in
the best neighborhood, but it was only four blocks from the courthouse. It
was their first real home.

Both Abraham and his wife recognized that he had married up. Mary
was a woman who "loved to put on *Style*," and while she had absolute faith
in her husband's political future, she was less convinced that he knew what
he was doing in some other aspects of life. She recognized, well before her
backwoods husband did, that success in Springfield required a certain level
of polish and decorum. Springfield wasn't New York, of course, nor was it
Mary's own hometown of Lexington, but the professional class of Springfield had pretensions to refinement, and although Lincoln was oblivious to
those standards, Mary was not. She set to work upgrading Lincoln's wardrobe in an attempt to make him "look like somebody"—lengthening his
pants, coordinating his outfits, and insisting that he purchase a new suit of
"superior black cloth," the most expensive purchase of the Lincolns' first
year of marriage.[14]

She started tutoring him in etiquette, demonstrating how to receive
guests at dinner and how to interact with servants, begging him please not
to come to dinner in his shirtsleeves. Some members of her family thought
she had gone too far. One told her, "If I had a husband with a mind such as
yours has, I would not care what he did." But Mary persisted, if only with
limited success. As long as Mary dressed him, he looked fine, but if left to
his own devices, Lincoln was sure to mismatch his clothes or use the wrong
fork at dinner. "I do not think he knew pink from blue when I married him,"
she told her sister.[15]

Lincoln took on a new law partner, William "Billy" Herndon, and the two
opened an office in the Tinsley Building, where the U.S. District Court of
Illinois met, not far from the capitol. With modest fees of ten to twenty-five
dollars per client and a reputation for honesty and hard work, the law firm
flourished. Although Lincoln had almost more work than he could handle,
his success as a lawyer allowed him to indulge in his passion for politics.
Throwing himself into the coming presidential election, he organized a

public meeting in Springfield to refute the charge that Whigs were hostile to foreigners or Catholics.[16] He also spoke in support of the Whig platform at the state convention in June 1844.

The young Whig volunteered to campaign for Clay across Illinois and into neighboring Indiana, and not incidentally build his own political base in the process. Lincoln was a brilliant storyteller, a natural in debates. He loved public speaking, and audiences loved him, something else he had in common with his hero. In 1844 he was already gaining a reputation as "the best stump speaker in the state." Clay's positions were entirely Lincoln's own: credit, tariffs, internal improvements. Like Clay, he generally avoided the subject of Texas, but at one appearance in Springfield he declared annexation of Texas "inexpedient" and supported Clay's position opposing it.[17]

As he rode from town to town young Abraham Lincoln undoubtedly felt baffled by the appeal of Polk's message among so many of his neighbors. He himself was indifferent about the possibility of annexing Texas. "I never was much interested in the Texas question," he admitted the following year. "I could never very clearly see how the annexation would augment the evil of slavery. Slaves would be taken there in about equal numbers, with or without annexation."[18] A pragmatist who believed that what a man needed to do in order to get ahead was settle down, work hard where he was, and develop the resources at his disposal, Lincoln couldn't muster up much enthusiasm for expansionism. He had learned from watching his unlucky father and shiftless stepbrother, who were constantly moving from place to place in search of better land, that success did not lie just beyond the frontier.

To Lincoln's mind, Manifest Destiny was a smoke screen designed to obscure the superiority of the Whig platform, and Polk's campaign themes were merely fodder to solidify the Democratic base. The United States would naturally expand its boundaries over time, no doubt, due to the superiority of its social and economic systems. But Lincoln understood the American dream as economic: technological development, access to credit, the growth of markets. Those, he determined, would be the elements of his message when he finally got to campaign for himself. And they would be his issues as a U.S. congressman.

The Whigs were a decided minority in Illinois in the early 1840s, but there were enough of them around the capital that redistricting in 1843 created a safe congressional seat for the party. Lincoln openly coveted it, and wrote to a friend, "Now if you should hear any one say that Lincoln don't want to go to Congress, I wish you, as a personal friend of mind, would tell him you have reason to believe he is mistaken. The truth is I would like to go very much."[19] To run, though, he would have to maneuver around a distinct obstacle.

The formidable John J. Hardin was a year younger and had a far loftier pedigree. Lincoln was, by his own description, "a strange, friendless, uneducated, penniless boy" when he arrived in Illinois. Untutored, self-made, and a backwoods campaigner, Lincoln was the original hick, never having traveled east of Kentucky, never even having had the leisure to take a vacation. Hardin was a southern gentleman. He was the stepnephew of Henry Clay, and son and heir of Martin Hardin, U.S. senator from Kentucky, member of the Kentucky Supreme Court, and decorated veteran of the War of 1812.[20]

He was also, notably, the namesake of his grandfather John Hardin, a Revolutionary War patriot who became famous for his military exploits against Native Americans and the British. The original John Hardin was a man of "great firmness of character, and a ready self-devotion to dangerous enterprises when . . . country called." He was also an expert marksman, "famous for the rapidity and accuracy of his shots." When he first heard the call for troops to "resist" Great Britain, he began recruiting. He joined Daniel Morgan's Rifle Corps with the rank of lieutenant and became a colonel in General Horatio Gates's campaign against General John Burgoyne's British troops. Gates offered him a public thanks for his "distinguished services" at the Battle of Saratoga.[21]

But the original John Hardin's prowess as a Revolutionary War soldier was far outstripped by his career as an Indian killer. As a lieutenant colonel in the Kentucky militia and a colonel in the Northwest Indian War in the Ohio Territory, Hardin was involved in almost every action against Indians in the region from 1786 to 1791. He was shot in the groin by an Indian at age twenty, and carried both the bullet and thoughts of vengeance with him for the rest of his life. He led a mistaken attack against a friendly tribe, the Piankeshaws, destroying a village near Vincennes, Indiana, in 1786. He brought home twelve scalps from an attack on a Shawnee village in 1789. In a campaign against the Miami in the fall of 1790, Hardin led 180 men into a Miami trap that resulted in 22 American deaths. In response, Hardin's men burned all the Miami villages near the forks of Indiana's Maumee River: 300 houses and 20,000 bushels of corn in total. The campaign was a failure, but this persuaded neither Hardin nor the U.S. Army to change tactics. The following year Hardin burned a Kickapoo village along with its cornfield and gardens at the mouth of Big Pine Creek in southern Illinois. It was widely said that "he commanded both the fear and the hatred of the Indians."[22]

So perhaps it is not entirely surprising that in April 1792, while he was traveling under President George Washington's orders to negotiate a peace treaty with the Shawnee, tribal members murdered him and his slave while they slept. He was only thirty-eight when he died. Before the news made it back to Washington, Kentucky entered the Union as the fifteenth state and the first state west of the Appalachians. John Hardin was posthumously named general of the First Brigade of the Kentucky Militia, and Kentucky, Ohio, and Illinois all named counties in the hero's honor.[23]

Abraham Lincoln knew the Hardin name well. Not only was Mary Todd third cousin to young John J. Hardin, but he himself had been born in one of the counties named after the famed Indian killer: Hardin County, Kentucky. Coincidentally, Lincoln was also named after an immigrant from Virginia to frontier Kentucky who was killed by Indians, "not in battle, but by stealth," as Lincoln later put it.[24]

Like his grandfather, John J. Hardin turned heads. Tall, handsome, and elegantly dressed, he walked with a military swagger and cut an "attractive, manly figure." He had a "winning and amiable character" and, although "somewhat impulsive," was widely popular among men and women. And he made the most of his advantages. He was a successful lawyer and army officer who upheld the family tradition by burning an Indian village to the ground in the Black Hawk War. He was elected brigadier general of the state militia in 1840. Although he lost an eye in a hunting accident not long afterward, he continued to impress and intimidate. College educated, rich, and well married, as patrician as you could get in the backwater state of Illinois, General Hardin was a natural at politics.[25]

Lincoln and Hardin had arrived in Illinois at the same time, both eager for advancement. The two got to know each other well while serving in the Illinois House of Representatives. The older man admired the younger and cultivated his friendship, and Hardin seemed happy to include Lincoln in his more elevated social circle. Before courting Mary Todd, Lincoln "never got on well with women" and was "curiously shy, ill at ease, and even perplexed in their presence." But the debonair Hardin provided a model of how to flirt and win women's favor. The two men jointly signed a letter in 1839 to one woman promising "as a gallant knight to give you the privilege of hanging up on a peg in my closet whenever it may seem convenient." Hardin and Lincoln may have been competitors for her favor as well as for political advancement, but the competition was a friendly one. Lincoln declared that Hardin was "more than his father" to him. Hardin repaid him in 1842 by stopping Lincoln's one and only duel before anyone was injured.[26]

Hardin, Lincoln, and a third state senator named Edward Baker, a large

Brigadier General John J. Hardin, as he appeared around
1840. J. G. Nicolay and John Hay, "Lincoln in Congress
and at the Bar," *The Century: A Popular Quarterly* 33, no. 4
(Feb. 1887): 517.

and easygoing British-born lawyer and good friend of Lincoln's who also
served in the Black Hawk War, were the leading young Whigs in the heav-
ily Democratic state. Once the young men found a route to Congress open
to them, all three began to jockey for position. Hardin, the best known of
the three thanks to his name and military exploits, won election to a short
term in Congress (1843–44) after redistricting took place. Baker received the
nomination the following year. As for Lincoln, he won the "honor" of serving as delegate to the nominating convention, which left him, as he wryly
wrote a friend, "fixed a good deal like a fellow who is made a groomsman to
a man that has cut him out and is marrying his own dear 'gal.' "[27]

To ensure that he would not again be jilted at the altar of Congress, he
turned to Baker and Hardin, asking that they agree to a rotating arrangement in which each would get a turn. Baker was game, and Lincoln believed
Hardin understood the agreement as well. In 1844 Lincoln couldn't be sure
what the future would bring, but he watched the surge of support for Polk
with dismay. He knew that his fate and the fate of Henry Clay were linked.
As one Illinois Whig wrote that fall, nothing less than "the nation's glory

or shame—the destiny of an empire" was at stake. "Henry Clay shall be the Joshua of our Army . . . and lead his chosen people to the chosen land" of peace and prosperity. It was imperative that Henry Clay win the election.[28]

Polk's supporters weren't leaving anything to chance in their effort to prevent that from happening. The Democratic Party had a domestic agenda of its own, focusing on low taxes, a small federal government, and states that protected the interests of their residents. But it wasn't much, and Polk acknowledged its limitations when he allowed supporters in the key manufacturing states of New York and Pennsylvania to undercut the Whigs with the promise that if elected, President Polk would support a protective tariff to help industry.

But all that was secondary to foreign policy. Democrats made territorial expansion their signature issue, proclaiming the dawn of a "Young America" that would surpass the old and enervated nations of Europe in strength and vitality, spread across the continent, and become the great empire of the future. They contrasted the Whigs, who, "advocating centralization, must wish & have ever wished to narrow our territory," with their own party, which, thanks to a wise faith in "State's Rights, know no limit to the possible extent of the Federal Union."[29] They would bring Texas into the Union, but wagered that they could hold the North with a promise to take the entire Oregon Country, including British Columbia, even at the risk of war with Britain.

It was a smart bet. After the Senate's rejection of the annexation treaty in June, the national clamor for Texas became almost deafening. "*Poke & Texas, that's the thing,*" concluded one demoralized Mississippi Whig, "it goes like wild-fire with the folks as kant rede, nor don't git no papers." Polk recognized what Clay and Lincoln did not: that Manifest Destiny was everything in 1844. One Illinois Democrat, who admitted that he "dreaded the annexation of Texas" because it "would increase the slave territory" of the country, explained his support for Polk, saying that "a glance at the map was enough to convince one that sooner or later the United States must extend to the Rio Grande." Manifest Destiny made annexation appear inevitable—"only a question of time"—and the Democratic platform look like simple common sense. Territorial expansion had become the "*great and new element which has entered in to this momentous contest, and which by its superior importance, is enough of itself, to determine the vote of every freeman.*"[30]

This election, Polk argued, was really about whether the country would grow or stand still, reach for its future or protect its past. How did America see itself, and what was it willing to risk? Was the nation with God and Manifest Destiny, or would this chosen people simply tend to their garden? Did

The United States of Mexico in 1847. J. Disturnell, New York. Library of Congress Prints and Photographs Division.

not Americans owe it to less enlightened nations to guide them to enlightenment? Polk was ambitious for his country, and he was not averse to a call to arms. So it was natural that his eye wandered from Texas to Mexico.

Mexico was certainly vulnerable. The nation won its independence from Spain just a generation after the United States threw off its own European oppressor, but the subsequent development of the neighboring republics differed strikingly. In 1800 the two nations boasted similar populations of around five million people. But the United States, politically stable and economically vibrant, expanded in both population and size, while Mexico's population stagnated. Mexico emerged from its brutal war for independence a shell of its colonial self. Six hundred thousand people died between 1800 and the end of the revolution in 1820, most from starvation and disease. Agriculture and industry were decimated, and mining output decreased by more than half. In 1845 Mexico's per capita income was less than half of what it had been in 1800, and its population of seven million was only a third of that of the United States.[31]

The people of the new Mexican nation were divided by region and by race, and there was no compelling ideology that drew them together. They lacked the faith in national destiny and the superiority of their nation's political and social forms that unified the citizens of the United States. The vast majority were Indians, living in relatively autonomous communities that had existed prior to Spanish conquest three centuries earlier. Their identities were grounded in patriarchal kinship networks. While Mexico's constitution declared all men citizens of Mexico with equal rights under the law, few Indians felt any allegiance to the nation or considered themselves Mexicans.[32]

Nor were the small percentage of Mexicans of European origin, known as *criollos*, united in a shared vision for the future development of Mexico. The elite proved unwilling to contribute to Mexico's tax base during the first decades after independence, and different political factions proved unable to fashion a stable political system. Turmoil became the norm, and frequent coups made any hope of developing the nation's resources a fleeting dream; between 1821 and 1857 the presidency of Mexico changed hands at least fifty times, almost always by coup d'état. A centralized economy and highly limited trade benefited few outside the capital and provided residents of frontier provinces with little opportunity for profit. Nor did the federal government provide residents of the northern provinces with protection from hostile Indian tribes who regularly robbed, kidnapped, and murdered Mexicans. While the United States was thriving in the 1830s and 1840s, Mexico was foundering.[33]

Polk's good friend Sam Houston put bluntly what most Americans, particularly in the South and West, believed to be true: that "Mexicans are no better than Indians." It appeared evident to Americans that the people of Mexico were incompetent at governing and administering, so much so that the citizens of the country's northern provinces were eager to break away and merge with the United States. Who wouldn't want to trade impoverishment for the lifestyle of the American immigrants, settlers who'd brought with them consumer goods and medicines unavailable in northern Mexico? Protestant Americans believed the Catholic inhabitants of Mexico to be inferior in both race and religion and desperately in need of enlightenment.[34]

Then there was California. Like many Americans, Polk had had his appetite for Mexico whetted specifically by that territory. In 1840 Richard Henry Dana's best seller *Two Years Before the Mast* had described in glowing detail the wonders of a beautiful, fertile land on the Pacific Coast, with magnificent harbors, a lucrative cowhide trade, and countless sea otters, whose dense pelts were in great demand in Asia. From California, the United States could gain easy access to the whaling ports of Hawaii, and ultimately to Asia. California should belong to America.

Out on the campaign trail, Polk broadcast in no uncertain terms his determination to remake the American map. His 1844 campaign was the most uncompromisingly expansionistic in American history, with the candidate promising that if elected, he would wrestle the entirety of the Oregon Country from England. "Fifty-four forty or fight," the Democratic slogan about seizing Oregon, encapsulated his vision of an America that spanned the continent. He offered an openly pugilistic platform and evinced no hesitation about putting U.S. soldiers in harm's way in order to fulfill what he saw as the nation's destiny. His was a well-formulated political agenda pumped out by a spirited campaign and an energized Democratic Party. "The Union of our party seems to be perfect," he marveled to a friend in June. "The greatest enthusiasm is everywhere prevailing."[35]

By midsummer the inexpediency of Clay's Raleigh letter opposing annexation had become clear even to the Sage of Ashland. He began to hedge his bets, to backtrack. He published two letters in July in Alabama suggesting that perhaps his Raleigh letter had been premature and that if annexation could take place without national dishonor or war, and if the country as a whole wanted it, well, then as president he would be happy to bring Texas into the Union. He wasn't opposed to the annexation of Texas in the abstract, only to the annexation of Texas right now. He also attempted to assuage southern voters by asserting that the questions of annexation and slavery were separate in his mind, that they were not related "one way or the other."[36]

Clay's Alabama letters swayed few voters, but they offered ample fuel for the Democratic charge that Prince Hal could not be trusted. "There is a vein of dishonesty and of double-dealing creeping thro' Henry Clay's course on the Texas question, unworthy of an American Statesman," concluded a Massachusetts paper. "He evinces traits of character which make him an unsafe man to trust with the destines of the nation." Democrats in Michigan placed his letters on a broadside as a prime example of "that political consistency which has ever characterized ROTTEN HEARTED POLITICAL DEMAGOGUES in all ages of the world."[37]

One constituency remained unmoved by all the commotion: Clay's female supporters. Perhaps because Texas had never fired their imaginations as it had that of their husbands, fathers, and brothers, they remained as devoted to Clay and his protective tariffs as ever. As one popular "Workingman's Song" asserted,

The Ladies—bless the lovely band—Our country's joy and pride,
They go for Harry, hand in hand, Maid, matron, belle, and bride,

> To gain "Protection" for themselves; They'll marry, and marry away,
> And tell their lovers and husbands, and sons, To vote for Henry Clay.[38]

Women around the country sewed flags and banners for Clay processions regardless of their husbands' political leanings, attended Whig meetings and conventions, and took the lead singing Whig songs. As one favored ditty from the Clay Club in Germantown, Pennsylvania, asserted, "There's not a lass in this broad land but vows she'd scorn to marry / The lad who don't give heart and hand to glorious gallant Harry!" In Litchfield, Connecticut, "3000 Whig ladies" turned out in matching outfits for a pro-Clay rally, while in Bangor, Maine, a young mother taught her eighteen-month-old daughter Agnes to answer the question "Who's going to be president?" with "Henry Clay." The wife of the president of the Democratic National Convention made her Pennsylvania home a meeting place for Clay women and proudly told her husband's Democratic friends that "though my husband is a *Polk* man, I am a *Clay* man; in fact the ladies are all Clay men."[39]

The problem was that none of these female "Clay men" could vote, and not enough of the voting men favored Clay. The candidate was now sixty-seven, repeating the same message that had driven him for decades. He'd had a heart attack two years earlier, and now looked old and worn-out. He discounted the "colds" that frequently attacked him, but quite likely Clay was suffering from the early stages of tuberculosis, known at the time as consumption because of its wasting effects on the body. Tuberculosis, a slow and relentless killer that attacks the respiratory system, was widespread, untreatable, and misunderstood in the nineteenth century. Virtually no one realized it was communicable, but everyone recognized the symptoms. Clay's grandson Martin Duralde was a sufferer. He had been living at Ashland at the height of his contagiousness, but Clay might have caught the disease at any point during the campaign or years earlier.[40]

In the face of Polk's determination to remake the American map, both Clay and his message seemed faded. The Democrats took note and, playing on Clay's reputation as the cunning "old coon," taunted:

> Their coons are dead, their cabins down,
> Hard cider grown quite stale, sirs,
> And at the people's with'ring frown,
> Their leader grows quite pale, sirs.[41]

The election results were remarkably close, a difference of just 38,000 votes out of more than 2.7 million cast. Polk carried the South, with the exception of North Carolina, Kentucky, and Tennessee. At another point in his life, Polk would have mourned this third rejection by his home state, but not this year. He did well in the West. Despite Lincoln's best efforts, everything west of Ohio went Democratic. Polk did surprisingly well in the Northeast also.

Polk won Pennsylvania, not because of any groundswell of support for Texas in the Keystone State but because of the repeated promises of native son George Dallas that Polk would pass a protective tariff. Polk also won New York. His victory there was achieved by a razor-thin margin of only 5,000 votes. Abolitionist James Birney, candidate of the antislavery Liberty Party, earned almost 16,000 votes. Had just 5,000 Liberty Party supporters voted for Henry Clay, whose views they most certainly preferred to Polk's, Clay would have won the state, and with it the electoral vote and the national election.[42]

Henry Clay was at a wedding in Lexington when he heard the news. The daily mail from the Northeast to the Southwest traveled through Cincinnati, on the Kentucky border. It reached the Lexington post office around ten at night. Several guests, anxious for election news, left the wedding for the purpose of retrieving the mail from the post office the moment it materialized. They returned with a letter, consulted among themselves, and then brought it to Clay, who was, as usual, surrounded by a group of women. Among them was Abraham Lincoln's mother-in-law, Betsy Todd. She described Clay's reaction in a letter to her stepdaughter, Mary Todd Lincoln:

> He opened the paper and as he read the death knell of his political hopes and lifelong ambition, I saw a distinct blue shade begin at the roots of his hair, pass slowly over his face like a cloud and then disappear. He stood for a moment as if frozen. He laid down the paper, and, turning to a table, filled a glass with wine, and raising it to his lips with a pleasant smile, said: "I drink to the health and happiness of all assembled here." Setting down his glass, he resumed his conversation as if nothing had occurred and was, as usual, the life and light of the company. The contents of the paper were soon known to everyone in the room and a wet blanket fell over our gaiety. We left the wedding party with heavy hearts. Alas! Our gallant "Harry of the West" has fought his last presidential battle.[43]

The daily eastern mail made it to Nashville about the same time it arrived in Lexington. The Nashville postmaster, a personal friend of Polk's, discovered a handwritten note from the Cincinnati postmaster attesting to the election results when he opened the mail package that night. He quietly called the Democratic proprietor of a "large livery service" and asked him how quickly he could get a letter to the Polks' home in Columbia, fifty miles away. James Polk was called from bed before dawn the next morning with the news. For the twenty hours between when the Polks learned of their altered circumstances and the regular delivery of the mail from Nashville, James and Sarah went about their business as usual, without letting on that they had any special news or any reason to celebrate.[44]

No doubt they were enjoying their last moments of serenity. When the election results became public, "the joy of the Democrats knew no bounds." Skinned raccoons hung from trees on major thoroughfares, and torchlight victory processions illuminated towns and cities across the country. Polk received a delegation of Democrats who had come all the way from Alabama to congratulate the president-elect in person, and orators at public meetings in Nashville and Columbia answered the question "Who is James K. Polk?" by introducing the new president. Congratulatory letters came from around the country, including one from Harry, a slave owned by Polk and hired out as a blacksmith in Mississippi. "I have been betting and lousing on you for the last several years but I have made it all up now," Harry wrote. "I am in hopes that you will come to this state before you go to the white house & let me see you once more before I die."[45]

James K. Polk, demonstrating the unwavering self-righteousness that would mark his presidency, embraced the slim victory as a mandate. Like Old Hickory, he believed his election reflected the will of the virtuous citizenry. Polk would ensure that their will would be done.

Nor was it only Polk who saw a mandate in the 1844 election results. On February 26, 1845, after elaborate maneuvering and several dubious promises made on behalf of both Tyler and Polk, Congress passed a joint resolution to admit Texas as a state. It was a controversial tactic, since a joint resolution enabled passage with a simple majority in both houses of Congress, as opposed to the two-thirds of the Senate constitutionally required for the adoption of treaties. Democrats had failed to muster the support of two-thirds of senators and might not have gained a majority of both houses were it not for the fact that so many opponents of annexation understood further objections as futile once Polk became president-elect. On March 1, just days before leaving office, a vindicated John Tyler invited Texas to join the United States.

President-elect Polk began his journey to the White House with an overnight stop at the Hermitage to pay his respects to General Jackson. Jackson, racked by old wounds, tuberculosis, and diarrhea, was barely hanging on, sustained only by rice and milk. But Polk's election had made him blissfully happy. Jackson was confident that Polk would not let him down, that he would "fearlessly carry out all his principles." Both men knew that it was the last time they would meet.[46]

As Polk continued on to Washington he no doubt remembered the trip the two Hickories had made in the opposite direction at the close of Jackson's presidency in 1837. Miraculously, Jackson's prophecy to Sarah Polk that she would one day be queen had come true. It would now be up to James Polk to fulfill Jackson's legacy during his own term in office.

Andrew Jackson passed away just four months later. Some of his final words to his family were about Texas and Oregon. He hoped both could be settled amicably, but if not, "let war come. There would be patriots enough in the land found to repel foreign invasion come from whatsoever source." He also mused that one of his few regrets in life was that he "didn't shoot Henry Clay."[47]

The weather on Tuesday, March 4, 1845, was inauspicious for an inauguration. Overcast skies had turned into a steady rain by the time the soon-to-be eleventh president of the United States made his way down Pennsylvania Avenue in an open carriage drawn by four horses. A record crowd was on hand to witness the ceremony. His escorts carried batons of young hickory. The First Lady, dressed in a gray and red striped satin gown, carried an elaborate ivory-handled fan, wholly unnecessary given the weather, but too beautiful to lay aside. On one side it featured portraits of all the presidents, including James, and on the other a picture of the signing of the Declaration of Independence.

Polk mounted a platform on the steps of the Capitol and in a clear, firm voice offered his vision of the future to the assembled mass of umbrellas. The greatest portion of his speech focused on Manifest Destiny, the issue that had won him the presidency. Predictably, he promised to bring the annexation of Texas to a speedy close, but he made it clear that Texas was hardly the extent of his vision for America. "Our title to the country of Oregon is clear and unquestionable," he asserted. And although he said nothing about California specifically, the most lyrical portion of his address involved "pioneers" and "distant regions" and how "our people, increasing to many millions, have filled the eastern valley of the Mississippi, adventurously ascended the Missouri to its headsprings, and are already engaged in establishing the blessings of self-government in valleys of which the rivers flow to the Pacific."[48]

At that very moment, U.S. ships were en route to the Gulf of Mexico to protect the newest state from its southern neighbor. Polk knew well that Mexico was unlikely to accept the new political reality. But he had no fear for the future. Here he was, about to enter the White House, and the opportunity to dismember Mexico was being handed to him like a gift.

As for Henry Clay, he retreated to his Kentucky plantation, humiliated and deeply bitter. No matter—he was convinced he'd already beheld the future. In Raleigh, North Carolina, almost a full year earlier, Clay had written that "annexation and war with Mexico are identical."[49] Those words had cost him the presidency. Now it looked like his prophecy was about to come true.

PART TWO

Mr. and Mrs. Polk's War,

1845–46

What cannoneer begot this lusty blood?

He speaks plain cannon fire, and smoke and bounce.

—SHAKESPEARE, *KING JOHN,* ACT 2, SCENE I

4

Speaking Cannon Fire

POLK ENTERED OFFICE with big plans and poor people skills. His vision for the nation was audaciously outsized; he had hardly hinted at it in his inaugural address. Not only would he embrace Congress's passage of the joint resolution admitting Texas as a state, but he would attempt to make the most of the newly annexed republic's territorial claims. He would uphold Texas's claims to the land between the Nueces River and the more southwesterly Rio Grande, however laughable those claims might be. The truth was that virtually none of the inhabitants in the disputed area considered themselves Texans, and despite repeatedly rebuffed excursions to the south and the west, the Lone Star Republic had only managed to establish one small settlement, Corpus Christi, at the mouth of Nueces Bay at the northern edge of the territory. And of course Mexico still hadn't recognized Texas's independence. Yet Polk would make it happen, and he would also face down the world's superpower, Great Britain, in order to gain Oregon, as the northern wing of his party demanded, despite the fact that the *Princeton* and its big gun "Peacemaker" had thus far done far more damage to Washington's political class than to Britain's naval supremacy.

Polk would do this, yes, but he would go further. Young Hickory's true plan, the one he had shared only with Sarah, was nothing less than wresting away Mexico's prized Pacific territory. Alta California was a land of unparalleled ports and unfathomed natural resources, "the richest, most beautiful, and the healthiest country in the world," as the U.S. minister to Mexico had described it the year before. According to the U.S. consul, annual exports from this magical land included 85,000 cowhides, 16,000 bushels of wheat, 1.5 million pounds of tallow for candles, 1 million feet of lumber, 20,000 beaver and otter skins, and 100 ounces of gold. True, Mexico had firmly rejected all previous offers to purchase California and had been particularly sensitive on the subject since the fall of 1842, when a doltish U.S. commodore, mistakenly believing that war between the United States and Mexico was imminent, seized the California port of Monterey and informed the shocked residents that the United States was annexing California. Tyler had apologized and assured Mexico that it was all an innocent mistake—there was no plot afoot, and of course the rogue commodore would be removed from his position. But after something like this, who could blame Mexicans for questioning U.S. motives in the region? When Americans "invaded" their country and continued to act "as though it were their home," Mexicans knew they could never rest secure.[1]

But for Polk that was all in the past; there was destiny to consider, and California was "destined to control the destinies of the Pacific." The lauded commander of the newly returned U.S. South Seas Exploring Expedition, America's first great voyage of discovery, had proclaimed it so. If the election of 1844 had proved anything, it was that James K. Polk could accomplish what lesser visionaries considered impossible. Through force of will and hard work, because no one worked harder than he, Young Hickory would conquer the continent. And he would do it in one term.[2]

But first he needed to assemble a cabinet. This wasn't as simple a matter as it might appear, and three days before his inauguration he had filled only two of the six cabinet posts. There were powerful blocs in the Democratic Party that needed to be appeased, supporters of Van Buren in New York and of Calhoun in South Carolina—men whose relations with one another were less than cordial. He needed to strike a pose of sectional balance in the cabinet, and he definitely needed a Pennsylvanian to help calm the storm that would inevitably erupt when the good people of the commonwealth discovered that Polk's tariff plans were miles away from what he promised during the campaign. He also needed to purge all of the Tyler supporters from the administration, as well as from the government jobs that were now his to distribute, thanks to the spoils system so brilliantly instituted by Andrew Jackson. Jackson had claimed that replacing Washington office employees would help prevent corruption, but it was also a wonderful way to reward one's own supporters.

There were other complicating factors. Despite his remarkable victory, far too many in Washington still saw him as a little man. Not just physically, although those who had known him in his congressional days noted that he had lost weight, and his coats were now two or three sizes too large. "He would be but the merest tangible fraction of a president," one woman noted, "if his clothes were made to fit." They questioned his political stature and told one another, quietly, that he "*cannot* go through what is before him without some strong man to lean on." Van Buren had the gall to say as much to his face, warning him that "the man who is suddenly & unexpectedly raised" to the presidency "has to remove apprehensions which will in such cases always arise" about his fitness for the job.[3]

If someone had dared insult Henry Clay this way (not that anyone would, because nothing could be more expected than for Henry Clay to become president), he might find himself embroiled in a duel, or so mocked that a duel might seem preferable to the social death Clay was so expert at imposing. But Polk wasn't one to lose his temper. Unlike other politicians he could name, Polk knew how to control his emotions. He felt the insult nonetheless, and under no circumstances could he allow a "strong man" or the supporter of a "strong man" into his cabinet.

There was also his promise to serve only one term. Polk certainly couldn't allow any presidential candidates in his cabinet, because that person would naturally put his personal advancement ahead of the good of the administration. What Polk needed, and would have, was nothing less than absolute loyalty and subservience from "a united and harmonious" cabinet, one that put "the existing administration and the good of the country" first. "In any event," he wrote longtime political crony Cave Johnson, "I intend to be *myself* President of the U.S."[4]

Given this long list of considerations and the slowness of the mail system, perhaps it isn't surprising that Polk's cabinet was at once striking in its mediocrity and offensive to many important members of his party. Three able men who had been instrumental in his success at the nominating convention in Baltimore won plum positions: dapper bachelor James Buchanan of Pennsylvania became secretary of state, brilliant Massachusetts historian George Bancroft was named secretary of the navy, and aggressive expansionist and proslavery ideologue Robert J. Walker of Mississippi became secretary of the Treasury.

Few found much to praise in the rest of Polk's appointments. In a supposed attempt to appease Van Buren supporters, Polk appointed William Marcy, the former governor of New York, to be secretary of war. Perhaps Polk was oblivious to the fact that Martin Van Buren hated the man. He

Polk's cabinet in 1846. Photo by John Plumbe Jr. When the early photographic technique known as daguerreotype was less than ten years old, Sarah Polk arranged for a photographer to be present just after a cabinet breakfast. The result was the first photograph ever taken in the White House, and the first of a presidential cabinet. From left to right: Attorney General John Y. Mason, Secretary of War William Marcy, Postmaster General Cave Johnson, President Polk, Navy Secretary George Bancroft, and Treasury Secretary Robert J. Walker. Secretary of State James Buchanan is absent. Courtesy James K. Polk Memorial Association, Columbia, Tennessee.

appointed college chum John Mason of Virginia as attorney general and Cave Johnson as postmaster general, rounding out a cabinet that many, and particularly Van Buren's supporters, did not view as being particularly well rounded. But whatever the liabilities to the harmony of the party, Polk's appointees were assets to his political program. Each man believed in Manifest Destiny. Walker, in particular, could be counted on to enthusiastically support any plan to divest Mexico of its territory. His brother had been a Texas settler who died after serving time in a Mexican prison.

In the appointment of his cabinet, Polk displayed a tendency that would prove to be one of his trademarks. He would solicit advice, appear to assent to it, and then, as often as not, do the exact opposite. He snubbed important members of his party with seeming reckless abandon. He would be *himself* president. "He had no confid[a]nts except from calculation and for a purpose," one contemporary noted. "His secretiveness was large, and few men could better keep their own secrets."[5]

But it wasn't just that Polk was secretive. In the chilly first months of 1845, many Democrats came to believe that the president-elect had a predilection to make promises, or appear to make promises, that he had no intention of keeping. At least five senators agreed in February to vote in favor of admitting Texas as a state after Polk privately convinced them that he would force Texas to back down from the Rio Grande boundary claim. They left his office believing that just as soon as he was president, he would send skilled diplomats to Texas in order to implement a compromise. When asked why he voted in favor of annexation, newly seated senator John A. Dix of New York explained that Polk's "assurance was given to others as well as myself" that negotiators would be sent to Texas. Dix trusted Polk, because "his honor is a sufficient Security" to prevent him from lying.[6] Dix believed Polk, because he assumed that the president, like other men of his profession and class, cared about his reputation as an honorable man. Honorable men did not lie, at least not without plausible deniability.

Dix and many others quickly learned, however, that James K. Polk's "honor" offered very little security. Of course Polk had no intention of negotiating with Texas and had never had any such intention; remarkably enough, he seemed uninterested in providing cover for his dishonesty. Before he was even inaugurated he had won a reputation as a man who couldn't be trusted. It was becoming clear that Polk's "mind was narrow, and he possessed a trait of sly cunning which he thought shrewdness, but which was really disingenuousness and duplicity." No Democrat would dare say it out loud, not yet anyhow, but the new president was a liar.[7]

But he didn't lie to everyone. Polk took a strikingly different approach with his cabinet than with the external political world. Rather than preside in an authoritarian manner, the president strove for consensus, and generally achieved it. Polk's cabinet became a remarkably cohesive unit, and he made the most of it. The president held twice-weekly meetings that all members were expected to attend, and he made it clear that every member had the right to speak on any issue. He delegated work to members, and felt free to take over their duties when necessary. There were markedly few divisions among cabinet members on issues of importance, in large part, perhaps, because the men of the cabinet shared Polk's worldview. Polk referred to his cabinet as his "own political family," and his cabinet proved crucial to his success in office, second only, perhaps, to his real family: his wife, Sarah.[8]

When Polk was first nominated, one wise advisor encouraged him to put Sarah to work. James might lack the "time or tact, to conciliate and please," but Sarah had plenty of both. "The wife of a man aspiring to the white house is no minor circumstance," he pointed out. "Mrs. Polk should be visited by Whigs and by Democrats of her own sex . . . as the ladies of the other side uniformly speak well, and generally highly of her." Even Polk's allies recognized that Young Hickory's personality required management. Fortunately, Sarah Polk, unlike her husband, "was ever a good listener."[9]

The candidate didn't need prompting; he already knew his wife's political value. She took her job seriously and was willing to work every bit as hard as her husband to advance their agenda. Washington hadn't forgotten Sarah Polk. Her self-possession, conversational skills, and elegant appearance impressed virtually everyone. A young antislavery Whig from Massachusetts named Charles Sumner seemed surprised when "her sweetness of manner won me entirely." During her husband's tenure in Congress, Sarah became such a favorite among the political class that when the couple left Washington a justice of the Supreme Court wrote a poem in her honor, praising her "playful mind." Members of both parties knew that Polk's election would be a two-for-one, and that it was Sarah alone who could counter Polk's political isolation.[10]

In fact, her influence had only grown during the dark years of James's political career. By the time he became president he depended upon his wife to read and analyze all the national news, and he left her piles of newspapers each day. Sarah diligently worked through them all, and then, "carefully folding the papers with the marked pieces outside, where a glance might detect them, she would place the pile beside his chair, so that whenever a few moments of leisure came, he could find and read without loss of time."[11]

He asked her to write letters for him, delegating to her virtually all of the work that a less secretive chief executive would give a secretary. On evenings when they entertained, the two worked late into the night, regularly putting in twelve to fourteen hours of work. "None but Sarah knew so intimately my private affairs," Polk admitted near the end of his life. But even at the height of his power, President Polk was open about the degree to which he and his wife had always worked as a team. Typical was his comment when Sarah broke up an impromptu concert given by Democrats in his honor on the Sabbath: "Sarah directs all domestic affairs, and she thinks that is domestic.' "[12]

Though her religious piety required that she shun the "follies and amusements of the world," and therefore ban hard liquor, dancing, and card play-

Sarah and James Polk. This daguerreotype portrait of the Polks was taken in 1849, during their last months in the White House. Their close relationship and Sarah's concern for her husband's health are apparent in their posture and her gesture. Courtesy James K. Polk Memorial Association, Columbia, Tennessee.

ing from the White House, she managed to pull off entertaining executive dinners at which gracious hospitality shamelessly combined with ceaseless lobbying. Dressed in simple but meticulously tailored gowns of deep-hued velvets and satins, Sarah cultivated a restrained elegance in keeping with her democratic ethos. She held two regular evening receptions every week, and added a third on Saturday mornings when Congress was in session. When James was unable to attend, she hosted these events alone. Powerful men cultivated her goodwill: more than one leading politician openly declared that he would rather discuss the issues of the day with her than with her dour husband.[13]

She was a brilliant entertainer but had little interest in other domestic matters. Lucretia Hart Clay, by contrast, who rarely left Kentucky, was renowned for her domestic prowess. She gave birth to eleven children and was said to cure the best ham in the county. During the presidential campaign a "lady remarked to a friend of Mrs. Polk's that she hoped Mr. Clay would be elected to the presidency, because his wife was a good house-keeper, and made fine butter." When Sarah heard this story she proudly replied, "If I should be so fortunate as to reach the White House, I expect to live on twenty-five thousand dollars a year, and I will neither keep house nor make butter."[14]

Twenty-five thousand dollars was the president's salary and would have been a fortune, except that the president was expected to pay most of the expenses of the White House, including the salaries of fifteen or twenty servants. The Polks, far from rich, had gone into debt during the presidential campaign. Sarah's plan for living within their income was simple, but it didn't include making her own butter. She replaced the White House staff with her slaves, moving them into the basement, which she renovated for the purpose.

The Polks' slaves shocked northern sensibilities but allowed Sarah a certain freedom from the day-to-day details of household management, or at least she acted as though this was the case. "She said the servants knew their duties, and she did not undertake the needless task of directing them." But social events didn't always run as smoothly as they might had the First Lady been in the kitchen rather than in the parlor with Mr. Polk. She once presided over a dinner with no napkins on the table, and failed to notice. On another occasion, when Senator Thomas Hart Benton came to dinner and the appointed hour had passed with no sign of a meal, he asked Sarah if he had come at the right time. "Colonel Benton," she responded, "have you not lived in Washington long enough to know that the cooks fix the hour for dinner?"[15]

Yet despite her strengths in what was then known as the male sphere of politics and her weakness in the women's sphere of domestic matters, Sarah Polk seemed to threaten no one. This was because, as one approving commentator put it, "she lived behind her husband as a politician." In an era of increasing agitation for women's rights, Mrs. Polk cultivated a persona of subservience that powerful men found intoxicating.[16]

Sarah was careful to always downplay her political skills. "She was better informed than it was her disposition to make known . . . early learned to be silent where anything was at stake . . . never told more than she knew, and seldom made an effort to display what she said as wisdom." She conferred about matters of national importance with her husband's associates but was always careful to say "Mr. Polk thinks so" when expressing her opinions to them. She was "familiar with the great matters exercising the minds of public men" and was sure to read books by writers visiting the White House so that she could converse with them about their work. But she also had what a contemporary called "intuitive tact." She was "too delicate and reserved to proclaim political opinions, or to join in the discussion of party differences. Being so intelligent and well informed, yet so unobtrusive, she was a charming companion."[17]

Sarah's talents did not go unnoticed by the public. She was held in high esteem by Americans of both parties and during the first year of the presidency garnered nothing but positive coverage in the daily press. Some Whigs who were skeptical or outright hostile to her husband's election hoped that she might have a positive influence on his administration. Sarah Preston Hale of Massachusetts, a forty-eight-year-old supporter of Henry Clay, wondered if "perhaps Mr. and Mrs. Polk together will make a very good President."[18]

Sarah was a woman who venerated the work of men, and excelled at it, in large part because she publicly embraced an almost reactionary standard of female subservience. By brilliantly manipulating the gender codes of the day, Sarah Childress Polk became one of the most powerful First Ladies in history. Were it not for her political skills, James Polk might never have won office. Together they made, if not a good president, certainly a successful one.

Among the politicians most enchanted by Sarah was George Bancroft, the new secretary of the navy. Bancroft was in many ways a strange choice for the cabinet, an aristocratic Harvard intellectual who held a Ph.D. from a German university and wrote serious works of history. Despite hailing from a stronghold of Whig power, Bancroft commanded respect within the Democratic ranks, but he probably wouldn't have made it into the cabinet had he not helped mastermind Polk's nomination in Baltimore. He yearned for a diplomatic appointment in Europe and was uninterested in the cabinet. But Polk ignored Bancroft's requests, despite the fact that they were reasonable and easy to fulfill.

Not long after the inauguration, Polk called him into his office. Bancroft had no suspicion that anything out of the ordinary would be said, since it was already obvious that "no man was the depository" of the president's "secrets, further than he chose to entrust them for his own purpose." But Polk had something singular to say, and he wanted Bancroft to hear it. Slapping his leg for emphasis, Polk told him that "the acquisition of California and a large district on the coast" was one of the priorities of his administration. It was God's will that Mexico's richest lands, especially the fertile stretch by the Pacific, pass from its current shiftless residents to hard-working white people better able to husband their resources. Bancroft was shocked. Did the president intend to start a war?[19]

Polk didn't really believe all-out combat would be necessary to realize the expansionist agenda that Democratic editors had begun calling America's "Manifest Destiny." He certainly didn't want to be blamed for sparking a war. No, he was counting on some bullying, and just a bit of brinksmanship, to create a messy little incident that would do the trick. Like most Americans, Polk felt a deep disdain for the racially mixed population of Mexico, and confidence that they would capitulate when faced with the resolution and might of the United States. He was furthermore convinced that their leaders were both corrupt and cowardly. When faced with war, they would certainly sell him California.

Mexico was already more than halfway there. Tyler's resolution to annex Texas was met with outrage both north and south of the Rio Grande. Henry Clay had warned that Texas annexation would lead to war, and by 1845 that view had become commonplace in New England. Abolitionists and ministers went on the offensive to warn America of the coming danger. Immediately after the election a series of fifteen passionate letters, intended to "awaken . . . fellow citizens to the national peril" of annexation, began to appear in the Boston *Atlas*. These letters, anonymously written by an eminent Unitarian minister in Massachusetts named George E. Ellis, continued through March 1845, and were reprinted around the country. They were designed to stop annexation on the grounds not only that it was "derogatory to the national character, and injurious to the public interest" but also that it would unquestionably lead to war. On January 15, with a joint resolution for the annexation of Texas before Congress, Ellis argued at great length, and with masses of supporting detail, that "no individual in power in Mexico would dare to entertain the idea of surrendering Texas—nor could such a surrender be obtained except by force."[20]

Events in Mexico supported this view. Angry partisans demanded that the Mexican president, José Herrera, vindicate this unprecedented action by the "implacable enemies of our race" in Texas and the United States. Attempting to cool their martial ardor, Herrera lodged a formal protest about the legality of annexation, to which the United States replied dispassionately that since both Texas and the United States were independent nations, neither needed consult with a foreign power before formalizing a union. Recognizing an insult when dealt one, Mexico's U.S. minister gravely left the country, officially severing diplomatic relations between the two countries just weeks after Polk's inauguration. When Texas formally accepted the U.S. offer of annexation, on the Fourth of July, 1845, Mexican jingoism reached a fevered state. "Defeat and death on the Sabine would be glorious and beautiful," a once moderate Mexico City newspaper declared, but peace under these conditions could only be "infamous and execrable."[21]

During his first spring and summer in office, Polk made preparations for war without really believing that war was imminent. He ordered the navy to assemble in the gulf, within striking distance of Mexico's ports, and directed Commodore J. D. Sloat, the commander of the naval flotilla in the Pacific, to immediately seize San Francisco and other ports in California if war should break out. He also sent word to a sixty-one-year-old major general named Zachary Taylor, commander of troops in the Southwest, to be ready for action. In June 1845, Taylor got his directions: march his four thousand soldiers to Corpus Christi, on the northern edge of the disputed territory, and await further orders.

Despite all the bluster in the Mexican press, the country neither attacked nor declared war. On the contrary, Herrera appeared willing to negotiate, because, as his minister of foreign affairs, Manuel de la Peña y Peña, admitted, given the precarious state of Mexico's finances, the nation would have to make enormous sacrifices "simply to avoid annihilation" in a war with the United States. Polk dispatched a party hack by the name of John Slidell on a secret mission to Mexico with instructions to treat Texas independence as a "settled fact . . . not to be called into question," to resolve the boundary dispute by offering to forgive two million dollars in outstanding claims by American citizens against the Mexican government, and to buy California in the process.[22]

Slidell was perhaps not the best choice for such a delicate mission. A Louisiana congressman "utterly untrained in formal diplomacy," Slidell was notable primarily for his violent support of slavery and his submission to both Old and Young Hickory. He was astounded that he had been approached for the job. "I have no very exalted idea of the caliber of Mexican intellect," he admitted to Secretary of State Buchanan before offering his view that the Mexicans would certainly come to terms.[23]

Slidell was loyal and accepted his mission with good grace, asking only that Polk provide some plausible excuse for his absence from his congressional duties in the administration paper, the Washington *Union*. James Buchanan put the chief clerk of the State Department, Nicholas Trist, to work on drafting an article that explained Slidell's absence without revealing any sensitive details of his mission.

Trist, a beneficiary of the spoils system in 1845, was in many ways a typical Polk appointee. A lifelong Democrat, he had been raised on a sugar plantation in Louisiana and had served in several previous administrations. Trist and Slidell had become friends in Louisiana. It was no coincidence that both hailed from the plantation South. A southern shift was palpable across Washington in the winter of 1845, and not only because of the Polks' slaves in the White House. As Democrats replaced Whigs in all the federal offices, the proliferation of southern accents was notable. Slidell also wrote Trist directly to impress upon him the importance of explaining his unusual mission to the people of Louisiana.

All parties, from the president to the diplomat to the clerk appointed to write an article in the diplomat's interest, understood what was riding on the outcome of this trip. Polk was explicit in his directions to Slidell. If he failed in his mission to "effect a satisfactory adjustment of the pending difference between the two countries (which I will not anticipate) we must take redress for the wrongs and injuries we have suffered into our own hands." In short, Polk would "call on Congress to provide the proper remedies" and declare war.[24]

Polk was putting on an excellent show of negotiating, but in fact everything about Slidell's mission, from his title to his terms, was intended to incense the Mexicans and to ensure that diplomacy would fail. Herrera had put a great deal of his political capital on the line by agreeing to receive a U.S. envoy to discuss the boundary of Texas. Mexico would never sell California while the issue of Texas was unresolved.

Nothing more clearly demonstrates the intended provocation of the mission than Polk's appointment of a known spy by the name of William Parrott as Slidell's assistant. Mexican authorities had made it clear that Parrott was an enemy of the state and that he was unwelcome in their country. Yet the president made the appointment despite the fact the Mexican government specifically asked that no one offensive be sent as minister. Polk was "essentially perpetrating a fraud in sending Slidell to Mexico in such a capacity and with such instructions as he did."[25]

Quite predictably, Slidell's mission failed, and it did so before he could even present the offensive terms to Mexico. Herrera recognized that receiving a minister from the United States would have signaled the restoration of diplomatic ties with the country, which would not only deprive Mexico of a bargaining chip but also prove fatal to his fragile regime. He refused to meet with Slidell. The rebuffed envoy withdrew from the capital and watched as Herrera was overthrown by hard-liner General Mariano Paredes, who campaigned on the promise to take all of Texas back from the United States. Although the possibility that Paredes might meet with an American diplomat was nearly unthinkable, Secretary of State Buchanan ordered Slidell to remain in Mexico a bit longer. He needed to maintain the charade of diplomacy in order "to satisfy the American people that all had been done which ought to have been done to avoid the necessity of resorting to hostilities." This was particularly important given that the "energetic measures against Mexico" that Polk would demand upon Slidell's return "might fail to obtain the support of Congress" if the United States appeared to be in the wrong.[26]

Slidell, for his part, was disgusted by Mexico. His failed mission provided much evidence to his mind that the country was both "feeble and distracted." In limbo outside the capital, he vented his anger in letters home. On December 29, 1845, he wrote the president directly with his advice for how to move forward. "A war would probably be the best mode of settling our affairs with Mexico," he told Polk.[27]

Had it had been a year earlier, Henry Clay would have watched Polk and guessed his next move. But not now: his own woes were too distracting. He had been in seclusion at Ashland, his Kentucky estate, since his defeat. Ashland was Clay's refuge, an eight-hundred-acre working farm and showpiece that was second to none in both beauty and productivity. Since his purchase of the original property in 1805, Clay and his wife had devoted themselves, and the forced labor of an average of fifty slaves, to the improvement of the groves, pastures, outbuildings, and extensive fields of corn, wheat, and particularly hemp that helped support the Clay family. They had a stone cheese house and a stone butter house, allowing Lucretia Clay to oversee the production of vast and profitable quantities of "the best butter and cheese in the Lexington market."[28] Lucretia's dairy business brought her $1,500 a year, some of which the indulgent mother privately distributed to her children and grandchildren. There was a chicken house and dove house, stables, barn, and sheds, "all in perfect repair, spacious, neat and in order." A greenhouse was full of "rare and choice plants . . . from every section of our country, and also exotic shrubs from almost every clime." Even the slave quarters, according to a contemporary report, were "white-washed, clean and well furnished, and plenty of flowers in the windows and about the dwellings."[29]

The main residence was a brick mansion that managed to look both "very

Ashland, the Home of Henry Clay, *by T. Sinclair. Eight-hundred-acre Ashland was one of the finest estates in Kentucky, a testimony to Lucretia Hart Clay's household management, Henry Clay's good taste and worldly success, and the labor of fifty slaves, none of whom appear in this image. Ashland was Clay's refuge from the stress of Washington.* Library of Congress Prints and Photographs Division.

venerable, and strictly republican," meaning obviously rich without seeming ostentatious. The two-and-a-half-story structure, situated on a small elevation commanding a "delightful view of the city of Lexington . . . towards the setting sun," was flanked by wings designed by the great architect Benjamin Latrobe. It was a large building, 120 by 60 feet, and featured a glorious octagonal library, paneled in ash and lit by skylight, as well as spacious dining and drawing rooms, a billiards room, office, and sufficient bedrooms for the large family and the Clays' frequent guests. The interior of the mansion was described as "plainly, but well furnished," but the French china and "choice and valuable" gifts from Clay's many admirers testified to the family's refinement. A visitor to Ashland, drinking fine Madeira wine served in cut crystal glasses on a silver tray, was made fully aware that the statesman was used to "living in the best society here and in Europe." There was a sizable carriageway, and great lawns of bluegrass. A meandering tree-lined path connected the mansion to an excellent macadam road that led straight into Lexington, a mile and a half away.[30]

If Clay was likely to find peace anywhere, it would be at Ashland, surrounded by his fields, his family, and the household furnishings and rare plants given him by his many admirers. It was said that "Mr. Clay has more ardent personal friends . . . than any man living." From the steps of his home, Clay could look out over Lexington, the city he had helped to make great, and know that "among his neighbors, at home, where he has spent a long life, he is *loved*."[31] But even in this idyllic spot, Clay found the trials of the period nearly insurmountable.

Lucretia was a great comfort. After the election they wept in each other's arms, and then resolved to move forward. But the good people of Lexington were making it difficult. Many of them seemed to take his loss as hard as he did. There was that bride and groom whose wedding was spoiled by news of Polk's victory. They had intended to honeymoon in Washington, but "abandoned their Eastern tour, and took a boat for New Orleans instead." Their boat carried the news of Clay's loss down the Mississippi, and at New Orleans "the expression of grief was appalling." The groom fell ill and a physician was summoned. When the doctor inquired if the young man had "suffered any great shock," he was told of Mr. Clay's defeat. "The physician, who was also a Clay man," embraced his patient, "and they wept together."[32]

Letters of sympathy and testimonials of grief, which Clay received in droves, were hard enough to face. Clay admitted that some of them were so painful that "my heart bleeds, for the moment, for my Country and my friends." But much worse were the people who insisted upon delivering their condolences in person, sitting in his drawing room with sorrowful expressions, demanding that Clay display his emotion, that he supply "all the capital of conversation . . . a monosyllable is all that I can sometimes get from them." He longed for an escape. "I am occasionally tempted to wish that I could find some obscure and inaccessible hole, in which I could put myself." For the most part, Clay maintained his composure, but when the electors of Kentucky gathered outside his house, by the time Clay had finished thanking them, all were in tears.[33]

Clay focused on the farm, tending his garden. For the first time in his life, he began to read theological works in earnest. And only a month after the election he emancipated his valet, Charles Dupuy, the slave who went everywhere with Clay, who was known on a first-name basis in Washington, and whose father had served the same function before him. When Clay was at home, Dupuy took charge of the household management, and when he was away, Dupuy was ever by his side. Dupuy helped Clay dress, shaved his face, slept in the same room. He was the closest man in Henry Clay's life.

Clay felt deeply ambivalent about slavery. He was one of the largest slaveholders in the Bluegrass Region of Kentucky, but also president of the American Colonization Society, which was determined to solve the problem of slavery by sending freed slaves to a colony in Africa, despite the fact that slave owners were unwilling to part with their very valuable property, and very few free black men or women were interested in moving "back" to a continent where neither they nor their parents had ever lived. Over the years, Henry Clay freed eight or ten of his slaves, including Dupuy's mother, Lottie, and his sister Mary Anne. But his liberation of Charles Dupuy in the winter of 1844–45 was exceptional, not only because there was no slave more crucial to Clay's well-being but also because Clay freed him at the very moment when he suddenly found himself in dire need of money.[34]

Clay's personal property was worth almost $140,000 in 1839, but by 1844 it was valued at only $51,000. Like many other men of his class, Clay carried some debt. The expenses of the election hadn't helped matters. Clay had cosigned a loan with his son Thomas, but when Thomas's business collapsed, the statesman found himself on the verge of bankruptcy. Henry Clay was now responsible for his son's debt. He struggled to pay his property taxes, liquidated his land holdings in neighboring states, took a mortgage out on his home and estate, and searched for ways to economize. But as of March 1845, Henry Clay owed $40,000 and was on the verge of losing Ashland.[35]

Only the generosity of his friends saved Clay from destitution. Merchants and businessmen around the country took up a collection upon hearing about Clay's financial distress and anonymously paid off his debt. The president of the Northern Bank of Kentucky wrote Clay with the good news, assuring the statesman that his benefactors considered their generosity "only part of a debt they owe you for your long and valued Services in the cause of our country and institutions."[36]

With his debt cleared, Polk's inauguration over, and the crowds of condolence-wishers dispersing to some degree, April 1845 should have been a better month for the Clay family. There were milestones to celebrate. April 10 would be the thirty-fourth birthday of Henry Clay Jr., the "pride and hope" of his family. A quick and clever child with his father's pale hair and eyes, young Henry had been born in Ashland's dining room not long after it was constructed. His two older brothers had been grave disappointments, but thus far the namesake, now a serious and perhaps overly somber young man, had lived up to his father's high hopes. "If you too disappoint my anxious hopes," Clay once threatened his son, "a constitution, never good, and now almost exhausted, would sink beneath the pressure. You bear my name." He was thinking of running for Congress from Louis-ville, a move his father entirely approved of, but in truth the burden of his father's expectations weighed on him. "How difficult it is for a young tree to grow in the shade of an aged oak," the younger Henry admitted to his diary. His parents were to celebrate their forty-sixth wedding anniversary on April 11. And on April 12, Henry Clay Sr. would celebrate his sixty-eighth birthday.[37]

But instead spring brought more misery. The Clays' youngest son, twenty-four-year-old John, grew despondent after an unrequited love affair and began acting erratically at the end of March. The Clays knew the symp-toms of mental illness too well to discount what they saw. Their eldest son, Theodore, had suffered a head injury as a child, and gradually degenerated into "violent insanity" before being permanently institutionalized at the Lunatic Asylum of Kentucky in 1831.[38]

John's "derangement" grew until one evening he took to the woods until 2:00 a.m., threatening to take his own life. On April 8, Henry and Lucretia were forced to place their youngest son in the lunatic asylum alongside their eldest. The patriarch poured out his anxiety and sorrow to John's brother Henry Clay Jr. "I find it extremely hard to bear this last sad affliction," he wrote. "I am afraid that John's case is hopeless."[39]

John's case wasn't hopeless. In a month he would be rational enough to return home, but his mental health would never again be perfect, and his parents would catch themselves watching his behavior for signs of return-ing instability. The stress on the family was great. And Clay was not in good health himself. A chronic cough, shortness of breath, and extreme fatigue were clear but unmentioned symptoms of his developing tuberculosis. Clay regretted the annexation of Texas and feared for what would happen to his country under Polk's guidance, but as 1845 wound down, Mexico was far from his thoughts.

Polk, on the other hand, could think of little else. He'd been in office nearly a year and his great push to the Pacific had gone nowhere. In Novem-ber he turned fifty. There was no party for the president. His birthday fell on a Sunday, and if there was any celebration, he failed to make note of it. Instead he went to church, where the minister delivered a "solemn and forcible sermon" from the Acts of the Apostles 17:31, on the coming Day of Judgment.[40]

James K. Polk was not a particularly deep thinker, but as the minister hammered into his audience that God "commands that all people every-where should repent" and that "he has appointed a day in which he will judge the world," he found himself shocked into introspection. The sermon, he wrote in his diary that night, "awakened the reflection that I had lived fifty years, and that before fifty years more would expire, I would be sleeping with the generations which have gone before me. I thought of the vanity of this world's honors, how little they would profit me half a century hence, and that it was time for me to be 'putting my house in order.' "[41]

Polk did not repent, at least not publicly, and he didn't join a church. But he did increase pressure on Mexico. On January 13, 1846, he ordered Taylor's forces to march to the Rio Grande and take up a defensive position deep in the heart of the disputed territory. The navy would blockade the Rio Grande. Surely this would force Mexico's hand, Polk thought. Either the Mexicans would throw the first punch, so to speak, or they would back down. Either way, Polk would gain California.[42]

It was his third attempt to provoke Mexico to war, and Democrats were solidly behind him. John Slidell was still in Mexico, performing a charade of diplomacy while advising the use of force. Comparing Mexico to an unruly woman, Slidell wrote the secretary of state in March 1846, "We shall never be able to treat with her . . . until she has been taught to respect us."[43]

While he awaited word from Taylor, Polk turned to the issue of Oregon. He was not so cocky as to believe his army could fight two wars at once, or easily defeat Britain, but Polk had made certain promises in 1844 about vanquishing the British from the Pacific Northwest that were proving inexpedient at the moment. Anglophobia was rife in the young nation, and many Americans imagined a vast British conspiracy to control North America and free their slaves. Northwestern Democrats believed all of Oregon, including British Columbia, rightfully belonged to the United States. Congressional representatives offered scathing attacks on England, and calls for war if Britain did not acknowledge U.S. rights in the region. To many in the North, full title to Oregon was more clearly America's Manifest Destiny than was Texas.[44]

Martial fervor grew in intensity, but even in the North there were Whigs willing to point out that taking "all of Oregon" would lead "inevitably to war." Robert Winthrop, Whig of Boston, quoted Shakespeare's *King John* on the floor of Congress in response to "the reckless flippancy with which war is spoken of in this house." In the 1840s, *King John,* which relates the struggle over the throne of England in the thirteenth century, was one of Shakespeare's more popular historical dramas. Near the end of the play the protagonist declares that England will be conquered by foreign invaders only if it is first torn apart by internal strife. The greatest Shakespearian actor of the day, Charles Macready, who was also a friend of Winthrop's, had recently performed *King John* in London to great acclaim. Many in Congress, particularly Whigs from the Northeast, knew all about Macready's forthcoming New York production of the play, which promised to be one of the most elaborate and expensive theatrical productions of the year. They were well aware of the reference when Winthrop compared those congressmen who threatened to "whip Great Britain" to the "swaggering citizens" in the play.

> *Here's a large mouth indeed,*
> *That spits forth death and mountains, rocks and seas;*
> *Talks as familiarly of roaring lions,*
> *As maids of thirteen do of puppy dogs.*
> *What cannoneer begot this lusty blood?*
> *He speaks plain cannon fire, and smoke and bounce.*[45]

No one spoke cannon fire more lustily than Polk, but the smoke and bounce of the Oregon debate was proving almost too hot to handle. With Taylor on the march to the Rio Grande, time was of the essence. In a masterstroke of diplomacy and domestic politics, Polk appeased northern expansionists by publicly claiming that Oregon belonged to the United States and asking Congress to terminate the joint occupation, while at the same time secretly inviting compromise. Polk was indeed putting his house in order, and it would be a continental empire big enough for young America to grow to adulthood.

Abraham Lincoln was not one of those Clay worshippers who took the "severe disappointment" of 1844 particularly hard. Having stumped for his hero around the state, he was dismayed by the outcome, but Lincoln rebounded quickly. Other Illinois Whigs were less fortunate. "I do not suppose that in all the union greater mortification of heart & spirit has been experienced than with myself, and my grown sons here on the doleful issue of the last struggle," one man wrote to John Hardin nearly a month after the election. Another confessed that he "suffered mentally more than human tongue can ever describe" and that Clay's loss "has unmanned me for everything like business." But Lincoln was by nature resilient, and high hopes for the future buoyed his spirits.[46]

Lincoln, like Clay, paid little attention to Polk's expansionism in 1845. He hadn't lost sleep over annexation: "inexpedient," he'd called it, but that was all. He ignored the war talk. What held him right now was his Springfield life. Mary was pregnant again. There was the rambunctious two-year-old Robert to control. The cow needed milking, and there was firewood to bring in to heat the family's most cherished possession, their first house, which under Mary's expert guidance had become a real home. Mary bought china, carpets, and furniture, and the couple entertained regularly, although Mary's simple Kentucky cooking, "loaded with venison, wild turkeys, prairie chickens and quail and other game," marked the couple as decidedly less than aristocratic.[47]

Mary's third cousin John Hardin and his wife, Sarah, would never serve their guests such fare. They were vastly richer than the Lincolns, and owned a spacious brick mansion in nearby Jacksonville. It was surrounded by groves and fields with plenty of room for the blooded Kentucky horses that John delighted in breeding and riding. These distinctions meant less to Abraham than to Mary. His law practice was thriving, and like Clay, Lincoln discovered that the ability to weave a tale and entrance an audience was of invaluable use in winning over juries regardless of the merits of the case.

Lincoln was still thinking about Congress and was determined to "test the temper of the winds again." Before Baker was seated in the Twenty-ninth Congress, Lincoln went to work winning nomination to the Thirtieth, bombarding the Seventh Congressional District with letters designed to advance his candidacy. One important Whig to whom he wrote two ingratiating letters was John Hardin, then finishing up his short congressional term. He let Hardin know that "one of our best friends" was irritated with the congressman, and suggested how he might right things with the man. He also offered some political gossip about how "the Texas question" was playing among local Democrats.[48]

But in the summer of 1845 Lincoln discovered that Hardin was contemplating a return to Congress in 1846. This was a major blow to Lincoln. Hardin did everything well, and his congressional term was no exception. He lodged the first vote ever by an Illinois representative against the slave power when he voted against the gag rule, which tabled all petitions about slavery without consideration. He set aside party interests by voting to reimburse ailing Andrew Jackson for a fine incurred many years earlier. He gave a very good speech in favor of protective tariffs. And he actively represented the interests of westerners generally. All these were popular measures with the good people of the Seventh District.

But Hardin went above and beyond the call of duty while in Washington. He demonstrated his singular ability to manage a crisis aboard the *Princeton* that fateful day in 1843. He was on deck, "forty or fifty feet off looking on and elevated so as to see all on deck," when the gun burst. "I was neither shocked or hurt," he explained to a friend, "and therefore in a condition to see and learn all about that most dreadful catastrophe." He took command of the wounded and dead visitors, and stayed on the ship for nearly a week.[49]

Hardin's sangfroid impressed everyone, and he emerged from the disaster not quite a hero but certainly something close. His reputation for bravery and leadership renewed by this tragedy, General Hardin was invited to help superintend the examinations of cadets at the military academy at West Point.[50]

He also made a splash among the Whigs of the East Coast, many of whom he got to know well while attending Clay's nominating convention in Baltimore. His supporters claimed that it was Hardin who wrote the first Whig song about James K. Polk, and he was the first in Congress to "give their Polk-stock a good shaking" when he delivered the inaugural speech of the campaign in the House against the "pigmy" presidential candidate. He was noted for his invective and sarcasm, and invitations to speak in support of Clay began to pour in from around the country. Abraham Lincoln stumped for Clay around Illinois, but Hardin, now an honorary member of Boston Clay Club Number One, was in demand from Philadelphia to Georgia.[51] When Hardin left Congress he claimed to be glad to be free of the place's bullying and arguing, which produced scenes that "would have disgraced the meanest western grocery." Washington wasn't much: "a long string of good buildings a mile in length," he wrote his daughter. "And when you leave this street one hundred yards you are out in a very poor country." His life there had been "pure drudgery." By the summer of 1844, he was more than "ready to surrender my honor . . . without a sigh or regret."[52]

He felt himself above politics. He had concluded, he told his wife, Sarah, that politics was an "amoral" way of life. He was anxious to get back to his home and law practice. But with characteristic confidence he also asserted that "no member of Congress" had been more "applauded by his constituents, or by his political friends through out the Union, than myself. Without arrogance I may say, [I] have already left my mark among the public men of this Congress." Hardin had a healthy sense of self-regard, but the enthusiastic public celebrations held in his honor across his district upon his return suggest that he was every bit as revered by the Whigs of that state as he believed.[53]

Now he was back in Illinois, but still acting like a politician. Worse yet, he was winning acclaim across party lines as a proponent of Manifest Destiny. The controversy over Oregon was raging hard. When Illinois Democrats held a public meeting in Springfield in June 1845, in support of the annexation of the entire Oregon Country, Hardin was a featured speaker. In a rousing patriotic speech, he called on listeners to present a united front in support of the annexation of not only Oregon but also California, which "at the proper time" would be "re-annexed" to the United States. It was the duty of all citizens to sustain the president on these matters, and should "the call to war be sounded . . . it would become the duty of every American citizen to rally to, and uphold the government." And he would be with them. His listeners could find him "at the battlefront . . . in any such contest, as long as the United States government existed, or a drop of blood still flowed" in his veins. He promised the people of Illinois that, "right or wrong, he would battle for his country, and for his country alone." The applause was deafening.[54]

That fall Hardin gained more acclaim, and a renewal of his brigadier generalship, when he helped quell violence between Mormon settlers in far western Illinois and their intolerant Gentile neighbors. The Mormons had been the object of persecution almost from the day in 1823 that Joseph Smith first announced that the angel Moroni had delivered to him golden tablets inscribed with scripture for the restoration of Christianity. Since 1839, twelve thousand members of the religious community had existed uneasily in Nauvoo, Illinois, protected from the wrath of non-Mormon neighbors in large part by the Democratic Party, which supported religious freedom and appreciated the reliable votes the Mormons cast in their favor.

But after news of Mormon polygamy appeared in a local newspaper in June 1844, Smith was killed by an Illinois mob. When word of a major assault against the sect and countermeasures by Mormons against Gentile neighbors made their way to the governor in the fall of 1846, Hardin led four hundred members of the militia to break up the conflict. That spring he also oversaw the expulsion of the Mormons across state lines. Mormons might not agree, but the Gentiles of Illinois praised Hardin's "wise and skillful management" of the Mormon displacement. Hardin was credited with putting a stop "to the lawlessness and bloodshed their presence engendered." The displacement of the Illinois Mormons was hardly fair, but quite likely Hardin prevented a full-scale slaughter of the oppressed minority.[55]

This paragon of virtue was Abraham Lincoln's competition for the Whig nomination to the Thirtieth Congress. Lincoln began writing letters to editors and lobbying delegates on his own behalf. In early September he went to Hardin's house to ask him directly: Was he intending to run in 1846? Hardin refused to commit himself one way or another. Lincoln realized that in order to win the nomination he would have to go on the offensive. "Hardin is a man of desparate [sic] energy and perseverance; and one that never backs out; and, I fear, to think otherwise, is to be deceived in the character of our adversary," he wrote one friend. Lincoln would not be deceived, and he would not back down. This election would be his. In other circumstances, perhaps, "if Hardin and I stood precisely equal—that is if *neither* of us had been to congress, or, if we *both* had," Lincoln would have given way. But "turn about is fair play," and it was Lincoln's turn now.[56]

By January 1846, as John Slidell's diplomatic mission slid into farce and General Paredes was inaugurated as president of Mexico, Lincoln's efforts to line up delegates had become almost maniacal. He knew General Hardin had all the advantages in the contest, but he would not let his chance at Congress slip by again. He wrote personal letters to "three or four of the most active Whigs in each precinct," made trips throughout the district, and demanded that his friends lobby everyone they knew: "let not opportunity of making a mark escape." When Hardin suggested that the two of them stop actively electioneering and instead submit their names for party election among Whig voters, Lincoln rebuffed his old friend. "I have always been in the habit of acceding to almost any proposal that a friend would make; and I am truly sorry I can not in this." It would have cost him the election, for everyone knew John Hardin's name but few knew Lincoln's.[57]

Hardin withdrew from the contest in disgust. In February 1846, as Polk plotted his next move with Mexico, Hardin published a public letter in which he firmly denied any agreement with Lincoln or Baker to rotate the office, as Lincoln had claimed. "I deem it an act of justice to myself," he wrote, "to state that his report is utterly without foundation. I never made any bargain, or had any understanding . . . respecting either the last or any future canvass for Congress." He also published his offer to let the Whig voters decide the issue, along with Lincoln's rejection of that seemingly democratic proposal, and accused Lincoln of improper campaign practices.[58]

With that, Lincoln's path to Congress was finally open, but the cost had been great. Hardin would never again be "a father" to Lincoln: the two men were no longer on speaking terms. And Lincoln had lost something more. He could no longer pretend to the voters, or to himself, that "if elected I shall be thankful; if not it will be all the same," as he had claimed six years earlier.[59]

For Hardin it was no great sacrifice. His heart wasn't in the contest, and his withdrawal from the race might have had little to do with Lincoln's success lining up delegates. Lincoln's attention that spring extended no further than the perimeter of his congressional district, but his opponent's view was far more expansive. He had his eye on California. Back in June 1845, Hardin had told the largely Democratic audience at the meeting in favor of annexing Oregon that "if he decided to run away from Illinois, he could be found in California."[60]

Now he was watching events in Mexico with great care. Several weeks prior to his clash with Lincoln, Hardin wrote to a highly placed military friend in order to gain confirmation of the "insult" offered the United States when Mexico refused to receive John Slidell. "If Mexico does not give every explanation & satisfaction which our govt. should demand under the circumstances," General Hardin saw "no resort but to take up arms." Hardin wasn't naive. He recognized that it might be all "diplomatic smoke" by the Polk administration. And if that were the case, his friend should feel free to burn his letter. But if there was going to be a war, Hardin wanted to be first in line for a commission. However he might feel about the president personally, "in our foreign relations I acknowledge no . . . party but one country, & believe it to be the duty of all true patriots to strengthen the hands of the govt. . . . against the aggression & insult from foreign nations." Hardin was itching for a fight, and he suspected he didn't have long to wait.[61]

Polk's policy of leaving Slidell in Mexico in order "to satisfy the American people that all had been done which ought to have been done to avoid the necessity of resorting to hostilities" was having its intended effect, and not only among military men such as Hardin. At the end of April, just one week before the state Whig convention met to nominate Abraham Lincoln for Congress, rumors of a military maneuver at the border spread across the state. It appeared that Zachary Taylor's troops, sent recently to the Rio Grande to protect Texas, had retreated. "We do not like the appearance of Gen. Taylor moving from under the guns of the Mexicans," proclaimed the local Whig paper. "Surely fear could not have induced him to abandon his position." Something needed to be done about Mexico, the paper concluded. "We think that the Mexican authorities have insulted our government, and robbed our people sufficiently, to call for some other policy than that of suing at their feet for our just rights."[62]

With the fate of Taylor's army in doubt, and passions against Mexico running high, Abraham Lincoln was nominated for Congress. He was on the verge of achieving his dream, with no premonition of the crisis about to engulf the nation.

5

"The Mischief Is Done"

NICHOLAS TRIST WAS not indifferent to expansion. As chief clerk of the State Department, second in command to Secretary of State Buchanan, he had been appointed by Polk to help him accomplish his goals. He was an excellent choice: his Spanish was impeccable, and his understanding of the "Spanish Character" and internal politics of Mexico set him apart from most other diplomats. Trist distinguished himself in other ways as well. Tall and handsome, with enviable posture and formal manners, the chief clerk radiated poise and confidence. He was fully aware that he was not only one of the best-pedigreed Democrats in the United States but also one of the most capable.

Trist also brought a little glamour to the administration. Thomas Jefferson had been responsible for his legal education, personally tutoring the young man for two years, sixteen hours a day. Jefferson and Trist's grandmother, Elizabeth, were old friends, and he early recognized a nascent intelligence in young Nicholas that commanded his attention. Trist's essential character and beliefs had been shaped by Jefferson: religious skepticism, love of logic, and commitment to abstract notions of justice. Just as important, Jefferson had blessed Trist's marriage to his granddaughter, Virginia, and made him his private secretary. Trist's intellect, abilities, and love more than repaid Jefferson's investment. He served as the aging Jefferson's companion on rides through the Virginia countryside, long walks around the grounds of Monticello, and countless conversations in the president's

Nicholas Trist. *Portrait by John Neagle, 1835. Nicholas Trist was thirty-five years old when this portrait was painted by the fashionable artist John Neagle. Trist was on a visit home from his duties as U.S. consul to Cuba. Although he had held the position for only a year, he had already decided that foreign service, particularly in the tropics, did not agree with him. He longed for a posting back in the United States.* Courtesy Thomas Jefferson Foundation, Inc., at Monticello.

library, the contents of which Trist catalogued. And at the end of his life, Nicholas and Virginia Trist provided Thomas Jefferson with a great-granddaughter, named Martha and called Patsy like Jefferson's daughter. Jefferson acknowledged his dependence on Trist by naming him an executor of his will.

After Jefferson, Andrew Jackson took him under his wing. Jackson thrilled to Trist's stories of life with the first Democratic leader, and treasured him as a conduit to the president he venerated above all others. Nicholas and Virginia Trist were frequent guests at the executive mansion, and the president often summoned Trist to discuss issues of the day.

Trist, like so many other Democrats, found Jackson's powerful personality intoxicating. He gleefully recorded an instance when Jackson announced, "I care nothing for clamors, sir, mark me! I do precisely what I think just and right!" Trist greatly approved of the statement. For his part,

Jackson grew nearly as dependent on Trist's intellect and fine penmanship as had Jefferson. He made Trist his personal secretary, provided him lodgings at the White House, and traveled with him. Jackson later named Trist American consul in Havana. Nicholas found the posting onerous—he worried about catching a tropical disease, and Virginia found the Havana climate intolerable. The Trists returned to Washington.[1]

In the spring of 1845, Jackson convinced Polk to hire Trist as chief clerk of the State Department. For a man who had never really wanted to work hard, whose priorities were family life and reading, the forty-five-year-old Trist had built himself a nice career.

Polk saw in Trist a man who shared his values. They were both southerners and slaveholders, true believers in the party and the expansionist agenda first advocated by the two Democratic giants. Both speculated in southwestern land, and both owned plantations where slaves grew staple crops, although Trist's sugar plantation in Louisiana was never remotely as profitable as Polk's cotton plantation in neighboring Mississippi. Trist, moreover, had attended West Point, suggesting that he understood the power of the military to advance American interests. Along with experience and competence, Trist was also known for the attributes Polk valued most: loyalty and discretion.

But there was no personal relationship between the two. There is no evidence that Polk ever as much as asked Trist about either Jefferson or Jackson, a fact that can only be attributed to Polk's singular reserve. He never invited the chief clerk for dinner. Secretary of State James Buchanan was a frequent and enthusiastic guest at Sunday dinners at the spacious Trist family abode in Washington, but Polk never visited. Buchanan became well known to Thomas Jefferson's great-grandchildren; Polk never met them. Had Polk followed the lead of Jackson and Jefferson in befriending Trist, history might have turned out differently. But as it was, Polk never got to know Nicholas Trist well enough to recognize two traits that Jefferson left to his grandson-in-law: the conviction that he was smarter than almost everyone else, and an innate distrust of war.

The distrust of war was perhaps more his grandmother's doing than Jefferson's. The president's struggles to keep the United States out of war with England and France during the last years of his presidency were well known and had been widely condemned at the time, but Jefferson had also encouraged a somewhat aimless eighteen-year-old Trist to attend the fledgling military academy at West Point. His grandmother, however, did not want Nicholas to become a warrior. While she initially agreed with his course of study (she rarely disagreed with Jefferson about anything), during his second year she sent her grandson a letter that clearly condemned both war and those who waged it. "I would as soon hear of your turning Highway man as to join any army, from ambitious motives," she told him. "War is at best a horrid calamity and those who wage war for the purpose of sub-jugating nations to their will are guilty of a heinous crime." She reminded "Dear Nicholas" that "when the hour arrives that you must quit this World let not your conscience upbraid you with having done any thing to dishonor humanity." Reminding him of the mental suffering that his father had expe-rienced after killing a man in a duel, Elizabeth Trist asked, "What must be the reflection of those who are instrumental in heaping misery on thou-sands, how many Widows and Orphans are thrown into the world destitute and wretched"?[2]

Not that he required a great deal of convincing on this point. Trist excelled in academics at West Point and made a number of lifelong friends, including Andrew Jackson Donelson, Old Hickory's nephew and namesake. But neither the spartan living conditions nor the intense physical demands of the military academy agreed with him. Painfully thin and prone to hypo-chondria, he worried constantly about his health. And he had trouble sub-mitting to authority. As he explained to Donelson, "I claim the liberty of regulating my own conduct by what I deem right."[3] Not surprisingly, Trist gradually came to the conclusion that he was unsuited for a military career. He left West Point without graduating and returned to Monticello deter-mined to marry Virginia Randolph and serve Jefferson any way he could.

A quarter of a century later, Trist found himself in a far less pleasant posi-tion in James K. Polk's administration. The chief clerk had had no idea that working for this president would prove so arduous. Trist enjoyed books, music, long dinners, and quiet time with his family. Polk, on the other hand, fully believed that "no president who performs his duty faithfully and con-scientiously can have any leisure." Trist's workload was staggering. "There has never been one day in which I had not on hand some subject (or several subjects) to dispose of which require . . . deliberate thought and research. And these subjects have all had to be disposed of by snatches," he wrote mis-erably. The "enormous mail" was overwhelming, and he was responsible for overseeing the work of the entire staff of the State Department. "Every-thing that comes passes through my hands in the first instance, anything that goes passes though my hands in the last instance."[4]

He struggled to meet Polk's high standards. The perfectionist president was convinced that if he handed over "the details and smaller matters to subordinates constant errors will occur." With no little sense of pride, Polk admitted that "I prefer to supervise the whole operations of the Government myself rather than entrust the public business to subordinates, and this makes my duties very great."[5]

It also made Trist's duties great. The chief clerk frequently found his letters returned to him for correction. The hours were endless, the intensity stressful, and Trist felt his health declining. "Without a single day's intermission," he wrote, "by the time I get away from the office I am *broken down* for the day." He began fantasizing about a less onerous posting somewhere far from the center of power. Instead, since James Buchanan, the secretary of state, was frequently out of the office, he found himself running the department.[6]

Thus he had quite a clear view of Polk's provocation of Mexico, and the president's latest move ordering Zachary Taylor a hundred miles into the Nueces Strip. Polk had already decided that if this tactic failed, he would risk the consequences and simply declare war. On April 25, 1846, he told his assembled cabinet that the time had come to "take a bold and firm course toward Mexico," and that "forbearance was no longer either a virtue or patriotic." Employing a language more common to dueling and other affairs of honor among southerners than to high diplomacy, Polk was adamant that the United States "take redress for the injuries done us into our own hands." According to him, by rejecting minister John Slidell, by refusing to pay claims put forward by U.S. citizens, and above all by refusing to recognize Texas's ownership of the Nueces Strip, Mexico had insulted the United States to such a degree that honor required the southern neighbor be punished.

As for the many injuries done to Mexico by the United States—the annexation of Texas, the occupation of the Nueces Strip, the repeated insults offered by America's incompetent and offensive minister—none of them factored into Polk's analysis. Mexico, inferior in both race and power, must necessarily bend to the will of its neighbor. To those who suggested that it might be unseemly, even un-Christian, to attack a weaker nation, Polk argued that "we must treat all nations, whether great or small, strong or weak, alike."[7]

Polk's concept of justice was unquestionably shaped by his experience as a slave master. Some slaveholders, such as Henry Clay, or Thomas Jefferson a generation before, struggled with the knowledge that slavery was wrong. But like most intensely conservative slave masters in the 1840s, Sarah and James Polk believed the domination of white over black was part of God's plan. James may have been influenced by his wife's views on this point. He liked to repeat evidence of Sarah's "acumen" on the topic by relating a conversation the two had had on a hot July afternoon in the White House. Gazing out the window at slaves working the grounds, Sarah interrupted her husband from his writing with the assertion that "the writers of the Declaration of Independence were mistaken when they affirmed that all men are created equal." When James suggested this was just "one of your foolish fancies," Sarah elaborated. "There are those men toiling in the heat of the sun, while you are writing, and I am sitting here fanning myself . . . surrounded with every comfort. Those men did not choose such a lot in life, neither did we ask for ours; we were created for these places." Domination of the strong over the weak, and white over black or brown, was not just the reality of slavery, it was also, in their perspective, right.[8]

That James K. Polk viewed international relations through the lens of slaveholding and dominance is notable but not particularly surprising for a southerner who modeled himself on General Andrew Jackson. Newspapers throughout the South echoed the belief that national honor, like personal honor, was a matter of highest significance, one that sometimes required the physical reprimand of inferiors. Just days before Polk addressed his cabinet, the New Orleans *Bulletin* explained that "the United States have borne more insult, abuse, insolence and injury, from Mexico, than one nation has ever before endured from another. . . . They are left no alternative but to extort by arms, the respect and justice which Mexico refuses to any treatment less harsh." If not, other nations would lose all respect for the United States. The New Orleans *Delta* warned that if the United States did not take "active measures" against Mexico, "every dog, from the English mastiff to the Mexican cur, may snap at and bite us with impunity."[9]

Sarah Polk, as fervent a believer in Manifest Destiny as her husband, agreed that the nation's honor must be upheld at all costs. "Whatever sustained the honor and advanced the interests of the country, whether regarded as democratic or not," she stated at a dinner party in defense of war, she "admired and applauded."[10]

These southerners were not alone. There were certainly northerners who believed in April 1846 that Mexico deserved punishment for the insults it had offered the United States. Walt Whitman, editor of a Democratic newspaper in Brooklyn, declared that "Mexico must be thoroughly chastised. . . . Let our arms now be carried with a spirit which shall teach the world that, while we are not forward for a quarrel, America knows how to crush, as well as how to expand!"[11]

But the threats and bluster were loudest from the South. It was the men of the South, that group that referred to themselves as "the chivalry," who specialized in what Massachusetts Whig Robert Winthrop called "gasconading bravadoes." The *Milwaukee Daily Sentinel and Gazette* saw Slidell's mission for what it was: a plot to insult Mexico and then demand satisfaction for an insult supposedly done by Mexico against the United States. It was, in the newspaper's judgment, a typically southern response. On April 29, the paper predicted that although Mexico "acted with becoming spirit and self respect" in dismissing Slidell, the United States "will insist upon 'satisfaction,' and as it is a question between us and a weaker nation on *the South,* the 'chivalry' will, doubtless, back up his demand and call upon the President and Congress to declare war against Mexico." Northerners, far more than southerners, were likely to agree with the paper that "it will be an evil day for Human Progress, Civilization and Christianity when America disturbs the peace of the world."[12]

Nor was everyone in the cabinet ready for war in late April. Only Secretary of State Buchanan seconded the proposition that Polk "recommend a declaration of war" against Mexico to Congress. There was still the tricky matter of the Oregon boundary: surely it should be resolved before attacking Mexico. The cabinet agreed to discuss the matter further the following week. Two days later, Congress passed a joint resolution to end the joint occupation of Oregon with England, and invited the two countries to settle the matter amicably. Polk signed the bill and, with a clear message that he was willing to compromise and hand over the northern portion of the territory to England, had it sent across the Atlantic. Fully expecting the British to comply with a settlement that was very much in their interest, Polk turned his attention to Mexico. He began drafting a war message to present to Congress.[13]

In Illinois, one politician was almost as anxious as Polk for hostilities to begin. The Illinois press was full of rumors of hostilities at the border, and on May 2, John Hardin inquired if his good friend, Congressman Stephen A. Douglas, had any inside information about affairs with Mexico. Douglas was one of Illinois's most powerful politicians and a leader of the state's Democratic Party, but the secretive president wasn't about to share with anyone, not even leaders of his own party, the fact that he had determined to go to war. "We are in a state of quasi war with that country, and are left to conjecture as to what is to be the sequel," Douglas wrote his friend. Hardin was fixated on California. He suggested to Douglas that in the event of war, troops immediately march to California from the Midwest and seize California by land. And Hardin himself should be the man to organize those troops. Douglas was supportive but noncommittal, for in truth he knew no more than Hardin. "The intentions of the administration in this respect are a profound secret. No one pretends to know what course will be pursued," he wrote Hardin.[14]

Much depended on one unprepossessing man; a potbellied, undereducated, slave-owning career military officer from Virginia. Zachary Taylor favored civilian clothes and a large straw hat, and his résumé was exceedingly modest, consisting primarily of a victory over the Seminole tribe in 1837 and several decades of garrison duty. He was no intellectual, and had heretofore shown little genius for the science of war. Many of his junior officers questioned his abilities. But the enlisted men adored him for his lack of pretension and common touch. Astride his beloved mount, Old Whitey, Taylor inspired veneration among the troops, despite the fact that the steed's appearance was a bit nobler than the rider's.

Zachary Taylor. Photograph by Mathew Brady, ca. 1847. Taylor, known as "Old Rough and Ready," was ordinarily dressed less formally than in this daguerreotype portrait taken during or soon after the war. General Collection, Beinecke Rare Book and Manuscript Library, Yale University.

Taylor may have felt ambivalence when Polk ordered him to leave Louisiana for Texas in the summer of 1845. Like most officers, Taylor supported the Whig Party over the Democrats. While neither side advocated a large peacetime army, Whigs repeatedly pushed for increased funding for the army and were steadfast supporters of the military academy at West Point. The Democratic Party feared the consolidation of power associated with a standing army, and wistfully believed state militias capable of protecting the nation. They didn't trust professional military men, and suggested that West Point might as well be disbanded. Army officers were suspicious, as well, of Democratic schemes for expansion. Less than four years had passed since the United States withdrew from a brutal guerrilla war of attrition against the Seminole Indians of Florida. The seven-year-long war, which failed to remove the tribe from their ancestral home, was fought in the blistering heat of the Everglades' swamplands. It was remarkably unpopular with officers and enlisted men alike, many of whom sympathized with the Seminoles and grew to hate the white settlers of the region. Many West Point officers resigned as a result of service in the Seminole War. Taylor, like most other Whigs, had serious misgivings about the annexation of Texas. According to one of his officers, Taylor privately denounced annexation as "injudicious in policy and wicked in fact."[15]

But Taylor followed orders and marched his troops to the edge of the contested territory. Not long after his arrival along the banks of the Sabine River, he received a novel map of Texas from the quartermaster general's office. It superimposed a new boundary mark at the Rio Grande over the earlier boundary mark at the Sabine. Lieutenant Colonel Ethan Allen Hitchcock of Vermont marveled in his diary at the "impudent arrogance and domineering presumption" of both the map and the administration that made it. Hitchcock, a close friend of Taylor's for twenty-five years, was the grandson of Revolutionary War hero Ethan Allen, and had served as both commandant of cadets and assistant professor of tactics at West Point. He would soon celebrate his forty-eighth birthday, and as a man born at the close of the eighteenth century, he had seen many things in his life. But he was sickened by the implications of this map for the future mission of the troops. "It is enough to make atheists of us all to see such wickedness in the world, whether punished or unpunished," he wrote in his diary.[16]

Fall in Corpus Christi was better than expected. The town itself was a disgrace, a ramshackle settlement of twenty or thirty structures that existed primarily for the purposes of illegal trade across the Nueces. Most of the population was involved in smuggling to some degree or another. But there were excellent opportunities for fishing and swimming in the bay. The men broke up the monotony of drilling with horse races and light amusements, including a performance of *Othello* in which another West Point officer, a young lieutenant named Ulysses S. Grant, was cast as the daughter of Brabantio. On October 16, the secretary of war directed Taylor to move "as close as circumstances will permit" to the Rio Grande, subject to his own judgment. Taylor's judgment told him to stay where he was, and so the troops remained in Corpus Christi.[17]

Winter was less pleasant. A severe cold snap at the end of November took everyone by surprise. The sun didn't shine for two straight weeks in December, and the men shivered in raised tents designed for use in balmy Florida. It was the coldest weather anyone in the region could remember. In an ominous preview of things to come, dysentery and diarrhea caused by poor sanitation began to ravage the camp. Some of the men took out their frustrations on local residents. After a spate of "outrages of aggravated character" against Mexicans living nearby, Taylor restricted his men to camp at nighttime.[18]

On February 3, 1846, Taylor received direct orders to march his men 150 miles south, all the way to the Rio Grande, also known as the Rio del Norte. He was understandably unenthusiastic. Secretary of War Marcy had earlier suggested to Taylor that the army's mission was defensive. The new orders reiterated that Taylor should not consider Mexico "an enemy" unless, of course, it should act that way. But if Mexico fired the first shot, Taylor should take advantage, and "not act merely on the defensive." Clearly the administration was hoping Taylor would shoulder some of the blame if hostilities ensued. And how could he not? Why was he deliberately marching four thousand men deep into territory that was widely understood, by everyone other than fervent U.S. expansionists, to belong to Mexico? "The 'claim,' so called, of the Texans to the Rio Grande, is without foundation," Colonel Hitchcock wrote in his diary. "She has never conquered, possessed, or exercised dominion west of the Nueces."[19]

Taylor had done almost nothing to prepare for future operations while in Corpus Christi. Now he sat on news of the impending move for three days. But conditions in the camp had degenerated, and Lieutenant Ulysses Grant summed up the reaction to Taylor's orders: "Fight or no fight evry one rejoices at the idea of leaving Corpus Christi." On the eve of their departure, General Taylor issued orders to the troops governing relations with civilians. He enjoined "all under his command to observe, with the most scrupulous regard, the rights of all person who may be found in the peaceful pursuit of their respective avocations, residing on both banks of the Rio Grande. No person, under any pretence whatsoever, will interfere in any manner with the civil rights or religious privileges of the people, but will pay the utmost respect to both." Taylor had these instructions translated into Spanish and posted along the route to Matamoros, on the Rio Grande. Taylor wrote a new will before starting the long trek to an unknown fate.[20]

In March 1846, Taylor marched his four thousand men through the Nueces Strip. It was "dreary, desolate, dry, and barren" countryside, a land better suited for snakes than people. The nearer they got to the Rio Grande, "the more dwarfed and thorny the vegetation—only the cactus more hideously large." And it was hot. "The sun streamed upon us like a living fire," one soldier recorded. Despite Taylor's proclamation asserting the "friendly intentions" of the U.S. Army, many of the inhabitants fled when they caught sight of the American troops. By no means did this feel like American territory. One American soldier who marched out of Corpus Christi expressed his disorientation in a letter back home to Illinois. Sitting in "the shade of a sort of white thorn," he reflected that "all about me are cactus, God knows how many kinds. It is impossible to describe them. All plants here have thorns, all animals stings or horns and all men carry weapons and all deceive each other and themselves."[21]

Mexican forces, meanwhile, had begun to mass at Matamoros on the southern bank of the Rio Grande, near the mouth of the river. From time to time the U.S. soldiers caught sight of them, marching in the distance. The Americans on the ground grasped better than most what was happening. Colonel Hitchcock wrote in his diary: "We have not one particle of right to be here. . . . It looks as if the government sent a small force on purpose to bring on a war, so as to have a pretext for taking California and as much of this country as it chooses."[22]

Taylor took up a position directly across the Rio Grande from the fortified port town of Matamoros and placed his cannon in clear sight of the stone and adobe buildings of the town square. He directed naval units to blockade the city and prevent food or supplies from reaching either the city of sixteen thousand or the occupying Mexican army. Cuban-born General Pedro Ampudia, a veteran of the Alamo and San Jacinto, sent Taylor a message giving him twenty-four hours to break camp and return to Corpus Christi. He also had handbills smuggled into the U.S. camp promising good treatment and high pay to any immigrants who chose to desert to Mexico.

Taylor explained that he was under orders, and suggested that responsibility for the war would rest with the nation that fired the first shot. Taylor would regret war, but he would not avoid it.[23]

His men weren't so sure. In one night fifty swam across the river and disappeared into Mexico. Taylor posted guards to prevent further desertions. Two weeks after Taylor's arrival, forty-two-year-old General Mariano Arista, a former Mexican governor who had once lived in Cincinnati, assumed command of the Mexican forces, which now numbered eight thousand. The following day, April 24, Arista sent a detachment of cavalry across the river. Taylor dispatched a small squadron of dragoons to meet them. The Americans were overwhelmed, and after a short firefight they surrendered to the Mexicans. Eleven U.S. soldiers were killed. Polk had his reason for war, although he didn't know it. Given the lack of communication between the Mexican frontier and the rest of the world, it would be two full weeks before the tidings would reach Washington.[24]

Polk spent those two weeks preparing for a war he was intent on beginning, regardless of conditions on the Rio Grande. On May 3, he called Senator Thomas Hart Benton to his offices in order to press the Democratic leader on the issue. Benton was one of the nation's most outspoken expansionists, a former Tennessean who, like Polk, modeled himself on Andrew Jackson and preached the gospel of Manifest Destiny. A physically imposing man with a temper that matched his bulk, Benton had served under Jackson in the War of 1812 and loved a good fight. He had killed a man in a duel, and shot his onetime mentor Jackson in the arm. He left Tennessee to get out of Jackson's shadow, and was now the West's most powerful politician.

Polk needed Benton's support, but also had reason to believe he would be sympathetic with Polk's approach. "I told him we had ample cause for War," Polk wrote in his diary. Benton "expressed a decided aversion to a war with Mexico" and particularly "advised delay" until negotiations with England over Oregon were "either settled" or "brought to a crisis, one of which must happen very soon." Polk agreed that if war could be avoided "honourably," that would be ideal, and he promised Benton that he would wait until John Slidell's return from Mexico to take action.[25]

Two days later, Polk and his cabinet agreed that they should wait for an update from General Taylor (from whom nothing had been heard in a month) before declaring war. On May 6, they received the erroneous news that Mexico had not yet attacked the United States. Two days later John Slidell returned from Mexico. He had no more idea than did Polk that Taylor had been fighting Mexico for over a week.

The failed diplomat and the president spoke privately for an hour, Slidell impressing upon Polk his conviction that "but one course toward Mexico was left to the U.S. and that was to take the redress of the wrongs and injuries which we had so long borne from Mexico into our own hands, and to act with promptness and energy." Polk agreed, and told Slidell that he had "made up" his mind to send a declaration of war to Congress "very soon."[26]

The following day, Saturday, May 9, Polk called his cabinet together and asked, again, whether they agreed to "recommend a declaration of war against Mexico" despite the fact that, as far as they knew, Mexico had not attacked the United States. Polk told them "that in my opinion we had ample cause of war, and that it was impossible that we could stand in *statu quo*, or that I could remain silent much longer." After all, "the country was excited and impatient on the subject."[27]

Polk was right on the last point. For weeks Democratic newspapers had been predicting that "war will be immediately declared against Mexico." The *Mississippian* declared that "our government has exhausted all measures for peace and conciliation" and thus "no alternative is left but a resort to arms." In Brooklyn, Walt Whitman was sure that "the people here, ten to one, are for prompt and *effectual* hostilities." Polk explained to his cabinet that since the country wanted war, if he failed to rise to the call, "I would not be doing my duty." All but Bancroft agreed that a recommendation of war against Mexico should be made to Congress the following Tuesday.[28]

Four hours later, Polk finally received news of the attacks on Taylor's forces. The president threw himself into composing a declaration of war over the course of that evening and throughout a long Sunday. He stopped work only long enough to attend a two-hour church service with Sarah, consult with important members of his party, and sit down to Sunday supper. At ten thirty he finally went to bed. "It was a day of great anxiety to me," he wrote in his diary, "and I regretted the necessity which had existed to make it necessary for me to spend the Sabbath in the manner I have."[29]

Polk had been composing this declaration in his mind for weeks, but it remained unfinished. He refused to see company on Monday morning and continued revising the message to Congress. Polk didn't like doing things at the last minute. It bothered him that he "had no time to read the copies of the correspondence furnished by the War & State Departments" that would accompany his message. For a man who assiduously checked the work of even minor clerks, the fact that a document of this importance was leaving his office without a final proofreading must have been anxiety-provoking.

With just hours to spare before he addressed Congress, he called Democratic senators Lewis Cass and Thomas Hart Benton to his office. Cass read the message and "highly approved it." Benton was not impressed by Polk's war bill. He told the president that "he was willing to vote men and money for defence of our territory, but was not prepared to make aggressive war on Mexico." Furthermore, he "disapproved the marching of the army from Corpus Christi to the left Bank of the Del Norte." When Benton left Polk's office, the president was not at all sure the senator would support his war. Polk "inferred, too, from his conversation that he did not think the territory of the U.S. extended West of the Nueces."[30]

At noon Polk sent his message to Congress. In the strongest possible language he excoriated Mexico, elided the truth, and demanded not that Congress declare war but that it recognize a war already in existence. He informed them that "now, after reiterated menaces, Mexico has passed the boundary of the United States, has invaded our territory and shed American blood upon the American soil." None of it was true—but Polk didn't consider it lies. There was a greater truth at stake, and he spoke in its service: "As war exists, and notwithstanding all our efforts to avoid it, exists by the act of Mexico herself, we are called upon by every consideration of duty and patriotism to vindicate with decision the honor, the rights, and the interest of our country."[31]

Democratic congressional leaders attached this declaration of war as a preamble to a bill authorizing funds for the troops, placed it in front of Congress, and demanded assent. It was a shrewd but contemptible move, and new in American history. By bundling the authorization of war funds with a declaration of war attributed to Mexico, Democrats ensured that any opponent of the measure could be accused of betraying the troops. Polk's supporters skillfully managed to stifle dissent in the House by limiting debate to two hours, an hour and a half of which was devoted to reading the documents that accompanied the message. The flabbergasted opposition was caught completely off guard and struggled to amend the bill. Powerless and voiceless, they watched helplessly as Polk's supporters ruthlessly stifled debate and foisted war on Congress and the country.

Just before the final vote, Garrett Davis, the Whig representative from Clay's district in Kentucky, gained the floor by a subterfuge, and then launched into an attack on Polk's statement and the rushed proceedings. "The river Nueces is the true western boundary of Texas," thundered Davis. It wasn't Mexico but "our own President who began this war. He has been carrying it on for months." Although repeatedly interrupted by Democrats and called to order by the Speaker of the House, Davis alone was able to voice what many of his colleagues believed: "that if the bill contained any . . . truth and justice," it would acknowledge "that this war was begun by the president."[32]

There were few men in Congress who took Polk's claims at face value. For weeks, newspapers had asked their readers "for what purpose . . . our Army of Occupation has been ordered down from Corpus Christi to the Rio del Norte," and concluded that Polk both "contemplated and desired" war. If not, "why was the United States army thrust upon the very lines of the Mexican?" The fact that he had provoked war by moving U.S. troops into an area long claimed by Mexico was self-evident. But the war bill offered the opposition a cruel choice: either assent to Polk's lies or vote against reinforcements for Zachary Taylor's troops, who, as far as anyone knew, were at that very moment engaged in battle with a much stronger Mexican army. Nor was Polk the only politician to recognize that "the country was excited and impatient" for war.[33]

Seventy-eight-year-old John Quincy Adams was having none of it. As secretary of state under James Monroe, Adams had been one of the nation's

John Quincy Adams. Antislavery activist John Quincy Adams headed the congressional opposition to war as leader of the "Immortal Fourteen," the select group of antislavery congressmen who voted against Polk's war bill. National Archives.

foremost expansionists, a firm believer since the 1810s that the entirety of North America was "our natural dominion." He wrote the Monroe Doctrine, which made a claim for U.S. influence throughout the hemisphere. He secured U.S. access to the Pacific with his Transcontinental Treaty. And he continued to maintain that the United States should control the entirety of the Oregon Country.[34]

But in the years since his presidency, his energies had increasingly focused on America's domestic perils, and the fate of American slavery was now his biggest concern. Adams was not opposed to war in general. There were "times and occasions of dire necessity for war," he wrote. But this was not one of them. He was adamant that "war for the right can never be justly blamed; war for the wrong can never be justified." His opposition to "this most outrageous war" was total. Just before the vote he told his fellow Massachusetts representative, Robert Winthrop, that he "hoped the officers would all resign, & the men all desert, & he would not help them, if they did not." When it was time to cast his vote, Adams loudly shouted no. But there were only thirteen men who followed his lead, all of whom, along with their constituencies, believed slavery to be the greatest peril facing America.[35]

The rest took the path of least resistance. Robert Winthrop was one of them. A Brahmin descendant of Puritan John Winthrop representing an antiwar district, Winthrop was not an abolitionist. But neither did he have to fear a public backlash, as did many southern and western Whigs who acceded to Polk's lies. He voted yes to war, but he was severely shaken by the proceedings and not at all sure he had made the right decision. "I found it hard to swallow so unjust a representation of the fact as the preamble of the Bill contained, & I did what I could to prevent it being prefixed to the Bill," he explained in a plaintive letter to a close friend. "But when the condition of things was so critical, I could not allow the insertion of a false fact to prevent my being found on the side of the National Defenses. I do not blame any of my colleagues for differing from me. It was one of those cases, where one could not vote either way with any satisfaction."[36]

In 1844 the Whig Party warned that Polk's election would lead to war with Mexico. Many reacted to the fulfillment of that prophecy with a sense of fatalism. "Heaven knows my heart is sickened at the idea of a War with any Country, & at a War with Mexico especially," Winthrop wrote. "I fear it will lead to mischief of every kind. But the thing was inevitable. Annexation was War. . . . If we had not recognized its existence this week, we must have done so next week." Many newspapers agreed. "The Congress of the United

States have adopted the War with the Republic of Mexico in which the President has, without their consent or authority, involved the country. . . . THE MISCHIEF IS DONE," the *Cleveland Herald* announced.[37]

Whig leaders felt strongly that it was time to look to the future. Winthrop claimed he supported the war bill not only because he believed opposition to be "fruitless" but also because "if I can do anything to moderate the War spirit, either in relation to Oregon or to Texas, it must be by exhibiting myself wil[l]ing, when War comes, to vote men & money for defense." Many in the Whig press agreed: "It will now and henceforward be the business of all good men . . . to mitigate the evils before us."[38]

Winthrop's friends reassured him that he had made the right choice. "You need give yourself no uneasiness about the wisdom of our course in that matter or its impression upon the public mind at home," one wrote. Even in Plymouth, "the very source & centre of all peace influences," the leading Whigs "all took the ground that anything that looked like opposition to a most liberal and vigorous preparation" for war "on the part of the Whigs would be fatal to their future ascendancy . . . Your ground is not only right in itself" but "will be found to be the only safe one for a statesman to occupy . . . What a fearful account this administration will have to settle."[39] Winthrop would also have an account to settle: although he couldn't know it at the time, he would spend the rest of his career attempting to justify that vote for war.

Matters were nearly as chaotic in the Senate, but under Thomas Hart Benton's leadership opponents of the bill managed to adjourn debate until the following day. At eight that evening Benton returned to the White House, full of questions and not at all happy. Polk called Buchanan and Marcy in as reinforcements for what he knew would be a contentious meeting. With a clear sense of outrage, Benton let all of them know that "in his opinion in the 19th Century war should not be declared without full discussion and much more consideration" than it had received in Congress that day. Marcy and Buchanan tried to reason with the Senate leader. Perhaps not realizing that Benton had dismissed U.S. title to the Nueces Strip in a private conversation with the president the previous day, the two men repeated the specious claim that "war already existed by the act of Mexico herself." This could only have infuriated Benton. Polk remained silent. He "saw it was useless to debate the subject further."[40]

After Benton left, Polk, Marcy, and Buchanan agreed that the Missouri senator would oppose the passage of the bill, as would South Carolinian John C. Calhoun, and "two or three other Senators professing to belong to the Democratic Party." In combination with the united Whigs, this coalition could defeat the bill in the Senate. Were that to happen, "the professed Democrats . . . will owe a heavy responsibility not only to their party but to the country." Polk went to sleep convinced that "all that can save the bill in the Senate is the fear of the people." The public wanted war. Polk hoped their elected representatives recognized the cost of opposing the will of the people.[41]

Debate in the Senate the following afternoon was heated. John C. Calhoun charged the president with provoking a war on Mexican soil, and Senator John M. Clayton of Delaware argued that Taylor's maneuvers within clear view of Matamoros were "as much an act of aggression on our part as is a man's pointing a pistol at another's breast." But Polk's fears proved misplaced. Virtually all of them capitulated, and at 6:30 p.m. the bill passed the Senate by a vote of 42–2. Had it "been deliberately put to a vote, whether it was right to order Genl Taylor" to the Rio Grande, or for him to plant "his cannon" at Matamoros, or for Slidell to be "sent to Mexico, when he was & under the circumstances he was," Calhoun was sure that "not a tenth part of Congress" would have voted "in the affirmative, & yet we have been forced into a war." Apparently "fear of the people" was an animating force. Even Senator Benton, who mocked the idea of a Texas boundary at the Rio Grande in a scathing speech to the Senate in 1844, agreed that in the end, "he was bound to stick to the War party or he was a ruined man." Robert Winthrop had cast his vote with thoughts of his own manhood in mind. He argued that to have "shirked the vote" would "have been hardly manly." Southerner John C. Calhoun clearly didn't see it that way. He abstained from voting.[42]

And with that, the U.S. Congress assented to war with Mexico. They did not declare war; Polk stole that privilege from them. John C. Calhoun recognized the implications of this constitutional usurpation. "The prescedent [sic] is pregnant with evil," he wrote. "It sets the example, which will enable all future Presidents to bring about a state of things, in which Congress shall be forced, without deliberation, or reflection, . . . to declare war, however opposed to its conviction of justice or expediency." But with near unanimity that in no way reflected the true feelings of their body, or of the nation, they condoned what would soon be called "Mr. Polk's War."[43]

Polk was not one to gloat. He remained as dour and subdued as usual at the large White House reception that evening. But the Democratic press was united in their celebration. "We have the pleasure of announcing orders for the prosecution of the war with Mexico that will be hailed by our countrymen with a burst of universal enthusiasm," wrote the New Orleans *Tropic*. "The American people are taking hold of it as becomes their energetic character. A great and powerful movement is about to be made, in which we see a glorious triumph of arms."[44]

The cabinet got straight to work implementing plans for the long-awaited war. There was a flood of volunteers to organize, officers had to be named, and everything from supplies to strategy demanded immediate attention. Polk's first action was to request "all the orders and letters of instruction to our squadrons in the Pacific & Gulf of Mexico" and ask that these be read to the Cabinet. Polk "desired to refresh" his memory about the exact orders that he had given Commander J. D. Sloat when, back in the president's third month in office, he had ordered Sloat to immediately seize San Francisco and other ports in California if war should break out. Perhaps he was also worried about how these orders would look in retrospect if subpoenaed by Congress.[45]

Polk hardly could have been clearer about his territorial ambitions, but Secretary of State Buchanan somehow missed the hint. In a remarkable display of obliviousness, Buchanan drafted a message to the great powers of Europe disavowing interest in Mexico's territory and presented it to the cabinet. Polk was flabbergasted when Buchanan read "that in going to war we did not do so with a view to acquire either California or New Mexico or any other portion of the Mexican territory." Polk "told him that though we had not gone to war for conquest, yet it was clear that in making peace we would if practicable obtain California and such other portion of the Mexican territory as would be sufficient . . . to defray the expenses of the war . . . it was well known that the Mexican government had no other means of indemnifying us."

This was not what Buchanan had hoped to hear. The secretary of state insisted that war "with England as well as Mexico, and probably with France also," would be the result, "for neither of these powers will ever stand by and [see] California annexed to the U.S." Growing ever more animated, Polk responded that "I would meet the war which either England or France or all the Powers of Christendom might wage, and that I would stand and fight until the last man among us fell in the conflict," before he would ever agree to Buchanan's pledge.[46]

The men argued for two full hours, with the rest of the cabinet lining up behind the president. Finally, at close to 11:00 p.m., Polk rose, demanded that Buchanan strike out the offending paragraphs of his message, and sent the speechless secretary of state out of the room. Polk rarely had to exert his will so bluntly within the cabinet, and there was no longer any doubt among the men in the room that Polk intended to take California. The discussion "was one of the most earnest & interesting which has ever occurred in my Cabinet," Polk wrote in his diary. But it wore him out. The president retired to bed "exhausted after a day of incessant application, anxiety and labor."[47]

Polk's bluster aside, he hardly believed it necessary to fight "all the Powers of Christendom" for California. He didn't even believe that he would have to fight Mexico. Polk's brinksmanship with England was vindicated on June 6 when word arrived in Washington of a British-proposed compromise over Oregon, agreeing to a boundary at the forty-ninth parallel, along with possession of Vancouver Island. England had sent it off just ten days before learning about hostilities on the Mexican border. Polk forwarded the proposal to an enthusiastic Senate, shifting responsibility for the compromise away from himself, and the Senate ratified the treaty nine days later. If speaking cannon fire worked with England, surely it wouldn't fail with feeble Mexico. When Polk's younger brother wrote from Europe during the summer, inquiring about the possibility of serving as an officer in Mexico, Polk told him to "abandon" any thoughts of joining the fight. "In regard to the Mexican war, my impression and hope is, that it will be of short duration. I doubt whether there will be much more fighting unless it be in a guerrilla warfare. . . . It is probable that the war will be over very soon."[48] A quick battle or two, and Mexico would surely capitulate.

PART THREE

The Crucible of Conscience,

1846–47

Although I was for annexing all of this part of Mexico

to the United States before I came here, yet I now

doubt whether it is worth it.

—CAPTAIN JOHN J. HARDIN,
PARRAS, MEXICO, DECEMBER 16, 1846

6

A Tame, Spiritless Fellow

IT IRRITATED ABRAHAM LINCOLN that the voters who came to his campaign rallies weren't more interested in tariffs. Congress had just passed an act that drastically reduced import levies, and Lincoln was incensed. The tariff was "in greater dispute than ever." Clearly, this should have been the leading issue of the campaign. Congressional candidate Abraham Lincoln covered eleven foolscap half sheets with notes for a brilliant, technical, inspiring speech on the matter. But he never got to deliver it. All the good voters of Illinois wanted to hear about was war.[1]

He supposed it made sense: Illinois was the center of western expansionist fervor, full of voters who had moved west in search of opportunity, and who might move again given the right circumstances. It hadn't been long since Illinois was the frontier. Lincoln's district, though majority Whig, was full of pro-war constituents who believed that the conquest of Mexico was part of God's plan. Mexicans "are reptiles in the path of progressive democracy," the Illinois *State Register* declared, who "must either crawl or be crushed."[2]

Immediately after authorizing the war, Congress had called up twenty-five thousand volunteers from the states closest to Mexico to aid Taylor at the border for a term of three months; forty thousand more volunteers were to be allotted evenly among the remaining states. Their term of enlistment was one year, which seemed ample, since almost everyone north of the Rio Grande expected a swift conclusion to the whole business. Illinois's quota of volunteers, three regiments of a thousand men each, filled almost instantly. Thousands more men clamored for an opportunity to fight. Some crossed into neighboring states for a chance to enlist.

First among Illinois's volunteers was John J. Hardin. He had been itching to fight Mexico, pestering Congressman Douglas for news about hostilities throughout the spring, and repeatedly volunteering to lead troops to California. Hardin's cousin, Kentucky representative John McHenry, broke the news to him the day after Polk's war message to Congress. McHenry was a Whig, but decidedly not one of the "Immortal Fourteen" congressmen who openly opposed the president. Like almost all other members of his party, he voted in favor of the war, despite admitting that it contained "palpable falsehoods." The entire business disgusted him. "No good reason has been applied and none can be applied to why our army was sent to entrench themselves & . . . their batteries opposite Matamoros—a child could have told it would lead to war," he fumed to Hardin. Making no attempt to moderate his views in order to suit his hyperpatriotic cousin, McHenry pronounced it "useless to disguise the fact that we have been brought into this war by the weakness or wickedness of our pres[iden]t . . . while we must all stand by the country right or wrong it is grievous to know that when we pray God defend the right our prayers are not for our own country." As for "those who have brought it on," McHenry declared them to "have a fearful responsibility even in this world and in the next."[3]

McHenry knew full well how desperately his cousin wanted to fight Mexico, even if he didn't quite understand it. He thought Hardin's patriotism and willingness to sacrifice all for the mendacious Polk were naive, and he let him know as much. The political climate in Washington was so poisonous, he warned, that "I can think no Whig would stand the least possible chance of getting any post where he can do honor to himself or service to his country" except where it would benefit the Democrats. But if "under all the circumstances" Hardin was still intent on supporting this war, McHenry offered lukewarm encouragement: by all means "raise your men & go at it."[4]

Hardin did. The governor appointed him colonel of Illinois's volunteers, and he set to work organizing his troops with typical efficiency and intensity. Colonel Hardin led the call for men at a rally in Springfield. "Let us not say that Taylor and his brave men can whip Mexico without our aid," Hardin proclaimed. "This is not the language of brave men. Let us have a hand in whipping her." He placed a call for troops in a local paper. "Illinoians should respond to the call which has been made upon them, promptly and with spirit," he wrote. "The General [meaning himself] asks no one to go, where he is not willing to lead." Always at his best when he felt the call to arms, Hardin was in his element. "You stand very high here with all our Military men and volunteers," one admirer told him.[5]

Hardin was inundated with letters from young men anxious to fight. "I have somewhat of an inclination for Glory, and to engage in such an expedition as I understand you have," wrote one when offering his services. Nor was adventure the only thing on their minds. Manifest Destiny was at stake. Like Hardin, many of them hoped to go to California. Several expressed the opinion that "the government aught not to lose the present opportunity of conquering New Mexico and California. Such an other may never occur."[6]

Others worried that if the men of Illinois did not volunteer in great enough numbers, they, or their state, would be shamed. "Excuse me for expressing my humble tribute," wrote one grateful admirer, "expressive of the thanks due from all good citizens, for your anticipated efforts to redeem them from the suspicion" that "our state has proven less gallant and patriotic than her neighbors." Hardin also warned the men of the state that "the fame of this state" might "be tarnished" if there was "either difficulty or delay in raising the requisite number of troops."[7]

National honor was at stake too. Even those inclined to dismiss Polk's claim that Mexico started the war couldn't help but feel that much depended on the outcome of America's first foreign war, that it could offer "a lesson" to "nations which jeer at the power and energies of a Republican people." The local Whig paper in Lincoln and Hardin's district, the *Sangamo Journal*, steadfastly denied that Mexico had started the hostilities, but in June it heartily endorsed the war, warning that "the eyes of all European nations will be upon us. . . . If we dictate terms to Mexico within her own dominions;—we shall be respected;—if not every petty power in the world will spit upon us." Fortunately, Mexico seemed unlikely to put up much of a fight. The people of Mexico were clearly racial inferiors, "but little removed above the negro," according to the Democratic Illinois *State Register*. Or perhaps closer to the Indians that the nation had successfully banished west of the Mississippi less than a decade earlier. One friend of Hardin's declined the call to arms because he imagined there would be "nothing to whip but a parcel of blankeded half-breeds armed with bows and arrows."[8]

And men had practical reasons for volunteering. Illinois's economy was in tatters, the state was struggling under an enormous debt obligation, and jobs were scarce in 1846. The pay for a private worked out to $15.50 a month, twice what a common laborer could earn (assuming he could find a job in the first place).[9]

Whigs were also worried about their reputation and were determined to avoid any charges of disloyalty. The Federalist Party had been totally discredited by their opposition to the War of 1812, and collapsed as a national party after holding a convention in Hartford to discuss means of bringing that conflict to a close, including the possible secession of New England. The disgrace of the Federalists was so intense that thirty years later Democrats, including Polk, referred to the Whigs as "the Federal Party" as a means of disparaging them.

In truth, Clay's party shared a great deal with the earlier Federalists, including a faith in a strong central government, widespread support in New England, and what Democrats regarded as a haughty elitism. They could hardly afford to justify linking themselves with the Federalists by offering only lukewarm support of a foreign war. "The Whigs here are much more ready to turn out than the real annexation party—they say it is to show our country and they are ready to Protect it," wrote a friend to Hardin. "There is no doubt in my mind but that a majority of those who turn out will be Whigs."[10]

Whigs also feared association with abolitionists, antislavery radicals who believed it was God's will that slavery end immediately. Even in their two areas of strength, New England and the upper Midwest, abolitionists were only a small minority in the 1840s. But they were vocal, motivated, and seemingly fearless. From the outset they loudly condemned the war with Mexico as unjust and part of a plot to strengthen slavery, just as they had condemned Texas annexation and the Texas Revolution before that. Immediately after the passage of Polk's war bill, the abolitionist *Boston Whig* proclaimed it "one of the grossest National lies that has ever been told." From his post as editor of the *Liberator,* William Lloyd Garrison impressed upon readers that the "chief anti-slavery work" was to end the war: "Endeavor to paralyze the power of the government, that Mexico may be saved, and the overthrow of the Slave Power hastened." Antislavery ministers condemned the war from their pulpits, and antislavery citizens in New England and the upper Midwest protested the war by writing dozens of antiwar petitions to Congress.[11]

Democrats perennially linked Whigs with abolitionists, but in truth a mainstream Whig like Henry Clay or John Hardin had little more in common with an abolitionist like Garrison than did James Polk. The defection of a segment of New York's Whigs to the Liberty Party in 1844, a defection that may well have cost Clay the election, should have made this obvious. While Whigs (particularly southern Whigs) were more likely than Democrats to personally disapprove of slavery, they were just as willing as Democrats to allow the South its own institutions, particularly given the centrality of slave-grown cotton to northern manufacturing and trade. Cotton was the most valuable national export, and New York's wealth was closely tied to its control of the transatlantic cotton trade. In the eyes of moderates such as Henry Clay, who linked manumission with the colonization of freed black people in Africa, the agitation of abolitionists was counterproductive, actually setting back the cause of ending slavery by alienating slave owners. And a national party in the 1840s simply couldn't win a majority on an abolitionist platform. Whigs had to distance themselves not only from their disloyal Federalist forebears but also from antiwar abolitionists. Tempers ran high. When abolitionists in Bloomington said publicly what many in Congress were saying privately, that the war was unjust, volunteers, most likely belonging to both the Whig and Democratic parties, smashed their windows.[12]

The Whigs of Illinois more than rose to these challenges. Edward Baker, currently the sitting Whig congressman from Lincoln's district, also decided to enlist. After receiving permission to raise a fourth regiment of volunteers, he rushed home without even resigning his congressional seat. He made the trip from Washington to Springfield in just six days, and within a month marched with his men out of Springfield through a gathering of thousands of well-wishers.[13]

This couldn't help but have affected Abraham Lincoln deeply. Hardin and Baker were his two main rivals in the congressional district. Both had now chosen war over politics, dismissing as petty concerns, unworthy of a patriot, the issues and contests that still enchanted Lincoln. And while there was no love lost between Lincoln and Hardin since the contested nomination, Edward Baker was one of Lincoln's closest friends. The Lincolns had revealed the depth of their esteem for Baker when they named their second son, born just months earlier, after him. Young Eddie hadn't yet sat up when his namesake left for the Halls of the Montezumas.

Thousands of Whigs followed Hardin and Baker's lead, but Abraham Lincoln was not among them. Although he had enjoyed his three months of military service as a young man during the Black Hawk War, and claimed in 1858 that his election as captain by his fellow volunteers "gave me more pleasure than any I have had since," Abraham's priorities in the summer of 1846 did not extend to Mexico. There was the new baby at home, he had finally won the nomination for Congress, and all his energy was focused on winning the election in August.[14]

Nor was Lincoln alone in withstanding the call to arms. There were

many powerful public men who found the pro-war hysteria and the enlistment of Hardin and Baker baffling. David Davis, a member of the state
legislature and occasional business partner of both Lincoln and Hardin,
marveled that "the only Whig Congressman (Col Baker) from this state
left his post in Congress and has the command of the 4th Regiment of Volunteers." Davis refused to speak at an enlistment rally on the grounds that
since he was not going to enlist he couldn't very well ask others to do so.
For her part, his wife, Sarah Davis, couldn't bear "to think of the sacrifice
of human life—mourning families and all the evils and miseries attendant
on war."[15]

John Hardin's law partner and closest friend, David A. Smith, was also
open in his disdain for the military life. When Hardin tried to entice him
to Mexico, his response was definitive. "I would not give the glory and gain
of spending one week quietly at home with my wife and children for all the
laurels, honor, and enchantments of whatever name or nature that you or
all Old Rough & ready will reap on the fields of Mexico," he wrote Hardin
that summer. He had no fear of Hardin's disdain. "You will most likely say
that I am a tame spiritless fellow and will never make any stir in this world.
That is very likely and I am content that should be so." Perhaps, Smith suggested, it was Hardin who had his priorities wrong, and Mexico was the
last place a man should look for honor. "The greatest thing to us after all is
to conquer ourselves and then we shall be more than the most successful
Military chieftains. We shall be conquerors in the highest and best sense of
the term."[16]

If David A. Smith was a "tame spiritless fellow," so too was his friend
Abraham Lincoln. Like Smith, Lincoln much preferred life with his wife and
children to the "enchantments" of Mexico, and like Smith, he had long held
that a man needed to conquer himself, to become disciplined, in order to be
a conqueror "in the highest and best sense of the term." "Internal improvements," a phrase beloved by Whigs, had two meanings. And Lincoln subscribed to them both. An individual needed to master his or her impulses,
work diligently, and focus on the moral improvement of the family, just as
surely as a community needed to create institutions such as schools, libraries, and churches, and a state needed to finance bridges and good roads, in
order to improve the lives of everyone. It was Whig doctrine. It was also
Abraham Lincoln's creed. Manifest Destiny held an allure, but new land
was no substitute for sustained effort and economic development, either for
an individual or for a state.[17]

Lincoln never seriously considered following Hardin and Baker to Mexico. The invasion of Mexico distracted America from what he believed was truly important—a Whig vision of America's future glory built on economics and not territorial expansion. This was not Abraham Lincoln's war.

Fortunately, his Democratic opponent in the congressional race was a Methodist minister, another "tame spiritless fellow" as lukewarm about the war as he was. But at the moment, the public cared for neither economics nor religion, just Mexico. It was beginning to dawn on Lincoln that if he was going to get to Washington, he'd have to either avoid discussing the conflict or at least give the impression of speaking in its favor.

Lincoln was sorry about the war but not especially worried about the outcome. Though foreign observers questioned how a small force comprising mostly down-and-out immigrants and untrained volunteers would perform against a better-prepared and well-organized Mexican army fighting on the defensive, the news from the battlefield was all good. Mexico's soldiers wore elegant uniforms, but the army was burdened with outdated armaments, political instability, and poorly paid and fed conscripts.[18] Even before the Illinois volunteers left the state, news of thrilling victories filled local papers. In the first regular engagement of the war, on May 8, Taylor's force of two thousand defeated General Arista's army of six thousand near a watering hole north of the Rio Grande known as Palo Alto. The Mexican column, shattered by Taylor's efficient artillery, was driven from the field with a loss of two hundred men, nearly four times that of the Americans.

The following day, Arista assumed a defensive position along a dried-up riverbed and waited for Taylor. Taylor's frontal assault at the Resaca de la Palma was a complete success. The regular forces proved experts at the deployment of the bayonet, and the dragoons were magnificent on horseback. Twelve hundred Mexicans were killed, and only 150 Americans. The remains of Arista's army fled across the Rio Grande to the safety of the well-laid-out brick town of Matamoros. The Mexican general was forced to abandon his personal papers when the Americans gleefully ransacked them. They found orders from the Mexican government to send General Taylor to Mexico City as a prisoner of war. Taylor prepared to cross the Rio Grande and finish off the Mexican army.[19]

Arista wanted to hold Matamoros, but his demoralized troops left little hope of withstanding the now imminent attack. On May 17, he began to move supplies and guns from the city. On May 18, U.S. soldiers waded across the river "up to their armpits," and as "the band struck up yankee doodle the first time it was ever played south of that river," the men "raised a cheer that made the woods ring." The U.S. Army marched into Matamoros without opposition and raised the Stars and Stripes above the city, Taylor appointed one of his officers military governor, and the residents of Matamoros had the decidedly unwelcome honor of being the first in Mexico to experience U.S. Army occupation.[20]

Everyone recognized the monumental nature of the occasion. Captain R. A. Stewart, an ordained minister, sugar planter, and commander of the Louisiana volunteers, set aside his military garb on Sunday, June 1, to address the victors of Matamoros on Jeremiah 7:7: "Then I will cause you to dwell together in this place, in the land I gave to your fathers forever and ever." In his view, the occupation of the U.S. Army was "calculated to shed light over the dark borders of Tamaulipas—to make its inhabitants embrace the blessing of freedom." And Taylor's remarkable victories "showed most plainly and beautifully, that it was the order of providence that the Anglo-Saxon race was not only to take possession of the whole North American continent, but to influence and modify the character of the world." The emotional men embraced his affirmation of Manifest Destiny. The "eyes of many sunburnt veterans . . . were filled with tears" by the end of the reverend's discourse.[21]

Americans at home agreed that the "many daring deeds" and "brilliant impetuosity" of the American troops proved the superiority of the United States and "sustained nobly the character of the Anglo-Saxon race." Even the anti-Polk congressman John McHenry expressed a bit of glee in a letter to his cousin Hardin after the capture of Matamoros about "how our army have whipped the Mexicans." The press went wild in their celebration of the "heroic little army" that had achieved such "matchless victories." "The prowess of our brave soldiers has made the perfidious Mexicans bite the dust," cheered an Illinois paper. "The serpent of the Mexican arms now writhes in death agony in the beak of the American eagle." Another paper gushed that "since the eventful days of our Revolutionary struggle no battle has been fought in which the heroes who march under the Star Spangled Banner, covered themselves with more glory, than did the little band who pressed forward at the command of the heroic Taylor, and charged an enemy of vastly superior numbers, in the very teeth of their roaring, death-dealing cannon!"[22]

No one received more acclaim than Zachary Taylor. Letters from the battlefront universally praised the "cool and gallant manner" in which Taylor led his troops, and noted that he "won the hearts of his soldiers by his willingness to share with them the most imminent perils." Journalists insisted that "there are few instances of a popularity so suddenly acquired,

yet so universal and well founded, as that of Gen. Taylor." It wasn't simply his "brilliant" victories and military "genius" but "the display of gal-
lantry, coolness, and conduct which won those victories" that "gained him
the hearts of his countrymen." Immediately after the battles on the Rio
Grande, soldiers in the field began composing and singing "Taylor songs."
By early July, newspapers were already speaking of General Taylor, "Old
Rough and Ready," as a presidential candidate, while the public gathered at
rallies designed to advance his candidacy.[23] Polk simmered, convinced the
acclaim belonged to him and not to his Whig general.

By midsummer, news from the front, or fronts, was even better. At the
start of the war, Polk, with the military counsel of Major General Winfield
Scott, had decided on a two-pronged attack on Mexico: Taylor's forces were
to drive south through Texas and Monterrey toward Mexico City, while
a second force, under the direction of Brigadier General Stephen Watts
Kearny, would capture Mexican lands to the west, into New Mexico and
Chihuahua and on to California. A third, smaller central division, under
the command of Brigadier General John Ellis Wool, was added to secure
Chihuahua in north-central Mexico. Polk ordered the navy to blockade the
port of Veracruz, and sent word to Commodore Sloat in California to put
his earlier order for the capture of California into action.

Polk's plans were spectacularly successful. Kearny marched the fifteen
hundred frontiersmen who made up his Army of the West a thousand
miles, averaging a hundred miles a week, from Fort Leavenworth in Kansas all the way to the provincial capital of New Mexico. Despite bluster on
the part of Manuel Armijo, governor of New Mexico, in six weeks the Yankees marched unopposed into Santa Fe. On August 16, New Mexico and
its eighty thousand inhabitants were in American hands. After Kearny
promised to protect the inhabitants and their property and to respect their
religion, the majority of the proud citizens of Santa Fe took an oath of allegiance to the United States. Unaware of the extent of simmering hostility
to American occupation that existed in the province, Kearny took leave
of New Mexico for California, after directing a Missouri lawyer under his
command, Colonel Alexander W. Doniphan, to head south to Chihuahua
to reinforce Taylor.

The Army of the West was accompanied by a thousand Missouri volunteers and a battalion of Mormon soldiers, serving in the only religiously
based unit in American military history. After John J. Hardin directed the
expulsion of Mormons from Illinois, Brigham Young determined to move
beyond the reach of American persecution. Mere days after Congress's

assent to war, a church elder asked Polk for federal assistance for a migration to Mexican territory beyond the Rocky Mountains. Polk agreed, provided the Mormons also fight Mexico. Polk authorized Kearny to receive "as volunteers a few hundred of the Mormons who are now on their way to California, with a view to conciliate them, attach them to our country, & prevent them from taking part against us." The five hundred men of the battalion contributed their uniform allowance to the purchase of wagons and provisions that enabled the Mormon exodus. Seventy women and children accompanied the soldiers all the way to California. By the end of the summer, the American public was convinced that New Mexico was safe in American hands, as headlines proclaimed, "Santa Fe Taken, Without the Firing of a Gun!"[24]

The news from California was even more brilliant. Nearly a year before provoking war with Mexico, Polk had authorized a "scientific expedition" to California under the command of famed explorer Captain John C. Frémont, Thomas Hart Benton's son-in-law. Frémont arrived in California in January 1846, where the suspicious actions of his men drove the Mexican authorities to order him out of the country. They decamped for Oregon, but when a special courier from Washington brought news of worsening hostilities with Mexico, Frémont returned to California, fought several modest skirmishes, and raised a flag in Sonoma featuring a crudely drawn picture of a bear. They declared California independent on July 4, 1846, only days before gaining confirmation that Mexico and the United States were in a state of war. Then Frémont's men lowered the Bear Flag and replaced it with the Stars and Stripes.

Commodore Sloat, receiving the same news of war, captured Monterey on July 7, and three days later the navy occupied San Francisco Bay. California's major ports were secured. On August 16, Commodore Robert Stockton, who succeeded Sloat, took Los Angeles without opposition, and declared himself governor of the territory. By the end of the summer, papers were confidently reporting that "the whole of Upper California is now in the possession of the Americans" and "forever lost to Mexico." As in New Mexico, papers reported, "the capture of California seems to have been effected without bloodshed or resistance."[25]

This was not entirely true. While bloodshed was minimal, there were countless episodes of robbery and intimidation that left much of the populace disenchanted with the Yankees. In Santa Barbara, a picturesque town of approximately two hundred adobe houses with red tile roofs laid out between a placid bay and the mountains, U.S. troops made the mistake of imposing upon the powerful de la Guerra family. José de la Guerra, the richest man in the county, "offered to help" the Americans by lending them ten to twelve horses out of the approximately fifty-eight thousand on his quarter-million-acre ranch. After the ranch manager's wife prepared and served them breakfast, eight U.S. soldiers seized forty-three horses and threatened the life of ranch employees, claiming that "they were enemies of the government and the troops could take anything and everything." Three lieutenants ended up in court as a result. But most *californios* lacked the connections and resources of the de la Guerras and had no recourse when their property was taken.[26]

Stockton gloated about his triumph in a letter to the president. "All is now peaceful and quiet. My word at present is the law of the land. My power is more than regal. The haughty Mexican Cavalier shakes hands with me with pleasure, and the beautiful women look to me with joy and gladness, as their friend and benefactor. In short all of power and luxury is spread before me, through the mysterious workings of a beneficent Providence."[27]

America's mood verged on the lighthearted: embedded journalists traveling with the troops turned battles into entertainments and idealized both America's hero-soldiers and their triumphs. The public was so anxious for news from Mexico that some unscrupulous newsboys and the papers themselves manufactured stories to get people to buy papers. One newspaper with its own correspondent in the field celebrated the enthusiasm for war news.

> The newsboy hits the streets and shouts out "here's the extra 'Erald—got the great battle in Mexico." The merchant rushes from his store and buys an extra . . . cartmen draw up to the sidewalk and stop with their loaded carts while they read . . . the clerk, on his way to the bank, reads a full account. . . . The dandy on the hotel steps, the cabman on the stand, the butcher at his stall, the loafer on the dock, the lady in the parlor, the cook in the kitchen, the waiter in the barroom, the clerk in the store, the actor at rehearsal, the judge upon the bench, the lawyer in the court, the officer in attendance, even the prisoner at the bar, [read] of the victory and rejoice![28]

The war was going so brilliantly that even Lincoln was forced to take part in a pro-war rally. At the statehouse in June, he found himself, along with four other distinguished speakers, supporting "prompt and united action" to "sustain" America's honor and "secure her national rights." The local paper lauded the "warm, thrilling, effective" speeches in favor of war.[29]

The speech was strictly political. Lincoln had had no change of heart, and he made no further public statements about the war. He was intent on winning the election. Abandoning his law practice entirely, Lincoln ran a disciplined campaign that summer. It helped that his opponent was an indifferent public speaker. But Lincoln "kept his forces well in hand," and one supporter remembered that "long before the contest closed we snuffed approaching victory in the air."[30]

Henry Clay made no speeches about the war in the summer of 1846. He was still so adored in his home state that he could have returned to office in 1846, had he wished, or he could have traveled the country, delivering addresses to enthusiastic Whig audiences. But Clay showed no interest. Seemingly retired forever from the world of politics, he roused himself only enough to bemoan the nation's fate in a letter to a friend in June. "A war between two neighboring Republics! Between them because the stronger one has possessed itself of Territory claimed by the weaker!" It was almost too much to believe, made worse for Clay because he had "foretold" what would happen. "This unhappy War never would have occurred if there had been a different issue of the Presidential contest of 1844."[31]

The "trumpet of war" sounded as loudly in Kentucky as in Illinois. Three regiments of Kentucky volunteers were mustered into service in May and June, and as in Illinois, Clay noted, "a vast proportion" of the volunteers "are Whigs, who disapproved of the measures which have led to this unfortunate war." Among them was Clay's favorite son and namesake, Henry Clay Jr., who was appointed lieutenant colonel in the Second Kentucky Volunteers. The father tried to keep up a strong front in a letter to his best female friend, Octavia LeVert: "We cannot but admire and approve the patriotic and gallant spirit which animates our Country men, altho' we might wish that the cause in which they have stept forth was more reconcilable with the dictates of conscience." But it was a painful parting. The young volunteer was the most gifted of his sons, the one for whom he had the greatest expectations. How bitter it was that Henry Junior was risking death for a president his father detested and a conflict he despised. Clay presented his son with the family dueling pistols and wept as he bid him goodbye.[32]

Nor was that the full extent of difficulties faced by Clay that summer. While the rest of the nation rejoiced at the news of American victories in Mexico, Clay's family was "laboring under a severe domestic affliction." His son John suffered another breakdown in August, requiring a second hospitalization. Clay sought relief at a nearby spa for a few days, but returned home to the devastating news that his first and favorite grandson, Martin Duralde, was dead. Duralde, just twenty-three, had been suffering for eigh-

War News from Mexico, 1848. *Richard Caton Woodville of Baltimore was just twenty-three when he produced his ambivalent painting of Americans reading the news from Mexico. This widely circulated image reflects the intense public interest in the war as well as the role that newspapers played in spreading news from the front. The 1846 conflict was the first American war covered by embedded journalists, whose reports offered Americans around the country what would have seemed like intimate access to the experiences of the troops on a nearly daily basis. Woodville's concern about the impact of the war on the future of slavery can be inferred by the presence of African Americans in the forefront. That the figure to the left is thoughtlessly dropping a match into a barrel suggests that the war may have devastating and unintended consequences.* Library of Congress Prints and Photographs Division.

teen months from a "hoemorrage of the lungs" due to tuberculosis, and had finally succumbed to "frightful convulsions from a congestion of the brain." Duralde had grown up in the Clay household after his mother's death at age twenty-two. Clay poured out his grief in a letter to Duralde's doctor. "Death, ruthless death, has deprived me of Six affectionate daughters, all that I ever had, and has now commenced his work of destruction, with my descendents, in the second generation."[33]

Lieutenant Colonel Henry Clay Jr. Henry and Lucretia's third and most promising son volunteered to lead Kentucky troops to Mexico, despite his father's hostility to the war and his own Whig principles. Courtesy of Ashland, the Henry Clay Estate, Lexington, Kentucky.

September brought more alarming news. Henry Clay Jr., who had joined Taylor's forces after his victories along the Rio Grande, had "met with a serious accident." Perhaps the elder Henry never heard the rumor that Lieutenant Colonel Henry Clay's injuries were sustained in a riding accident while drunk. He was charged with drunkenness in the accident, but his subordinates maintained the charges were false. He admitted to his father that "I have not and probably shall never recover the perfect use of my arm." Clay's nerves may have been at a fevered pitch over the safety of his son that month, but September also brought the most brilliant victory yet for U.S. forces.[34]

Monterrey, a provincial capital of fifteen thousand, sat on a key transit route in northern Mexico and was considered of strategic importance both to Mexicans and to Americans, who envisioned the city as an anchor in a defensive line across northern Mexico. After his embarrassing losses along the Rio Grande, General Arista was stripped of command. His replacement was ordered to concentrate his forces in Monterrey and defend the city from invaders. Given the setting of the town, nestled in the foothills of a mountain range and extending along a river, and the layout of the city, with straight and easily barricaded streets, this seemed straightforward. In July and August, the seven thousand Mexican troops now gathered in the area, under the command of General Ampudia, constructed impressive fortifications around the city.

Taylor, meanwhile, marched his six thousand men from Matamoros to Monterrey. On September 19, he reconnoitered the mile-long city, seemingly unconcerned that he was about to attempt to storm a virtual fortress. On Sunday, September 20, U.S. troops deployed into a line of battle. During the three-day battle that followed, they accomplished the seemingly impossible. Taylor divided his forces, and half, under the command of Brigadier General William Jenkins Worth, took advantage of a driving rain to seize the main road into town by surprise. They then stormed the town, first seizing earthworks from the Mexicans, then capturing a stone fort with the use of an artillery barrage, and finally driving the Mexicans from their

Heroic Defense of the City of Monterey. *Mexicans produced few images of the invasion of their country during or directly after the war. This rare lithograph depicts the chaos and destruction of the street fighting during the third day of the siege of Monterrey from a distinctly Mexican perspective. Mexican soldiers heroically defend their city with the help of civilians and a priest. From* Album Pintoresco de la República Méxicana (Mexico: Hallase en la estamperia de Julio Michaud y Thomas), *ca. 1848–50.* Yale Collection of Western Americana, Beinecke Rare Book and Manuscript Library.

interior fortifications. The other half of the American forces, under Taylor, attacked from the opposite direction. On the morning of September 23, Taylor's forces were fighting in the streets of Monterrey, smashing through the walls of houses and bayoneting Mexican soldiers. The destruction was terrible, and horrified residents watched as "Monterey was converted into a vast cemetery. The unburied bodies, the dead and putrid mules, the silence of the streets, all gave a fearful aspect to this city."[35]

The following morning, Ampudia surrendered. The Americans were getting dangerously close to his munitions storehouse, and the general feared an explosion. All public property in the town was handed over to Taylor's forces, and Mexican troops agreed to retire from the field. The U.S. Army settled into an extended occupation of the town. Ampudia requested, and was granted, an eight-week armistice, which each government had the right to veto.

The terms were generous on Taylor's part—far too generous, in Polk's eyes. "It was a great mistake of Gen'l Taylor to agree to an armistice," the president wrote in his diary when he heard. "He had the enemy in his power & should have taken them prisoners." He immediately, and angrily, vetoed the armistice. The cabinet agreed that had Taylor "captured the Mexican army, deprived them of their arms, and discharged them . . . it would have probably ended the war with Mexico." But Taylor's actions made sense given the situation, which Polk wholly failed to comprehend. The American troops were exhausted, hungry, and low on ammunition. They were in no state to continue the grueling hand-to-hand combat that would be required to secure the city.[36]

Taylor was also fairly sure the war was now over. The United States had secured Texas and had taken the fight into Mexico itself. His job was now done. Five hundred U.S. soldiers had perished in the capture of Monterrey, and Taylor had no interest in seeing that number increase. Had the war been about the Mexico-Texas boundary, it would have been over.

But Polk's ambitions involved more than Texas alone, and they were growing larger with each U.S. victory. At a cabinet meeting on June 30, Secretary of State Buchanan tried, once again, to convince the president of the folly of dismembering Mexico. When Secretary of the Treasury Robert Walker argued in favor of taking everything north of the twenty-sixth parallel (including most of Sonora, Chihuahua, Durango, and Baja California, as well as a good portion of Nuevo Léon and Tamaulipas; in total, a third of modern-day Mexico), Buchanan protested. "If it was the object of the President to acquire all the country North of 26° . . . it should be known," he insisted. And "the opinion of the world would be against" us, "especially as it would become a slave-holding country." Walker responded "that he would be willing to fight the whole world sooner than suffer other Powers to interfere in the matter." Polk agreed with his belligerent secretary: "I remarked that I preferred the 26° to any boundary North of it."[37] And no one in the cabinet questioned Buchanan's assumption that these new lands would become slave territory.

The war, then, was far from over.

As the summer turned to fall, American newspaper readers might have noticed a subtle shift in war news. After the initial euphoria of America's stunning victories dissipated, the nearly universal response in favor of the war began to fray. In late May, the Philadelphia *North American,* a staunch Whig paper, had cheered that "all party distinctions" had been "lost—all hearts heated and fused into one fiery mass against the foes of the country."[38]

But news of mounting casualties led many in the United States to ask why the war had not yet been brought to a conclusion. Because the army did not censor the letters of soldiers, both volunteers and regulars wrote home with vivid reports of overcrowded, unsanitary camps and outbreaks of communicable diseases in the regiments. Many of these were published by their families in local papers. One October 1846 letter from Monterrey, published in the New Orleans *Picayune,* admitted that "the health of the army is bad, a very heavy proportion of the officers and men being on the sick list. . . . Our sufferings are intolerable." A correspondent to the New Orleans *Times* noted in November that "disease was very common with the officers and the men" stationed along the Rio Grande. Volunteers, particularly from the countryside, lacked the previous exposure to communicable diseases that might have provided some immunity, and as a result they suffered from this disease at a higher rate than did the regulars. Unused to standards of camp sanitation, and more liable to undercook their rations or overindulge on the novel tropical fruits they encountered, they were also more prone to illness caused by tainted water and poor diet.[39]

The women of Baltimore formed a benevolent organization "to assist the poor sick and wounded soldiers" with donations of preserved food, and journalists made similar appeals to the "patriotism" of women in other towns, but the bad news kept coming. When a shipload of sick and injured soldiers arrived in Louisiana, a journalist marveled that half of the passengers "were wounded or sick, some having lost their legs, others their arms, and others being wounded in their arms and legs. . . . Will you believe me when I tell you that with all these sick and wounded and dying men, not a surgeon or nurse was sent along to attend upon them, not a particle of medicine furnished, not a patch of linen for dressing wounds." David Davis wrote to a Massachusetts friend that the Illinois volunteers "have been treated worse than dogs & one half either die, or return home, emaciated & with constitutions wholly broken down."[40]

The public evinced quite a bit more concern about the volunteers than the regulars. Although serving in the same army, they were dramatically different groups, and were perceived that way at the time. More than twice as many volunteers as regulars served in Mexico, 59,000 versus 27,000. The vast majority of enlisted men in the peacetime regular army were poor, uneducated, and unskilled. Forty percent were recently arrived immigrants (many not yet naturalized), and 35 percent could not sign their name. Their average age was twenty-five. Service in the army was neither particularly remunerative nor honorable; in a democratic culture that upheld freedom and independence as precious American rights, soldiers were considered overly servile. They were subjected to harsh corporal punishment, including whipping, and forced to labor under conditions they considered degrading, often alongside slaves. Most men who enlisted in the regular army did so because they had no better options in the sluggish and unpredictable economy in the decade following the Panic of 1837. Even those poorly paid jobs open to unskilled laborers, such as digging ditches and canals or hauling coal, were hard to come by. Not surprisingly, many of these men deserted when the opportunity presented itself.[41]

Volunteers, by contrast, tended to come from the middle and upper echelons of society. Their ideas about discipline were decidedly more lax than those of the regular army, and they insisted upon being treated with respect, like citizens. They demanded (but were not legally entitled to) the right to withdraw from service when they chose.

There was no love lost between the two groups. Volunteers looked down upon the regulars and often failed to conceal their contempt. Their disdain was not simply grounded in a conviction of their social superiority. Like most Americans, the volunteers questioned whether a democratic republic like the United States had any need for a standing army, and doubted that men serving for wages could be relied upon in a fight. Both beliefs had long histories. Soon after the Revolution, Congress declared that peacetime standing armies were "inconsistent with the principles of republican government" and "dangerous to the liberties of a free people," since they could easily be "converted into destructive engines for establishing despotism." As for paying men to fight, this too seemed suspicious to Americans. In the 1840s Americans still venerated the volunteer ethos as particularly admirable and trustworthy, while professionalization would not take on the positive attributes of skill and expertise until after the Civil War. One could practice as a doctor or lawyer in the 1840s without a great deal of training or any formal certification, and all firefighting was conducted by volunteers, even in large cities. Americans were hesitant to employ paid firemen because they questioned whether men motivated by financial interests would be willing to risk their lives at a fire. Paying soldiers seemed equally problematic.[42]

The regulars, by contrast, found preposterous the idea that volunteers could defend the United States, let alone conduct an offensive war like that in Mexico. They resented their extra rights and privileges, as well as the fact that volunteers won a disproportionate amount of praise for victories that by rights belonged to the regulars. Zachary Taylor, who found the volunteers impossible to control, believed them more trouble than they were worth. Perhaps he was right. Volunteers, lacking both training and discipline, were not only less reliable under fire than the regulars, and disproportionately susceptible to communicable disease, in part because of their poor sanitation practices, but also committed atrocities against Mexican civilians that would come to shock Americans back home.

The occupation of Matamoros and Monterrey did not go smoothly. Captain R. A. Stewart, the minister, had hoped the American occupation of Matamoros would "make its inhabitants embrace the blessing of freedom." But Lieutenant Ulysses S. Grant recognized how unlikely that was. He wrote to his fiancée, Julia, of the "great many murders" and "weak means made use of to prevent frequent repetitions. Some of the volunteers and about all the Texans seem to think it perfectly right to impose upon the people of a conquered City to any extent, and even to murder them where the act can be covered by the dark. And how much they seem to enjoy acts of violence too! I would not pretend to guess the number of murders that have been committed upon the persons of poor Mexicans and the soldiers, since we have been here, but the number would startle you."[43]

None of this should have been surprising. As youths, most of the volunteers had thrilled to tales of Texas heroism and Alamo martyrs. Even enlightened U.S. soldiers were, by modern standards, racist. They saw Mexico as an immoral nation and Mexicans themselves as an inferior race practicing a suspect religion. Many who volunteered felt deep enmity for the people of Mexico, and conflated them with Indians and African American slaves. Lacking training and discipline, with little knowledge of military codes, many ran wild. Texas Ranger Buck Berry, whose three-month term of enlistment actually expired before the battle of Monterrey, continued on with Taylor because "some of us had traveled six hundred miles to kill a Mexican and refused to accept a discharge until we got to Monterrey where a fight was waiting for our arrival."[44]

Soon this was national news. On October 6, the New Orleans *Picayune* reported that "eight Mexicans, including two women, had been killed" a few miles outside nearby Camargo, "an old dilapidated-looking town" on the San Juan River. "The murder was attributed to some of the volunteers." The story was picked up by other papers. The following week the *Charleston Mercury* broke news of atrocities in Monterrey. "As at Matamoros, murder, robbery, and rape were committed in the broad light of day, and as if desirous to signalize themselves at Monterey by some new act of atrocity, they burned many of the thatched huts of the poor peasants. It is thought that one hundred of the inhabitants were murdered in cold blood, and one . . . was shot dead at noon-day in the main street of the city." This story was picked up and circulated in other papers as well. By late May, news of volunteer depradations had made it to London.[45]

Many Mexican citizens had fled Monterrey as soon as U.S. forces arrived, having heard news of affairs in Matamoros, while the Mexican press complained that "the volunteers, the most unprincipled and ungovernable class at home, have been let loose like blood-hounds on Mexico." Lieutenant George Gordon Meade agreed. On October 20, he wrote his wife that the volunteers "have made themselves so terrible by their previous outrages as to have inspired the Mexicans with a perfect horror of them."[46]

Even sympathetic voices admitted the truth of these stories, but they blamed the carnage on the people of Mexico. Violent volunteers were simply seeking "revenge" for the "outrages committed on the persons and property of American soldiers." Ohio volunteer Frank Hardy, stationed in Matamoros, explained to his brother that although "for a while it was thought that many of the Mexicans were favorable to the institutions of the United States. . . . it is now pretty generally believed that they are almost without exception *snakes in the grass*, and are at heart strongly attached to their Government. . . . they profess friendship to the Americans merely for the purpose of being protected and making money—They are in short a treacherous race and have hearts the most of them as black as their skins." He admitted that many of his fellow soldiers "are in favor of prosecuting the war—when hostilities shall again commence—upon different principles, and plunder, and ravage, and give them a taste of war in all its horrors, and see if that will bring them to a sense of their folly in contending with the United States."[47] It was a lesson learned over decades of Indian wars back home; when faced with a "treacherous race," the rules of war did not apply. Vengeance, in their eyes, was justice.

In the late fall, the New Orleans *Delta* reported on a "war between the Kentuckians and Mexicans" in which "not less than forty Mexicans have been killed within the last five days, fifteen of whom, it is said, were killed in one day, and within the scope of one mile." Attempting to justify the actions of the volunteers, a correspondent to the *Delta* explained that "ever since the occupation of Matamoros by our troops the Mexicans have been cutting off our men . . . and the compliment has been invariable returned, generally two for one . . . in many cases the innocent is made to suffer for crimes committed by their guilty countrymen."[48]

The Kentuckians may have been bad, but they were not nearly as bad as

General Wool and staff in the Calle Real, Saltillo. This early daguerreotype shows Brigadier General John Ellis Wool and his staff in the streets of Saltillo, Mexico, his headquarters from December 1846 to November 1847. Wool attempted to curb volunteer abuses against Mexican civilians in northeastern Mexico, but with limited success. Fully aware of fierce local opposition to the U.S. occupation, Wool was careful to travel with a large escort, as seen here, for purposes of security. Yale Collection of Western Americana, Beinecke Rare Book and Manuscript Library.

Congressman-elect Abraham Lincoln. Portrait by Nicholas H. Shepherd, 1846–47. The first picture ever taken of Abraham Lincoln reveals a well-groomed gentleman seemingly aware of his importance as a newly elected congressman. Mary Todd Lincoln also posed for a photo the same day at Shepherd's Springfield studio. Library of Congress Prints and Photographs Division.

the Texans. Taylor expressed regret in a letter on June 30 for "outrages committed by the Texas volunteers on the Mexicans and others" and claimed he was unable to contain the "lawless set." While he admitted that many in the unit were skilled, he also believed that they were "too licentious to do much good." Reliable information reached Washington "almost daily" about "atrocities" committed by "the wild volunteers." General Scott appealed to the secretary of war: "Our militia & volunteers, if a tenth of what is said to be true, have committed atrocities—horrors—in Mexico, sufficient to make Heaven weep, & every American, of Christian morals, blush for his country. Murder, robbery & rape of mothers & daughters, in the presence of the tied up males of the families, have been common all along the Rio Grande." General Wool wrote to Senator Lewis Cass of Michigan that deserters had not only robbed the citizens of the region with impunity but also "ravished women, two of whom had died in consequence of their brutality."[49]

The Philadelphia *North American* was just one of many newspapers at the start of the war that celebrated "the spirit of the country" where the government "can rely for its wars upon the volunteers . . . men abandoning a better and brighter lot for the honor of striking a blow for the land of their love." But it also had warned that "should the lust of conquest, or the passions of revenge" rear their heads, "public opinion will fall away from" the war "as good men shrink from crime."[50] By the autumn of 1846, there were plenty of reports of crime for good men to shrink from.

On August 3, 1846, Abraham Lincoln was elected to Congress. In the end, the race wasn't even close. Lincoln surpassed his opponent by 1,511 votes, the largest margin of victory ever for a Whig congressional candidate in the district, and substantially larger than Henry Clay's in the presidential contest two years before. He would be the only Illinois Whig in the Thirtieth Congress, which would not convene until December 6, 1847, sixteen long months after the election. Mary was thrilled, but Abraham was subdued. He admitted to his friend Joshua Speed that "being elected to Congress, though I am very grateful to our friends, for having done it, has not pleased me as much as I expected."[51]

One Whig who did not congratulate Lincoln on his election was John J. Hardin. He and the rest of the Illinois volunteers were mustered into service on July 10. On a bright summer day thousands of people, including Hardin's wife and three children, gathered at the Mississippi River port of Alton to say goodbye to the 877 members of the First Illinois Regiment. The troops looked splendid in dark blue roundabout coats trimmed with yellow, light blue pants, and blue cloth caps with glazed covers. In the panoply of state-specific volunteer uniforms, this would help the men of Illinois identify one another, and men of other states to identify the origins of heroes and cowards. Each man carried modern weaponry: a government-furnished carbine and percussion-lock pistol. The dragoons also carried sabers. Hardin's thirteen-year-old daughter Ellen later recalled that the "glitter of the scene" and "hopefulness of the soldiers" reassured the crowd. "Tears of parting were suppressed" and "forebodings of danger were silenced." The First Illinois Volunteers crowded onto the "great white steamer" *Missouri* and then were gone, borne away, it seemed to Ellen, to "some unreal world." She never forgot the sight of the steamer, and her father, disappearing from view.[52]

Hardin spent August 3 in Port La Vaca on the Gulf coast of Texas, overseeing the disembarkation of his men from their ship and helping them set up camp. It was a chaotic business, and one he found taxing. Perhaps it reminded him of taking charge of the wounded on the *Princeton* in 1844, after the big gun "Peacemaker" exploded. He had won praise on that occasion for his leadership and calm in the face of disorder. Now those skills would be tested daily.

He wrote his wife, Sarah, that evening, exhausted and somewhat homesick. A great adventure lay before him, but his mind was still back in Jacksonville with his family, horses, and fields. "It is late Monday night, and election day in Illinois," Hardin mused. "I should like to know how you are all getting along at home. You seem to be a long way off."[53] Perhaps Hardin regretted missing an election that might have been his. If he did, those feelings didn't last for long. The First Illinois wasn't yet in Mexico, but each of the volunteers believed personal glory was on the horizon. And they were right. It would take longer than any of them expected, but they would ultimately take part in a battle that tame, spiritless fellows couldn't possibly imagine.

7

Buena Vista

COLONEL JOHN HARDIN was tired of Texas, tired of marching, and tired of drills. It had been only a month since he had assumed command of the First Illinois Volunteers. Since then, Brigadier General John Ellis Wool, the commanding officer of the Central Division, or the Army of Chihuahua, had taken note of Hardin's ability to lead, and immediately after his arrival in August had given him the command of the Second Illinois as well as the First. After a 160-mile march from the coast, Hardin's Illinois regiments reached Camp Crockett, outside San Antonio. The once-lively city was decaying and nearly deserted. Hardin wrote his sister that he felt as though he had landed in "the most out of the way place in the world."[1]

There the Illinois volunteers waited, along with regiments from Kentucky and Arkansas, for orders to move to the front. "There is much monotony in camp life," Hardin admitted in a letter home to Sarah. The food was bad, the weather worse, and his men were growing antsy. The nearby ruins of the Alamo beckoned, but pilgrimages to the most holy site of the Texas Revolution only stoked the men's desire to meet their enemy.[2]

San Antonio was a desolate place, but it offered every temptation for a young man to get into trouble. Hardin, a temperance advocate with no more taste for cards than for whiskey, had "trouble stopping drinking and gambling" among his men, but his vision of himself as a great leader did not extend to dealing with the endless squabbles and differences that seemed to plague the "wild young men" of his regiment. "I get along with

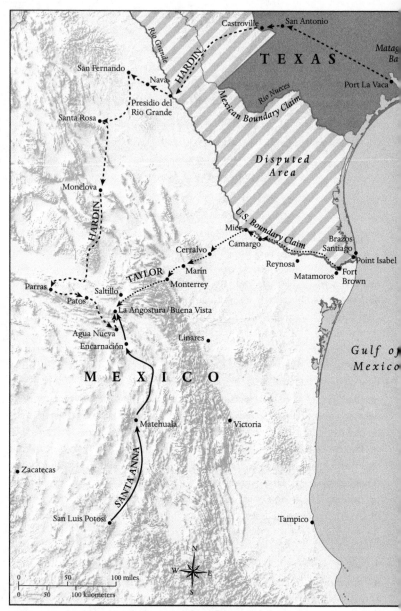

GENERAL TAYLOR AND COLONEL JOHN J. HARDIN IN TEXAS AND MEXICO

my command as well as I could expect, considering the incongruous materials of which it is composed," he wrote his wife from camp, "but still I have
more difficulty in settling other peoples troubles than with anything else."
Reports of unruliness among Hardin's volunteers had already appeared in
newspapers in Boston and Milwaukee.[3]

They sat at Camp Crockett just long enough to miss the excitement in
Monterrey. Hardin was livid and blamed his commanding officer. General
Wool, a New Yorker and veteran of the War of 1812, appeared to Hardin to
lack the needed vigor for the job at hand. "Expect nothing great or striking
from this column of the army—it moves with too much of the pomp &
circumstance of war & far to stately to overtake Mexicans," he fumed to
his law partner. But Wool was waiting for instructions from Taylor, who
himself was waiting for instructions from Polk. Those instructions failed
to materialize. Taylor, already overwhelmed by the "lawless" volunteers
from Mississippi and Texas, was in no hurry for Wool to bring more to the
front. In August, he expressed the idle wish that the two Illinois regiments
in Texas "be sent to some other" place.[4]

Hardin's daughter Ellen, who had trouble imagining Mexico when her
father first departed, now repeatedly saw it in her sleep. She wrote him that
August, "Last night I dreamed that you and all your men came back but
were raving mad because you did not get to fight the Mexicans." The eldest
of the Hardin children, Ellen understood her father quite well. At the end of
September, they finally received orders to march to Mexico. "I start to seek
my destiny beyond the Rio Grande," Hardin rejoiced. "What it may be is
uncertain, but I would like to help to form it myself."[5]

On the first of October, Hardin and his men began their arduous march
to Mexico. Each man carried a knapsack full of food, a tin cup and plate,
a spoon, a small table, and a "bread board" to sit upon. They also carried
two blankets that would provide their bedding during the march; one
blanket served as a mattress, the other as a covering. Each company had a
mule-drawn wagon carrying equipment. In addition, the officers had servants to carry their knapsacks.[6] Personal servants were considered invaluable for maintaining the respect due officers, who were, by law, gentlemen.
The federal government reimbursed officers for servant hire and provided
them a clothing allowance and extra rations. The army also specified how
many servants each officer class was entitled to bring with them. Generals
Taylor and Scott were each entitled to four servants, and each brought four.
Colonels were entitled to two, but John Hardin brought only one.

Most of the servants taken to Mexico were African American. Although the army excluded all black men from service in the 1840s (the navy imposed a 5 percent quota), and militia companies also forbade the membership of black men, servants were part of every American army unit, a fact that received no publicity at the time. Officers in Mexico hailing from the South brought their slaves with them, and many northerners either hired freed slaves or attempted to obtain Mexican help once across the border. When Lieutenant Ulysses Grant was ordered to the Rio Grande with Taylor in 1845, he wrote his fiancée, Julia, "I have a black boy to take along as my servant who has been to Mexico." Colonel Robert Hunter, a Louisiana state senator who volunteered in May despite promising his wife, Sarah Jane, in April that he would never "serve the people" again unless it was "for money and not for honor," brought his slave Milly with him to Matamoros. Sarah Jane Hunter told Milly to take "good care" of her husband before she sent her to Mexico. Like other servants, Milly shopped and cooked for Hunter, cared for his horses, cleaned his clothes, and ministered to him when he was ill.[7]

While there is anecdotal evidence of black soldiers following volunteer units and fighting in battles alongside whites, it more frequently happened that black servants took up arms out of necessity. One of Taylor's slaves told a historian some years later that he saved the general's life at Monterrey. "A Mexican was aiming at the General a deadly blow, when he sprang in . . . and slew the Mexican, but received a deep wound from a lance."[8]

John Hardin's servant was most likely a slave from Kentucky named Benjamin, who was around twenty-one years of age. Hardin purchased Benjamin, described as a light-skinned "mulatto boy," as a personal servant from Mary Todd's Kentucky relatives in 1833. He was offered Benjamin's entire family but chose instead to separate Benjamin, described at the time as "too small to ride . . . far on horseback," from his mother and siblings. Benjamin was one of several African Americans working in the Hardins' Jacksonville mansion at the start of the war. The Hardins brought slaves with them when they moved from Kentucky in 1831 after their marriage, and others were left to the couple when Sarah's mother died. Although they lived north of the Mason-Dixon Line, the legal status of these African Americans was far from clear.[9]

Illinois was, of course, a free state. It was formed out of territory designated free in the Northwest Ordinance of 1787. But particularly in southern Illinois, slavery was very much a reality. According to law, adult slaves became free when they moved to the state. Those under age passed through a period of indenture before earning their freedom. In reality, however, a form of indenture not unlike slavery was the norm in southern Illinois among adults as well as young people. African Americans in Illinois were usually coerced into signing indenture contracts for years at a time. They could not leave the service of their master, could be whipped if disobedient, and were even referred to in legal statutes as "slaves." Many of these individuals were sold back into permanent slavery before their indentures expired.[10]

There is little evidence of African Americans in Illinois becoming free after their period of indenture was up, but there is evidence that African Americans with the legal status of slaves were still living in the state at the beginning of the U.S.-Mexican War. The 1818 state constitution outlawed the importation of slaves into Illinois but did not free the slaves already there; in 1840 there were still 331 listed in the federal census. The Hardins purchased an eight-year-old girl named Dolly in the mid-1840s, around the same time that the Illinois State Supreme Court declared that slaves could no longer reside in the state. Dolly signed her mark to a ten-year indenture contract, but she was still working for Sarah Hardin decades later. She was, in fact, buried with the family.[11]

The fact that Illinois sent more volunteers to Mexico than any other "free" state, indeed more than any other state except Missouri, may have had nearly as much to do with its coercive labor system as it did with the fact that it was a western state, full of believers in Manifest Destiny who themselves had moved west looking for opportunity. "Illinois . . . should not be numbered with the free states," the *Liberator* declared in 1854. "It is, to all intents and purposes, a slaveholding state." It is not surprising that many white men in Illinois had less of a problem with a war that could enlarge the area of slavery than did the white men of Massachusetts or Ohio.[12]

John Hardin was far from the only wealthy man in Illinois exploiting the state's indenture statutes in order to provide his family with the comforts of servile labor. If anything, the Lincoln family's unwillingness to employ black indentured servants set them apart from other upwardly mobile families in the southern half of Illinois. While there is no need to account for Abraham Lincoln's unwillingness to engage in coercive labor, it is worth pointing out that Mary Todd grew up in a slaveholding family and certainly could have imported slaves from Kentucky as the Hardins did, had she wished. The fact that she did not may have reflected her father's evolving antipathy for slavery, a view he shared with his good friend Henry Clay, as well as her husband's.[13]

The embedded journalists who traveled to Mexico frequently condemned the country's system of debt peonage, which produced an under-class trapped in lifelong involuntary servitude because of debt. But those journalists virtually never mentioned the ubiquitous servants of American officers unless they committed a crime or, as more often happened, deserted to Mexico. So many crossed the river when Taylor was camped opposite Matamoros that one Kentucky officer concluded, "If we are located on this border we shall have to employ white servants." The image of the hearty American volunteer headed to Mexico in order to secure the honor of his country and to gain new territory for America's free institutions left little room for the hundreds of employed and enslaved African Americans who served their needs. Nor did John Hardin mention Benjamin (assuming that the unnamed servant traveling with him was the same personal servant he had purchased fourteen years earlier) in any of his letters home. Just as slavery in Illinois remained invisible to most white Americans, so too were the black servants in Mexico "invisible" to the public.[14]

Even with Benjamin's help, Hardin found his trip through the Nueces Strip quite a trial. The area was as foreboding as ever. Hardin kept a diary, noting that "after crossing the Nueces the quality of the soil & the appear-ance of the country changed very much for the worse . . . rattle snakes, wolves, and turkey abound. This land is worth nothing." The area near the Rio Grande Hardin found particularly "desolate" and rightly attributed it to "the invasions of the Comanche Indians, who . . . drive off or killed the inhabitants." He noted that "the Mexicans are very much afraid of the Indi-ans & along the Rio Grande complain justly of their government that it affords them no protection against Indian incursions." Hardin was travel-ing through a man-made "desert," the product of ten years of devastating attacks by Indian warriors on the Mexican inhabitants of the region that depopulated settlements and inhibited economic growth. The easy con-quest of northern Mexico by U.S. forces was in large part attributable to the power that Native American people held in the area; the Mexican residents had neither the energy nor the will to fight two wars at once, particularly since one of the wars was against a country that promised to protect them from their more immediate enemies, "the barbarians."[15]

Water and grass were scarce, the soil parched. A greater contrast to the well-watered prairies, groves of trees, and fertile ink-black soil of central Illi-nois could hardly be imagined. And there was little to break up the monot-ony besides the men's own hopes for adventure. On October 16, Hardin and his men marched twenty-four miles without locating water. It was a relief to reach the neatly laid-out mining town of Santa Rosa, which boasted an attractive central square. In this town of twenty-five hundred, Hardin purchased trinkets for his wife and children: a "Mexican blanket and cushion" and "a small hand bag . . . with a silver crop appended to it, & which was attached to a string around a Mexicans neck. It was very tasteful." Three weeks and 150 miles after leaving San Antonio, they finally made it to Monclova in Coahuila, another orderly town that was home to eight thousand residents. And there they waited, again.[16]

Hardin was desperate to see action. Convinced that Wool preferred drilling to battles, he wrote directly to General Taylor, requesting a transfer to Taylor's command. Taylor refused his request and admitted to Hardin that he himself was under orders from President Polk to stay put and remain on the defensive. The president had a new plan for achieving victory over Mexico, and it did not include Taylor, Wool, or the Illinois regiments.

Polk's snub of Taylor was deliberate. Envious of the general's growing political prestige, and furious that Taylor had agreed to an armistice with Mexico, the president stripped Old Rough and Ready of four-fifths of his troops, including almost all the veteran forces, and transferred them to the new commanding general of the army, Winfield Scott. Taylor lost his closest advisors and skilled officers: Ethan Allan Hitchcock, Ulysses S. Grant, and other men who had been with him since they first marched into Texas.

Scott had an audacious campaign plan: he would invade the very heart of Mexico. The navy would transport U.S. troops to the Gulf Coast port of Veracruz. They would storm the strongest fortress in the Western Hemisphere and then march directly to the capital. It was the same route that Hernan Cortés had taken in 1519, on the way to conquering the Aztec Empire, although Montezuma lacked Mexico's artillery and garrisons.

Taylor would play no role in any of it. Polk had slapped Taylor down, in no uncertain terms. Taylor was certain that the intention behind the "outrage" of pulling his troops was "that I would at once leave the country, in disgust & return to the U. states which . . . would have been freely used by them to my disadvantage" politically.[17] Polk might only serve one term himself, but he was determined to keep a Whig from inheriting the White House. His orders to Taylor had the merit, in his eyes, of discrediting Taylor both as a general and as a political candidate.

Not that General Scott was any great friend of the president's. Yet another presidential hopeful from the Whig Party, Scott was almost six and a half feet tall, of enormous girth, and remarkably patronizing. None of this endeared him to the diminutive president. As Polk fumed in his diary, "These officers are all whigs & violent partisans, and of having the success

Major General Winfield Scott at Vera Cruz, March 25, 1847. *Lithograph by Nathaniel Currier, 1847. "Old Fuss and Feathers" looks neither old nor fussy in this heroic representation of his siege of Veracruz.* Yale Collection of Western Americana, Beinecke Rare Book and Manuscript Library.

of my administration at heart seem to throw every obstacle in the way of my prosecuting the Mexican War successfully."[18] But at the moment Scott was the lesser of two evils.

Taylor, humiliated and angry, was left with the shell of an army holding a defensive position outside Monterrey. Polk's need to micromanage everything, and the disrespect he showed to General Taylor, won him no friends in the army. Henry Clay Jr., serving on Taylor's staff while he recovered from his riding accident, expressed the feelings of most of Taylor's junior officers about the transfer of troops when he wrote home to his father, "This Army sympathizes with him. For one I must confess I consider the manner of the thing very improper to say the least."[19]

Colonel Clay didn't know it, but his father had dined with General Scott in New Orleans while Scott was en route to Mexico. Clay fled Ashland for the winter, in search of warm sun and some distance from his crushing familial commitments. The tubercular flare-ups that Clay referred to as his chronic "colds" and his son John's continuing mental struggles left him incapacitated at the close of 1846, and both he and Lucretia worried incessantly about young Henry in Mexico. Clay sought a geographic cure in New Orleans. He always felt better in the Crescent City.

Clay stayed, once again, at the home of Dr. William Mercer, and while the doctor's high-ceilinged mansion was as comfortable as ever, New Orleans seemed somehow washed-out. The weather was terrible. Clay wrote Octavia LeVert that the city seemed "less gay" than usual, and he attributed it to the war. But certainly Clay was less gay than he had been in the past. The optimism and overwhelming self-confidence of candidate Clay just before Valentine's Day in 1844, when he strolled the streets of New Orleans convinced the presidency was in hand, were gone. "This unhappy War with Mexico fills me with anxious solicitude," he wrote not long after arriving in New Orleans. "When is it to terminate? How?"[20]

The commanding general's visit provided Clay a singular opportunity to assuage his fears. They dined at the Mercer home, and given the love of elegant dining, fine food, and wine that Clay and Scott shared, it was no doubt a lavish repast. Almost certainly the two men discussed Henry Clay Jr.

Three days later the elder Clay was invited to deliver a toast at a dinner in the company of several military men. Attempting to make a joke out of a very serious matter, the Sage of Ashland admitted that he "felt half inclined to ask for some little nook or corner in the army, in which I might serve in avenging the wrongs to my country." The applause of his listeners encouraged him. He announced to even greater whoops and cheers that "I have thought that I might yet be able to capture or to slay a Mexican." Of course the aged Clay was not about to join the army; he was referring, with apparently indiscernible sarcasm, to the early enthusiasm for volunteering. Clay concluded his toast with his sincere hope that "success will crown our gallant arms, and the war terminate in an honorable peace." Clay's remarks were reprinted in the New Orleans *Picayune* the following day and were quickly picked up by newspapers of every persuasion.[21]

While Prince Hal's spontaneous and thoughtless remarks hardly reflected his true feelings about the war, this toast was the first public statement he had made about Mexico, and almost no one got the joke. Not that it was very funny. "What will some of his friends in Congress say?" asked the Democratic *Mississippian*. What they said was that it appeared the great

Henry Clay was pandering to public opinion, inflaming bloodlust at the very moment that the nation appeared to be tiring of the war. "Poor stuff," pronounced the *Journal* of Lowell, Massachusetts, while the Quaker-edited *Worcester Spy* conceded, "If Henry Clay is possessed of the blood-thirsty spirit therein shadowed forth, then he is not the man we have ever taken him to be."[22]

Democrats reveled in the gaffe. "The Federal [Whig] papers of New England continue to throw out their bitter denunciations on account of the present war with Mexico," one Vermont Democratic paper crowed. "Their slang seems to correspond poorly with the views of the great 'HENRY'. . . at a late dinner at New Orleans." Abolitionists pointed to the gaffe as evidence that they had been right to forsake Clay in 1844. "The whole history of his life," the *Emancipator* wrote, proved "that he was too demon-like for any christian man to support without sin."[23]

Papers were still debating Clay's toast on Valentine's Day of 1847. Clay had imagined what it would be like to be on the front, but on that day many of the volunteers found their minds wandering in a very different direction. Twenty-seven-year-old Thomas Tennery mused in his diary, "This being Valentine's day no doubt the young folks at home are employing it in making love, or visiting, or receiving company, and making merry." This was as it should be, since "it is the duty of all nature to enjoy the time as well as possible."[24]

The state of Coahuila was full of Americans desperate to kill a Mexican, and it seemed that most of them were fuming in the Army of Chihuahua. Hardin blamed General Wool for the fact that he hadn't seen a battle, but in fact Wool was just as anxious to fight as his men were. He was still waiting for orders. In late November 1846, Wool wrote Taylor requesting a move from Monclova to the village of Parras, 125 miles west of the colonial town of Saltillo. "Inaction is exceedingly injurious to the volunteers," Wool wrote Taylor, "I hope the general will not permit me to remain in my present position one moment longer than it is absolutely necessary."[25] The subtext would have been clear to Taylor: the volunteers were out of control, and Wool feared for the safety of local residents.

The volunteers needed to move on, and gathering the greatly diminished army in the five-thousand-person town of Parras, a spring-fed oasis in the semidesert of Coahuila, made sense. The climate was "unsurpassed in the world," according to one volunteer, with air "so pure that flies and mosquitos are unknown." Famous for its wine and women ("Such enchanting

General Antonio López de Santa Anna. Photographic
print on carte de visite *mount. General Santa Anna*
held the rank of president of Mexico on eleven separate
and nonconsecutive occasions between 1833 and 1855. He
was fifty-two years old and living in exile in Cuba when
the United States declared war on Mexico. Polk, believing
him willing to negotiate with the Americans, allowed
him transit back to Mexico. Library of Congress Prints and
Photographs Division.

glorious eyes! and black glossy hair! What little feet and hands and divinely
graceful shapes!"), Parras may not have been the safest place to house the
troops.[26] But it both fit within Taylor's plan to control northern Mexico
defensively and also guarded against a possible attack by Mexican forces,
which were now under the command of the charismatic General Antonio
López de Santa Anna, the one man who could unify, inspire, and lead his
diverse and fractured country to victory. And it was all James K. Polk's fault.

Like so many Americans, Santa Anna's first important military service
was against Indians, in his case in the land that would eventually become
the American Southwest. He quickly rose through the ranks in the army of
New Spain, joined the rebels in the independence movement, and became a
towering personality in the history of early national Mexico.

After his failed 1836 campaign against Texas (it was Santa Anna who led the charge against the Alamo, ordered captured Americans shot at Goliad, and signed a treaty of Texas independence), he retired in disgrace to his estate, Manga de Clavo, on the road between Veracruz and Mexico City. Manga de Clavo was Santa Anna's Hermitage, a showpiece property (eventually boasting forty thousand head of cattle) that provided not only a convenient location for meetings of his friends and allies but also physical proof of his status. At 483,000 acres, however, Manga de Clavo was vastly larger than Jackson's domain. One could travel thirty miles along the main road between Veracruz and Mexico City without leaving Santa Anna's property.[27]

But an imposing estate can only do so much to repair a reputation. In 1837 it appeared unlikely that the people of Mexico would ever forgive Santa Anna his incompetence, or forget how quickly he had turned despot a year earlier. Another international crisis soon returned him to his countrymen's good graces, however. In 1838 the French landed in Veracruz in an attempt to force repayment of Mexican debt. Santa Anna rode to the port from his estate, led Mexican forces against the French, and lost a leg in the process. He appealed to the people of Mexico to forgive his mistakes and grant him "the only title I wish to leave for my children: that of a good Mexican." Santa Anna's heroic self-sacrifice in the "Pastry War" catapulted him back into power. But after another dictatorial stint as president, Santa Anna was imprisoned, then banished to Cuba in June 1845.[28]

To Americans raised on stories of the Alamo, Santa Anna was as pure a devil as walked the face of the earth. But Polk saw things differently; he believed he could manage Santa Anna. Thomas Hart Benton later wrote about the Polk administration that "never were men at the head of a government less imbued with military spirit, or more addicted to intrigue." From his initial directions to Slidell before the war through the closing days of the conflict, Polk repeatedly demonstrated his faith that secret dealings could bring Mexico to terms. Given Polk's assumption that Mexicans were cowardly and corrupt, it isn't surprising that he thought the deposed leader corruptible. U.S. envoys persuaded him that Santa Anna was so desperate to return to power that he would settle on almost any terms the United States might dictate. The president of the United States allowed Santa Anna, Mexico's greatest leader, free transit from Cuba back into Mexico in August 1846.[29]

Polk's faith that the war would be a brief one may have stemmed from his belief that Santa Anna would sell California to the United States once he was back in power. Polk repeatedly asserted, "I am strongly inclined to believe that *Santa Anna* desires peace, and will be prepared to re-open negotiations as soon as he feels himself secure in his power."[30]

Polk operated under the assumptions that Santa Anna was an opportunist and that he was addicted to power. Both were true. But the general was also a patriot, or as he himself had put it, "a good Mexican." Once safely in Mexico, Santa Anna evinced no interest in negotiating with the United States, and instead promised to avenge the loss of Texas. At first Polk refused to believe it. "Though I have reason to think that he is disposed to make peace, he does not yet feel himself secure in his position, and is cautious in his movements," he wrote in October. "I have but little doubt but that he will ultimately be disposed to make peace."[31]

But in November Santa Anna started organizing troops to confront Taylor's small army. "Ten thousand rumors reach us that Santa Anna is marching with a large force, some say 20,000 on this place," Henry Clay Jr. wrote his father. If an army of this size was really marching north, Taylor recognized that their best chance to defeat it was to gather the combined forces of his and Wool's troops near Parras.[32]

Before hearing back from Taylor, Wool began his march south, while Taylor, who was directly disobeying orders from Polk to stay where he was, also began to move toward Parras. Hardin was thrilled to be on the move, but he complained to his wife about the "long tedious & tiresome march" and the weather along the way: "extremely hot in the middle of the day, the nights are quite cold." They reached Parras on December 5. The Illinois volunteers had marched seven hundred miles since they first landed in Texas. They had yet to see action, and Hardin was shocked by the poverty and desolation of northern Mexico. "Occasionally a Hacienda is found in a day's march, on a small stream but beyond all is 'a vast howling wilderness' yielding nothing for the support of man or beast," he wrote his wife. "Not an acre in 100 is or ever can be worth a cent in all Mexico we have traversed."[33]

Sad to say, they seemed no closer to a fight in Parras than they had back in Texas. "We have supplies of wheat here for 4 months for 3000 men, & of corn for 2 months & of Brandy and rum for 10 years," Hardin complained to David Smith, his fellow temperance advocate. The troops were getting restless, and to Hardin's dismay, "our men use the liquor rather freely when they get a chance."[34] General Wool ordered Hardin to post a guard to prevent the "plundering" of Mexican civilians in the vicinity. Hardin took offense at the "imputation" that his men were stealing, or worse. Wool backed down: it wasn't the Illinois volunteers he was worried about, "it was the Arkansas troops." But the damage was done. Hardin threatened to march his men home—an idle threat. Wool said he would be happy to see Hardin leave, "but your men cannot, and *shall not go*." If there was ever any question in their minds, the volunteers of the First Illinois now realized they were stuck in Mexico for the duration of their yearlong enlistment.[35]

Henry Clay Jr. faced similar problems with his own troops camped nearby. According to one publicized report, the men of the entire Second Kentucky "were incompetent from inebriation," although Clay assured his father that the reports were overstated and that, upon his "honor," he himself was sober. "My own habits have not for years been so good as during this campaign," he wrote his namesake, assuring him that he had "not for a single moment been incapacitated for my duties" by alcohol. But Colonel Clay admitted that the strain of keeping the Second Kentucky volunteers in line was "making me prematurely old. I long for a battle that it may have an end."[36]

As they sat in camp Hardin's patience began to wear thin. He had not received a letter from his family since September. He wrote to Smith in early December, "I have seen a good deal of the world since I left home. . . . I want now to see a squirmish, a fight & a battle, & then will be ready to go home & attend to other business than arms, unless there is a call for troops at home." His feelings were nearly universal among the soldiers gathered in northern Mexico under Wool's command. Archibald Yell, a disciple of Andrew Jackson's and close ally of Polk's since the 1830s, gave up his congressional seat to lead the First Arkansas Volunteer Cavalry to Mexico in 1846, only to wait around in camp. He wrote Polk in early November that "I now dispare of being able to do my country much service or myself much credit—I wish to God I was with Kearny or Taylor but so it is my destiny is sealed, and without remedy, I never murmur, but posibly the time may come when I can expose the *folly* and *imbecility* of this collum." Captain Robert E. Lee of the Army Corps of Engineers, just weeks shy of his fortieth birthday, also worried that his "ambition for battle would be permanently thwarted" by the bad luck of being assigned to Wool's division.[37]

Noting the great "dissatisfaction in his com[man]d," Taylor admitted at Thanksgiving that "Genl Wools column had turned out an entire failure, which, I expected from the first would be the case." Taylor had, in fact, predicted back in June that the vast number of volunteers being sent to northern Mexico "will from design or incompetency of others, have to return to their homes without accomplishing anything commensurate with their numbers . . . The question will be asked why did the troops lay idle, & why did they not march against the enemy no matter where he was, find, fight & beat him."[38]

Meanwhile, as Hardin's frustration over "missing" the war grew, he began to question America's future in the region. Back in October, when he first reached Mexico, he had seen potential for U.S. development. He had written in his diary that the silver mines near the town of Santa Rosa "are reported to be amongst the richest in Mexico." They were abandoned because of the "ignorance of the Mexicans" but "would require only a little skill and energy to make very valuable."[39] Hardin could easily envision the mines, and territory, in the hands of the United States.

But the longer he spent in Mexico, the less he liked it. He believed the land, for the most part, to be worthless. In early December he wrote David Smith that "there is not an acre in 500 that a man in Illinois would pay taxes on." The people of Mexico were far worse. "I have never seen a drunken Mexican," he admitted. "That is the only good thing I can say about them—they are a miserable race, with a few intelligent men who lord it over the rest ¾ of the people, or more are Paeons and as much slaves as the negroes of the South—Treachery, deceit & stealing are their particular characteristic—They would make a miserable addition to any portion of the population of the United States." A week later he informed another friend that the only difference between the "paeons" of Mexico and "the slaves of the South is, their color, & that the bondage of the father does not descend to the son—as for making these Paeons voters & citizens of the United States, it should not be thought of until we are . . . to give all Indians a vote." As for Mexico's women, they "are not pretty enough to please a man who has not seen a white faced lady for 4 months—in fact, they are generally most decidedly homely."[40]

When Hardin had volunteered for Mexico he was infused with ideals of Manifest Destiny. But three months in the country had radically changed his views. "Although I was for annexing all of this part of Mexico to the United States before I came here," he told a friend, "yet I now doubt whether it is worth it. . . . So much for Mexico. Its people are not better than the country—not more than 1 in 200 is worth making a citizen of." John Hardin's evolution from an avid expansionist to xenophobic cynic was a rapid one. Gone were his early professions of destiny and national greatness. Hardin's single goal in December 1846 was to see action.[41]

Hardin's views were shared by many in the army. *The Genius of Liberty*, a newspaper published by and for U.S. troops in Veracruz, attributed the dramatic decline in volunteering to soldier disillusionment. "At the commencement of the war . . . many of us entertained extravagant notions of the country which we were about to invade. . . . We were to rove in the delicious gardens of the south, basking in the charms of some beautiful maiden

Group of Mexicans with a soldier, 1847. This daguerreotype was most likely taken in Saltillo, Mexico, in the late winter or spring of 1847. The soldier has been identified as Abner Doubleday, the New Yorker who is often said to have created the modern game of baseball while a student in Cooperstown. A first lieutenant in the army, Doubleday was stationed in Saltillo with the First Regiment of Artillery from February 1847 to the end of the American occupation in May 1848. Doubleday spoke Spanish well and showed more sympathy for the people of Mexico than most American soldiers. His irregular uniform reflects the widely varied costumes worn by volunteers. Yale Collection of Western Americana, Beinecke Rare Book and Manuscript Library.

as she wreathed the flowers, or offered the fruits of her native soil. . . . But a few days in Mexico soon dispelled the illusion. . . . The gardens turned out to be vast forests of palm, maguey and cactus." Exposure to the land and people of northern Mexico led them to question the future of Manifest Destiny in the region, and with few opportunities to prove themselves in combat, many volunteers wondered exactly why they had signed up in the first place. "A right hard fight with the enemy, followed by a riddance of this pestilent country, would be hailed by the whole regiment as a consummation of too much happiness," one Georgian volunteer wrote home. "I would willingly forego [sic] the possession of all the rich acres I have seen to get back from this land of half-bred Indians and full-bred bugs."[42]

But soldiers also regretted the deaths of Mexican civilians, the "friendly" inhabitants who "always treated us with kindness," in the words of *The Genius of Liberty*. "It is painful for us to reflect upon the fact, that many of those who fell before our invincible soldiers . . . sacrifice[d] their lives in a warfare which is as inglorious as it is useless." Of course America was turning away from the war. "A powerful nation may be compelled to prosecute a war with a weaker one, and destroy the innocent with the guilty in order to secure its own rights, but the more civilized its citizens will be, the more reluctantly will they engage with it," the paper wrote in October. In December Taylor remarked that the volunteers "are beginning to look many of them to their homes with much anxiety, & will leave the moment if not before their time expires."[43] For most of the volunteers, the great adventure in Mexico had turned out to be anything but.

Rumors of Santa Anna's march increased in early January. Mexican civilians gleefully reported to the American troops that they should expect "mucho fandango pocotiempo" or "a big party coming up soon." Taylor ordered Wool's column of the army to a wide valley south of the town of Saltillo, at the base of a mountain pass known as Angostura, or the Narrows. A hacienda named Buena Vista was close by. At last a battle seemed imminent, but again, nothing happened.[44]

Hardin wrote his daughter Ellen a long and lonely letter soon after arriving at Buena Vista. Ellen, now fourteen, was five years older than her brother Martin, and eight years older than the baby of the family, Lemuel. She was a studious girl whose love of both books and horses had been nurtured by her father. He had taught her to ride before Martin's birth, placing her on a horse in a great pasture adjoining their home and issuing the warning, "Now my daughter, don't let him throw you off."[45]

The two had been unusually close before he entered national politics. When she was young she "always followed him about, as a little child more frequently follows the mother. He never checked this following and I was in great happiness when sometimes he would take my hand as I trudged about, or would turn and tell me about some object, tree, pond, bird or other animal." One of her most vivid childhood memories was standing perfectly still in the corner of the family's sitting room, unseen by the adults, while her father had a bullet removed from his eye after a hunting accident. "I held my breath while the physicians were at work—I thought my father was so brave to utter no sound, that I must not cry, although I seemed to realize his suffering—for even then I had an unbounded devotion to him."[46]

The two remained close, or as close as they could be given her father's repeated absences from Illinois. When they were together they took long rides on horseback. When he was in Congress he talked about bringing her out to Washington "for a few days," so she could see the "splendid" Capitol and other sights. But it didn't happen. Ellen was still devoted to her father, however, and although Hardin never put his family before what he saw as his "duty," he was clearly fond of his daughter as well. "Very gladly would I exchange a few days or weeks of camp life to be by the sides of my sweet children and their mother," he wrote her.[47]

He had visited the elegant late eighteenth-century cathedral in Saltillo, famous for its carvings of Quetzalcóatl, the Aztec rain god, and columns of intricately carved gray stone. Like most other Protestants, he was distinctly unimpressed. The church was "gaudy" and full of "contemptable" wax figures. "Just think of the virgin Mary stuck up on the side of the wall over an altar in a glass case looking like the 'Belle of Philadelphia' or some other beauty and dressed in the finery of 15 years ago," he wrote Ellen. "If I could only show you a mountain vista & a church you could see all of Mexico worth seeing & these are much better to look at than to be amongst." He wistfully admitted to his daughter that Mexico had failed to live up to his imagination. "The rich, beautiful, lovely & Indian, this valley which I expected to find in Mexico & which I thought I might be tempted to live, has not yet been seen."[48]

At last he received news from his wife, who was, as he suspected, staying at her brother Abram Smith's cotton plantation in Princeton, Mississippi. In a long letter, written just before Christmas, she revealed her concern for her husband. "I know you will never knowingly or wantonly commit an act that will make me blush for you or myself and to know that the Father of my children is a man of spoilless character and of unblemished morals is a comfort indeed, now that you are exposed to the demoralizing influence of a soldier's life." Sarah had heard the stories of the behavior of America's soldiers, and while she trusted her husband, she was also frustrated at being left alone. She need not have worried. John didn't touch liquor, and he appears to have avoided the fandangos that entranced his men.

Sarah resented her husband's absence, but she was also proud he was no tame, spiritless fellow. He had chosen to go to war. Her brother Abe was another story. He appeared to be "a perfect Patriarch," she wrote John. Abe was master of a prosperous plantation and owned sixty-one slaves. He had a thriving law business, had served in the state legislature, and had earned a reputation as a Shakespearian scholar of some note. But he had not gone to Mexico. This gave Sarah license to belittle her brother. She confided to her husband that, appearances aside, Abe was "a complete henpecked husband." Her evidence? "He would like to go to Mexico but his wife wont let him even though he wants to go."[49]

Did she wish her own husband were slightly less spirited, or somewhat more henpecked? Between his term in Congress and his service in Mexico, the couple had seen very little of each other over the past three years. The children missed their father, and the boys were running wild. Her brother's plantation, she complained to John, was "decidedly the last place to raise children." She felt free to mock Abe in a letter to her husband, but in a moment of anger she wrote her soldier husband, "life is too short to be wasted in the way you are living."[50]

John responded in an emotional letter the week before Valentine's Day. Home seemed very far away to him as well. When he had first arrived in Texas, his mind was still in Illinois. He had been aware that it was election day, and he had mentally framed his duties as a soldier in the context of his previous work as a lawyer and politician.

But in February 1847, that was no longer the case. "I have been so long freed from the noise & hustle of politics & law that I think of them as 'things that were,'" he told his wife. "I feel no distinction to participate in them again—especially is this the case with Politics—Afar off in Mexico in a foreign land we cease to feel an interest in party struggles & only desire to see our Country triumphant & prosperous." While Hardin's dreams of Manifest Destiny had faded, he still craved a battle. "I will not conceal from you, what indeed you well know," he admitted to Sarah. "I am anxious to see more of Mexico, and some real service. If I see that I have accomplished my goal, if not it will have been a year thrown away."[51]

What John did not tell Sarah was that only three days earlier he had written Stephen A. Douglas, now a U.S. senator, in the hopes of obtaining a transfer to General Scott's army. Perhaps he was inspired by the good luck of Robert E. Lee, who learned on the eve of his fortieth birthday that he was being transferred to General Scott's expedition. Both Hardin and Lee were convinced that glory awaited them in Veracruz.

Hardin told Senator Douglas that if there was any opportunity for him to join the departing soldiers and march to the heart of Mexico, he would grab it. Otherwise he was sure he "would get no battle" and had no wish to continue with his regiment after his term of enlistment ended.[52] Rumors of a great Mexican army on the march were, by early February, "so frequent and so groundless" that "we now disregard them," Hardin admitted.[53]

A week later rumors were arriving "every few hours" that Santa Anna was "about to be on us with 20,000 men." But Hardin didn't believe "one word of the whole story." His "dull and stagnant" life in camp was only alleviated by the arrival of "many old acquaintances" in Henry Clay Jr.'s Second Kentucky Regiment. Socializing with Clay and the other Kentucky officers provided some distraction, but not enough.[54]

Hardin had one other matter to write home about: a shocking massacre. At the close of 1846, a sergeant in the Arkansas regiment of volunteers stationed with Taylor's troops admitted in his diary that "a portion of our Regiment are assuming to act as *Guerrillas*, and have been killing, I fear *innocent*, Mexicans as they meet them." Not long afterward, Mexicans killed an Arkansas volunteer in retribution for a Christmas Day raid on a local ranch at Agua Nueva where Arkansas volunteers robbed and raped the inhabitants.[55]

On February 13, the Arkansas cavalry took revenge. They rounded up civilians and commenced "an indiscriminate and bloody massacre" of twenty-five or thirty Mexican men in the presence of their wives and children, utilizing tactics learned in Indian wars. An Illinois volunteer named Samuel Chamberlain heard gunshots and rushed to the scene. He later described the shocking sight: "The cave was full of volunteers, yelling like fiends, while on the rocky floor lay over twenty Mexicans, dead and dying in pools of blood, while women and children were clinging to the knees of the murderers and shrieking for mercy . . . nearly thirty Mexicans lay butcherd on the floor, most of them scalped. Pools of blood filled the crevices and congealed in clots."[56]

Archibald Yell, Polk's friend and commander of the Arkansas "Rackensackers," as they were now known, refused to discipline the guilty troops; Taylor was ready to send the whole crew home, except that he desperately needed troops. He, unlike Hardin, knew there was a greater battle than this in store for the men of the Army of Chihuahua.

Indeed, Hardin was proved wrong the very day he wrote to Sarah. Through a stroke of luck, General Santa Anna's troops had intercepted a letter from General Scott to Taylor revealing the transfer of troops from one commander to the other, as well as details of the proposed invasion of Veracruz. Santa Anna could have concentrated his troops in Veracruz and prepared for the American onslaught of central Mexico. But instead he envisioned a singular opportunity to wipe out Taylor and his remaining forces when the invaders were at their weakest. On February 2, the commander marched out of the great mining center of San Luis Potosí, three hundred miles northwest of Mexico City, with an army of twenty thousand men.

Samuel Chamberlain, Rackensackers on the Rampage. *Samuel Chamberlain of the Second Illinois Volunteers witnessed the massacre of unarmed civilians by the Arkansas Volunteers on February 10, 1847. His painting of the gruesome scene highlights the violence of the volunteers, who appear deaf to the pleas of women and children. A company of U.S. dragoons at the mouth of the cave has arrived to end the slaughter.* Courtesy San Jacinto Museum of History.

The Mexican army suffered incredible deprivation during the three-week, two-hundred-mile march to Buena Vista. The winter weather was brutal, the desert terrain unyielding. Food, sleep, and water were in short supply. On February 21, Taylor received confirmation that Santa Anna and his army were just sixty miles to the south. He directed General Wool to lay out defenses at La Angostura between a high plateau laced with ravines on the left and a network of gullies on the right. Santa Anna arrived later that day to offer Taylor the chance to surrender. The American forces were vastly outnumbered, Santa Anna told Taylor; surely he recognized the untenable nature of his position. Taylor declined.

The American forces left under Taylor's command, almost all volunteer, numbered less than five thousand. Santa Anna's army of twenty thousand had been weakened by the forced march. Perhaps a quarter of his men, a shocking percentage, had died along the route. But the odds were still daunting. Hardin's regiment, along with a Pennsylvania battery, was stationed in the pass, a mile in front of the other troops. On the frosty morning of February 22, the Mexican forces came into view. Taylor informed Hardin that unless he held the pass, the battle would be lost. Hardin's moment had arrived. He addressed his men: "Soldiers: you have never met an enemy, but you are now in front. I know the 1st Illinois will never fail. I will see no man to go where I will not lead. This is Washington's Birthday—let us celebrate it as becomes true soldiers who love the memory of the Father of their Country." It was a false alarm. The irregular fire that occurred that day did not involve the volunteers from Illinois. Santa Anna gave a moving speech to his troops in the evening, and the strains of his band could be heard clearly by Hardin and his men.[57]

The American troops woke on the morning of the twenty-third to the astounding sight of the Mexican army celebrating a pre-battle mass. "Twenty thousand men, clad in new uniforms, belts as white as snow, brases and arms burnished until they glittered in the sunbeams like gold and silver," marveled Illinois volunteer Samuel Chamberlain. It was obvious that the Americans were vastly outnumbered. Santa Anna attacked immediately after mass, and his forces quickly pushed back the U.S. troops and threatened to surround them. By nine that morning Taylor's small army was in desperate trouble, but America's light artillery, vastly superior to the Mexican cannon, staved off defeat. The American guns "poured a storm of lead into their serried ranks which literally strewed the ground with the dead and dying," according to one eyewitness. The Pennsylvania battery deployed alongside Hardin's regiment held off five thousand troops with artillery, but several thousand more Mexican infantry attempted to flank their position. Hardin took five of his companies and, "himself always in front," advanced under cover of a hill, shouting, "Remember Illinois! Give them Blizzard, boys!" The infantry was driven back. His soldiers later claimed that that charge saved both the First Illinois and Clay's Second Kentucky regiment from being flanked.[58]

A fierce charge by the Mississippi troops, led by Jefferson Davis, combined with the ceaseless efforts of the artillery, drove the Mexicans back by the early afternoon. At 4:00 p.m. Taylor attempted to seize the initiative. He ordered the Illinois men and the Second Kentucky to advance. "This, like all of Hardin's moves, was quickly made," and approximately a thousand men pushed ahead, triple-speed, over broken ground in the face of a heavy fire of grape from a Mexican battery. In a frenzy of optimism, Hardin brashly announced, "We will take that battery." He drew his sword with a shout, and the men of Illinois charged the battery directly behind their fearless colonel.

They almost made it. When they were only a few yards from the battery, "some fifty yards to our right their whole reserve—some six or seven thousand infantry, opened fire." Hardin had unknowingly rushed into the path of Santa Anna's final assault. Ten thousand men, including several thousand fresh troops, emerged from a ravine armed and ready to crush the American advance. They advanced across a plateau in a blaze of fire. Many who were there later recalled that "no man but Hardin would have attempted to fight with such odds as 15 to 1." The men could hear the colonel's voice above the din, shouting, "Boys, remember the Sucker State; we must never dishonor it! Give them Blizzard! They fall every crack!"[59]

Hardin's bluster could not disguise the fact that both he and Taylor had badly misjudged the situation. Because of his ill-considered charge, Hardin's troops were now beyond supporting distance and were surrounded on all sides by Mexican infantry. His position was untenable. The Second Illinois and Henry Clay's Second Kentucky pushed forward to support Hardin, and the regiments became the focus of the Mexican attack. "The Mexicans, with a suddenness that was almost magical, rallied and returned upon us," a participant reported. "We were but a handful to oppose the frightful masses which were hurled upon us, and could as easily have resisted an avalanche of thunderbolts."[60]

Taylor called for Hardin to retreat.

"Now came a desperate time," remembered a survivor of the battle. The men sought shelter in a gorge and had to retreat down a "deep ravine—rocky and broken—in which no order could be kept." All semblance of discipline evaporated as each man fought for himself. "There were infantry a few yards above us on each side of the ravine, and several thousand lancers had cut off our retreat at its foot." To the retreating men it appeared that the entire edge of the gorge was darkened by a great mass of Mexican soldiers firing down on them. At this point, "every voice appeared to be hushed but Col. Hardin's—we could distinctly hear him shout . . . 'Remember Illinois and give them Blizzard, boys!' " Twenty Mexican lancers charged at Hardin, firing at the same time. A private in his regiment reported that "Hardin fell, wounded; with his holster pistol he fired and killed one lancer—and I think he drew, or attempted to draw, his sword—but in the melee I could not be sure, for as many lancers as could approach him, surrounded, and threw their lances in him—and thus perished an officer, than whom none was ever more beloved."[61]

The charge decimated the First and Second Illinois, as well as the Second Kentucky. The three units accounted for 45 percent of the fatalities that day, with ninety-one Illinois men and forty-four Kentuckians killed, and greater numbers injured. At two the following morning, the surgeon attached to the Second Kentucky wrote home to his family that he had "just finished dressing the wounds of my regiment. I have been in blood to my shoulders since 9.00 this morning."[62]

In total, more than seven hundred Americans were either killed or injured, including a number of officers, some of whom, like Hardin, had national reputations. Rackensacker commander Colonel Archibald Yell was killed while attempting to counter a Mexican charge in the morning. Colonel William McKee, commander of Clay's regiment, was also killed in the retreat down the ravine. A sudden rainstorm in the late evening brought the fighting to a close. A rainbow followed. Taylor's forces had maintained their defensive position, but it was far from clear whether they could continue to do so. Neither commander could claim a victory that night, but the numerical superiority of the Mexican forces argued in their favor come the following morning. Taylor's little army was far from optimistic at the end of the bloody day of battle. They shivered during the frosty night as coyotes feasted on the bodies strewn across the field.

Remarkably enough, the Mexican army chose not to fight another day. Santa Anna instead decided to retreat under cover of darkness, later claiming that he had been called back to Mexico City to quell a political uprising. In fact, he received no such order. He was almost back to Mexico City when he learned that five national guard battalions, supported by clerics tired of paying for the war, had rebelled against the liberal government.[63] Santa Anna had simply had enough. He had stopped the Americans, and his forces had suffered horrific casualties, with more than thirty-five hundred killed, wounded, or missing. But during the day's battle they captured flags and artillery, and those Santa Anna carried with him back to central Mexico as proof of Mexico's victory.

Americans, of course, viewed Santa Anna's retreat differently. Despite being outnumbered and without the help of the veteran troops, they had miraculously prevailed. When news of the victory arrived in the United States, spontaneous celebrations occurred across the nation, in small towns and great cities. When news reached Illinois, church bells pealed and cannon were fired. There were bonfires and parades from New Orleans to Boston. "Flags are flying from all the public buildings, and one universal spirit of joy and gladness pervades all patriotic hearts at the success of old 'Rough and Ready,'" a reporter in New York gushed.[64] Printmakers immediately prepared images of the battle for sale, many of which emphasized the intimate and seemingly heroic hand-to-hand nature of the combat.

The Battle of Buena Vista became the signature victory of the war, proof

Battle of Buena Vista. *Lithograph by Nathaniel Currier, 1847. This popular representation of the American victory at Buena Vista highlights the hand-to-hand combat of the battle.* Library of Congress Prints and Photographs Division.

that a small band of brave American volunteers could outfight a Mexican army four times its size. It was immediately conceded that there could be no higher "aspirations of military fame" than to say of a "fellow-citizen, *he was at Buena Vista.*" From his post as editor of the *Brooklyn Daily Eagle,* Walt Whitman proclaimed that the victory "will live . . . in the enduring records of our republic," and that "whatever may be said about the evil moral effects of war," victory at Buena Vista "must elevate the *true* self-respect of the American people." Caroline Kirkland, the editor of a new literary magazine, admitted that even those such as herself who found war "abhorrent and revolting" couldn't help but feel "pride" for the "gallant self-devotion" of the troops.[65]

It was the battle that the volunteers and American public had longed for. Then the casualty lists began to roll in.

8

Inscrutable Providence

ON MARCH 29, Henry Clay returned to Ashland after a four-month absence. Despite the "very bad" weather in New Orleans, it had been a good winter. His health had been fair, and he had enjoyed the parade of politicians and businessmen who sought his counsel at Dr. Mercer's. But it was delightful to be home. Flowers were blooming, the air was fresh, and the "bright sun shine beaming all around" reflected Clay's own joy at being reunited with his family. For the moment he forgot about the "anxious suspense" he had felt since news of "hard fighting" in Mexico made its way to New Orleans two weeks earlier.[1]

Clay's joy was short-lived. The following day his son James burst into the room during dinner "with grief depicted in his countenance," and announced that Colonel Henry Clay had been killed at the Battle of Buena Vista.[2]

Colonel Clay was shot through the thigh just before John Hardin's death, when the Illinois and Kentucky volunteers attempted their retreat down the deep ravine. Badly wounded, Clay handed his father's dueling pistols to one of his men for safe return, and ordered his regiment of Kentucky volunteers to retreat without him in the face of the advancing enemy. Then, brandishing his sword to the last, he succumbed to an onslaught of bayonet-wielding Mexicans. Clay's body was rescued by two unfree black men serving the company. Joel, an enslaved body servant and son of a prominent Lexington barber well known to the Clay family, was himself injured in the process. "No man ever fell more nobly, or more deeply regretted by his brother soldiers," a fellow soldier wrote to the senior Clay. He sent a lock of his son's hair shorn immediately after death.[3]

Colonel Clay had always stood out in the large Clay brood. He had graduated second in his class at West Point and had, his father imagined, a fine political future ahead of him. The senior Clay loved Henry deeply, but he also placed huge expectations on the son he considered most likely to succeed. All six of Clay's daughters had met early and tragic deaths, but this new loss he found almost insurmountable. "I find it extremely difficult to sustain myself under this heavy calamity," he wrote to William Mercer. "I was greatly attached to him, and he had high qualities, well known to me, entitling him to my warmest affection." In a life "full of domestic afflictions," Clay found that "this last is the severest among them."[4]

The soldier left behind three young children, whose mother, Julia, had died in 1840. The oldest was just thirteen. It was all "excruciatingly painful" to the family's patriarch, particularly since normally stoic Lucretia "bears the affliction with less than her usual fortitude." The couple was particularly "tortured by account after account" of "the manner of his death, and the possible outrages committed upon his body by the enemy."[5] Clay's body had been stripped of its clothes and repeatedly bayoneted. He was just thirty-five when Polk's war took his life, a little more than a year younger than John Hardin and only two years younger than Abraham Lincoln.

Newspaper accounts of the battle highlighted the martyr-like deaths of John Hardin and Henry Clay Jr.; as one report had it, "the representatives of each state seemed to vie with each other in the honorable ambition of doing the best service for their country." Readers learned the details of how "the noble Hardin met his death gloriously while conducting the last terrible charge. . . . Lieutenant Colonel Clay was cut down at almost the same moment with Hardin and McKee, while giving his men the most brilliant example of noble daring and lofty chivalry."[6]

If there was any consolation to gain from his son's death, Clay repeatedly stated, it was that "if he were to die, I know that he preferred to meet death on the field of battle, in the service of his Country." But the thought failed to provide solace. "That consolation would be greater," he admitted to one friend, "if I did not believe that this Mexican War was unnecessary and of an aggressive character." But Colonel Clay had seen things differently. "My poor son did not however stop to enquire into the causes of the War. It was sufficient for him that it existed in fact, and that he thought the Nation was entitled to his services."[7]

Because of the fame of his father and the drama of his passing, Colonel

Clay's death became a media spectacle, with the elder Clay playing a leading role. It was widely reported that Colonel Clay's last words before his death were to his father. With the enemy bearing down, the injured officer handed over the family pistols and gasped, "Tell him that I used these to the last! They were his gift." Clay's heroic demise, as one association of young Whigs in New York concluded, was equal to "that of the last of the heroes of the age of Chivalry." There could be no higher subject for the "poets and historians and artists of our country" than the "events and scene of our young hero's fall."[8] The outpouring of celebration over victory at Buena Vista was heightened by the heroic demise of Clay, Hardin, Clay's commanding officer McKee, and Archibald Yell. Colonel Clay, in particular, was inevitably mentioned in the many poems written about Buena Vista, and almost always linked with John Hardin. Albert Pike's epic and widely reprinted "Buena Vista" was written directly after the battle.

> Ho! Hardin breasts it bravely! . . . the Foe swarm ten to one:
> Hardin is slain; McKee and Clay the last time see the sun.[9]

In Horace Hoskins Houghton's "Battle of Buena Vista":

> Mercy Trembled at the sight
> And came from heaven, sad change to tell—
> When Clay, and Yell, and Hardin fell;
> And, weeping at the piteous sight,
> Drew down the curtains of the night—[10]

Newspaper reports lauded the fallen:

Clay—the young, the brave, the chivalrous—foremost in the fight, the soul of every lofty sentiment—devoted to his friends and generous to his enemies. He fell in the flower of his age and usefulness, and has left no worthier name behind him. If he was not the "noblest Roman of them all," few will deny that in him—

> Were the elements
> So mixed, that Nature might stand up and say
> To all the world—THIS WAS A MAN.[11]

Americans also clamored for visual representations of the deaths of the Buena Vista martyrs. Hardin's national fame was indicated by the fact

Death of Col. John J. Hardin: Of the 1st Regiment Illinois Volunteers. *Lithograph by Nathaniel Currier, 1847. Hardin's national reputation is indicated by the fact that the leading U.S. printmaking firm produced this image of his death at Buena Vista.* Library of Congress Prints and Photographs Division.

that the preeminent lithographers of the era, Currier and Ives, produced a hand-colored print in his honor.

At least seven lithographs of Henry Clay's heroic demise on the battle-field were produced by leading printmakers, most of them tastefully colored and all suitable for framing. While one popular image showed demonized Mexican soldiers bayoneting the prostrate officer, most chose instead to represent the dying Clay calmly handing the family dueling pistols to a comrade for safe return to his father while Mexican troops advanced in the background. These images highlighted the bond between father and son but also invited viewers to share in the Clay family trauma, making their private tragedy openly public. "Take these Pistols to my father," young Clay exhorts his comrades in one image. "Tell him, I have done all I can with them, and now return them to him."

While the media frenzy probably struck Lucretia as heartlessly invasive, her husband seems to have welcomed the public to share his grief. Zachary Taylor wrote Clay a moving letter of condolence just days after the battle. "No one ever won more rapidly upon my regard" than the "manly and hon-orable" Colonel Clay, he assured the father. "Under the guidance of himself and the lamented McKee, gallantly did the sons of Kentucky, in the thickest

Death of Lieut. Col. Henry Clay, Jr. *Butler and Lewis, 1847. At least seven prints were produced by major printmaking firms of the death of Henry Clay. Almost all highlighted Clay's relationship with his famous father by representing the return of the family dueling pistols. The caption below this print reads, "Leave me, take care of yourselves. Take these Pistols to my father and tell him, I have done all I can with them and now return them to him."* Library of Congress Prints and Photographs Division.

of the strife, uphold the honor of the State and of the country. . . . When I miss his familiar face, and those of McKee and Hardin, I can say with truth, that I feel no exultation in our success."[12] Clay allowed the letter to be published, and it appeared in newspapers across the country.

Clay also allowed a New York printmaker, who sent Clay a lithograph of the Battle of Buena Vista, to quote from Clay's thank-you note in newspaper ads for his firm. The image, Clay wrote, was "a rich and beautiful specimen of the lithographic arts." Clay admitted that it "will constantly remind me of a sad loss which I sustained on that memorable occasion," but he was consoled "by the consideration that my lamented son, I know, if he were to be prematurely taken away, preferred such a death as he encountered."[13] Neither printmaker nor public saw anything wrong with exploiting Clay's grief for purposes of commerce.

As Henry and Lucretia mourned, expressions of condolence poured into Ashland from around the country. Friends wrote; but so did strangers. The wife of a lawyer in Danville, Pennsylvania, lamented the loss of "your Son your own name, your noble gallant Son . . . And O how like his father so self-sacrificing." Her son was serving in Mexico as well, but she "could not partake in the rejoicing manifested by many in our town—by illuminations and other demonstrations of joy over the victory atchieved at Buena Vista" because of her sorrow over Clay's loss. She apologized for sending her letter. "Excuse me Mr Clay for I could not refrain for attempting to write to you your life and Character are so familiar to us that I cannot deem you a Stranger."[14]

The Louisville Bar Association, citing the "irreparable loss which his little orphans now sustain," and "the tear that steals down the manly cheek of his honored father," determined to wear mourning for thirty days. An association of Philadelphia merchants sent their condolences as well.[15]

And of course Clay heard from his political colleagues. His onetime opponent Martin Van Buren was one of many Democrats who sent condolences for Clay's "severe affliction."[16] But President Polk, proving his consummate ability to hold a grudge, sent nothing. Nor did Polk see fit to record the news of Colonel Clay's death in his diary. Polk's war had taken a shocking toll on the Clay family, and it was not over yet.

Polk's slight hardly registered in Clay's grief. His son's death shook him deeply and forced him to reexamine his life. Although Clay's reputation for high-stakes gambling and drunken excess was based on behavior abandoned decades earlier, he had never been a churchgoing man, despite the entreaties of his pious wife. Now, however, he turned to religion for solace. He wrote a friend in May that he could "cease to mourn for him if consolation could be drawn from any human source," but felt "that He only can heal the wound which has been inflicted, who permitted it, and to Him I strive to bow and submit, in meekness and humility." Clay was baptized an Episcopalian on June 22, at Ashland. On Independence Day, as he noted in his own prayer book, he took "the sacrament of the Lord's Supper" for the first time in the chapel of Transylvania University, in Lexington.[17]

Later that month, a Buena Vista survivor returned the Clay family pistols to Ashland. The nation learned that Clay was still "very much bowed down under a sense of deep affliction, brought upon him by the death of his son, the lamented Col. Clay." The return of the pistols reopened the wound, and "the emotions of Mr. Clay were truly painful to witness."[18] Clay intended to pass the pistols on to his grandson.

On July 20, the family performed "the sad and melancholy duty" of attending Colonel Clay's funeral. Fifteen to twenty thousand people gathered at the State Cemetery in Frankfort to honor the remains of Clay, McKee, and others whose bodies had been returned from the battlefield. The Clay fam-

ily's grief was highlighted in newspaper accounts of the proceedings, particularly the tears shed as "Mr. Clay was surrounded by the orphan children
of his lamented son." The undertaker presented Henry Clay with a "breast
pin" made of his son's hair, and gave Lucretia Clay a locket, also made of her
dead son's hair. Clay assured the man that the "delicate and touching" tributes were "more highly prized by us than 'rubies and diamonds,' and will be
carefully preserved by us, and transmitted to his children."[19]

Henry Clay's tasteless joke about killing a Mexican was not forgotten,
and New England abolitionists were quick to point out the irony, or justice, of Clay's own loss. Theodore Parker, Boston's leading radical abolitionist and theologian, was brutal in his assessment. "There stood one of the
foremost men of America, hoping to 'capture or slay a Mexican!' the son
of some woman that never injured him," Parker intoned. "Alas—could he
have known it—vain man, how soon is he doomed to weep at the 'inscrutable Providence,' by which his own son, the dear one, lies slain in battle."

As for the supposed nobility of Colonel Clay's death, Parker pointed out
that it was "some vulgar bullet of a nameless soldier" that brought Colonel
Clay down. Furthermore, it was the nameless Mexican, not young Clay,
who was in the right. Clay's killer "fought for his country, her altars and her
homes, while the American volunteer fell inglorious and disgraced, a willing murderer, in that war so treacherous and so cruel."

Parker offered no solace for "the father who had hoped to 'slay a Mexican.' " Henry Clay "shall find but sad consolation kissing the cold lips of his
only [sic] son." And this, according to Parker, was due justice. "Is Providence
so 'inscrutable'?" the theologian asked. "He who would deal death upon the
sons of other men—shall he not feel it in his own home?"[20]

The Sage of Ashland watched as Kentucky's surviving twelve-month volunteers returned home after Buena Vista. They were feted with elaborate dinners, public barbecues, and parades. Many were physically injured, while
others had less obvious injuries to their minds and spirits. The Kentucky
legislature voted to build a memorial in honor of those who did not return,
a towering commemorative marble monument overlooking the Kentucky
River, inscribed with their names.

At the dedication ceremony, a young veteran who had fought at Buena
Vista recited a poem he had written for the occasion, titled "The Bivouac
of the Dead." Theodore O'Hara wrote specifically about the "doubtful conflict" that "raged / O'er all that stricken plain," and about the "vengeful

blood of Spain." He mourned the men who died in Mexico. But it was his evocation of the futility of death that led both northerners and southerners to embrace "Bivouac of the Dead" a little more than a decade later in the Civil War.[21]

O'Hara was one of the few Kentucky volunteers who served with both Taylor and Scott, and he participated in Scott's march to the capital. Kentucky's hard fighting concluded at Buena Vista. This was not the case for the men from Illinois. Only two of Illinois's four regiments fought under Hardin and returned home from northeastern Mexico. Edward Baker's Fourth Illinois Volunteer Regiment joined Scott's army. As they sailed off to Veracruz along with eleven thousand other U.S. soldiers, one Illinois volunteer recorded that they were "in the best of spirits as if they were going to a ball." On March 9, they took part in the first amphibious landing in American naval history. Without any idea of the strength of the Mexican force awaiting them in the walled city, the men crowded into specially designed surf boats and stormed the beach at Veracruz, rifles held over their heads to keep them dry.[22]

Remarkably, they met almost no opposition. Political disorder in Mexico City and Santa Anna's decision to fight Taylor before dealing with Scott prevented the Mexican army from sending crucial reinforcements before the invasion. This was one of the few times in the war when Mexicans would be outnumbered by their invaders. But with less than four thousand men at his command, General Juan Morales faced odds not unlike Taylor's at Buena Vista.

There was still the matter of the walled city to penetrate, however. The venerable and elegant city of fifteen thousand was surrounded by high walls of coral and brick cemented with lime, forming a hexagon approximately one-quarter by one-half mile in size. It presented an imposing appearance. Scott spent a week building fortifications on the beach and establishing a tactical plan. It was imperative that U.S. forces move on to the healthier altitudes near Mexico City quickly; the swampy lowlands of Veracruz were full of mosquitoes, and yellow fever was already weakening his forces.

Scott decided to bomb the city into submission. They sealed the route out of town and cut off the water supply, communications, and rail network into the city. On March 22, Scott informed the residents of Veracruz that they had no choice but to surrender. Confident that help from Mexico City was on its way, they refused to comply.

Then Scott's army received the emotional news of Buena Vista. John Hardin's loss, not surprisingly, "cast a gloom over every man in the Illinois Regiment." Colonel Edward Baker had succeeded Hardin in Congress, and the two men had known each other for over a decade. He was "deeply affected" by the news and issued a regimental order that "a life of such unsullied honor, and a death of such proud distinction has given his name immortal renown."[23]

The men of the Fourth Illinois, like the rest of the troops gathered on the beach of Veracruz, realized they had missed the greatest battle of the war. They determined to earn as much glory as those they had left behind at Buena Vista. "We are going down on Vera Cruz like a tornado," one Wisconsin soldier wrote home. "Not only the eyes of America but all Europe are looking on this greatest conflict that has occurred in modern times. . . . We cannot fail, we will not fail, we shall not FAIL."[24]

They didn't fail, but neither did they match the glory of the Buena Vista dead.

When the Mexican army refused to surrender, Scott ordered his artillery to fire. For forty-eight straight hours shells descended on the people of Veracruz, smashing homes, churches, and schools indiscriminately. On March 24, foreign consuls stationed in Veracruz appealed to Scott for mercy. They asked that the women and children of the city be allowed to evacuate. Scott refused their request and stated that there would be no truce without surrender. The general intensified his bombing the following day, and, as Scott expected, the demoralized army came to terms. The civilians who left the city were in a pathetic state. "They were nearly starved to death when they surrendered," a twenty-one-year-old volunteer from South Carolina wrote his family; "they had got to eating their donkeys." It was a sobering vision for many of the soldiers. "To see the Mother with her infant on her back and with what little clothing she could carry toddleing along to seek a home unknown" made one Pennsylvania volunteer wonder how it would feel to be in her place. "There was not much sport made of them as would be supposed."[25]

The following bright and cloudless day the soldiers in Veracruz marched out of the walled town and surrendered their arms. As U.S. soldiers marched in, both volunteers and regulars had their first opportunity to see the effects of the 463,000 pounds of shot and shell that had rained into the city over the past four days. Their pleasure at witnessing "our flag planted on one of the best fortified castles in the wourld" was somewhat decreased by the scene inside the walls of the city. As a twenty-nine-gun salute rang out, the soldiers looked out on a city that was "virtually in ruins. Some buildings were set afire and nothing remains but blackened walls. Others are shattered and scattered in fragments. Street pavements are torn up from end to end." Those houses that were not destroyed flew flags "of some neutral nation," the residents fearing that "the *voluntarios* would break into them."[26]

The casualties were staggering. Mexico estimated that up to 500 civilians and 600 soldiers were killed in the bombardment. The U.S. estimate of Mexican casualties was 100 civilians and 80 soldiers. U.S. forces lost only 13. General Scott clearly chose civilian deaths over U.S. casualties or any delay in his plans. This was not the first time he had made such a choice. In 1838 he presided over the forced removal of the Cherokee in Georgia. Although the tribe offered no violent resistance, over a quarter of the Cherokee died on the Trail of Tears while under Scott's supervision. When Santa Anna heard news of Veracruz, he concluded that the people of Mexico had brought "this disastrous misfortune upon ourselves," the result of "interminable discords." He called on his fellow citizens to "die fighting" and promised to do the same himself. Stationed in Veracruz in the week after the siege, Ethan Allen Hitchcock found the "stench" of the dead "intolerable." He moved his tent out to the "suburbs" in order to get away from the smell.[27]

Scott's official report of the victory was on its way back to the United States that same day, carried on the steamship *Princeton*.[28] Abel Upshur would have been proud. Before he met his death aboard the vessel, in an explosion not unlike those that destroyed Veracruz, he had dreamed that the *Princeton* would prove America's might to the world.

But also winding their way back to the United States were reports of a different sort: accounts by embedded journalists from half a dozen American papers of the carnage in Veracruz. The correspondent for the New Orleans *Picayune* decried the "deplorable" effects of the bombing. "Hardly a house had escaped, and a large portion of them were ruined. The shells had fallen through the roofs and had exploded inside, tearing everything into pieces—bursting through the partitions and blowing out the windows." William Tobey, a Pennsylvania volunteer who wrote under the pen name "John of York," told the Philadelphia *North American* that if the people of Pennsylvania could "know, see and feel" the carnage, "you would all turn Quakers." Just "one glance" at the population leaving the city "would show how grossly wrong" it was to direct a war at the people. A correspondent for the New Orleans *Delta* agreed. "Women and children, old men and lame ones, hobbling off . . . and although they are, and should be, the enemies of every American, my heart bled for them. Their treachery and cruelty to our people was lost sight of in their humiliated looks. . . . On my soul I could not help pitying them."[29]

Scene in Vera Cruz During the Bombardment. *E. B. and E. C. Kellogg, 1847. This lithograph of the bombing of Veracruz, produced by a Hartford, Connecticut, firm, is one of the few American-made images of the war that visually represented the suffering of Mexican civilians. This vision of the widespread destruction of the city by American artillery and the deaths of women and children was most likely based on reports by soldiers and embedded journalists that appeared in American newspapers after the battle.* Yale Collection of Western Americana, Beinecke Rare Book and Manuscript Library.

The journalists also reported that U.S. troops rioted immediately after entering Veracruz, setting fire to a nearby settlement, Boca Rio, after robbing and raping the inhabitants. Scott resorted to the public hanging of a rapist and issued an order establishing military courts to try Americans for crimes against Mexicans. His actions restored order, but not before the American people realized that American atrocities would not be limited to northern Mexico.

Veracruz was the most widely reported battle of the war, and the most negatively reported. The carnage within the walls of the city, and the disorder outside it, led the press to issue open criticism of the American government for the first time during the war. After contemplating the "hideous corpses, staring the living in the face" in Veracruz, many of the entrenched journalists began to question when "the war fiend" would be "tired of his sport, or sated with blood," and how many "thousands of human lives" would yet "be sacrificed to the ambitious aspirations of man, or the just or unjust requirements of nations." The public might not trust everything they read in the papers, but they couldn't help but notice the new skepticism of the embedded reporters.[30]

The criticism hurt Polk. Democrats had fared badly in the elections of 1846, and Polk's plan to invade central Mexico was forged in the hopes that it might bring an increasingly unpopular war to a speedy end. But Veracruz had hardly appeased his critics. Unlike Henry Clay, however, Polk never questioned providence. He belonged to no church, but his purpose in life was clear. He was the agent of Manifest Destiny. He ignored the naysayers who wondered out loud why Mexico hadn't yet capitulated. He left unanswered reports from his commanding officers about atrocities on the front. The mounting death toll among American troops seems to have made no impression on him. When Santa Anna betrayed him and fought like a good patriot, Polk simply moved on and redoubled his efforts to win the war through sheer will and unending labor.

But the hard days and long nights of work, his obsessive attention to detail, and the relentless control he exercised over every department and clerk were taking a toll. "In truth, though I occupy a very high position," the president lamented in his diary, "I am the hardest working man in this country." Back in the halcyon days before his inauguration, James Polk had warned potential cabinet members that he would "remain constantly at Washington" during his term in office. He kept that promise. Nine months after his inauguration he admitted that he hadn't yet left Washington for a single day. "I find the Presidential office no sinecure," he wrote a friend. "My labours and responsibilities are very great." In total he spent less than six weeks of his entire four-year term away from the White House.[31]

His stress was evident. In July, Brigadier General John Quitman noted "a haggard and careworn look" about the president. By Polk's own admission, his "constant confinement to my office and great labour for many days past" left him increasingly "enfeebled and prostrated." Sarah begged him to take a vacation, but his deep sense of duty made it impossible. Although in "the habit of taking exercise on horseback all my life," Polk stopped riding soon after learning of Taylor's armistice following the Battle of Monterrey. He was "so incessantly engaged in the onerous and responsible duties of my office" that he didn't mount a horse for the next six months.[32] Even an hour a day for himself was an impossible luxury with an invasion of central Mexico to manage and duplicitous Whig commanders to keep in line. His once dark brown hair was now almost completely white.

Polk was perfectly aware that he was destroying his health. But he would not stop. Providence had made clear that he could not stop until the nation's destiny was secure. And that required bringing the war to a close. It was now in its second year. Someone had to negotiate a peace treaty with Mexico. It had to be an official of high public stature, it had to be a Democrat, and it couldn't be a presidential candidate. Polk refused to take sides in the battle to name his successor; he could not afford to further alienate any powerful Democrats. Given the unsettled state of affairs in Mexico, as well as Mexico's unwillingness to negotiate, whoever left on the mission might be gone for a very long time. Polk received the "joyful news" of Scott's capture of Veracruz on April 10, and at a meeting of his cabinet a few hours later, he argued in favor of immediately appointing a commissioner to join Scott's army and "take advantage of circumstances as they might arise to negotiate for peace."[33]

It was James Buchanan who recommended Nicholas Trist, the impeccably credentialed chief clerk of the state department. Thomas Jefferson's protégé was "an able man, perfectly familiar with the Spanish character and language," and trustworthy. He was a personal friend of Buchanan's, a southerner, and a slave owner. He was not running for office and had no public name to speak of. Polk could be sure to receive any acclaim for a treaty negotiated by the chief clerk. And Andrew Jackson himself had vouched for Trist's "talents, integrity, and honor." Trist could be counted on to follow whatever "well defined instructions" he was given. The suggestion struck Polk "favorably." Trist had been open in his criticism of Polk's Whig generals and appeared to dislike Scott as intensely as did the head of his party. Nicholas Trist was as thorough a Democrat as could be found in Washington.[34]

Or so he appeared. Trist had been privy to all the negotiations between Mexico and the United States since his friend John Slidell's charade of negotiation in 1845. He had spent long hours in Polk's office in the year since, translating messages into and out of Spanish for his superiors. Working unconscionably long hours that didn't nearly match those of the president, Trist had seen the machinations of the administration firsthand.

Trist supported his country's war in Mexico, but had not forgotten what Jefferson had taught him: the importance of justice and morality. Nor had he set aside his beloved grandmother's words to him when he was a cadet at West Point: "Those who wage war for the purpose of subjugating nations to their will are guilty of a heinous crime."[35] Trist loved his country, but he was not a man to blindly follow orders when his conscience told him otherwise. Perhaps he already had doubts about the justice of this war.

Wasting no time, Polk ordered Buchanan to fetch Trist. It was a Saturday afternoon, but the clerk was hard at work at his desk when Buchanan invited him to walk over to the White House. At the time, Trist had "as little thought of going to Mexico as of going to the moon." He was astounded when the president conveyed his instructions. Trist was being dispatched to Mexico, incognito, to join up with Scott's army in Veracruz. His secret mission: to negotiate a peace treaty including an ample territorial settlement. While Polk never wavered from citing Mexican aggression as the war's cause, he had by now subtly added the necessity of expansion to his reasons for fighting. There would be no peace without territory, and the more abject the enemy's defeat, the more land the United States could claim. Trist's instructions specified a major territorial cession, not only the disputed Nueces Strip but Alta California and New Mexico as well, for which the United States would pay twenty million dollars. Polk authorized up to thirty million if Trist could obtain Baja California and additional territory to the south. Trist accepted his assignment, and suggested a possible reward for his service: a minor posting somewhere far from the capital that would yield a decent income without making many demands on his time. Trist dreamed that the end of the war would bring him some leisure.[36]

No one, Polk felt, would be more reliable or loyal than Trist. But the president had no idea whom he was dealing with. "Had he been at all capable of attaining insight into character," Trist later wrote, the president would have "obtained at least a glimpse into mine. But it remained a sealed book for him."[37]

One of Polk's colleagues observed that the president's "knowledge of men was imperfect, and when he required services from others they were made to understand that it was for their interest to serve him." There is no better example of this than Polk's closing promise to Trist. As the diplomat left his office, Polk told him, "Mr. Trist, if you can but succeed in restoring peace, you will render a great service to your country and acquire great distinction for yourself." Trist took exception to the remark. "The service shall be rendered, sir, if it be possible for me to do that. But as for the distinction, I care nothing for that." Assuming that most men craved glory, Polk was visibly irritated by Trist's rejoinder, which struck him as profoundly insincere. It was an awkward parting.[38]

As James Buchanan walked Trist out of Polk's office, he elaborated on Polk's suggestion. "If you succeed in this," Buchanan told him, "we shall have to take you up as our candidate for the Presidency." Trist laughed in response, but with "derision and heavy heartedness" rather than "merriment and satisfaction." In truth, he was dismayed. How Buchanan, a man he considered a friend, could possibly think he was motivated by a quest for political office was beyond him. What Trist craved was time with his family, and the opportunity to read and reflect, as he had back with Thomas Jefferson at Monticello. "How far you are from being capable of understanding me," he thought. It was the last conversation the two men would ever have.[39]

Four days later, Trist was on his way to Mexico. He had not sought his assignment. He had no interest in leaving his wife and children, even for a month, and he knew his absence would be far longer. But having accepted his duties, he embraced them fully. He would be the agent of peace. It never entered Polk's head that his envoy had doubts about the war. Nor did it occur to him that Trist was very much like himself. Polk assumed that, like most men, Trist was driven by hopes of money and acclaim. But both were driven by idealism. Polk's highest allegiance was to Manifest Destiny. Trist's allegiance, as would become clear, was to justice.

9

Needless, Wicked, and Wrong

NO FOURTEEN-YEAR-OLD should have to break news like this to her mother. Ellen Hardin had been enjoying the winter in Mississippi. With her father so far away, she particularly appreciated the attention lavished on her by her indulgent uncle Abe. "The Patriarch" might be an object of mockery to her parents, but he and Ellen got along well. In many ways he was like her father: a successful attorney and man of substance, wealthy, respected, and once elected to public office. Both kept extensive libraries, where Ellen indulged her growing interests in history and English literature.

But of course Abe had not gone to Mexico, despite wanting to. As a result, he now had plenty of time for his niece. Ellen's brothers were still children, but she was nearly an adult. Ellen and Abe discussed Shakespeare. He took her with him on business trips around the state and to New Orleans, where she delighted in the cosmopolitan atmosphere. Her explorations of the Crescent City with her uncle "opened up a new world of observation and experience" for her.[1]

Those experiences did not include bumping into Henry Clay, although he was in residence that winter at William Mercer's home. She certainly would have recognized him. Not only was he the leader of her father's party, but they were related through both business and marriage as well. When John Hardin's father died, his mother married Henry Clay's brother. This made the Whig leader John Hardin's uncle and Ellen's great-uncle. John Hardin

Ellen Hardin, age sixteen. The eldest of John J.
Hardin's children was devoted to her father. As a young
child Ellen "always followed him about, as a little
child more frequently follows the mother." She dreamed
about him when he left for Mexico and treasured the
letters he sent home. On vacation in New Orleans, she
was one of the first people in America to learn the news
about Buena Vista. Courtesy Saratoga Springs History
Museum.

also served as Henry Clay's business agent in Illinois in the 1830s. The blue-grass elite of Kentucky kept tight company.

Virtually all war news from northeastern Mexico arrived in the United States via the port of New Orleans. The lag time was generally two to three weeks. Reports had to be carried by courier from the interior of Mexico over poor roads, and often through hostile populations, to the port of Matamoros. News then traveled by boat to the mouth of the Mississippi River, and from there to New Orleans. The fastest route from New Orleans to Washington included a steamboat to Montgomery, Alabama, and from there a combination of local trains and horse-drawn post carriages to a Georgia train depot that connected to the Northeast. As for the telegraph, in 1848 it extended no farther south than Petersburg, Virginia. The American public's access to battle reports during the first year of the war was inversely proportional to their distance from New Orleans.

News from central Mexico was even slower in arriving in the United States. It sometimes took six weeks or two months for Polk to receive official battle reports from General Scott. To his chagrin, President Polk often read about events in Mexico in newspapers days before reports arrived via official diplomatic routes. Embedded journalists and their special couriers proved more efficient at navigating the difficult and complex transportation routes than the army did.[2]

A report of the "great victory at Buena Vista" arrived in New Orleans on Sunday afternoon, March 21, nearly a month after the battle. This was a week later than it might have appeared, but it took Taylor's battered army eight days to regroup, bury their dead, and locate a courier willing to brave the guerrilla-controlled roads to the rear of Buena Vista before an American-authored account of the battle left Coahuila. The embedded journalists who had covered Taylor's earlier victory at Monterrey and had an interest in scooping other papers had all left with Scott's army for Veracruz. Along with virtually everyone except General Taylor, they assumed the fighting in northern Mexico was done.

A special edition of the New Orleans *Mercury* appeared at five thirty that Sunday evening. The *Picayune*'s special edition appeared an hour later. Ellen Hardin, in New Orleans with her uncle, was thus one of the first people in America to learn of her father's death. President Polk received his report two days later. Henry Clay received the news in Ashland a week after that. Had he extended his stay in New Orleans one week longer, he would have learned of his son's death without Lucretia by his side.[3]

Ellen and Abe immediately left for Vicksburg, where Sarah was visiting friends. It was in Vicksburg that Sarah Hardin's daughter and brother told her that her husband was dead. The widow put her affairs in Mississippi in the best order she could, packed up her children, and returned home. By coincidence, an Illinois volunteer returning from Buena Vista traveled up the Mississippi on the same steamship as the Hardins, bound for the same destination. He carried with him some of the dead colonel's personal effects, including a Mexican battle flag Hardin had captured in Buena Vista and which he had specifically requested should be "sent home as a last memento for his wife."[4]

They returned to a community that embraced them and their grief. The news from Buena Vista was difficult for the people of Illinois to wrap their heads around. For fifteen years the former congressman, militia general, and now Mexican War hero had built a reputation on a steely invincibility. He had vanquished Illinois of her Indians and Mormons, taken charge of the survivors after the explosion on the *Princeton,* and been the first to volunteer for Mexico. His constituents had grown to revere "Colonel John J." Suddenly "no Hardin was there . . . his manly form, his proud, glorious smile greeted not the throng of his admiring friends." A good portion of the first two Illinois regiments of Mexican war volunteers were also gone, but when news of Buena Vista made it to Illinois, it was "Col. Hardin's death" that the papers predicted "will shed deep gloom over the state" and "be regarded as a national calamity." The loss of "one of the noblest specimens of man" couldn't help but "be felt in all the circles of society."[5]

When Hardin's death was announced in his courthouse, an Illinois judge reported that there wasn't "a dry eye" in the court. "He was too brave," wept the major in charge of Hardin's remains. Sarah was deluged with letters, from friends, from acquaintances, from admirers. They came from Illinois and Mississippi, St. Louis and New Orleans. Democrat Thomas Hart Benton sent his condolences despite his political differences with John. None of this was much consolation, not even the letters from women who wrote simply to reassure her that while they had never met, they sympathized with her. Virtually every letter asserted that her husband was a great hero. True, he had "died a glorious death." But he was still dead, and at age thirty-six she was left with three children to raise. "My heart dies within me," she admitted to her sister. "How can I live, how dark and lonely will be the journey of my life."[6]

Abraham Lincoln was in Illinois when he heard. The two men had parted as enemies over an election that Hardin was only half interested in and which Lincoln now looked back on with ambivalence. A year later, Lincoln was congressman-elect, still in Illinois. He understood what was required from a man in his position: he would take the lead in honoring Colonel Hardin. On Monday, April 5, he convened a memorial meeting in the state capital in honor of the state's first volunteer. His introductory address praised Hardin's many virtues, and then, speaking for the assembled multitudes, Lincoln proclaimed that "while we sincerely rejoice at the signal triumph of the American arms at Buena Vista . . . it is with the deepest grief that we have learned of the fall of the many brave and generous spirits there, and especially, that of Col. J. J. Hardin." Lincoln made sure the meeting, and his words, were reported in the local paper.[7]

Lincoln spoke for the people, as befitted their elected congressional representative. But did he speak for himself? Hardin had once been, in Lincoln's own words, "more than a father" to him, yet Lincoln couldn't help but notice that Hardin's death vastly improved his own political prospects. "The death of Hardin was not detrimental to Lincoln," noted one Illinois jurist, as Hardin had been the "strongest" politician in the state. Nor was this jurist the only observer to recognize that had Hardin survived the war, Lincoln would have been hard-pressed to match the colonel's "high aspirations, strong convictions, resolute purposes," and "great military renown." Hardin was "the most popular" Whig politician in the state even before the war, and some said his "personal popularity was greater" than that of almost anyone else in Illinois. David Davis, later Lincoln's campaign manager, also concluded that had he lived, Hardin would have "controlled the politics and offices of the state."[8]

What none of these men knew was that Hardin had repudiated "the noise & hustle of politics & law" just weeks before Buena Vista, when he assured his wife he felt "no distinction to participate in them again." That letter arrived posthumously. But John Hardin had just celebrated his thirty-seventh birthday. In political terms he was still a young man, and more than entitled to change his mind. His interest in "party struggles" might very well have revived once he was back in Illinois. He certainly could have returned to Congress had he chosen, and Stephen Douglas might have found the war hero a far more difficult challenger than Abraham Lincoln in the 1858 Senate race. Had Hardin lived, Lincoln would have been overshadowed.[9]

As spring turned to summer, Lincoln had multiple opportunities to measure himself against his deceased rival. He didn't have a great deal else to do; he was a year into an interminable sixteen-month wait between his election and the start of the Thirtieth Congress. There was year-old Eddie to deal with, and his legal practice could be demanding, but Lincoln was basically waiting for his future in Washington to begin.

The brightest spot on his immediate horizon was the upcoming River and Harbor Convention in Chicago in early July. President Polk had predictably vetoed an act passed by the closely divided Democratic Congress to provide federal funding for river and harbor improvement. Such federal action was anathema to his small-government views. Whigs responded with a call for a great national gathering in Illinois's burgeoning metropolis, the midwestern transportation hub of Chicago.

It would be Lincoln's first visit to the city; he was going as a convention delegate from Illinois, and he would deliver a speech. He would finally have the opportunity to promote his ideas about the importance of federal action in the interest of internal improvements, an opportunity denied him during the election when Illinois was focused on war. He would brilliantly unmask the shortsightedness of Democratic policies in the presence of thousands of like-minded and politically connected Whigs from around the country. He had high hopes his speech would bring him positive publicity, perhaps even the beginnings of a national reputation.[10]

But Hardin's name remained in the papers. A meeting called to support Taylor for president adopted a resolution that with the death of John Hardin, "the whole country has lost a statesman of exalted patriotism." Far from Illinois, Hardin was proclaimed "one of Nature's noble spirits, a soldier tried and true, a rare union of the best qualities of the head and heart."[11]

Hardin was lauded by Zachary Taylor and by General Wool, who issued an order naming Hardin's sacrifice essential to the victory at Buena Vista. This assertion was patently false, for Hardin died in vain, blundering into a trap set by Santa Anna. The deaths of ninety-one Illinois men in a Mexican ravine served no strategic or tactical purpose. But this was too painful to contemplate, let alone verbalize. It was far better that Hardin's mourners focus on his bravery, leadership, and patriotism, rather than on his willingness to die a pointless death in a war he no longer understood or endorsed.

There were the many poems about Buena Vista that reminded readers of his particular heroism. In May a returning veteran stated that it was Hardin and not Taylor who so brilliantly chose the army's position at Buena Vista. Taylor chose not to contradict him. In June news of Sarah Hardin's plans for the funeral was reported as far away as Baltimore, and when the town of Frankfort, Kentucky, asked Sarah Hardin for the right to return her husband's remains to the "same soil" that held the remains of the Kentucky Hardins, the correspondence was reprinted in distant Albany and New Orleans. Writing for the widow, Hardin's law partner David Smith insisted that Hardin's grave rest in Illinois, "where he is admired and beloved." The use of the present tense appeared to be deliberate. The Kentucky state legislature chose to inscribe Hardin's name on their memorial to the war dead anyhow. Calhoun County, Illinois, on the banks of the Mississippi and Illinois rivers, renamed its county seat Hardin in honor of the colonel, despite the fact that there was already a county in Illinois named after John Hardin's grandfather, the Revolutionary War hero and Indian fighter.[12]

The public outpouring of grief reached a crescendo in July, just as the River and Harbor Convention came to a close. The twelve-month volunteers recruited at the start of the war had completed their year of service, and most of them returned home. The First and Second Illinois volunteers, retracing the same route that had taken them to Mexico, arrived by the steamer *Missouri* in St. Louis on July 7. They bore with them the remains of their beloved colonel. Hardin's funeral became a multiday, two-state affair, its account reprinted in papers large and small around the nation. His coffin, along with that of a Missouri officer, was loaded on a hearse, followed by Hardin's beloved "war mount"—the "beautiful grey charger" that accompanied him through Mexico.[13]

Leading Hardin's charger was Benjamin, the African American servant who had accompanied Hardin to Mexico. Slavery was illegal in Mexico, and from the start of the war the coerced black servants traveling with the army understood that Mexico offered economic and social opportunities denied them in the United States. Many black men taken to war discovered that, for them, Mexico was the real land of freedom. They escaped into Mexico and never returned.[14] But Benjamin did not desert. He showed a striking loyalty to Hardin, given the fact that the colonel never mentioned his name in a letter home. Although he was a young man, he not only marched alongside the colonel in life but accompanied his horse home after Hardin's death, carrying "his clothes, sword, saddle, and other articles" with him through Mexico and Texas.[15] And yet, like virtually all the other unheralded servants in Mexico, Benjamin received no public acknowledgment. He received none of the acclaim accorded the white American men of his age who left for Mexico. Nor, in fact, did he receive as much acknowledgment as Hardin's horse. In reports of the funeral, he was simply Hardin's unnamed servant.

Benjamin escorted Hardin's horse and body through the streets of St. Louis in a grand parade accompanied by a military band. Their destination was the courthouse rotunda, where the entire second floor had been decorated in what reporters deemed "excellent taste," both "solemn and imposing." The darkened room was lit only by lamps, while military banners and black crepe hung from the columns. Hardin's coffin, along with that of the officer from Missouri, were placed on a bier, draped in black and edged with white lace.

Thomas Hart Benton addressed the crowd. His comments were brief but highly emotional. He praised the volunteers for fulfilling the "pious and sacred" duty of returning Hardin's "earthly remains" over three thousand miles, and, ignoring the fact that the rest of the Illinois dead remained in Mexico, he stated that the graves of Americans "should not be trod by foreign feet." He confirmed that all of Washington, including the president himself, had been absorbed by "anxiety" over the fate of Taylor's army before learning the "glorious news of a great and almost unparalleled victory." And he reflected that both Illinois and Missouri had contributed more than their share of the dead at Buena Vista. Pointing to the coffin, he intoned, "The brave, lamented and beloved Hardin lies there!" On behalf of the state of Missouri, he offered thanks for the opportunity to pay tribute to the great hero of Illinois. On the "bloody and glorious field of Buena Vista," Benton assured them, the "American character . . . immortalized itself by valor."[16]

It was largely a political performance. Hardin's remains didn't need to visit St. Louis. But their return provided an opportunity for a leading Democratic politician to glorify the cause of war. With the twelve-month volunteers returning from service, the army was desperately in need of new bodies. Recruiting posters papered the walls of St. Louis that July. The courthouse remained in its mourning garb for two days to allow the "very many who have not yet seen it" an opportunity to experience the "very solemn effect" and "highly impressive character" of the funeral rites. As for Hardin, his coffin was returned to the steamboat *Defiance,* which delivered the colonel, his horse, and Benjamin to Illinois.[17]

A week later, John Hardin was laid to rest in his hometown of Jacksonville. It was Bastille Day, a fitting date to bury a man who many believed sacrificed his life for the cause of liberty. It was a hot, dry day, and by midmorning Jacksonville was overflowing with a crowd of fifteen thousand admirers from around the state. There was a festive air in the town, with rural families decked out in their best clothes and parasols "as plenty as blackberries."[18]

Jacksonville was a small town, but it was the seat of one of the most fertile counties in the state, and among its eight thousand residents were many men of means originally drawn from New England and Kentucky. It had certain pretensions to both sophistication and what the Whig ruling class considered right-minded reform. It boasted the State Asylum for the Deaf and Mute (procured through John Hardin's efforts while in the state legislature), along with a small college founded by one of the sons of renowned theologian Lyman Beecher, a Plato Club, an art association, and the "flourishing" Jacksonville Female Academy, where Ellen Hardin was educated. It boasted a number of fine brick homes, the oldest of which had been built for John Hardin. The residents of the town were committed to providing "all the refinements of social life" and the "cultivation of . . . higher aspirations."[19]

Town residents liked to call it the "Athens of the West," but on the day of the funeral the public square felt more like Rome. Mounted marshals dressed in white sashes cavorted in front of the stores, hotels, and offices that lined the square, while a military band entertained the throngs. Jacksonville was a "dry" town, but many in the crowd were visibly drunk, either unaware or unconcerned that the man they arrived to honor had been a lifelong advocate of temperance.[20]

Among the crowd, but most likely sober, was the entire delegation to the Illinois state constitutional convention, which was then meeting thirty miles away in Springfield in order to revise the state constitution. Among the most serious issues they faced was whether to enshrine into the constitution the ban against the "immigration and introduction, under any circumstances, of free negroes into the state." That the new constitution would explicitly restrict voting to "white citizens" was a foregone conclusion. During Abraham Lincoln's first term in the state legislature, he voted in favor of a resolution that "the elective franchise should be kept pure from contamination by the admission of colored voters." That resolution passed, 35–16.[21]

Laws restricting the immigration of free blacks into midwestern states were long-standing and widespread, but they were enforced only sporadically before the 1830s. In 1819 and 1829 the Illinois legislation had attempted, and failed, to limit immigration to whites. But starting in the 1830s, rising racism led northern and western states under Democratic control to increase their enforcement and pass increasingly restrictive laws limiting the political and social rights of free African Americans. Black people in Illinois could neither marry white people nor testify against them in court. Public schools in Illinois excluded black children. Abraham Lincoln was on record as opposing the "injustice" of slavery in the legislature in 1837, but he was even more open in his opposition to abolition societies "and the doctrines promulgated by them."[22] Like virtually every other politician in Illinois in the 1840s, Abraham Lincoln appealed to racial prejudice in order to advance his political beliefs. In 1836 and 1840, he accused Martin Van Buren of favoring black suffrage. Had he still been in the statehouse, Lincoln might well have voted to ban black immigration into the state. But this was by no means a foregone conclusion. Amending the state constitution was a serious matter and required sustained debate.

Those attending the constitutional convention had a lot to deal with, but John Hardin's death took precedence. They took the week off to attend the funeral, and resolved to wear black crepe armbands for thirty days in Hardin's honor. Also in attendance at the funeral were "many members" of the Chicago River and Harbor Convention. The gathering, which editor Horace Greeley of New York declared to be the largest meeting held in America up to that time, would have fully met Lincoln's expectations, had his short speech in favor of internal improvements gained any attention at all. But it wasn't even reprinted in his local Whig paper. The convention concluded on June 7, and delegates to the convention from New England and the South went "many miles out of their course to be present" in Jacksonville for the funeral.[23]

Lincoln didn't have to go far out of his way to pay his last respects to John Hardin. He shared a stagecoach through the Illinois prairie with a writer for the *Boston Courier*, traveling from the convention to the funeral. When they reached the outskirts of Springfield the latter noted that Lincoln "knew, or appeared to know, every body we met, the name of the tenant of every farm-house, and the owner of every plat of ground . . . he had a kind word, a smile and a bow for everybody on the road, even to the horses, and the cattle, and the swine." However he felt about the colonel, the congressman-elect's attendance in Jacksonville would have been expected. Most likely Lincoln, along with his traveling companion from Boston, was part of the crowd jockeying for position in the Bastille Day heat. He would not have been drinking. Like John Hardin, Lincoln never touched the stuff.[24]

At ten o'clock, a formidable procession got under way. Taking the lead was a militia group named in Hardin's honor, followed by the governor and his retinue, the delegates to the Illinois state convention, and judges, academics, and doctors. A smartly dressed local volunteer fire company carrying a banner, members of the clergy, and the local Masonic fraternity marched ahead of the funeral car with pallbearers. Behind them was "the noble animal upon which the bold Hardin had ridden for many a weary mile, over many a desert and dangerous waste," again led by Benjamin. Sarah Hardin and Ellen and her two brothers followed, along with other relatives, and after them came the surviving members of Hardin's regiment. The assembled citizens trailed behind. A marching band provided a funeral dirge, "impressive and solemn beyond description," composed especially for the occasion. They stopped at the Hardin family's "large and hospitable mansion" at the eastern end of town and gathered beneath the "noble trees, reared by the hand now still in death." Before he was laid to rest by his "Masonic brethren," the assembled multitude heard a very peculiar eulogy, provided by Hardin's first law clerk.[25]

Richard Yates extolled John Hardin's many virtues. He spoke of his political prowess and the fact that "he was never unsuccessful before any people for any office for which he was a candidate." He made sure his audience heard all about Hardin's distinguished forebears in Kentucky, including the original John Hardin. George Washington had selected that John Hardin to negotiate with the Shawnee in 1792, he claimed, "on account of his great knowledge of Indian character, his firmness of purpose, and his fearlessness of danger." And the forebear died as he lived, "never avoiding the post of danger, and ever ready to serve his country." Yates also praised John J. Hardin's "classical education," "brilliant intellectual facilities," and "legal ingenuity." Yates had studied law under Hardin and had a somewhat inflated opinion of his abilities. "To his competitors, he was a powerful opponent," Yates stated. But Hardin was also beloved. "His uniform, courteous, manly and gentlemanly bearing" won "a warm respect and devoted friendship" among the legal community.[26]

What Yates focused on, above all, was Hardin's "firm, noble, manly" character. "Need I say he was brave? He could not be otherwise," Yates admitted. But unlike Thomas Hart Benton, Yates was not interested in extolling Hardin's martial virtues or vindicating the losses at Buena Vista. On the contrary, he was intent on remembering a man of "exalted purity of moral character" without a "single vicious habit" or "base appetite." What Hardin was notable for, Yates claimed, was not his martial virtue but his innate moral restraint. Hardin was "incorruptible" and "exemplary as a devoted and sincere Christian." In a claim that may have raised the eyebrows of more than one tame, spiritless fellow in the audience, Yates claimed that "never was a nature more fitted for the enjoyment of the pleasures of home" than John Hardin. Never was one "more adapted to the discharge of all duties of a kind father and devoted husband."[27] The Hardin eulogized at his funeral was not the man who raised Illinois's first regiment to fight America's war of empire. It was a man who had conquered himself rather than conquering others.

To be sure, John Hardin was a temperance advocate who took pride in his upright "habits." Just before leaving for Mexico he was elected an elder in the Presbyterian Church, and he had, in fact, donated the Jacksonville lot on which the church stood. His obituaries often contained the claim that "few men, amid the trials and temptations of public life, have been more successful at maintaining an upright and consistent character in all the walks of life" than had John Hardin.[28]

But to describe him as a restrained family man took some creativity, particularly at a military funeral. David Smith, whom Hardin had unsuccessfully tried to lure to Mexico, and Hardin's widow and children, were not the only ones in the audience who recognized that for Colonel Hardin, the possibility of military service always trumped the "enjoyment of the pleasures of home." He was martial to the bone. But this was not how Yates chose to remember him.

This was because Yates had his doubts about the war with Mexico, doubts so strong that he was willing to air them at a military funeral for a war hero, surrounded by the surviving soldiers of Hardin's regiment. "Differ as men may and do, as to whether the war could have been avoided," Yates admitted, "there has been but one common, patriotic, national American sentiment" in response. The volunteers turned out, despite the fact that not all supported the cause. "Be the opinions of men on the war what they may, surely none could fail to admire the exalted patriotism which induced our volunteers . . . to endure privation, to encounter the disease of a strange climate, and to face death."[29]

To what end? Buena Vista may have been a great victory to the nation, but "to us, my friends, this victory, however brilliant, is a sad defeat. To us the question comes at what cost?" The men of Illinois fell "in a strange land, far from kindred and home. There were no kind mothers, or sisters there—no wife to pillow their gallant heads." Yates noted what Benton had not: that the remains of the vast majority of the dead, unlike John Hardin, Henry Clay Jr., and other officers famous or wealthy enough to merit special treatment, had not been returned for burial to the United States. They had been buried where they fell, on Mexican soil, trampled by foreign feet.

And there they remained. Yates asked his listeners to identify with "the deep felt sorrow of the wife, who shall never look on that loved one again," as well as "the tears of the bright-eyed boys and girls whose father's form now fills a soldier's grave in a foreign land."[30] Yates could not bring himself to speak in favor of the war, even as he extolled a man he "loved" who sacrificed his life in Mexico.

The eulogy and funeral were followed by a light meal served under a nearby grove of trees. A series of military speakers attempted to outdo one another in their tributes to Colonel Hardin. Many praised the valor of the soldiers in battle. All agreed that a monument to the memory of the Buena Vista dead should be built as soon as possible.[31] As the crowd returned to the public square, Sarah Hardin invited the surviving members of the First Illinois to join her for dinner in their family home.

The writer for the *Boston Courier* who traveled with Lincoln through Illinois reported that the funeral was designed "to gratify a spirit of military ardor." Like most citizens of Massachusetts, the journalist opposed the war, and he imagined that Illinois, which had sent more volunteers south than any state except Missouri, was still gripped by a "military mania" for

Mexico. He noticed that Jacksonville, like St. Louis, was full of recruiting posters. "The fruit of to-day's pageant," he wrote of the funeral, "will be the enlistment of at least a thousand new victims to the insatiate ambition of our wicked and unprincipled government."[32]

But this reporter never actually made it to Hardin's funeral. He remained in the Jacksonville public square after the procession departed, and completely missed Yates's conflicted eulogy. He never learned how similar Yates's view of Hardin was to the antiwar views of New Englanders. That summer, a letter writer to the antislavery *National Era* also claimed that Hardin was a paragon of restrained manhood. He asserted that John Hardin opposed the war, and "confessed, from the outset, that the Mexican War was all needless, wicked, and wrong."

While Hardin's views of Mexico and Manifest Destiny evolved during his year of service, and by the time of his death he had come to question the wisdom of annexing Mexican land, by no means did Illinois's first volunteer ever say that the war was "needless, wicked, and wrong." He most certainly did not say this in 1846. But antiwar voices played fast and loose with the facts of Hardin's biography in their attempt to turn Hardin's death into a cautionary tale. Despite condemning the war, according to this account, Hardin foolishly let a misguided sense of patriotism, rather than his conscience, guide his actions. His decision to follow "that treacherous and illusive motto, 'Our country, right or wrong,' " became the cause of his undoing. "From that hour, the wrath of heaven seems to have overshadowed him."[33]

While Yates never went so far as to claim that Hardin thought the war needless, wicked, and wrong, his own views about the war were clear to everyone in the audience, and not far from those holding sway in New England. But because the Boston reporter missed Yates's eulogy and focused only on the pre- and post-funeral celebration, he believed that the people of Illinois continued to embrace the war. Had he been privy to the conversations between Sarah Hardin and her husband's men in the Hardin home after the funeral, he might not have claimed that the returning volunteers "express, at present, very little or no opinion at all as to their feelings."[34] But his assumption that the people of Illinois felt the same in the summer of 1847 as they had a year earlier was mistaken. The antiwar spirit that had moved Richard Yates was on the rise, even in the pro-war West. Yates hardly would have dared question the war otherwise.

.   .   .

Abraham Lincoln would not have made the same mistake as his traveling companion. He knew there was a change in the air.

It started long before the funeral. David Davis commented on the decline in war spirit in Illinois in December 1846: "Everyone around here was anxious to enlist in June last. Nothing was before the eyes of the young men then but the 'pomp and circumstance' of war. Now the drums might beat for a week & not a single man fall into line." Martial ardor cooled as the war dragged on, scores of volunteers died of disease, and reports of bad behavior on the front diminished the glory of volunteering. Recruiting meetings began to be met with indifference, or worse. When opponents of the war turned out for a "war meeting" in Chicago in February 1847, they vigorously debated the virtues of the war with the military speakers who hoped to drum up enlistment. A correspondent for the antislavery Liberty Party reported that one audience member introduced a resolution "declaring that all war is sinful and anti-Christian," while another "made some very sensible remarks on the iniquity of the war, notwithstanding a wild buffalo of a fellow attempted to bellow him down." The few recruits convinced to volunteer "made the tour of the grog shops before retiring to rest," the journalist reported. "One of them showed his bravery by kicking a small boy who happened to stand in his way. By the time he gets to Mexico he may be prepared to kill women and children. So much for volunteering in Chicago."[35]

It was obvious in the spring of 1847 that the new recruits were less impressive in terms of their character and accomplishments than the first men to turn out had been. One letter writer declared them to be "young and ignorant, some of them are utterly abandoned and worthless." Fifty "raw" recruits waiting to descend the Mississippi from Peru, Illinois, were so "excessively noisy and drunk" that a steamship captain refused to let them on board. As the twelve-month volunteers returned to Illinois in the summer of 1847, apathy toward the war turned into something closer to distaste.[36]

The returning volunteers, for the most part, looked terrible, even their officers. William Weatherford, who succeeded Hardin as colonel of the First Illinois, appeared on the streets of Jacksonville the week of Hardin's funeral, "very much emaciated by sickness, and darker colored than most Indians." His shirt was dirty, his pants "worn through in holes," and his shoes "nearly worn out." Worse yet, he seemed uninterested in conforming his appearance to the norms of civilized society. He wore his shirt "open in front, like a common frock coat," with no collar or necktie. The Boston reporter noted that descriptions "of the uncouth appearance of the Mexican

"Going to and Returning from Mexico." This antiwar cartoon, published in the popular New York humorous periodical Yankee Doodle *in late 1846, contrasts a new volunteer (who seems to be reconsidering his enlistment) with ragged and maimed soldiers returning from Mexico. Critiques of the appearance and behavior of the veterans were common by the summer of 1847, and many states struggled to fill their quotas of new volunteers.* Yankee Doodle *1, no. 6 (Nov. 14, 1846): 71.*

officers" hardly compared to "such a poverty-stricken and miserable specimen of a commander" as Lieutenant Colonel Weatherford.

What use did America have for such a "broken-down man, unfit for further service, and without much hope for the future"? The reporter predicted that "with scores of others in similar situations," Weatherford would probably become "a violent politician, an office-seeker and a demagogue." Critics of the war suggested that the returning veterans, corrupted by their military service, would, in turn, corrupt the political process.[37]

Lincoln had the opportunity of witnessing the growing antiwar sentiment in his state firsthand when one of Springfield's most eminent ministers, Albert Hale, of the Second Presbyterian Church, preached two sermons critiquing the war as "unjust" on the Sunday before John Hardin's funeral. Not content to simply elaborate on the waste of the war in human life, the "barbarous and inhuman cruelties" committed by both sides, and the "wicked" character of this war in particular, Hale also condemned the returning veterans. Those once upright and moral young men had returned to Illinois defiled. "When the war is over," Hale intoned, "the multitudes that remain—that have been schooled amidst its immoralities, its cruelties and its crimes—will operate, like a moral pestilence, over the length and breadth of the land."[38]

Albert Hale was a prominent figure in Springfield. Forty-seven years old, he had been educated at Yale, and moved to Illinois at the same time as Hardin and Lincoln in order to perform missionary work among the Sac, Fox, and Pottawatomie tribes. In 1839 he became pastor of Springfield's Second Presbyterian.[39]

But his sermons against the war did not sit well with many in the capital, and particularly not with the delegates to the constitutional convention who knew Hale from his official duties ministering to the assembly. All the delegates left for a week for Hardin's funeral immediately after Hale's sermons, but the controversy continued after their return. Lincoln and the delegates were back in Springfield on Monday morning, July 19, when Reverend Hale was scheduled to deliver a prayer to reopen the convention.

Hale's entrance into the convention hall was uneventful, but as he rose to the dais and began to address the assembly, he was interrupted with "hissing and clapping of hands" by a Democratic delegate outraged by Hale's critique of the war. Ignoring the outburst, Hale finished his prayer. The incensed delegate accosted Hale and, making sure he was clearly heard throughout the hall, warned the minister that "if he did not wish to be hurt, he must not come there again."[40]

The *Sangamo Journal* reported this exchange directly below a long article about John Hardin's funeral. The newspaper found the proceedings at the convention hall outrageous, "totally at variance with our free institutions," and a clear infringement on Hale's right to free speech, ultimately deciding to publish Hale's antiwar sermons in pamphlet form so that "the community may be able to form a correct opinion in the case." Starting in the summer of 1847, anyone in Illinois who wished to consider the "inequity" of the war needed only to pick up a copy of this pamphlet.[41]

Or they could simply read a newspaper. The embedded journalists traveling through Mexico with the army were, on the whole, as pro-war as any group in America. Most, if not all, felt antipathy for the people of Mexico, grounded in Americans' perceived racial superiority. William Tobey, the correspondent for the Philadelphia *North American,* traveled as a soldier with the Pennsylvania volunteers. He repeatedly informed his readers that they had no concept of how "different" the people of Mexico were from Americans. "The mass are ignorant, indolent, barbarous, treacherous and superstitious, given to thieving, cheating, [and] lying," he wrote. Sharing in

the day-to-day sufferings of U.S. troops, embedded journalists closely identified with them. Witnessing the results of Mexican resistance firsthand, the
dead bodies of U.S. soldiers killed by local guerrilla fighters, they were not
wholly unsympathetic to reprisals against the civilian population.[42]

And so at first they largely overlooked robberies, rapes, and even murders committed by soldiers. Reports of murders by American volunteers
that appeared in print in 1846 were generally drawn from letters written
home by enlisted men, and quite often only antislavery papers were willing
to print them. The *Ashtabula Sentinel* of Ohio claimed that not "a hundredth
part of the crimes committed by our troops are published, or ever come
to the knowledge of our people." A few journalists, including Christopher
Mason Haile, writing for the New Orleans *Picayune,* condemned the "dis-
reputable conduct" of some of the volunteers, including numerous "outrages against Mexican citizens" such as "robbing, assaulting the women,"
and breaking into houses. These offenses had been "too long neglected"
by the press, and Haile admitted it gave him "great pain" to condemn the
soldiers he traveled with.[43]

But by and large, antiwar reporting in the first year of the war was limited to abolitionist papers and mainstream Whig papers in New England.
This followed the model of war coverage set in the War of 1812. That war
was wildly unpopular in the Federalist stronghold of New England, the
region most likely to suffer economically from a disruption of trade with
England. Federalist papers in New England loudly opposed the War of 1812,
critiquing it in searing terms as an offensive war, thus immoral, and likely
to corrupt America's men by exposing them to the horrors of war.[44]

But Federalist papers outside New England were more circumspect.
Editors had to sell papers, and charges of disloyalty could have devastating
effects not only on sales but also on the health and welfare of the editors
themselves. When Baltimore's *Federal Republican* opposed the War of 1812
in the nation's most pro-war city, retribution was quick. A mob destroyed
the offices of the paper not once but twice over the course of the war, beating and torturing both the editor and his supporters. Federalist editors in
Savannah, Alexandria, Richmond, and New York City were also silenced by
the threat of mob action. Outside New England, opposition to the war was
viewed as treasonous.[45]

The Federalist Party was ultimately destroyed by its opposition to the
War of 1812, of course. While abolitionist papers such as William Lloyd Garrison's *Liberator* of Boston condemned the war with Mexico from its inception, Whig papers tended to be just as patriotic as Whig congressmen in

1846. Because of its economy, relatively strong antislavery sentiment, and Whig majority, New England continued to be the one region in which it was safe to express opposition to American war, whether against England in 1814, Native American tribes in the 1820s and 1830s, or Mexico in 1846, and mainstream Whig papers in New England proved more willing to oppose America's invasion of Mexico, and the behavior of U.S. troops, than papers elsewhere.

But by the summer of 1847, even hardened journalists from outside New England found themselves forced to report on and condemn American atrocities that left them questioning their assumptions about American morality. It appeared that "the harsh treatment and privations the men are subjected to soon make one callous to all but his own feelings and interests," one journalist explained.[46]

The February massacre at Agua Nueva, when the Arkansas Rackensackers killed at least twenty-five Mexican civilians in a cave, was a key turning point in the reporting of the war. Few soldiers who had witnessed the event and scalped corpses could refrain from discussing it, and some of those who died at Buena Vista, including John Hardin, described the murders in the final letters they ever wrote home. Nonetheless, the New Orleans *Picayune* originally dismissed General Santa Anna's report of the slaughter as "exaggeration." But when a correspondent to the *St. Louis Republican* reported the story in "horrible detail," the *Picayune* recanted and printed the *Republican* letter in full. "It is impossible to excuse the conduct of our volunteers on any plea of retaliation and it is wrong to conceal the facts of the case," the paper admitted. News of the "American atrocities" at Agua Nueva was reprinted from Milwaukee to Texas.[47]

The witness to the slaughter who wrote to the *St. Louis Republican* on Valentine's Day of 1847 concluded, "Let us no longer complain of Mexican barbarity—poor, degraded, 'priest ridden' as she is. *No act of inhuman cruelty, perpetrated by her most desperate robbers, can excel the work of yesterday, committed by our soldiery.*" As it became increasingly difficult to differentiate the barbarity of U.S. soldiers from that of the Mexican people, journalists wondered if perhaps the war really was degrading the American character. William Tobey wrote from Veracruz in April, "I daily witness painful spectacles of human degradation and selfishness that before seemed impossible to our nature." Reverend Hale's critique of the corrosive effect of the war on America's men was not so different from the reports that had been coming from Mexico for months.[48]

John E. Durivage, the correspondent for the New Orleans *Picayune* stationed with Taylor near Monterrey, was another embedded journalist whose

reporting changed over the course of the war. A Polk supporter with little
love for the Mexican people, he was initially highly defensive of American
actions. When two U.S. soldiers were "charged with having committed a
rape upon a Mexican female," Durivage was dismissive. "I hardly think it is
a possible case in this country, but the accused will be tried for the offense
nevertheless." Durivage never reported the outcome of the trial.[49]

But despite his unwillingness to believe that an American soldier would
rape a Mexican woman, he became increasingly concerned with the behavior of the troops. By April 1847, he too openly wondered at the "outrageous
barbarity" perpetrated "by persons calling themselves Americans." He
reported the "melancholy, incontrovertible fact" that another slaughter,
similar to that at Agua Nueva, had taken place in the town of Guadalupe.
"An American was shot two or three weeks ago, and his companions and
friends determined to revenge his death. Accordingly a party of a dozen or
twenty men visited the place and deliberately murdered twenty-four Mexicans. . . . Under pretext of revenging the death of a comrade, the inoffensive (for all we know) inhabitants of a rancho, who have been assured that
they should be respected and protected, have been willfully murdered in
cold blood." Durivage realized that "such foul deeds as these cannot but
be revolting to every good citizen," but he reported them anyway. And he
continued to report similar occurrences, such as the hanging of "upward
of forty Mexicans" by the Texas Rangers, which appeared in a Matamoros
paper in May. His final letters from Mexico openly discussed depredations
against Mexicans and the futile attempts of Taylor and other officers to keep
the volunteers in line.[50] These accounts, the prime source of war news, were
summarized and reprinted in papers across the country.

As the war dragged on, rumblings of protest began to spread. The fourteen congressmen who had voted against Polk's declaration of War in May
1846, including John Quincy Adams and Ohio's antislavery firebrand Joshua
Giddings, never ceased to speak out with vehemence against the war. Some
of the most explosive rhetoric emerged from the Senate. The spellbinding
fifty-two-year-old orator Thomas Corwin of Ohio shocked the nation when
he rose in the Senate in February and offered that "if I were a Mexican,
I would tell you, 'Have you not room in your country to bury your dead
men? If you come into mine we will greet you with bloody hands, and welcome you to hospitable graves.' "[51]

Polk considered his opponents guilty of treason, and said so in his annual
message to Congress six months into the war. "A more effectual means
could not have been devised," he warned, "to encourage the enemy and
protract the war than to advocate and adhere to their cause, and thus give

them 'aid and comfort.' " Polk's reduction of dissent to treason outraged many Americans, including some war supporters. The mobilized antislavery forces of New England were joined by increasing numbers of dissenters to "Mr. Polk's War." In February antiwar protesters held a mass meeting in Boston where Charles Sumner bitterly attacked Congressman Robert Winthrop for voting for the war. The Massachusetts legislature, which had already refused to outfit its volunteer regiment, declared in April that the war in Mexico was "so hateful in its objects, so wanton, unjust and unconstitutional in its origin," that it "must be regarded as a war against humanity."[52]

Henry David Thoreau spent a night in jail after refusing to pay his poll tax in protest against the war. He delivered a lecture titled "Civil Disobedience" calling for resistance against the government, which he declared had been "abused and perverted" in the service of war and slavery. "Witness the present Mexican war, the work of comparatively a few individuals using the standing government as their tool; for in the outset, the people would not have consented to this measure."[53] New England intellectuals such as James Russell Lowell and Ralph Waldo Emerson published trenchant critiques of the war.

The issue of slavery was not far from the surface of most of these critiques. Polk never wavered from citing Mexican aggression as the war's cause, and he insisted that the issue of slavery was irrelevant to the prosecution of the war. But when he submitted a request to Congress in August 1846 for two million dollars to negotiate a settlement with Mexico, it became clear to Congress that there would be no peace without territory. Most of that territory was coveted by slave owners. Northern Democrats were blindsided by the request. They had no interest in additional lands to the south, particularly after Polk's betrayal on Oregon.

Van Buren supporters in Congress, sick of Polk's dissimulations, lashed back. On the sweltering evening of August 8, a little-known Pennsylvania Democrat named David Wilmot gained the floor and introduced a rider to the bill banning slavery from any lands taken from Mexico. The Wilmot Proviso passed the House along strictly sectional lines but stalled in the Senate, where southerners had an advantage in numbers. Reintroduced in February 1847, it again passed in the House and stalled in the Senate.[54]

By the middle of 1847, it was clear to virtually everyone in America that the spread of slavery was intimately connected with the resolution of the war. In September, a "Captain of the Volunteers" stationed in California published a scathing indictment of Polk's war based on his personal knowledge of the administration's diplomatic and military efforts to gain California. His account argued not only that "the present administration . . . have acted with a design to" annex "the territories of the Californias, Sonora, Chihuahua, and New Mexico . . . a measure as fraught with evil to ourselves as unjust to the inhabitants of Mexico," but also that "the whole course of the administration" had been ordered to "insure" the possession of "the country of Mexico to the slaveholders of the South." New England antislavery activists had been repeating this accusation for over a year. The Wilmot controversy allowed more moderate Americans, including men in uniform, to see that they had been right.[55]

Walt Whitman, the editor of the *Brooklyn Daily Eagle*, was initially an enthusiastic supporter of the war, proclaiming that Mexico should be "thoroughly chastised." His support for the Wilmot Proviso led him to revise his views by the summer of 1847. In September he published an editorial, "American Workingmen, Versus Slavery," that framed his support for the proviso in both sectional and class terms, starkly contrasting the interests of the "workingmen," with whom Whitman identified, and slave owners. "If either the slaves themselves, or their owners, had fought or paid for or gained this new territory," he wrote, "there would be some reason in the pro-slavery claims" to Mexican territory. "But every body knows that the cost and work come, forty-nine fiftieths of it, upon the free men." Whitman's antislavery views, not shared by the paper's conservative Democratic owner, got him fired from the *Daily Eagle*. By arguing that the interests of workingmen and slave owners were opposed, Whitman learned that the interests of the Democratic Party and justice might well be opposed too.[56]

With the exception of Free-Soil advocates such as Whitman, Democratic editors and their papers continued to wholeheartedly support the president and his war. America's popular culture, which enthusiastically embraced the war at the outset, continued to celebrate both American Manifest Destiny and the valor of the American soldier in the months after Wilmot's proviso was introduced. Urban taverns rang with pro-war drinking songs, marching bands played "General Taylor's Quick Step" and other military airs, and readers devoured paperback accounts of "the success of American arms" and "Mexican treacheries and cruelties." Even the citizens of antiwar Boston willingly paid twenty-five cents a person (children under twelve were half price) to visit "Donnavan's Grand Serial Panorama of Mexico, delineating the Scenery, Towns, Cities, and Battle Fields" in spacious Boylston Hall.[57]

A casual observer could be excused for assuming that America was united in support of war, but many Americans were perplexed and angry. Antiwar

198 A WICKED WAR

petitions to Congress appeared from around the country, including Illinois, and no longer just from areas of antislavery strength. Whig newspapers from Maine to South Carolina asked when the war would end, what would happen to Mexico, and why the war had been begun in the first place. "We believe the public sober sense of the nation never desired war," a North Carolina newspaper stated in May. That same month a rising politician in Ohio wrote to his brother, Lieutenant William T. Sherman, stationed in Mexico, "There is no doubt that a large majority of the people consider it an unjust aggression upon a weak republic, excused by false reason, and continued solely for the acquisition of slave territory."[58]

Evidence of this view was clear around the country. Jane Swisshelm of Pittsburgh was just twenty-one years old when the United States declared war on Mexico. She was a deeply religious young woman, and already convinced that slavery was wrong. Although it was common for antislavery women to publish anonymous letters, Swisshelm's opposition to the U.S.-Mexican War, which she viewed as a natural outgrowth of slavery, convinced her to go further. In 1846 she openly published a series of scathing editorials against the war in a local Pittsburgh paper, a radical move for a woman at the time.

Swisshelm also refused to shake the hand of an old friend just returned to Pittsburgh after volunteering to fight Mexico. When the volunteer asked if it was "possible" that she would not take his hand, Swisshelm looked into "his manly, handsome face" and told him, "There is blood on it: the blood of women and children slain at their own altars, on their own hearthstones, that you might spread the glorious American institutions of woman-whipping and baby-stealing."[59]

Rebecca Gratz, a sixty-seven-year-old philanthropist in Philadelphia, wrote her sister-in-law, "I feel so much more sorrow & disgust, than heroism in this war. . . . When we were obliged to fight for our liberty—and rights—there was motive & glory in the strife—but to invade a country and slaughter its inhabitants—to fight for boundary—or political supremacy—is altogether against my principles and feelings." A doctor's wife in Pennsylvania declared that through "wicked deception" by Polk, "this war has carried Sorrow and dismay into every portion of our Country." After witnessing a military funeral for a local soldier in April 1847, a woman in Boston wrote in her diary that "our nation must be cursed for so unrighteous and needless a war. 'There really is a God who judgeth and will avenge.' " A man in rural Massachusetts was so enraged by the war that he suggested to his cousin in Vermont that "the best thing the free states can do is to withdraw from the slave states and establish a free government." He would just as soon "let the slave states support the accursed slave system alone."[60]

Not even Sarah Polk was immune from attack. A Massachusetts newspaper condemned her as a hypocrite who, despite "her piety . . . lov[ed] most cordially all plunder, robbery, murder, and every other sport for the sake of slavery." But James K. Polk came in for special abuse. Emily Huse, a wife and mother in the Wisconsin Territory, bemoaned the war in a letter in September 1847 to a female friend. "Was there ever the like of that Mexican War? Horrid butcherys—Mexico is harder metal than Polk thought." Huse's husband had recently learned that three local men were killed in the war, and as a result was unable to sleep. He told his wife that he "wishes President Polk dead. Pity he hadn't died 3 or 4 years ago."[61]

From his camp near Monterrey, Zachary Taylor was thinking similar thoughts. "A report has reached here that President Polk was dead, which, I do not credit," he wrote his son-in-law. But "while I regret to hear of the death of any one," he admitted, "I would as soon have heard of his death . . . as that of any other individual in the whole Union."[62]

10

War Measures

WHAT POLK FOUND most galling about the cacophony of voices raised against him was that the news from the front was good, remarkably so, and yet he received none of the acclaim. He complained to his cabinet and his diary about "the injustice of giving all the credit of our victories to the commanding General," and none to the regulars, volunteers, or commander in chief. Even so, he thought, it should have been apparent to everyone that matters in Mexico were progressing nicely.[1] General Scott was on the move, the Mexican army was on the defensive, and the plan to take the capital was falling into place.

Scott, like Cortés before him, had stormed Veracruz during Holy Week. Not long afterward, Manuel G. Zamorg, a major in the national guard of Veracruz, bemoaned the fact that "the Conquest of Mexico, to judge from present indications, was far harder to Cortez in 1521 than it is to the Yankees in 1847. What a miserable reflection!" Scott set off for Mexico City after securing Veracruz in April. He understood that there was no time to rest, or to lose sleep over the collateral damage. The troops needed to reach higher ground to stave off yellow fever, and General Santa Anna was on his way.[2]

Santa Anna had been kept busy by affairs in the capital. After marching back from Buena Vista, he quelled a rebellion in Mexico City, reestablished order, and promised the people of Mexico that he would defeat the invaders. Three days after news of the fall of Veracruz reached Mexico City, he was marching toward the coast with an army of twelve thousand. He

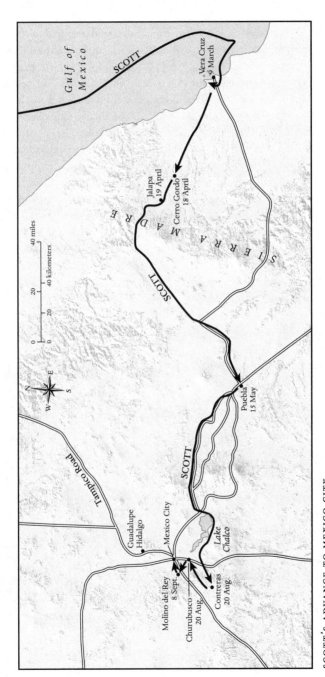

SCOTT'S ADVANCE TO MEXICO CITY

established headquarters near his summer estate and prepared to crush the Americans at a mountain pass called Cerro Gordo on the road to the capital.

When Scott's troops arrived at Cerro Gordo they found an impenetrable Mexican defensive line spanning two miles from the bank of a river across the pass and over two hills. "The hights of Cero Gordo looked almost as imposable to take as the hights of Gibralter," one soldier wrote home. Scott sent his engineers to search for a solution. Captain Robert E. Lee proved the hero of the day when he discovered a mountain path around Santa Anna's position. On April 18, the two armies battled on the road, and a portion of U.S. troops secretly moved around the Mexican left flank. They emerged in the rear of the enemy, causing instant confusion. As the Mexican troops began to flee, Santa Anna found himself face-to-face with Edward Baker's Fourth Illinois Volunteers. He barely escaped with his life and had to leave behind in his carriage $18,000 in gold, a lunch of roast chicken, and the artificial leg he wore after battling the French in the Pastry War nine years earlier. The men of Illinois turned over the gold, ate the chicken, and brought the leg back home with them.[3]

The battle lasted only a few hours. It was a decisive victory, and while no Buena Vista, it finally brought the volunteers some measure of the glory

"*Capture of Gen. Santa Anna's Private Carriage at Battle of Cerro Gordo, April 18, 1847.*" *Edward Baker's Fourth Illinois Volunteers had the good luck to capture Santa Anna's artificial leg during the battle. They brought the leg back to Illinois as a trophy of war, and it now resides at the Illinois State Military Museum.* J. Jacob Oswandel, *Notes of the Mexican War, 1846–47–48* (Philadelphia, 1885), 131.

they craved. "The American heart is again made to swell and throb with the emotions of joy and national pride and exultation, over another and not less glorious achievement of our indomitable army," the New Orleans *Delta* proclaimed. But it was a bloody battle. Writing in his journal that evening, a Pennsylvania volunteer reported seeing "no less than fifty dead Mexicans all on one pile . . . Some groaning. It was enough to move the strongest heart. . . . Although our enemy's[,] yet as an American I could not help having that sympathy which all soldiers should have for one or other especially when wounded in defense of their country."[4] The following day Scott continued the push forward toward the capital. Mexico's president issued an edict calling on the men of the region to form irregular units and drive the invaders back to Vera Cruz. A light corps of mounted lancers could, it was hoped, achieve what the army could not. Mexico embraced guerrilla warfare.[5]

Among the most tenacious soldiers fighting for Mexico were the U.S. deserters who made up the San Patricio (or St. Patrick's) Battalion. Desertions had been a problem for the U.S. Army since Taylor first entered Texas, particularly among the 40 percent of the regular army who were recent immigrants. Raised in foreign cultures, many immigrants looked at America's fantasy of Manifest Destiny with skepticism, if not outright hostility. One Prussian volunteer from Ohio, Otto Birkel, noted in his diary that "the Founding Fathers of the [American] Republic were right to . . . recommend the strongest neutrality in all world affairs to their grandsons; but these grandsons thought themselves wiser, and now there is talk of uniting the entire continent of North and South America into one enormous state." While anyone who had traveled through Europe "can very well see the madness of these plans," in the United States "the majority of the people . . . do not doubt the possibility of the undertaking, and are supported . . . by countless demagogues."[6]

Furthermore, while a significant proportion of immigrant soldiers were Catholic, the officers, for the most part, were Protestant, and the army reflected the virulent anti-Catholicism of American society in the 1840s. Anti-Catholic riots were common events in northeastern cities in the 1830s and 1840s. Just two years before the start of the war, objections by Catholics to the use of the King James Bible in public schools led to a major riot in Philadelphia and a national conversation about the place of Catholicism in America. There were plenty of soldiers who claimed "that the present war is favored by the Almighty, because it will be the means of eradicating Papacy, and extending the benefits of Protestantism." Catholic immigrants found it difficult to abide by some of the army's rules. Soldiers of all faiths were advised, or compelled, to attend the Protestant services offered by the army chaplain. They were often banned from attending Catholic mass. Not surprisingly, they had trouble justifying a war waged on fellow Catholics.[7]

Mexicans recognized their quandary. From the opening shots of the war, the nation encouraged desertions with promises of respect, public assistance, and eventual land grants. In June 1847, Juan Soto, governor of Veracruz, distributed a handbill, in both Spanish and English, that appealed to "Catholic Irish, Frenchmen, and German[s] of the invading army!" It stated, "The American nation makes a most unjust war to the Mexicans and has taken all of you as an instrument of their iniquity. You must not fight against a religious people, nor should you be seen in the ranks of those who proclaim *slavery of mankind* as a constitutive principle. The religious man . . . is not on the part of those who desire to be the lords of the world, robbing properties and territories which do not belong to them and shedding so much blood." Deserters would not be alone; "many of your former companions fight now content in our ranks. After this war is over, the magnanimous and generous Mexican nation will duly appreciate the services rendered, and you shall remain with us, cultivating our fertile lands. Catholic Irish, French, and German!! Long live liberty!! Long live our holy Religion!!" Two months later, Santa Anna issued a similar circular promising land and equality to American soldiers.[8]

More than a few Catholics found appeals like these persuasive, and decided to switch their allegiance. Under the leadership of a tall, blue-eyed Irishman named John Reilly, who deserted from Taylor's camp across the Rio Grande from Matamoros, 150 former U.S. soldiers became one of Santa Anna's greatest weapons, experts at operating the artillery that the U.S. Army employed with crushing effectiveness. Fighting under a shamrock-festooned flag, with promises of land and glory as a reward for their service, the St. Patrick's battalion knew that surrender to the United States was the equivalent of death. Although many members of the battalion were recent immigrants from Europe and not American citizens, the U.S. Army considered them all traitors.

The road north from Cerro Gordo passed through miles of jungle full of musical birds of all hues. A Pennsylvania volunteer declared it "the prettiest country that I have yet seen . . . like the Garden of Eden more than anything I can compare it to." Scott spent the first half of May in Jalapa, a scenic town of gardens and orange groves. The troops delighted in the temperate climate four thousand feet above Veracruz. Everything is "neat and clean," wrote a volunteer, "not only the streets and houses but also the citizens." It reminded many volunteers of home, and inspired fantasies of Americanization. One volunteer found it "easy to imagine ourselves in some thriving Yankee town." Another was "astonished as well as delighted to see such an intelligent set of people. I did not think that there was such people in all Mexico judging from those I had seen before. Business is done here in a neat and Yankee style. The females are beauty's they cannot be beat."[9]

But perhaps the similarity of Jalapa to the United States exacerbated their homesickness, for what most of the twelve-month volunteers imagined was being back in the United States. They were sick of Mexico. Carl von Grone, a Prussian serving with Scott, wrote to his brother in Germany that "the numerous thieving riff-raff" among the volunteers "committed the most shameless acts of depravity on a daily basis" in Jalapa, "including the robbing of women on open streets, thefts in their accommodations, break-ins, robbing of churches and so on."[10] Their enlistments were almost up, and despite Scott's entreaties and the recent victory at Cerro Gordo, virtually none of them wanted to continue fighting. As Colonel Pierce M. Butler, commander of the South Carolina volunteers, wrote to the governor of his state, "The contest is unequal and the service an inglorious one. The universal voice of the Army, Navy, and Volunteers, is for terminating this contest, and peace would be to them the most welcome news." Their terms of service over, the regiments left Mexico in droves, and American papers sought to justify their unwillingness to continue fighting.

The Milledgeville, Georgia, *Recorder* turned to John Hardin's memory for help. It claimed that the "universal" desire of the soldiers to come home was shared by "the heroic Col. Hardin, in a letter received at Washington just previous to his lamented fall." John Hardin had again become the unlikely spokesman for ending the war, having, in fact, written Senator Douglas just before his death asking for the chance to ship out to Veracruz, and stating that if he could not, he saw no point in continuing in the army.[11]

Scott's troops had had their battle and were now ready to return home with what they considered to be honor. Their honor was derived from participating in a fight, not from conquering Mexico or seeing the march through to its end. Few were as lucky as Colonel Edward Baker's Fourth Illinois, who returned to the United States not only with honor but with Santa Anna's artificial leg as well.

This left Scott deep in Mexican territory with less than eight thousand soldiers, three thousand of whom were incapacitated by illness. In mid-May he moved on to Puebla, halfway between Veracruz and Mexico City. The second-largest city in Mexico, Puebla impressed the troops with its scenic mountain setting, cathedral, tremendous bullfighting stadium, and "fine large stores." Scott's remaining forces spent ten trying weeks in Puebla over the summer of 1847, waiting for the arrival of reinforcements. Morale was low and the soldiers were continually harassed by irregular troops. William Tobey, writing for the Philadelphia *North American*, reported that thirty soldiers had been murdered by guerrilla partisans, whom Americans called "rancheros," since leaving Veracruz, "and they will hang on our skirts and continue to kill stragglers." Six Illinois volunteers were killed in three days.[12]

To the men of the army, the fault for all of this was clear. Polk was not supporting the troops. Scott asked for more soldiers, and Polk hadn't granted them. Tobey, writing explicitly from a "Loco Foco," or northern Democratic perspective, condemned Polk and the "quack warriors at Washington" for the halt in operations. Polk failed to send reinforcements in a timely manner, despite Scott's "warning advice," because of political resentment against the Whig general. The Polk administration's "power was fast crumbling and falling away, and though they could not arrest their own downfall," Tobey explained, they "would not consent to see others rise above them." As for the " 'right or wrong' supporters of Mr. Polk," the "brother democrats who have not yet discovered who James K. Polk is," Tobey assured them that "I do not know a democrat in the whole army, regular or volunteer, who does not execrate the man and his war measures."[13]

One of the "war measures" causing Scott particular irritation was Nicholas Trist. Trist arrived in Veracruz on May 6, well after Scott's departure. He carried with him two pistols (one of which was quickly stolen), the treaty, and a burning ambition to bring the war to a close. He was almost immediately stricken with the diarrhea that was plaguing the troops, and when he caught up with the army in Jalapa he was too ill to meet with Scott in person. Instead, while high on the large quantities of morphine he was "obliged to take . . . to save [his] life," Trist sent Scott a packet of papers. Included within them were an official letter asserting Trist's authority to negotiate a treaty and a letter to the Mexican foreign minister, which Trist ordered the general to deliver to the Mexican authorities.[14]

This was a mistake. Scott knew full well that Polk was doing all in his power to find a Democratic general to replace him. Polk had proposed that Congress create the position of lieutenant general so that he could elevate Thomas Hart Benton to a position outranking both his Whig generals. Congress demurred, which left Scott in charge but furious. And before Trist's arrival in Mexico, Scott had received "reliable information from Washington" about Trist's "well-known prejudice against me." This usurpation of military authority by a common clerk was too much for Scott to bear. Trist had the authority to negotiate a treaty, but surely not to issue commands to the commanding general. He refused to comply with what Trist insisted were the president's orders. Outraged by Scott's response, a drugged Trist began an imperious thirteen-page letter by candlelight that night in his tent. He bragged to his wife about the dressing-down he delivered to Scott: "If I have not demolished him, then I give up."[15]

Scott was not demolished, but he was angry. He moved on to Puebla without so much as speaking to Trist. But he was not one to step back calmly from an insult. Trist's letter was a "farrago of insolence, conceit, and arrogance," hardly the words of a gentleman, and Scott would have nothing to do with the so-called diplomat. Trist wrote his wife that Scott was an "imbecile" of "bitter selfishness and egregious vanity." And then he forwarded copies of his correspondence with Scott to the State Department. Scott, who was just as convinced as Trist that he was dealing with a particularly unreasonable individual, also wrote to Washington. Buchanan and Polk were astounded by the correspondence, particularly after Scott threatened to resign his post on account of "the total want of support and sympathy on the part of the war department." Trist was the last straw, Scott wrote. He couldn't be expected to conduct critical military operations with "such a flank battery planted against me" as this commissioner.[16]

Polk was tempted to accept Scott's resignation, and had there been a remotely capable Democratic general waiting in the wings, he would have done so. "The truth is that I have been compelled from the beginning to conduct the war against Mexico through the agency of two Gen'ls highest in rank who have not only no sympathies with the Government, but are hostile to my administration." All the good generals were Whigs, and Congress refused to do anything about it. He declined Scott's resignation and watched as the feud escalated. Privately, Buchanan reassured Trist that the administration supported him. In July and August, reinforcements in the form of new recruits finally arrived in Puebla, and Scott was ready to move on to the capital.[17]

Santa Anna, in the meantime, had recovered from his humiliation at Cerro Gordo. In the face of taunts and harassment on the streets of Mexico City, he reasserted his powers as dictator over the Mexican Congress and began organizing a defense of the city. Announcing to the people that he would fight a "war without pity unto death," he constructed fortifications around Mexico City and concentrated twenty-five thousand troops at three vulnerable points around the city.[18]

On August 7, the fourteen thousand men under Scott's command began their final seventy-five-mile march to Mexico City. As they crested a mountain pass, they looked down on the Valley of Mexico. Many were overcome with emotion. Illinois colonel George Moore, a good friend of John Hardin's, was one of the few twelve-month volunteers who reenlisted, despite his growing doubts about the war. He later wrote that the war "left a reproach upon" the United States "which ages upon ages will fail to remove." But in 1847 the view from ten thousand feet amply repaid his decision to stay on as an aide-de-camp. "A full and unobstructed view of the peerless valley or basin of Mexico, with its lakes and plains, hills and mountains, burst upon our astonished sight, presenting a scene of matchless prospective that would bid defiance to the pencil of the most gifted landscape painter." The troops then descended, intent on capturing a fortified city of two hundred thousand, surrounded by marshland, lakes, and a lava bed. And there was no retreat. The route back to Veracruz was riddled with murderous Mexican rancheros who wished them dead. The Duke of Wellington, watching events unfold from his lofty perch in England, declared that "Scott is lost—he cannot capture the city and he cannot fall back upon his base."[19]

It was the final stage of the American military plan, and it proved to be the bloodiest fighting of the war. As at Cerro Gordo, Captain Robert E. Lee discovered a route around the concentrated Mexican forces. This one led directly through a lava badland more than three miles wide. The Battle of Contreras on August 19 was a hard-fought struggle between evenly matched forces over jagged lava rock. Santa Anna was on the verge of crushing the Americans but pulled back abruptly, as he had at Buena Vista, taking a portion of the best soldiers off to defend the gates of the city. He missed another opportunity for victory.

That evening a cold, heavy rain began to fall, and troops on both sides spent a miserable night on the field. On the morning of August 20, desperate U.S. troops, braving lightning and pouring rain, divided their forces. They attacked the remaining Mexican troops from two directions and routed the enemy in minutes of fighting.

Scott had opened up a road to Mexico City. They marched into Churubusco, a small village of whitewashed adobe houses with red tile roofs and colorful bougainvillea vines. There they met Santa Anna. The Mexican troops, with the San Patricio battalion manning the artillery, fought valiantly on the muddy ground at the monastery convent of San Mateo. The San Patricios repeatedly tore flags of surrender out of the hands of their Mexican comrades, knowing that surrender meant death for their treason, but by the end of the afternoon Scott's forces had prevailed. The U.S. Army was now only three miles from Mexico City. Santa Anna had lost a third of his troops over the previous few days. The U.S. Army sustained a thousand casualties.

Seventy-two of the San Patricios captured by the U.S. Army were tried in two courts-martial. Seventy were initially sentenced to death by hanging, but Scott pardoned five and reduced the sentences of fifteen to jail, fifty lashes, and branding of the letter *D* for deserter. John Reilly, who had deserted before the war began, was one of the sixteen who were whipped and branded. Sixteen of the captured men were hanged soon after trial, a spectacle that both Mexicans and Americans found "revolting." The remaining thirty awaited execution.[20]

The last stand of Santa Anna's forces was at a line of interior defenses. Both armies were battered, and Scott's troops were in no position to continue fighting. On August 24, Scott and Santa Anna agreed to an armistice for the purposes of opening negotiations. When an American wagon train entered Mexico City under the flag of truce in order to pick up supplies, it was attacked by the populace. Santa Anna did nothing to quell the riot. On September 6, the Mexican government formally terminated the armistice, and Santa Anna issued a proclamation to the residents of the capital that he would "preserve your altars from infamous violation, and your daughters and your wives from the extremity of insult."[21]

Scott still had to capture two fortified positions, a mass of stone buildings called Molino del Rey, and the imposing Chapultepec Castle half a mile to the east. General Worth attacked the Molino at dawn on September 8 in a frontal assault with his whole division. Worth's hope that the mill was deserted proved to be mistaken, and Mexican artillery rained down on the Americans. It was the bloodiest battle of the war, as the infantry struggled and failed to storm the buildings and a sharp clash between rival cavalry decimated both sides. One column of Scott's forces lost eleven of its fourteen officers, and reports circulated among the men that Mexican soldiers had slit the throats of wounded Americans. U.S. troops continued the assault, however, and eventually battered down a gate leading into the buildings. They continued fighting, room to room, until their opponent eventually withdrew. The Mexicans suffered two thousand casualties, and seven hundred Americans fell.[22]

Four days later, Scott's artillery began to bombard Chapultepec Castle. He had seven thousand remaining troops. The castle once had been the residence of Spanish royalty but was currently occupied by a Mexican military school. The following morning, September 13, the guns began firing at dawn, for two hours. Then the Americans began to scale the castle walls. They found that six of the military cadets, all teenagers, refused to fall back even after the Mexican army retreated. According to legend, one of them wrapped himself in the Mexican flag and jumped to his death in order to prevent the flag's capture. In the aftermath of the defeat, *los niños héroes* were venerated by the people of Mexico.

The Battle of Chapultepec produced lasting heroes for Mexico but a crucial victory for the United States. As the victorious U.S. forces raised the American flag over the castle, the thirty remaining San Patricios were publicly executed in a mass hanging, despite pleas for clemency by priests, politicians, and "respectable ladies" of Mexico City. It left a "terrible impression" on the people of Mexico.[23]

Scott pushed forward to the walls of Mexico City, and after a loss of another nine hundred men, he took control of one of the city gates. Santa Anna found it impossible to hold the city, and fled with his army toward the northern suburb of Guadalupe Hidalgo. A delegation from Mexico City approached Scott's headquarters under a flag of truce and surrendered the city. At 7:00 a.m. on September 14, the American flag was raised in the capital, and General Scott, in his most elaborate uniform, rode proudly into the city to the cheers of his men and the terror of the civilian residents. According to twenty-nine-year-old Mexico City poet and journalist Guillermo Prieto, "demons, with flaming hair" and "swollen faces, noses like embers" roamed through the city, desecrating churches and turning houses "upside down."[24]

Military operations should have been over that day. Scott had conquered the Mexican capital after a dramatic series of military victories. But neither the people nor the government of Mexico were willing to negotiate. The army had no one to blame but itself for the Mexicans' intransigence. Despite the best intentions of most of the officers, when it came to "conquering a peace," U.S. troops were their own worst enemies. Northeastern Mexico was marked by "devastation, ruin, conflagration, death, and other depredations" committed by Taylor's men against the region's "inoffensive inhabitants." One Mexican general wrote Taylor directly in May 1847 to learn if

"General Scott Entering Mexico City, 1851." Carl Nebel captures the tension of General Scott's entrance into Mexico City's grand plaza on September 14, 1847. Dragoons cluster around Scott, protecting him from harm, while cannons face the square, ready to fend off attackers. A stone-throwing Mexican in the lower left and armed men on the roof make clear that the United States may have captured the capital but has hardly won the hearts and minds of its inhabitants. George Wilkins Kendall and Carl Nebel, *The War Between the United States and Mexico Illustrated, Embracing Pictorial Drawings of All the Principal Conflicts* (New York: D. Appleton, 1851), plate 12.

the U.S. Army intended to follow the laws of nations and fight in a civilized manner or continue to engage in warfare "as it is waged by savage tribes between each other."[25] Decades of Indian Wars had left their mark on U.S. combat.

With a stubborn enemy refusing to surrender, Scott's troops settled into a lengthy occupation. Volunteers, drunk on stolen liquor, committed rape and murdered unarmed civilians, and soldiers were in turn murdered on a daily basis. The two countries seemed no closer to a peace treaty than when Taylor had first crossed the Rio Grande. Bands of guerrilla rancheros formed and launched merciless attacks on Scott's men. At least twenty-five express riders, attempting to get news from central Mexico to Veracruz, were captured and killed, wounded, or tortured by Mexican guerrillas.[26] The war that was going to be over as soon as it began now seemed endless.

Yet suddenly, after two months of squabbling, Trist and Scott were on good terms with each other. After some initial attempts at negotiating without Scott's help, Trist realized that he needed the general on his side. Scott, also anxious for peace, reached a similar conclusion. Nicholas Trist was the only man in Mexico who could officially negotiate a treaty. When Trist again fell ill, Scott sent him a get-well note, a jar of guava jelly, and an invitation to move to his own much more comfortable lodgings for the period of his recovery. All three were gratefully accepted.

The two men discovered that they had more in common than they ever would have imagined, not the least of which was a belief that the war should be brought to a conclusion as quickly as possible. Each man wrote to Washington in order to take back the nasty things he had said about the other. Scott called Trist "able, discreet, courteous, and amiable," and asked that "all I have heretofore written . . . about Mr. Trist, should be suppressed." He regretted the "pronounced misunderstanding" and assured the administration that since the end of June his communication with the diplomat had been "frequent and cordial." Scott attributed the "offensive character" of Trist's earlier letters to the effects of morphine. Trist also asked that his insulting letters about Scott be stricken from memory; "justice" demanded that his previous letters be withdrawn from public view.[27]

Perhaps not surprisingly, given this chain of events, Secretary of War William Marcy had a nervous breakdown. In late August, he retreated from Washington for a monthlong recovery. In the meantime, the rapprochement between the general and diplomat became a friendship as the two men happily spent hours discussing literature, politics, and, above all else, the prospects for peace in Mexico. Trist had discovered Scott to be "affectionate, generous, forgiving and a lover of justice," he happily wrote his wife. This development was more disturbing to Polk than their previous argument. Scott, it was clear, could not be trusted. A friendship between him and Trist could only lead to trouble.[28]

So while there was ample reason for celebration, and plenty of ecstatic commemoration after the fall of Mexico City, for the most part matters were not going much better for James K. Polk than for the soldiers stationed in Mexico. The threat of guerrilla attack was one that Polk could fully identify with. His Democratic coalition had shattered over the Wilmot Proviso, and Democrats had lost control of the House of Representatives. Whigs would control the House when the Thirtieth Congress was seated in early December. The "growing unpopularity of the war" was news in London. Voices of protest against the war increased as the occupation dragged on through the fall, while at the same time a growing minority of Democratic expansionists began pushing for the annexation of the whole of Mexico as spoils of war. At a mass meeting in New York in support of annexing the entirety of Mexico, Sam Houston, the former president of the Republic of Texas, proclaimed the full "continent" a "birth-right" of the United States. "Assuredly as to-morrow's sun will rise and pursue its bright course along the firmament of heaven, so certain it appears to my mind, must the Anglo Saxon race pervade . . . throughout the whole rich empire of this great hemisphere." He was met with "great cheers" and cries of "annex it all" from the audience. The *New York Herald* assured readers that once annexed, Mexico, "like the Sabine virgins," "will soon learn to love her ravisher."[29]

Polk was sympathetic to Houston's vision, but the All-Mexico Movement, as it was known, did nothing to improve the prospects of peace. And peace, above all else, was what Polk dreamed about—on the rare occasions when he slept, that is. The vitriol and controversy combined with his ceaseless labor took an increasing toll on his fragile health. Night after night Sarah pleaded with him to stop work and come to bed, while members of his inner circle noted his "shortened and enfeebled step, and the air of languor and exhaustion which sat upon him."[30] Yet Polk kept going. What he needed was peace with honor, and as much of Mexico as he could take with it.

II

Duty and Justice

POLK'S FETISH for secrecy was open knowledge. But generally speaking, what he chose to hide remained hidden. The president, therefore, had every confidence that Nicholas Trist's assignment would remain a "profound secret." Commissioner Plenipotentiary Trist traveled as a special agent so that Polk could bypass the Senate, and he was paid out of the president's private funds. He adopted an alias, "Dr. Tarreau," a French merchant, so as to avert suspicion. And Trist was known for his discretion; Andrew Jackson had vouched for it.[1]

This mission was strictly classified. In the president's view, it was no one's business that he was making overtures for peace to a despised and diminished Mexico. Publicity could only bring criticism, both from the extremists in his own party and from the Whigs, who were clearly in the ascendancy. "The success of Trist's mission," he wrote in his diary, "must depend mainly on keeping it a secret from that portion of the Federal [Whig] press & leading men in the country who, since the commencement of the war with Mexico, have been giving 'aid and comfort' to the enemy by their course." With luck, Trist would be home, treaty in hand, before the hostile Thirtieth Congress was seated at the start of December. Until then, "the strictest injunctions of Secrecy" must be followed.[2]

But within three days of Trist's departure from Washington, the *New York Herald* disclosed both the details of Trist's mission and the terms of the proposed treaty, "with remarkable accuracy and particularity." Polk fumed to his diary, "I have not been more vexed or excited since I have been president." Worst of all, he had no idea whom to blame for the "treachery."[3] He suspected the secretary of state, whose ambitions for the presidency had positively crippled his objectivity and ability to do his job. Buchanan, in turn, pointed to Virginia Trist. Perhaps Trist himself was to blame.

It was impossible to determine who was at fault. The leaks continued. Just days after Trist "fetched up, to use a seaman's phrase, at Vera Cruz," his journey was so well publicized that Trist's own family and friends looked "to the newspapers" to learn of his progress. "He writes but seldom," Trist's brother wrote to Virginia, but "I see enough about him in the news papers."[4]

Soon the very pretense of secrecy appeared futile to virtually everyone except Polk. The embedded journalists spoke openly of Trist's movements, as did the press and common soldiers in Mexico. Whig newspapers accused Polk of sending Trist to Mexico in order to "spy" on General Scott or otherwise undermine his operations. And before the end of the year, both Trist and his peace treaty appeared as the subplot of popular author Charles Averill's *The Mexican Ranchero; or, The Maid of the Chapparal: A Romance of the Mexican War*. The pulp novelette was available for purchase for twenty-five cents at "periodical depots" throughout the United States and Canada, as well as from wholesale agents in cities throughout the Midwest and along the eastern seaboard. The "trade" was of course furnished with a "liberal discount."[5]

From a pro-war perspective there were worse places for Nicholas Trist to land, although Polk probably didn't see it that way. *The Mexican Ranchero* was one of the better works in the healthy genre of sensationalistic war fiction. Cheap potboilers printed on rough paper with eye-catching covers, war novelettes placed fictional characters in real battles and featured plenty of sex, violence, heroism, and racial stereotyping. A large audience of readers who appreciated convoluted plotting and nonstop action consumed them voraciously, particularly urban working men. *The Mexican Ranchero*, like many of its genre, featured romance between a white American soldier and a light-skinned Mexican woman. This romance helped readers imagine that the ultimate resolution of their violent war would not be theft, misery, and the forced displacement of Mexican citizens, but a sort of international marriage that would bring bliss to both husband and wife, United States and Mexico.[6]

This was a popular fantasy, particularly among the growing minority of expansionist Democrats who hoped to annex all of Mexico to the United

States. Sam Houston recommended that the crowd of men who gathered in New York City in support of annexing all of Mexico "take a trip of exploration there, and look out for the beautiful senoritas, or pretty girls, and if you should choose to annex them, no doubt the result of this annexation will be a most powerful and delightful evidence of civilization." Some who heard him almost certainly had read *Mexican Ranchero*. Perhaps they had a copy at home. The editor of the Philadelphia *Public Ledger* used the same reasoning in December 1847 in response to those who claimed Mexicans were too foreign to annex. "Our Yankee young fellows and the pretty senoritas will do the rest of the annexation, and Mexico will soon be Anglo-Saxonized, and prepared for the confederacy."[7]

Nor was this fantasy limited to politicians, editors, and novelists. Some in the occupying army had similar thoughts. One Indiana captain wrote his brother that in order to conquer the country "every man is required to give in his *mite* and I shall therefore commit matrimony with the first

Rejon the Ranchero. Rejon, the eponymous guerrilla partisan of the 1847 dime novel The Mexican Ranchero, *determined to kidnap Nicholas Trist to prevent peace between the two countries. Dime novels such as* The Mexican Ranchero *promoted both the war and annexation of Mexican territory with thrilling tales of adventure and romance on the front.* Charles Averill, *The Mexican Ranchero (1847), 53.*

decent, clean and *respectable, yellow* Mexican gall I can meet with—I will *annex* myself to this country by some such desperate act." What Houston and the *Public Ledger* both understood was that sex sells, and that the fantasy of sex with Mexican women, or "personal annexation," could help sell white American workingmen on absorbing Mexico, just as surely as it could sell novels. Given the increasing clamor for taking all of Mexico in the fall of 1847, the sales pitch appears to have been working.[8]

It was at this moment that Trist's mission was fictionalized, offered for sale for twenty-five cents, and avidly consumed by readers around the country. The fate of his treaty is a key plot of *The Mexican Ranchero,* secondary only to the romantic travails of three Mexican and three American characters hell-bent on personal annexation. At the start of the action a band of Mexican guerrillas, led by the skilled partisan Rejon the Ranchero, are doing their best to derail the peace process by killing U.S. soldiers. They take the Mississippi Volunteer Corps hostage and hatch a plot to kill General Taylor. They also decide to waylay Nicholas Trist, the only man who can bring peace to Mexico. Rejon sends a mysterious and beautiful cross-dressing female ranchero called the Maid of the Chapparal to capture the American minister.

Trist would have been flattered by his portrait in this novel. As imagined by the author, Trist is no ordinary diplomat. A sterling specimen of American Anglo-Saxon manhood, the fictional Trist stands tall, with a "muscular and well developed form," and a "face on whose every lineament was marked the impress of thought. That bold, open countenance and towering brow told at once of a powerful intellect and commanding mind." Diplomats were not usually elevated to heroic status in war novelettes. It is a testimony to the public's knowledge of and concern about Trist's peace mission in the fall of 1847 that Charles Averill was willing to endow diplomacy, and the making of a treaty, with the highest level of manliness and drama.[9]

The fictional Trist's personal virtues are not sufficient to keep his mission secret, however. The Maid of the Chapparal had no more problem locating Trist than did the American newspapers, which repeatedly enraged the president by reporting the details of his peace mission. "You are Mr. Trist, the American diplomatist, commissioned to negociate a peace? . . . You are even now on your way to the capital with peace propositions in your possession?" the female ranchero asked him. " 'You are strangely correct . . . , mysterious lady,' answered the wondering Trist.—'This mission was supposed to be a secret between myself and my government. How you have discovered it, senora, I can not pretend to surmise.' "[10]

Trist is eventually rescued by the escaped Mississippi Volunteers, and Rejon is revealed to be Ambassador Don Almora, not an enemy at all, but rather a friend to America. Mexican characters marry Americans, and the reader is assured that the eminently capable Trist is about to bring the war to a close with his skillful diplomacy. "The war is well nigh self-exhausted; Peace with its smiling face is treading close upon the bloody footsteps of the grim old King of Carnage."[11]

If only Nicholas Trist's reality had been so simple. In *The Mexican Ranchero* the only thing standing between diplomatist Trist and peace was a band of misguided rancheros. These Mexican partisans needed only to accept the love offered them by their American invaders to realize that they were all one family. Peace was on its way, but what kind of peace? The author never speculates on the ultimate fate of Mexico. How much of it would be absorbed by the United States? Would it continue to exist as an independent country? And the increasing discord in the United States between opponents of the war and aggressive expansionists demanding all of Mexico played no role in the drama. As Trist learned in the fall of 1847, guerrilla partisans were the least of his troubles. For in truth it was not the people of Mexico but his own president who was attempting to waylay him on his way to the capital "with peace propositions in his possession." And it appeared doubtful that anyone was coming to save him or his treaty.

Polk regretted sending Trist to Mexico as soon as he received his envoy's first petulant letter about Scott. The president complained that "because of the personal controversy between these self important personages, the golden moment for concluding a peace with Mexico may have passed." It was bad enough when Trist and Scott were quarreling like children. But when the two men reconciled, matters actually became more ominous. Scott was the last confidant he wanted for his agent; moreover, months went by without any official communication from the front, and early evidence suggested that the minister was easy to manipulate.[12]

Trist's initial negotiations with Santa Anna were not promising. In fact, he wasn't even supposed to be negotiating: his job was to see that the treaty Polk had stipulated was signed by Mexico. His "plain duty," as Polk put it, was "to submit the ultimatum of his Government." Yet Trist had the temerity over the summer to forward a Mexican proposal for a boundary at the Nueces River. Given that Polk's excuse for invading Mexico was that American blood had been shed on American soil when the Mexican army crossed the Rio Grande, nothing was more likely to embarrass him in front of his political opponents than news that a U.S. representative openly acknowledged a possible Mexican claim to the Nueces Strip. "You have placed us in an awkward position," Buchanan wrote Trist privately. "To propose" that the United States could possibly "abandon that portion of our country where Mexico attacked our forces and on our right to which the Whigs have raised such an unfounded clamor, will be a fruitful case of appeal against us in the next Congress."[13]

Polk was exceedingly irritated that "Mr. Trist has managed the negotiation very bunglingly and with no ability." No further progress toward peace appeared to have been made since then. Polk's imagination ran wild with visions of a conspiracy, Trist as Scott's "mere tool . . . employed in ministering to his malignant passions."[14] The two of them would undermine everything he had worked for.

After his hopes for a speedy treaty were dashed, the president, along with other expansionists, found that his appetite for Mexico was growing. He had originally directed Trist to settle for nothing less than a southern boundary at the Rio Grande, as well as the annexation of Mexico's provinces of Upper California and New Mexico. But now he imagined an American Sonora, an American Baja, and full command of the Gulf of California between the two. In September Polk told his cabinet that he was "decidedly in favour of insisting on the acquisition of more territory." The United States should take Tamaulipas and the line of thirty-one degrees. And twenty million dollars was too much to pay.[15]

Trist and his treaty had clearly become a liability. But there was no unanimity in the cabinet about how to proceed. Possibly Trist was making a treaty; perhaps he already had done so. Given the delay in communications, it was impossible to know what was happening. Matters were becoming strained in the cabinet. Buchanan was "nervous" and exhibiting "a degree of weakness" in his pursuit of the presidency that Polk found "almost incredible." Secretary of the Treasury Walker worked so hard that Polk was convinced that "his general health may be destroyed and his life endangered, if he continues to apply himself as he has heretofore done." Polk was particularly sensitive to this after "careworn and "overwhelmed" Secretary of War Marcy's nervous breakdown.[16]

This left Polk doing Marcy's job in addition to his own. He was already "devoting all my time & energies" to micromanaging the war and "examining all the details of everything that is done, as far as it [is] possible for me to do so." It was a "vast amount of labor" made worse by the fact that Polk didn't feel he could trust the subordinate officers in the War Department, almost all of whom were Whigs. "Many of them are indifferent and . . . take no sort of responsibility on themselves, and this renders it necessary that the Secretary of War & myself should look after them, even in the performance of the ordinary routine of details in their offices."[17]

Polk's health was visibly failing. The chairman of the House Committee on Foreign Affairs called on Sarah Polk to warn her that James "was wearing himself out with constant and excessive application, that if he did not take some recreation, he would die soon after the close of his term." He suggested that she "insist upon his driving out morning and evening; that she must order her carriage and make him go with her." Sarah, who understood

James Knox Polk. The exact date when Polk sat for this daguerreotype is unclear, but his haggard appearance and thin hair indicate that it was late in his presidential term or perhaps in the months after he left office. One letter writer who saw Polk in the summer of 1847 described his "fatigued and careworn countenance, which me-thought, might turn the hearts of some of his most violent opponents" (Sandweiss, Eyewitness to War, *241).* Daguerreotype with applied color, ca. 1847–49, 2¹³⁄₁₆ × 2⅜ inches. Amon Carter Museum of American Art, Fort Worth, Texas, P1981.65.12.

her husband's destructive work habits better than anyone, attempted to follow the advice. Day after day she ordered their carriage, "and the carriage waited and waited, until it was too late. It would have been obliged to wait all day, for somebody was always in the office, and Mr. Polk would not, or could not, come," she later recalled. It was hopeless. "I seldom succeeded in getting him to drive with me."[18]

In early October, Polk was struck by a serious attack of chills and fever. Bedridden, he "transacted no business of any kind" for nearly a week. Polk wasn't used to idleness, and long days in bed left him too much time to think about the war. How had things gone so wrong? And how could he salvage the coming presidential election for the Democratic Party?[19]

When he finally rose from bed, still too "feeble" to remain standing for more than a few minutes at a time, Polk's first decision was to fire Trist. He called the cabinet to his bedroom. He explained that if Trist remained in Mexico, it might well convince the Mexican government that "the U.S. were so anxious for peace that they would ultimate[ly] conclude one upon the Mexican terms." The cabinet was unanimous in agreement: Trist should be fired. Nor would Polk appoint any other negotiator. It would be up to Mexico to come to him, and the longer the Mexicans waited, the more it would cost them. Buchanan sent a recall letter to Trist. All negotiations were to be immediately suspended, and Trist was to return home at once.[20]

Just two weeks later Polk learned of Scott's capture of Mexico City. Rather than regret recalling Trist, however, the news only strengthened his conviction that Trist and the treaty he carried were woefully inadequate to the new reality. Matters now appeared in an entirely different light than they had back in April. The war was won, so why not escalate his demands? In October 1846, General Taylor had suggested that a boundary at either the Rio Grande or the "Sierra Madre Line," giving the United States the cities of Matamoros and Monterrey and the states of Chihuahua and Sonora, "was the best course that can be adopted." He told Polk that the Sierra Madre line would be easily defensible with small garrisons at Monterrey, Saltillo, Monclova, Linares, Victoria, and Tampico. This recommendation appeared sound, and it was conservative compared to the views of some in his own cabinet. Walker openly favored "taking the whole of Mexico." Although Buchanan had initially argued against taking any territory from Mexico at all, as a presidential candidate he now declared that annexing all of Mexico was "that destiny which Providence may have in store for both countries."[21]

But in Mexico City, matters looked very different. After an initial attempt at negotiations with Santa Anna collapsed, Trist found himself without recourse. Scott's victory had led to chaos in Mexico's government. Santa Anna had fled the capital and factions battled for control. Some argued for peace, while others demanded that the nation keep fighting, with guerrilla forces if necessary, until the invaders were ejected. Some of the wealthiest families supported the total annexation of Mexico by the United States as the option most likely to bring stability to the country. The occupying U.S. troops were set upon by guerrillas on a daily basis. Those irregular forces made it nearly impossible to get any news back to Washington.

Trist and General Scott spent long hours discussing the futility of occupying central Mexico. There were just too many Mexicans, and many of them understandably hated their occupiers. Out of the eight million inhabitants in Mexico, Scott wrote, "there are not more than one million who are of pure European blood. The Indians and the mixed races constitute about seven millions. They are exceedingly inferior to our own. As a lover of my country," he later explained, "I was opposed to mixing up that race with our own." Scott was adamant that "too much blood has already been shed in this unnatural war."[22] The situation was chaotic, unstable, and very likely to end in disaster.

America's soldiers found their first extended experience as an occupying army unsettling. Many, including Ulysses Grant, were shocked by Mexico's poverty. "With a soil and climate scarsely equaled in the world she has more poor and starving subjects who are willing and able to work than any country in the world," he wrote to his fiancée, Julia. "The rich keep down the poor with a hardness of heart that is incredible. Walk through the streets of Mexico for one day and you will see hundreds of beggars, but you never see them ask alms of their own people, it is always of the Americans that they expect to receive." And the occupying army was getting antsy. "The Mexicans swear they will not fite any more and they will not cum to any terms of piece and I can't tell how long we will remain here," complained one North Carolina volunteer. "We would much rather they would cum to some terms of piece or fite one or the other for we are getting tired of lying still and doing nothing."[23]

Mexico might not choose to fight, but plenty of its citizens were willing. Stone-throwing mobs set upon U.S. soldiers, who were in turn forced to break up riots, such as the one that resulted when a local man, accused of murdering an American, was publicly whipped. Embedded journalists no longer adjusted their coverage to protect the troops. The New Orleans *Crescent* noted that the army's morale began to decline during the occupation. "Robbery seems to be the order of the day," it reported. "I can trace this bad conduct on the part of some belonging to the army to nothing but the insatiable appetite for gaming that exists in this city. Men lose their money, then their credit, and self-respect. Some of them will stoop to most anything." The New Orleans *Picayune* reported that the night after a Texas Ranger was killed by guerrillas, "a company of Rangers went to the vicinity of the murder and killed 17 Mexicans, and wounded some 40 more." The article, titled "Massacre of Mexican Citizens!," was reprinted as far away as Albany.[24]

With a clear view of the reality of the American occupation, Trist's perspective on Manifest Destiny and America's mission began to change. Polk's instructions were nothing, he wrote, next to "the iniquity of the war." America's invasion of Mexico and its occupation of the capital were "a thing for every right-minded American to be ashamed of." And Trist was ashamed. He wanted to go home, and he hoped Polk might reward him for his service in a manner that would allow him some free time. But he also realized that he had to bring the war to an end, not just for his own sake, but for the sake of his country and the country that had been invaded. He determined to make peace with "as little exacting as possible from Mexico."[25]

Just weeks before Trist learned of his recall, prospects for negotiation began to improve. Santa Anna had, once again, been sent into exile, and the new president, Supreme Court justice Manuel de la Peña y Peña, who had opposed the war in 1846, was pushing for peace. Peña and his moderate supporters asserted that accepting America's terms offered Mexico the best opportunity for rebuilding the shattered country and preventing further encroachment by its avaricious northern neighbor. But these views were considered treasonous by many in Mexico who maintained that a sustained guerrilla war was a better, more honorable outcome than surrendering any land to the Americans. The majority of people in Mexico steadfastly believed that the Nueces River was the rightful southern boundary of Texas.

Peña's position was precarious. Another political coup seemed possible at any time, and the new administration would likely be far less amenable to compromise. A treaty of peace, signed by representatives of a legitimately recognized government, was clearly necessary to bring the war to an end. After all, the original dispute over Texas's independence was in large part the result of the fact that Texans never signed a peace treaty with Mexico in 1836.

As the occupation dragged on, the soldiers became more and more desperate. Ulysses S. Grant wrote Julia, "Mexico is a very pleasant place to live because it is never hot nor ever cold, but I believe evry one is hartily tired of war . . . I pity poor Mexico." Lieutenant John M. Brannan of Indiana, who like a number of his fellow officers in Mexico would go on to greater fame in the Civil War, had recently been brevetted to captain for "gallant and meritorious conduct" in the Battle of Contreras and Churubusco. But the honors hardly mattered. He and his men also wanted to go home. He bemoaned the seemingly endless occupation in a letter to his brother at the end of October. "There is no prospect of ever seeing a white face or the United States again," he complained. "You will soon hear what Congress intends doing in regard to this war. I have made up my mind that we have to conquer and occupy the whole country and regenerate this ignorant, super-stitious and vicious race."[26]

Brannan wasn't the only person waiting anxiously for the Thirtieth Con-gress to convene at the end of December and to make clear their intentions regarding the war. If and when Nicholas Trist came to some agreement with Mexico, Congress would have to ratify the treaty. If things contin-ued to drag on without a resolution, as seemed likely, it would be up to the Whig-controlled House of Representatives to take charge and force the president to do the people's bidding.

Across the United States that fall, congressmen were setting off for Wash-ington, wondering how the war would shape their terms. When Congress-man Lincoln looked east in the fall of 1847, he could visualize a number of different routes to Washington. None of them was simple, and neither he nor Mary had ever traveled east of Kentucky. With rambunctious and (oth-ers thought) badly governed four-year-old Robert and their toddler Eddie to tend to, the journey must have seemed especially daunting. Eddie had begun showing signs of the tuberculosis that would kill him less than three years later, and Mary had begun to suffer from debilitating headaches. But after all the years they had spent working toward this election, and nearly a year and a half of waiting since it took place, the Lincolns were ready for the journey. In October they leased their Springfield home for the year for ninety dollars, and two days later started for Washington.

There was no easy way to get to Washington from Springfield in 1847. You couldn't travel by train. Nor was there a route by water. Indeed, the general difficulty of getting *anywhere* easily from the remote towns and cities of western states such as Illinois, Kentucky, and Tennessee explains the appeal of the Whig vision of an activist central government among a population that otherwise venerated the frontier values and expansionist platform of Andrew Jackson's Democratic Party. What hope could there be for a fledgling community far from the seat of power, or for a young and penniless but ambitious man, without the helping hand of the government, with its protective tariffs and ability to extend credit? A number of mid-westerners were as angry about Polk's veto of the Rivers and Harbors Bill, which would have done so much to improve transportation and commerce in their portion of the country, as they were about the war with Mexico.

The shortest route to Washington from Springfield was 840 miles, mostly by stagecoach, which was a fantastically uncomfortable way to travel, particularly with small children. Overcrowded coaches bounced and jostled over rutted roads that were dusty in the summer and muddy in the winter. In difficult patches passengers were expected to get out and walk. Travel was totally unregulated and accidents frequent. Undergreased axles broke or caught fire; coaches collided with pedestrians and smaller vehicles, sank into streams or holes, or, dramatically, toppled over, often resulting in serious injuries. On the "splendid turnpikes in Kentucky" (financed with help from Henry Clay) travel was relatively safe, but on the "natural roads" virtually everywhere else, "the pitching from side to side was like that of a small steamer on a coasting trip." In the best of circumstances passengers could expect to arrive at their destination hungry, thirsty, sleepy, and covered with dust. Grisly accounts of less favorable outcomes were easy to find in local newspapers.[27]

But the Lincolns didn't choose the shortest route, and the reason had little to do with comfort. Mary wanted to visit her family in Lexington. And members of Congress were reimbursed for their travel at what was then the astronomical sum of forty cents a mile. It was the rare congressman who didn't choose a route that was, in the words of New York Tribune editor Horace Greeley, another Whig elected to the Thirtieth Congress, "exceedingly crooked, even for a politician."[28] Lincoln's chosen route was twice as long as necessary. It included lengthy trips by river steamer down the Mississippi and then up the Ohio and Kentucky rivers to Frankfort, Kentucky, followed by a train trip to Lexington to visit the Todds. They then returned to Frankfort, went by steamer to Pennsylvania, caught a stagecoach to Cumberland, Maryland, and from there traveled by train first to Relay Station, Maryland, and then by the Baltimore and Ohio to Washington. Lincoln's trip of 1,626 miles cost the taxpayers $1,300.80, approximately $30,000 today. Although his journey cost $878.80 more than the shortest possible route, Lincoln, like most congressmen, assumed he was entitled to inflated mileage to offset his low congressional salary. The wealthy didn't have to worry about such things, of course, but for a common man, mileage was one of the great benefits of serving in Congress.

The highlight of this meandering journey for Mary Todd Lincoln was visiting her family in Lexington. If she sometimes considered herself superior to the society she found in Springfield, it was because she measured everything about her current situation against the benchmark of Lexington. And Springfield just didn't measure up. It had some graceful trees and a few homes of architectural note, as well as a few markers of its emerging gentility, including a Thespian Society and a Young Men's Lyceum, although it wasn't nearly as genteel as Jacksonville.

But Springfield's most outstanding characteristic was its mud. During rainy periods the streets were virtually impassable by foot, particularly for ladies. To make matters worse, the numerous hogs who roamed the streets in search of scraps enjoyed uprooting the wooden sidewalks. Thanks in part to lobbying by Abraham Lincoln, the twenty-five-hundred-person town of Springfield had become the capital of Illinois on July 4, 1839. The unfinished statehouse sported classical columns, but the business district, full of shanties, was an eyesore. Illinois's new capital had ambition to spare, but in the 1840s it was still very much a work in progress.

Lexington was altogether different. It had grand homes in town and grander hemp plantations outside it (Mary's grandfather's estate was one of the nicest). Lexington also had Transylvania University, the oldest institution of higher learning west of the Alleghenies, and the alma mater of John J. Hardin, Jefferson Davis, and Mary's own father. Robert Todd was fortunate enough to have studied law there under Henry Clay in the first decade of the nineteenth century. Lexington had high society and families of long standing like her own, many of whom had originally migrated from the Piedmont region of Virginia, where they knew a thing or two about living well. They had brought their love of horse racing, gambling, and hard liquor to the Bluegrass Region, and prospered thanks to their many slaves.[29]

Lexington had a beautiful setting amid undulating hills, fertile limestone soil, and the highest concentration of slaves in the state. Kentucky was part of the border South, caught uneasily between the large cotton plantations that dominated the states to the south and the relative freedom of the states to the north. There were 210,000 slaves in Kentucky at the end of the 1840s, fully one-fifth of its population. But most of the state, including Hardin County, where Abraham Lincoln was born, was composed of small farms worked by families without the aid of slave labor.

Lexington, by contrast, was home to large plantations and a slave population with a density closer to that found in the Deep South. Slaves in Lexington, like those in Mississippi or Alabama, were likely to labor outdoors under the oversight and lash of white overseers, to sleep in separate slave quarters, and to interact primarily with other slaves. Most of the wealthy families in Lexington owned slaves. The Clays and Todds were no exception.

The landlocked city was in some ways on the decline in the 1840s, bypassed by Louisville since steamers opened up the river depot to the New Orleans trade via the Mississippi. Lexington no longer bid fair to take the seat of government away from Frankfort despite years of lobbying by Henry Clay, but it was still the cultural capital of the region. Lexington had a somewhat better claim than Jacksonville to the title "Athens of the West." Lexington was Mary's ideal of a city. She remained a Kentucky girl at heart, and throughout her years in Springfield she always subscribed to a Lexington newspaper.

The Lincolns arrived in Lexington on November 4, their fifth wedding anniversary, and passed three lovely weeks, ending on Thanksgiving Day, in the stately two-story brick home where she had lived as a teenager, complete with double parlors, coach house, and elaborate flower gardens leading to a gentle stream. It was Abraham's first visit to his wife's hometown, and his first introduction to her stepmother and small half brothers and half sisters. It was the first time the Todds had met Mary's children as well. Mary was proud to show off her two handsome sons and congressman husband. By all accounts Lincoln charmed his in-laws during that visit.

This was the first real vacation of Abraham Lincoln's life. It was also his first extended exposure to real slavery, as opposed to the indenture system of Illinois. During his sojourn in Lexington he had ample opportunity to study the "peculiar institution" firsthand. There were slaves in the Todd household, and separate slave quarters out back. Notices of runaway slaves appeared in the daily paper. Lexington was also the slave-trading center of the state. Slave auctions and shackled slaves were common sights, and Lincoln likely saw both during his visit. The jail of a slave trader was easily visible from the home of Mary's grandmother down the street. From the terrace of her lawn, Lincoln could look down over spiked palings into the yard of the slave pen and hear the cries of slaves tied to the whipping post. Five slaves were sold during his visit to Lexington to satisfy a legal judgment in favor of his father-in-law. Slavery became a reality for Abraham Lincoln in a new way during those three weeks.

The visit to Lexington was as much a highlight of the long journey to Washington for Abraham Lincoln as it was for his wife, although for very different reasons. It wasn't that Lincoln didn't enjoy the Todd family circle. He got along particularly well with her father, whom he had previously met in Springfield. They shared not only family interests, including young Robert Lincoln, named after his grandfather, but also political beliefs. Robert S. Todd was one of the most prominent citizens in the town, president of the branch bank of Kentucky, engaged in the cotton manufacturing business, and a twenty-four-year member of the Kentucky state assembly. Although Todd and Lincoln came from dramatically different backgrounds and only one was a slave owner, both were dyed-in-the-wool Whigs. There were a lot of Whigs in Lexington. American hemp, a plant related to marijuana that was grown for its fiber, was vastly inferior to that grown in Russia. Hemp became a profitable crop in Kentucky only because of a high protective tariff levied on Russian hemp passed by the Whigs. With its fledgling manufacturing concerns and remote location, Lexington was the center of Whig strength in Kentucky. Todd was on a first-name basis with all the leading Whig politicians in the state, including Lexington's favorite son, Henry Clay. Mary had known the Clays since childhood, when she once brought a pony to Ashland to show it off to Clay. She admired the statesman almost as much as her husband did.[30]

It was Clay who made this such a special trip for Lincoln. A lawyer who parlayed success at the bar into a political career on the national stage, a firm nationalist whose abilities to compromise were unparalleled, and an advocate of the interests of westerners, Henry Clay was an easy man for Lincoln to admire and identify with. And like the rest of America, he also thrilled to Clay's speeches. His cousin later attributed the fact that Lincoln initially became a Whig to the fact that he "always Loved Hen Clay's Speaches."[31]

Lincoln did indeed love Clay's speeches, but he had never heard the orator in person. All agreed that Clay's true genius as a speaker lay primarily in his animated, passionate delivery and deep bass voice. Listeners compared Clay's voice to "the finest musical instrument," which could be as "soft as a lute or full as a trumpet." It was a voice of "wonderful modulation, sweetness, and power."[32] Lincoln knew that reading Clay's speeches was like deciphering a musical score without ever having heard it performed. A few weeks before his marriage in 1842, Lincoln, as a member of the executive committee of the Springfield Clay Club, invited the Kentucky senator to deliver an address in Springfield. "The pleasure it would give us, and thousands such as we, is beyond all question," he wrote.[33]

Clay never made it to Springfield in 1842. But in 1847 Lincoln went to Lexington, and there, at last, he heard the music live. The very day he and his family arrived in Lexington, newspapers announced that Henry Clay would deliver an address on the war in Mexico, at a meeting presided over by Robert S. Todd. Lincoln had obviously picked a fortuitous time to visit

Clay's hometown. What he didn't yet know was that this speech, one of Clay's greatest, would change the course of both men's careers.

By the time the Lincolns reached Kentucky, the military occupation of Mexico's capital had already dragged on for two months. While agitation to "conquer and occupy" the whole country was becoming more avid the longer Mexico stalled, many Whigs had begun to argue that the best solution was to withdraw U.S. troops from Mexico without taking any territory, bringing a swift and not entirely shameful end to a bloody war that had started with a lie. This was what the Massachusetts House of Representatives called for in April 1847: "the restoration of an honorable peace, without further attempt to dismember the territory of the enemy, and upon terms of mercy and magnanimity becoming a great and brave people toward a sister republic."[34]

The war needed resolution, and the opposition Whig Party needed leadership and guidance. "Old Rough and Ready" Zachary Taylor was a growing favorite for the party's nomination in 1848, but not even his most fervent supporters imagined that the plainspoken general could provide the rank and file with direction in this crucial period. The general likely could rally the troops at election time, but his command of soldiers was far greater than his command of policy.

So the Whigs did what came naturally; they turned to Henry Clay.

Leading Whigs had been prodding Clay for some sort of statement on the war almost from its beginning. Now, at last, the Sage of Ashland agreed to speak. Clay was not doing well. His health was on the decline, and his son's death continued to haunt him. The loss of Henry Junior, he wrote a friend, was particularly "deep and so agonizing." He had been baptized in the hopes that it would provide some solace, but five months later Clay admitted that he had "been nervous ever since" hearing of his son's death, and still couldn't bring himself to look at "the partner of my sorrows," Lucretia, "without feeling deeper anguish." He found it painful to walk the grounds of Ashland, for the very trees reminded him of his son.[35]

Clay determined to oppose the war that took young Colonel Clay's life. Countless Americans had seen images of his son handing over his dueling pistols just moments before death, asking that the senior statesman learn that his son had "done all [he] could with them, and now return them." His son had sent a final message: it was up to Henry Clay to soldier on. He would condemn the extension of slavery and offer a solution to the ongoing immoral conflict in Mexico. And perhaps he would find peace. Whether primarily out of bitterness at the loss of the best hope for the next generation of his family or anger at the war he would have prevented had he become president in 1844, Clay decided, at age seventy, to speak out with conviction. He would let the American people know exactly what he thought, even if it cost him the Whig nomination in 1848. And he would do it at home, in Lexington, where pro-war fervor still ran high, but he knew he would always find an audience that loved him. Some things were more important than becoming president.

Yet perhaps, at the same time, this new path would finally lead him to the presidency. It wasn't impossible. He would have been the frontrunner for the party's nomination, but in the last letter he ever received from his son, written just weeks before Buena Vista, Henry Clay Jr. confided that General Taylor would run for president in 1848. "He feels his power," he told his father, and admitted that "except for yourself there are very few whom I would prefer to him." Clay had lost the 1840 nomination to William Henry Harrison. That war hero's death had delivered the nation into the hands of John Tyler and his disastrous presidency. Could Henry Clay allow another general to become president? Could he prevent it?[36]

From the day Clay's address was announced in the papers, excitement ran high, and not just in Lexington. News that Clay would speak out "created a sensation in the political circles seldom experienced," reported one New York newspaper. " 'What will he say?'—'What course will he pursue?' were the questions universally asked." A Milwaukee paper gushed that voters there were anxious to learn what "one of the first men of the nation, with no station or commitments to bias the soundness of his judgment" would say about "the topic which of all others now lies nearest the heart of the whole people."[37]

Papers across the nation picked up the news, and a series of notable figures announced their intention to be there for the event, including the governor and senators from Kentucky. Some audience members traveled hundreds of miles just to hear Clay's speech. Abraham Lincoln may possibly have visited Ashland earlier that week with his wife or father-in-law and met with Clay personally. If so, he might have had some sense of what Clay would say on November 13. But Clay held his cards tight. He knew the importance of surprise to a dramatic address. No one expected Clay to praise the war, but just what he would say was a mystery.

The address was originally scheduled for Lexington's courthouse, but as visitors and reporters from throughout the region poured into the city, it became apparent that the crowd would number in the thousands. The venue was changed to the new Market House, a cavernous brick building on Water Street.

On a dark and rainy Saturday morning, the crowd began to assemble outside. An immense assembly of men and women thronged the hall, "all ages participated, the father as well as the son—all classes and conditions of society." Many in that Lexington audience still supported the war. Some, no doubt, imagined that the dismemberment of Mexico by the United States was just and right. The vast majority unquestionably supported slavery. They were all ready to hear something remarkable.

Clay was not an original thinker, but he could energize and inspire an audience like few other men in politics. He knew the speech he was about to deliver was among the most important of his career, a speech that could save lives, perhaps change history. The American people still looked to him for guidance. After all, no other politician had proven as skillful as Henry Clay at delivering his nation from a crisis. And almost half of all voters had chosen him over Polk in 1844. Clay knew that many of them felt the loss nearly as acutely as he did. Much was at stake, both for him and for the nation.

At exactly eleven o'clock Clay mounted the podium with the supreme confidence that always accompanied the orator when he was in his element and an erect bearing that belied his seventy years. "The shouts of the assembled thousands" filled the room as General Leslie Combs called the meeting to order and a series of officers was elected, including Robert Todd as vice president. General Combs requested that the audience observe a "perfect silence" during the following address, "as it was probably the last time that" Clay "would ever address a populous assembly." Henry Clay had come before them, Combs said, out of his duty to the country. The "momentous question" of the resolution of the war now presented itself to the American people, and no man who loved his country could remain silent. Clay would not "allow any selfish consideration to palsy his tongue." Clay was there, Combs reminded his audience, because he would "rather be right than be President." The audience roared its approval.[38]

As Clay rose and faced the assembly, a silence descended over the room. Clay began his address on a subdued note. Speaking in measured tones, he noted how the dark and gloomy weather outside the lecture hall perfectly reflected the condition of the country. Anxiety, agitation, and apprehension were the rule, given the unsettled state of the "unnatural" war with Mexico. Clay's voice rose as he bluntly described the manner in which Polk had provoked an "unnecessary" war of "offensive aggression," laying blame on the president and detailing his many lies and deceptions.

Clay excoriated the president, but he reserved some of his wrath for the congressional Whigs who had capitulated in 1846 and voted in favor of the war. The United States never should have annexed Texas in the first place, since everyone had understood at the time that annexation would result in war. Yet the majority of congressional Whigs had voted in favor of a war declaration with "a palpable falsehood stamped on its face" that Mexico was to blame. "Almost idolizing truth," Clay intoned, "I would never have voted for that bill." And the audience could see that the great man meant what he said. Voting for a bill with a lie at its heart was exactly the kind of thing that the old, opportunistic Clay might have done, had he been in Congress. But not the man who faced them today. His sincere disgust at that vote, if not completely fair, was for the witnesses assembled in the Lexington Market House too evident for doubt.

With increasing intensity, Clay detailed the terrible results of that vote and the "frightful struggle" that ensued. Clay lingered over the mad "sacrifice of human life . . . waste of human treasure . . . mangled bodies . . . death, and . . . desolation." Thousands of Americans had already died, and many more soldiers had been disqualified by a "wild spirit of adventure" from returning to civil society. And whose fault was this? It was Mexico, not the United States, that was "defending her firesides, her castles, and her altars."

Nor was Clay done. Congressional Whigs had agreed to the war because they were afraid of appearing unpatriotic. But "whose hearts," Clay emotionally asked, "have bled more freely than those of the Whigs?" His voice nearly cracking, Clay asked an audience intimately familiar with his own grief, "Who have more occasion to mourn the loss of sons, husbands, brothers, fathers than Whig parents, Whig wives, and Whig brothers, in this deadly and unprofitable strife?" Clay held back his tears, but many in the audience did not. All knew he had lost his son. And it had been widely reported that Colonel John Hardin was Clay's nephew: two dead young men of promise in one family. Clay's losses, and the nation's losses, were nearly unthinkable.

But this address was not primarily about Henry Clay. It was about the country to whose service Clay had devoted his entire long career. And more than the youth of that nation had been lost in the past two years. With a deep and burning indignation, Clay told his audience that the United States had lost its "unsullied character" internationally. Other nations "look upon us, in the prosecution of the present War, as being actuated by a spirit of rapacity, and an inordinate desire for territorial aggrandizement." Even God himself must wonder at America's actions. His deep bass voice thundering, Clay leaned into the podium, warning his audience about the dangers of annexing Mexico and citing historical examples to prove that imperialism inevitably led to ruin for the conquering nation. He dwelt at great length on the "direful and fatal" consequences of emulating the Roman Empire, the ill effects on the character of the nation of becoming a "warlike and conquering" power, and the incredible expense of annexing Mexico.

Clay also expressed his reservations about the racial implications of inviting Mexicans to join the Union. "Does any considerate man believe it possible that two such immense countries, with territories of nearly equal extent, with populations so incongruous, so different in race, in language, in religion and in laws could be blended together in one harmonious mass, and happily governed by one common authority? . . . [T]he warning voice of all history . . . teaches the difficulty of combining and consolidating together, conquering and conquered nations." The Moors had failed to hold Spain, and England was struggling to hold Ireland. "Every Irishman hates, with a mortal hatred, his Saxon oppressor," and "both the Irish and the Mexicans are probably of the same Celtic race. Both the English and the Americans are of the same Saxon origin."[39] Appealing to the racist views of his audience, Clay proclaimed that annexing Mexico would doom the United States.

But he had a solution. Because war powers resided with Congress, Congress could end the war. It was up to them to quickly and honorably settle the Mexican boundary issue and then to demand the immediate withdrawal of all U.S. troops from Mexico, ending a disgraceful and immoral war without annexing a single acre of Mexico's land beyond the Nueces Strip. And Clay demanded that Polk comply. His audience, swept up in the moment, exploded in applause and implied agreement that Polk would be forced to comply, that they would see to it.

Not everything in this address was as universally pleasing as Clay's demand that Polk be held to account. Clay also addressed the issue of slavery. Although he was speaking in a slave state, to an audience full of slave owners, Clay clearly and sharply disavowed "any desire, on our part, to acquire any foreign territory whatever, for the purpose of introducing slavery into it." Heads turned when he said that, although no voices were raised in dissent. If anyone doubted his position on this subject, Clay added, in a voice of utter seriousness, that he had "ever regarded slavery as a great evil." The fifty enslaved men, women, and children back at Ashland might reasonably have argued otherwise, but no one in the audience that day would have dared. Slavery was a great evil. In the past, Clay had often stated his belief that slavery was wicked. But now he offered no concessions to slave-holding Whigs, and no hope that Henry Clay, if he had anything to do with it, would allow new slave states to be created out of Mexican land. It was a radical stand, a brave stand. Abraham Lincoln wasn't the only man in attendance that day who must have marveled at Clay's courage.

In a series of resolutions at the close of a speech that "carried conviction to every mind," Henry Clay challenged the incoming Thirtieth Congress to investigate and determine the purpose of the war, to loudly oppose the president if he attempted to annex or dismember Mexico, to prevent the extension of slavery into any foreign territory, and to redeem the honor of the nation in the process. His final resolution invited the people of the United States who were "anxious to produce contentment and satisfaction at home, and to elevate the character of the nation abroad," to hold meetings of their own in order to make their opposition to the war dramatically clear. The citizens of America must take upon themselves responsibility for ending the war. They must make their voices heard. Clay's resolutions, including those opposing the extension of slavery, were submitted and unanimously adopted.[40]

The thousands of people in the Market House exploded in applause, rising to their feet and filling the hall with their shouts and roars. Henry Clay had spoken for two and a half hours, but the crowd was energized rather than exhausted, called to action by "the great mass of truths" that Clay so powerfully presented. The speech they had heard was "rich, earnest, and true," and not one they were likely to forget. Certainly, Abraham Lincoln did not. As he and the thousands of others left the hall that afternoon, they filled the streets and homes of Lexington with their praise of the Sage of Ashland, their approval of his resolutions, and their amazement that the seventy-year-old Clay was still at the height of his powers.[41]

Thanks to the wonders of the telegraph, plus a reporter who immediately after the speech rode eighty miles (in a record five hours) to the nearest telegraph office in Cincinnati, Clay's speech and resolutions were in print across the country within days. The speech won immediate acclaim among northern Whigs, many of whom were both delighted and surprised by Clay's clearly stated principles. "He is not afraid to speak out," approved the Boston *Daily Atlas,* while another paper noted, "It is a high exercise of moral courage for Mr. Clay, living in a slave-holding State and addressing an audience composed mostly of the owners of slaves—to bear his testimony against any extension of this institution." Several papers reported that Clay had demanded Polk's impeachment if he didn't comply with Congress's wishes.[42]

Nothing about Clay's Lexington speech was radical, even if it was radical for Henry Clay. Almost all of it had been formulated by other Whig politicians in other contexts. But as so often was the case with Henry Clay, it was the way he said something that proved so inspiring. The "free simplicity, sound logic, and manly directness" of Clay's words "attest their truth and crown their excellence," noted one reporter. "The right thinking men of the country of all classes and parties will thank Mr. Clay for thus embodying in words that will not lie, the feeling of their hearts and the convictions of their judgments."[43]

Reactions to the speech in other quarters were less positive. A few abolitionist papers—but only a few—contrasted Clay's Lexington address with his boast in New Orleans a year earlier that he might "capture or slay a Mexican." This was nothing more than a typical Clay flip-flop. "Mould the clay which way you will, 'tis a very clay-god still," punned the *Liberator*.[44]

But Democrats and many western Whigs labeled the speech treasonous. The administration's paper, the *Washington Union*, condemned "the spirit of treason promulgated" by Clay, particularly his assertion that "the war has been brought upon us *by our own act*; and that we and not our enemies, are responsible for its evils and its guilt." It also quoted an army officer who claimed to see "no difference between the men who in '76 succored the British, and those who in '47 give arguments and sympathy to the Mexicans." Democrats in Nashville met to condemn Clay's resolutions as "incompatible with national honor" and "having the direct tendency to encourage the opponents of peace in Mexico to protract the war." The New York *Courier and Enquirer*, a conservative Whig paper, warned that adopting Clay's unpatriotic resolutions would be "suicidal" for the Whigs. Soldiers in Mexico wondered if Clay's stand signified advancing senility, whether "he has arrived at an age for the follies and errors of which he is no longer responsible."[45]

If the Lexington speech improved Clay's standing in New England, it badly damaged it in the South. Southern Whigs concluded that Clay had "done himself great injury in his late speech" and that they would "not rally on Mr. Clay, or *any* Whig who swears by his Lexington resolutions." Whigs in Georgia refused to hold a meeting to so much as discuss Clay's resolutions. Of course, Clay knew before his Lexington speech that his chances of winning the presidential nomination without the support of southern proslavery Whigs were slim to none. He had taken a gamble with his speech. But he had always been a gambling man. If his words helped end a "frightful struggle," then of course he hadn't lost a thing. He was still the man who would rather be right than be president.[46]

Clay's words shook Washington, the nation, and beyond. In London, Britain's foreign minister wrote approvingly about Clay's speech "against an aggressive policy in the conduct of the Mexican War." Clay asked his fellow citizens to join together against war in Mexico, and the people responded. Antiwar rallies inspired by Clay's call to action bloomed from Indiana to New Jersey, Kentucky to Maine. Newspapers as far away as Mexico City reported that Clay's call for meetings "is arousing the masses in all parts of the Union."[47]

Not surprisingly, the "views of Henry Clay were fully sustained" at a "great meeting" in Boston. A "peace" meeting held in the Broadway Tabernacle in New York was widely reported to be "one of the largest and most enthusiastic meetings ever held in that city." In Philadelphia, "hundreds of the most respectable of the citizens" called for a "town meeting" in support of Clay's resolutions, and "thousands went away who were unable to gain admission" when it occurred. The gathering was reported to be "one of the largest and most respectable public meetings ever called together."[48]

While it was primarily the Whigs of Trenton, New Jersey, who endorsed Clay's resolutions by acclamation, citizens of all political parties turned out in Cincinnati to oppose "the causes and character of the Mexican War, as well as its further offensive persecution." The first meeting in Cleveland opposing the war was such a success that antiwar protesters decided to hold another a week later. In New Orleans, agitation caused by the ex-senator's oration was so great that one of the first things a returning soldier wrote about after his arrival in the Crescent City from Mexico was "Clay's antiwar speech." At meetings in cities around the country, thousands of people denounced the war, condemned Polk for starting it, and adopted Clay's resolutions wholesale, "with a fervor of manner and earnestness of purpose that are rarely exhibited."[49]

The antiwar movement was no longer a New England phenomenon. The public meetings in the wake of Clay's Lexington speech proved beyond a doubt that a peace movement was now national. Henry Clay didn't create the movement, but his political stature, authority as a grieving father, and singular speaking abilities gave voice to masses of dissenters and offered a clear path to protest. It was a "great wave," according to a Philadelphia reporter, which "rolled from Lexington, upheaved by the mighty voice of

Henry Clay," and now "goes onward from us with renewed and more over-whelming force." And while Americans met in support of Clay's "principles, more than to the man," they appreciated Clay more than ever. "Henry Clay sat enshrined in their hearts—but they gloried in him most, because he had spoken forth the truth unshrinkingly. . . . They reverenced him because he had forgotten self in his love of country, and because he valued his country's welfare more than his chances of gain."[50]

Abraham Lincoln bore witness to Clay's courageous and principled speech, and to his dramatic gamble. When as a child he had pored over Clay's biography, and as a young man committed Clay's speeches nearly to heart, did he imagine the real thing would be like this? The oratorical brilliance he might have envisioned, but not the subject matter. Henry Clay had built his career on economic issues, and those issues had become Lincoln's: internal improvements, a strong national bank, tariffs, and credit. These were the issues that Lincoln campaigned on, that inspired him, that drove him to Congress. They weren't the issues that interested voters on the campaign trail in 1846, but still they were his issues. His issue was not the war, and it certainly wasn't slavery. Before his trip to Lexington, Lincoln seemed generally unconcerned about the institution of slavery, viewing agitation to end the "peculiar institution" primarily as a nuisance that unproductively split the Whig Party.

What Lincoln saw and heard that afternoon made him reconsider these positions. The Sage of Ashland, his Prince Hal, had described the horrors of the war with blinding clarity, struck down the president as a liar, and ordered the people to protest a war that they, and Lincoln, knew to be unjust. Speaking in a slave state, Henry Clay had condemned the expansion of slavery, and in no uncertain terms. He had linked the war in Mexico with the slavery issue in a way that few southerners dared. Lincoln could only guess at the reasons Clay had finally spoken out: those of a father still anguished at his son's sacrifice, those of a patriot acting in what he felt were the best interests of his country, those of a righteous man choosing justice before ambition. But he understood the political consequences. By criticizing the war, Clay had jeopardized his political base in the South, which still largely supported it. By condemning slavery in a proslavery state, he had risked devastating voter backlash. It was a great act of political bravery. And Clay had right on his side.

Clay had made it clear that Mexican land must not, and would not, become slave territory. Henry Clay had demonstrated to the assembled thousands, and the many thousands more who would read his words in their morning papers the following week, that he valued truth and justice more than political office. And in so doing, he had proven that he was no mere politician. He was a leader.

Was this a revelation for Abraham Lincoln? He knew that the war and the extension of slavery were wrong. But had he understood that they were so very wrong that nothing else mattered? William Herndon later said that his law partner "stood bolt upright and downright on his conscience." Was his conscience now alive to the moral wrong of the war? Lincoln saw clearly that his issues in Congress would not be economic ones. In this period of national crisis it was not the time to focus on tariffs. If Henry Clay could attack the war, the president, and the spread of slavery, so could he. Congressman Abraham Lincoln had a new mission.[51]

Nicholas Trist received Polk's recall order just two days after Clay's speech, and the following day read about it in the Mexico City press. He knew nothing about Clay's speech, of course, but he too understood that personal sacrifice would be necessary to bring this war to an end. Lincoln's mission had changed, but Trist's had stayed the same. There was much in Henry Clay's speech that the diplomat would have agreed with. He too believed that the people of Mexico and those of the United States were incompatible socially and racially, and that the United States could never effectively govern large portions of Mexico's territory. He saw the corrupting effects of service in Mexico on the morals of many U.S. soldiers. Young men who would never engage in such behavior at home drank, gambled, and visited fandangos. Some did much worse. Most of all, Trist had seen firsthand the violence done against Mexico. He knew the Mexicans were fighting to protect their homes and families. He had come to believe that the United States was at fault. And it made him "ashamed" to be an American.[52]

Trist believed that Peña's presidency offered the best opportunity to bring the war to an end without a total dismemberment of Mexico. Local papers were reporting that Polk was ready to annex the whole country, and Trist warned Mexico's diplomats that "a strong public opinion" in the United States was demanding that "the U.S. should select a line of boundary as may suit themselves." He had earned the trust and respect of the Mexican negotiators over the previous months. This was an opportunity that couldn't be squandered.[53]

"What is my line of duty to my government and my country, in this extraordinary position in which I find myself?" Trist wondered. He consulted with General Scott and with another confidant, the British chargé d'affaires Edward Thornton. Scott encouraged him "to finish the good work he had begun." Thornton begged for Trist's "charity for this unhappy nation, to lend a hand toward the preservation of her nationality. I look upon this as the last chance for either party of making peace." So too did James Freaner, an embedded journalist for the New Orleans *Delta*. "Mr. Trist, make the treaty!" he told him. "It is now in your power to do your country a greater service than any living man can render her. I know our country. . . . They want peace, sir. They pant for it. They will be grateful for it."[54] Scott, Thornton, and Freaner, three men with very different agendas, all argued for peace. The soldiers wanted peace. And Mexico deserved peace.

Trist did something unheard of in American diplomacy: he refused to come home. He was, he knew, the only man who could make a treaty. He owed it as a "solemn duty to my country" to at least try. As a nervous Buchanan asked British diplomats to help deliver a second copy of the recall notice, which he suspected may never have arrived, Trist composed a sixty-five-page letter explaining why he refused to be fired. He was convinced the president was unaware of the true state of affairs in Mexico. Continued occupation was unwise, annexation of the whole impossible, he asserted. It offered "incalculable danger to every good principle, moral as well as political, which is cherished among us." A conquered Mexico would ultimately corrupt and destroy America. Furthermore, Polk's treaty terms would strip Mexico of half of her land. "However helpless a nation may feel, there is necessarily a point beyond which she cannot be expected to go under any circumstances."[55] The United States could not ask Mexico to go further. He would not ask Mexico to go further.

Then he continued negotiations. The fictional Trist in *The Mexican Ranchero* faced down guerrilla partisans. But the real Trist faced down a president. The most creative novelist would have had difficulty coming up with a more heroic plot line.

Polk received Trist's letter mere weeks after the Thirtieth Congress convened. The president had been "much fatigued" with his "long and close confinement & constant labour." Now the news left him dumbstruck. Thousands of miles from his president, Nicholas Trist pressed his negotiations. The man was not naive: he knew he was risking his career. But as he later wrote, his course was now "governed by my conscience." His "sense of justice" directed him to end America's "abuse of power." The people of Mexico deserved justice. He would deliver it to them. And, just as important, he would protect the people of America from the impossible burden of annexing Mexico.[56]

Polk saw the matter differently. "I have never in my life felt so indignant," he wrote in his diary. "He has acted worse than any man in the public employ whom I have ever known. His dispatch proves that he is destitute of honour or principle, and that he has proved himself a very base man. I was deceived of him."[57] He wanted Trist physically thrown out of army headquarters.

Late one evening, two weeks after Clay's speech, the exhausted Lincoln family finally arrived in Washington and checked into Mrs. Spriggs's boardinghouse, on Carroll Row, just across from the Capitol Building. Mrs. Spriggs's came well recommended. Both Baker and Hardin had lodged there during their congressional terms. It had been more than a month since the Lincolns left Springfield, and in three short weeks Lincoln and six Democrats were to represent Illinois in the lower house of Congress. "During my whole political life," Lincoln later wrote, "I have loved and revered [Clay] as a teacher and leader." As Lincoln pondered his path in the Thirtieth Congress, Clay's speech and lesson were firmly in mind. "As you are all so anxious for me to distinguish myself," he wrote to William Herndon, "I have concluded to do so before long."[58] Congressman Lincoln would live up to his promise.

PART FOUR

Truth and Consequences, 1848

Would you have voted what you felt you knew to be a lie? I know you would not. Would you have gone out of the House—skulked the vote? I expect not. . . . You are compelled to speak; and your only alternative is to tell the truth or tell a lie.

—ABRAHAM LINCOLN TO WILLIAM HERNDON,
FEBRUARY I, 1848

12

To Conquer a Peace

SEAT 191 WAS one of the very worst in the entire House of Representatives, and starting on December 6, 1847, it was occupied by Congressman Abraham Lincoln. He was relegated to the middle of the back row in a section off to the left of the Speaker. Fortunately, Lincoln was tall. While his seat was hardly conducive to catching the eye of the newly elected Speaker, Robert Winthrop of Massachusetts, it did allow him an excellent view of his colleagues. Lincoln sat on the Whig side of the house. One row ahead of him sat his messmate at Mrs. Spriggs's boardinghouse, the irascible abolitionist Joshua Giddings of Ohio. Forty-four-year-old George Ashmun of Massachusetts, a second-term congressman with bright black eyes and a shining bald head, sat in the same row, almost exactly in front of the new Illinois congressman.

Lincoln also had a good view of eighty-year-old John Quincy Adams, seated in the center of the action. Adams, a fixture in the House of Representatives since 1831, was one of the few congressmen with a proper home in Washington. Virtually all elected representatives in both houses lodged in boardinghouses like Mrs. Spriggs's, a tacit acknowledgment of the transient nature of national political office, even among those with "safe seats," such as Winthrop, Ashmun, and Giddings. They led, for the most part, a bachelor's existence. Most left their wives at home, and Mary Todd Lincoln quickly realized why. Boardinghouse life was remarkably unpleasant for a woman with children. Mary was the only wife at Mrs. Spriggs's, and the

244 A WICKED WAR

male camaraderie shared by Lincoln and his partisan messmates made few concessions to women's interests and concerns. Dinner conversation was inevitably about politics, and after-dinner jokes too raw for a lady's ears. Robert was uncontrollable, Eddie still nursing. Mary had few social outlets. She reveled in Abraham's entrance into the national political scene but found life in D.C. intolerable. She lasted only a few months before returning to Lexington with the children.

There was nothing transient about John Quincy Adams. He had moved to Congress after his single presidential term, and there he remained, his wife, Louisa, by his side. The Whig leader was as alert and outraged as ever, but physically on the decline. He was still the public face of congressional antislavery activism, but he had recently relinquished control to Giddings, whose energy, fearlessness, and physically intimidating bulk (he was six foot two and close to three hundred pounds) made him better suited to parrying the thrusts of proslavery extremists. "It is the curse of our Country and our party that northern men are too Craven hearted to maintain their own rights," Giddings declared at the start of the war. The Ohio representative had no problem sticking up either for his own rights or for the rights of those without a voice in Congress, particularly slaves, but also, increasingly, the people of Mexico.[1]

Giddings, Ashmun, and Adams were proud members of the Immortal Fourteen, the representatives brave enough to vote against Polk's declaration of war. All three had continued their assault against Mr. Polk's war in the seventeen months since. Giddings repeatedly warned the House that the war would lead to a "flood of vice and immorality" and that patriotism demanded dissent from the "aggressive, unholy, and unjust war" engineered by the president for the conquest of Mexico. "In the murder of Mexicans upon their own soil, or in robbing them of their country," he asserted. "I can take no part either now or hereafter. The guilt of these crimes must rest on others."[2]

Speaker Robert Winthrop was not one of the Immortal Fourteen. He had voted in favor of declaring war on Mexico in May 1846, and had come to regret it. Although he had a staggering record of public service for a man still in his thirties, plus an impeccable family name, the people of Massachusetts were not pleased with his endorsement of the war. Abolitionists were particularly enraged, and lashed out at Winthrop with a vehemence that he had difficulty understanding. His seat was safe, but he was condemned in local papers and rebuked in a public meeting at Faneuil Hall by fellow Whigs.

Thirty-six-year-old Charles Sumner, a rising antislavery activist in Boston and close friend of Winthrop's since childhood, was among his harshest critics. Sumner not only chastised Winthrop in public but also admitted to writing an anonymous assault on Winthrop in the *Boston Courier*. He believed his actions were justified because, as he told Winthrop in an extremely self-righteous letter, "the War Bill was the wickedest act in our history."[3]

Winthrop was flabbergasted by the betrayal. Had such an attack on a man's character occurred in the South, it might well have resulted in a duel. These two Massachusetts men chose to settle their differences with words. Winthrop privately voiced to Sumner his anger at "the intentional offensiveness of these articles, & their obvious design, not to sustain a principle or vindicate the truth, but to rob me personally of that spotless reputation, which is the dearest treasure mortal times afford." Sumner was unmoved by Winthrop's appeal. "Towards yourself personally I have no feeling, except of kindness," he wrote him. "But the act, with which your name has been so unhappily connected is public property. Your conduct is public property." Just to make his outrage at Winthrop's actions crystal clear, Sumner concluded, "I would have cut off my right hand, rather than utter such a sentiment" as Winthrop had, "setting *country* above *right*." Even in seemingly unified Massachusetts, the war was fracturing personal relationships and political alliances.[4]

A year later, Winthrop was still justifying his war vote. He was shocked to discover that a number of abolitionists, including Giddings, openly opposed his election as Speaker in the Thirtieth Congress, in large part because of his war vote in May 1846. They appeared willing to hand the Speaker's position over to the Democrats before allowing Winthrop to have it. "There is no position more difficult to maintain," he wrote to one friend, "either with satisfaction to one's self or others, than that of a Member of Congress during the progress of a War to which he is opposed." As for Sumner, Winthrop was done with him. "Abolitionism seems to destroy all sense of justice or truth in those who embrace it," he complained to a mutual friend. As the war dragged on there seemed to be less and less room for men like himself, conservative Whigs who, in Winthrop's words, "go for the policy by which war may be averted; but when it is at the doors . . . know no way but to defend the Country." It was up to Winthrop to try to direct the energies of the divided factions of the Thirtieth Congress toward the peaceful resolution of the war.[5]

However abysmal his seat, Abraham Lincoln had no problem understanding the president's address to Congress on its first day in session. Polk's third annual message made no concessions to the fact that the House was now in Whig hands. If anything, Polk went on the offensive, intent on bending the will of the House majority to the greater cause of war. He reiterated his claim that Mexico had "involved the two countries in war by invading the territory of the state of Texas, striking the first blow, and shedding American blood on American soil." He justified the progress of the war thus far, and argued for the "necessity" of taking territory from Mexico. In reference to Henry Clay's Lexington address, Polk completely rejected "the doctrine of no territory." Were the United States to withdraw from Mexico without taking any territory, as Clay demanded, it "would be a public acknowledgement that our country was wrong and that the war . . . was unjust and should be abandoned." Such an admission would be both "unfounded in fact, and degrading to the national character." It was "manifest," Polk claimed, that Mexico would ultimately lose New Mexico and California, since these territories were "contiguous" to the United States. America's destiny was clear: the war would end with a good deal of Mexican land becoming U.S. territory.

And at last dropping his pretenses to secrecy, Polk also gave an account to Congress of the failure of Nicholas Trist's mission to Mexico. Trist was recalled, he said, because Mexico had failed to accept the terms that America offered. It was now up to Mexico to make overtures for peace; until then, no diplomat would be sent in Trist's place. In the meantime, the president argued, America's "national honor" required that the war be "prosecuted with increased energy and power" until a "just and satisfactory peace can be obtained."[6]

What Polk intended to do, what he had argued for all along, was to "conquer a peace." The Polk administration was inordinately fond of the phrase, and variations on the wording appeared repeatedly in official documents released by Polk and his cabinet during the years of the war. But what did it mean? The United States was conquering Mexico not in order to subdue and occupy it but to force Mexico into acknowledging American claims and agreeing to a "just" territorial settlement. How exactly this would be accomplished was no clearer in December 1847 than it had been in May 1846. Thus far the remarkable military victories of U.S. troops had failed to facilitate that elusive peace in the midst of a great deal of conquest. The behavior of America's volunteer troops had in fact done the opposite, turning the people of Mexico against an occupying force in both northeastern and central Mexico that robbed, raped, and murdered with seeming impunity. Taylor's army had burned down so many villages that it had utterly devastated northeastern Mexico. As one disgusted officer serving under Taylor put it, "They make a wasteland and call it peace."[7]

But it was the only plan Polk had, and he intended to stick with it. The United States would continue to kill Mexicans and occupy their cities until Mexico's political leaders came to their senses. With breathtaking self-confidence and the faith of a true believer, James K. Polk demanded congressional authorization for more troops, more funding for expenses, and unwavering support for a war that now threatened to carry on long into the future.

It was an audacious move, and the product of a great deal of consideration. For weeks, Polk had refused to see company so that he could revise problematic paragraphs of the speech. He had argued repeatedly with cabinet members, particularly the now radically expansionistic secretary of state, over the substance of important passages. Despite the explicit and repeated urgings of both Buchanan and Marcy, Polk did not call for the annexation of all of Mexico in his address. He held back. But for the newly empowered congressional Whigs, the president's address was no less a call to arms. They would most certainly not support Polk's war. Indeed, they would make it their business to bring the whole sordid business to an end.

Not that it would be easy. While national support for the war was on the wane, and the Whig Party felt empowered by its new majority to bring the war to a conclusion, there were plenty of Whigs and Democrats who believed, like Robert Winthrop, that it was wrong to condemn an American war while it continued. As the ambivalent reception of Henry Clay's speech proved, opposition to an American war was tantamount to treason in the minds of many Americans. Furthermore, the war continued to be popular in some portions of the West and South.

At the same time, agitation for the annexation of all of Mexico continued to grow, even in some quarters where enthusiasm for the war had previously been flagging. The people of South Carolina, for example, had never evinced much enthusiasm for the fight against Mexico. Relatively few South Carolinians responded to the call for volunteers, and their leading Democrat, John C. Calhoun, had vocally opposed the war from its outset. Calhoun had become a thorn in Polk's side, warning that an invasion of central Mexico would lead to a "war between the races" that would "end in the complete subjugation of the weaker power." He also cautioned Polk that to annex large portions of Mexican territory to the United States would "subject our institutions [meaning slavery] to political death."[8]

On October 13, 1847, the Georgetown, South Carolina, *Winyah Observer* declared the conflict "probably the most unfortunate and disastrous war" in American history. But three weeks later, after receiving news of Scott's capture of Mexico City, the newspaper changed its tune, recommending that the United States annex the entire country and "make Mexico do us justice." With Manifest Destiny seemingly vindicated by the conquest of Mexico, even many of Calhoun's supporters believed that the no-territory position was madness. Aggressive expansionists were happy to endorse Polk's plan to continue fighting if it brought the entire nation of Mexico under the American flag.[9]

Abraham Lincoln's Illinois was the center of western pro-war fervor. His state sent more volunteers to Mexico than any except Missouri. And he was representing "John Hardin's" district, as people annoyingly insisted on calling it. While there were western Whigs who were now willing to oppose the war openly, there were also some, such as George Grundy Dunn, a newly elected Whig representative of Indiana, who refused to speak out against the war because he believed it would cost him his seat. Lincoln knew what was at stake.

Yet Congressman Lincoln, the lone Whig in the Illinois congressional delegation, had been seated for less than three weeks when he was recognized by Speaker Winthrop and offered his first contribution to the antiwar movement. This was his first congressional resolution, a crucial moment in the political life of any representative, and he could have picked a different, less controversial topic. His entire career had been devoted to economic issues. No doubt as he yearned for that congressional seat over the years he had imagined himself addressing the august body about tariffs, or banking, or transportation.

But Lincoln chose not to discuss economics. With a confidence surprising in a newly seated freshman congressman, Abraham Lincoln chose instead, on December 22, 1847, to demolish Polk's claims about the start of the war. He offered a brutally logical discourse on the spot where the war had begun. The boldness of his approach offered a clear rejoinder to Polk: Congress would no longer be bullied into submission.

Mary was most likely in the audience for her husband's first congressional resolution, having left her children in the care of one of the enslaved black women who earned extra wages at Mrs. Sprigg's in order to buy their own freedom. She would have been fashionably dressed, and at least as anxious as her husband. As Lincoln rose to the podium in the elegant red and gold galleries of the House, she would have had a better sense than

Lincoln's fellow representatives of what to expect. The other congressmen could hardly be blamed had they been misled by the stranger's awkward frame and high-pitched voice.

But as Lincoln launched into his discussion of the Nueces Strip and offered a series of eight resolutions that called Polk on what was, in Lincoln's eyes, an obvious lie, they no doubt listened more closely. Lincoln demanded to know the exact "spot" upon which Mexicans troops shed "American blood on American soil." Acting every bit the lawyer he was, Lincoln offered a devastating rebuke to Polk and proved that it had been U.S. troops who began the war by making an unprovoked attack on Mexico. The land in question was Mexican, Lincoln proclaimed, both by historical fact and by occupancy at the time. In an accusatory tone, he asked rhetorically if "the people of that settlement, or a majority of them, or any of them, have ever submitted themselves to the government or laws of Texas or of the United States, by consent or by compulsion, either by accepting office, or voting at elections, or paying tax, or serving on juries, or having process served upon them, or in any other way." The answer, all knew, was no.

Lincoln went further. He reminded listeners that the residents of the "contested region" fled "from the approach of the United States army, leaving unprotected their homes and their growing crops." Clearly, then, the "American blood" shed at the Rio Grande, the blood that belonged to "armed officers and soldiers, sent into that settlement by the military orders of the President, through the Secretary of War," could not rightly be blamed on Mexicans. The president, not Mexico, was responsible for their deaths, and for the war.[10]

Lincoln's Spot Resolutions were argued with clarity and delivered with conviction. But they were not particularly novel. Many of Lincoln's ideas and phrases were drawn directly from Henry Clay's Lexington address: that the "spot" in question was "within the very disputed district," that the war resulted from Polk's order that Taylor move his troops to the Rio Grande, and that Polk had never made the purpose of the war clear. Clay's speech, of course, had echoed similar charges made by other Whigs in private and in public. Only the fiercest Democratic stalwarts in Congress ever accepted Polk's claims about "American soil" at face value. Lincoln's approach was unusually lawyerly, pointed, and eloquent, but the grounds of his attack were familiar by December 1847. Lincoln's Spot Resolutions were tabled by Congress and never acted upon. But Lincoln's debut congressional performance was by no means a failure.

During the first month of the session, other Whig congressmen offered resolutions of their own, some of which came to a vote. Two weeks after Lincoln, George Ashmun proposed a resolution affirming that "the war was unnecessarily and unconstitutionally commenced by the president." Lincoln voted in favor, and the Ashmun Amendment passed, 85 votes in favor, 81 against.[11]

Neither Lincoln's Spot Resolutions nor his vote in favor of the Ashmun Amendment went over well in Illinois. Western Democrats, as well as some Whigs, were inclined to agree with Robert Winthrop about the demands of patriotism in a time of war. William Herndon chastised Lincoln, lecturing his law partner that it was the president's "duty . . . if the country was about to be invaded and armies were organized in Mexico for that purpose, to go—if necessary—into the very heart of Mexico and prevent the invasion." Herndon warned Lincoln that his positions not only were wrong but would be politically costly back home. Indeed, they might leave Lincoln unelectable in the future.[12]

Lincoln dismissed Herndon's concerns and justified his actions not in terms of political expediency but in terms of the demands of truth. "If you had been in my place you would have voted just as I did," he wrote Herndon. "Would you have voted what you felt you knew to be a lie? I know you would not. Would you have gone out of the House—skulked the vote? I expect not. . . . You are compelled to speak; and your only alternative is to tell the *truth* or tell a *lie*. I can not doubt which you would do."[13]

Lincoln refused to lie. He would not back down, he would not "skulk" the issue. In short, the occupant of seat 191 was no tame, spiritless fellow. This was a man who had determined to tell the truth and to bring the war to an end. Rather than back down, Lincoln decided to throw himself further into the controversy that was engulfing his country.

On January 12, Lincoln returned to the podium for his first full-length congressional speech. Once again the packed galleries most likely included an anxious and excited Mary Todd Lincoln. Lincoln began his address by revisiting the question of the spot where American blood was shed, elaborating on his Spot Resolutions, and holding the president to his own standards of truth. Polk, he ordered, must "attempt no evasion—no equivocation" on the issue, since "a nation *should* not, and the Almighty *will* not, be evaded." Was the spot in the United States, or was it not?

As he warmed to his subject, Lincoln's gestures and voice became more animated. The larger issue, he insisted, was Polk's moral stature. What was the state of the president's conscience and soul? As he wrote his address out for publication, he savaged both the president and the man's address to Congress. Polk, Lincoln intoned, is deeply conscious of being in the wrong—that he feels the blood of this war, like the blood of Abel, is crying to Heaven against him. That originally having some strong motive—what, I will not stop now to give my opinion concerning—to involve the two countries in a war, and trusting to escape scrutiny, by fixing the public gaze upon the exceeding brightness of military glory—that attractive rainbow, that rises in showers of blood, that serpent's eye, that charms to destroy—he plunged into it, and has swept, *on* and *on*, till, disappointed in his calculation of the ease with which Mexico might be subdued, he now finds himself, he knows not where—How like the half insane mumbling of a fever-dream, is the whole war part of his late message![14]

In Lincoln's account, Polk was a coward, hiding behind his office in order to wage war against an unoffending neighbor. In the process he had been seduced by "military glory," the chance, at last, to link his own name to war and killing, as had so many prominent Jacksonian Democrats of his generation. Worse yet, the president had seduced thousands of ordinary American men with the "attractive rainbow" of patriotism, revenge, and victory of arms that military service seemed to offer. And it had driven him to a state of madness. Now he could only repent the vast loss of life for which he, alone, was responsible.

Lincoln's condemnation of the president was total, his attack on the man blistering, but other aspects of his speech were more cautious than either Clay's Lexington address or many of the addresses made by Giddings, Adams, Ashmun, or half a dozen other congressional Whigs over the previous year and a half. Lincoln was careful to praise the troops, and he avoided entirely the divisive question of territorial annexation.

At least this was true about the version of the speech he recorded for posterity. Lincoln may have been carried away while delivering the second half of his speech. According to the Democratic Illinois *State Register,* Lincoln actually claimed that "God of Heaven has forgotten to defend the weak and innocent, and permitted the strong band of murderers and demons from hell to kill men, women, and children, and lay waste and pillage the land of the just." It seems highly unlikely that Lincoln would have referred to U.S. soldiers as "demons from hell," but perhaps the influence of Joshua Giddings and other antislavery Whigs at Mrs. Spriggs's and in Congress led him to issue a more sweeping condemnation of the war than he preferred to see in print. Perhaps also, stories of American volunteers scalping Mexican civilians at Agua Nueva brought the horrors of the Black Hawk War to his mind. As a young captain he witnessed wartime atrocities against women

"Mexican Family." *According to a Democratic paper in Illinois, Congressman Lincoln referred to Mexico as the "land of the just" in his January 12 congressional speech, and to U.S. soldiers as a "band of murderers and demons from hell" permitted "to kill men, women, and children."* Daguerreotype, ca. 1847, 2⅞ × 3¹³⁄₁₆ inches. Amon Carter Museum of American Art, Fort Worth, Texas, P1981.65.18.

and children, and made the unpopular choice to prevent a revenge killing by his own men. He upheld the sanctity of civilian life even when American volunteers accused him of cowardice. Lincoln knew something about "defend[ing] the weak and innocent." He had, perhaps, earned the right to pass judgment about morality during wartime.[15]

Lincoln's stinging account of the president's "sheerest deception" raised an immediate response. Democrat John Jamieson of Missouri rose after Lincoln, and proclaimed that a patriot never questions his president. "Whether we are in a war that is right or wrong," he argued, wasn't even "a debatable question." All American wars should be upheld by all Americans. And he chastised Lincoln—or, as he called him, the gentleman "from the Hardin and Baker district"—for insulting the memory of his military forebears. "Yes, sir; look back and see what your Hardin did. He was a Whig, to be sure . . . and fell nobly at Buena Vista. You have a Baker, too, from your district, and that Baker went along under Gen. Scott, and he too was in the bloody battle, and at Cerro Gordo commanded. . . . Coming from the district that had thus been represented, both here and in Mexico, it is astonishing to me how the gentleman could make the speech here which he has."[16]

But the many newspapers around the nation that chose to report on Lincoln's antiwar oratory suggested that John Jamieson was wrong and that the freshman congressman from the Hardin District was in fact upholding the tradition of patriotic service by recognizing that patriotism, in early 1848, required something other than mindless consent to an endless war; that perhaps conquering a peace required forthright action and considered dissent.

Lincoln's speech received a surprising amount of publicity. Newspapers in Boston and Vermont printed Lincoln's January 12 speech in full, and an Arkansas paper printed the preamble and resolutions of his speech.[17] Papers in Boston, Virginia, Connecticut, and New Jersey offered descriptions of Lincoln's speech as well as a detailed description of the man they all described as "Col. Hardin's" replacement in Congress. He was "a tall, raw-boned, thin and spare, dark-complexioned man. He is six feet four or five inches high. He speaks with rapidity and uses a good deal of gesture, some of which is quite new and original. He was listened to, however, with great attention, and made a sound, sensible and manly speech. . . . Mr. Lincoln is probably about forty years old. He represents Col. Hardin's old district; he who commanded the Illinois Regiment, and who fell at Buena Vista."[18] The *Baltimore Patriot* concluded that "evidently there is music in that very tall, Mr. Lincoln."[19]

At least sixteen newspapers, from Augusta, Maine, to Augusta, Georgia, reported that "Mr. Lincoln, of Illinois," delivered a speech "combating the idea that the war was commenced by the shedding of American blood on American soil," some devoting a long paragraph to his speech, others a single sentence. The New Orleans *Picayune* reported on both of Lincoln's antiwar addresses, not unfavorably, alongside their increasingly critical war correspondence.[20] The "manly" Mr. Lincoln was speaking the truth, and a national audience was ready to sing his praises. The *Missouri Republican* lauded his speech as one "of great power" and "the strongest and most conclusive arguments." Lincoln "commanded the attention of the House, which none but a strong man can do."[21]

Lincoln's antiwar activism brought him his first taste of the national renown he had long craved, but his words ignited a firestorm in Illinois. The state's Whig press was largely supportive of Lincoln, but it was the Democratic press that evinced true enthusiasm for Lincoln's Spot Resolutions, which were precisely the evidence they needed to tar Lincoln as a new "Benedict Arnold." The *Illinois Globe* regretted that "a representative from our noble state, should thus disgrace her . . . Well may the patriotic people of the 7th district lament that they have not a HARDIN or BAKER to represent them at this important crisis! Alas, poor SPOTTY!"[22]

Borrowing language from the pulp fiction of the day, the Illinois *State Register* dubbed Lincoln the "Ranchero Spotty." The paper reported on a public meeting held in opposition to Lincoln's stance that resolved, "Henceforth will the Benedict Arnold of our district be known here only as the Ranchero Spotty of one term." The Peoria *Press* predicted, "What an epitaph: 'Died of the *Spotted Fever.*' Poor Lincoln." Illinois's Democratic newspapers were unified in agreement that the "miserable man of 'spots' " was following a "traitorous course in Congress." The Democratic press in neighboring states also joined the chorus of disapproval.[23]

By tarring Lincoln as the Ranchero Spotty, the Illinois *State Register* suggested not just that Lincoln was siding with Mexico but also that Lincoln's words were akin to the actions of Mexico's irregular fighters. The journalists who referred to Lincoln as a ranchero were aware that guerrilla activity was an intractable problem for U.S. troops. Mexican rancheros terrorized U.S. troops by "picking off every one who ventured alone at any distance from the camp," as one popular war novelette explained. Arguing by analogy that congressional critics of the war were endangering the troops with what they considered to be cowardly, vicious, and unmanly attacks, hostile journalists attempted to group those critics in the same category as Mexican partisans. President Polk had made a similar comparison early in the conflict when he publicly charged that any criticism of the war gave "aid and comfort" to the enemy. It was an accusation that Polk returned to repeatedly in private as well as in public.[24]

Nor was this solely the view of Democrats. William Herndon, for one, was openly critical of Lincoln's behavior. He warned his law partner about the "extensive defections from the party ranks, and the injury his course was doing him." His opposition to the war in Mexico was nothing less than "political suicide."[25]

But Lincoln appeared not to care that his reputation in his own district was in "exceedingly bad repair" as a result of his antiwar agitation. On February 2, he wrote Herndon again, not to reassure his law partner but to praise an antiwar speech delivered by "a little slim, pale-faced, consumptive man" named Alexander Stephens of Georgia. Stephens declared that Polk's abuse of power in prosecuting the war was "disgraceful and infamous," and asserted that "the mark" of an "unnecessarily and unconstitutionally" begun war "is fixed upon him as indelibly as that stamped upon the brow of Cain by the finger of God." He contrasted Polk's craven acts to the brilliant success of Zachary Taylor, the presumptive Whig presidential candidate.[26]

But Stephens also talked about the precious lives lost at the Battle of Buena Vista nearly a year earlier, deaths that rested on Polk's shoulders. In a moving tribute to the famous martyrs of the war, he mentioned McKee and Yell, as well as Henry Clay Jr., whom he described as having "a heart as pure, stern, inflexible and patriotic, as the great sire from whom he sprung." But Stephens saved his final praise for a man whom Lincoln could not help but think a great deal about during his first months in office, "a Hardin, Mr. Speaker, well known to you and to me, and many of those around me, and of whom, I take this occasion to say, I never knew a truer, firmer, or nobler man."[27] The speech moved Lincoln to tears.

In his letter to Herndon, Lincoln declared it "the best speech, of an hour's length, I ever heard," and admitted that "my old, withered, dry eyes, are full of tears yet." Alexander Stephens was the representative of a Georgia district at least as divided over the war as Lincoln's. But he held nothing back in his blistering attack on Polk. His speech at once vindicated Lincoln's course in Congress and provided a political path forward for the Whigs to condemn the war yet support a war hero, Zachary Taylor, as president. It also offered a moving tribute to the man who was still the most famous representative of Illinois's Seventh Congressional District. It was a speech that placed Hardin's heroism in a context of dissent against the president and the war he had begun. It connected Hardin's bravery in supporting the war with Lincoln's in opposing it.

Stephens's speech linked Lincoln and his old rival in a manner that Lincoln himself had previously been unable to achieve. The next time Lincoln rose to the podium to discuss the war, he stated clearly that with the death of John Hardin, "we lost our best Whig man." And he laid claim to part of the "proud fame" of those who fell in the war: "As an American I too have a share," he asserted.[28]

The freshman Whig from Illinois determined to circulate "a good many copies" of Stephens's speech in his district, to let "our people" see that he was not undermining Hardin's accomplishments in opposing the war, but vindicating that loss by bringing the war to an end. Lincoln would let the people of Illinois see that dissent could be patriotic, that his route forward was the best for the country and for his party. He would show them that John Hardin was not the only hero from the Seventh Congressional District, that there was more than one way to be a conqueror.[29]

13

A Clear Conscience

LITTLE DID ABRAHAM LINCOLN know it, but he was not far from the mark when he described the president as finding himself "he knows not where" in the middle of January. Polk probably wouldn't have admitted it to anyone but Sarah, but matters had spiraled out of his control. Trist was negotiating without authority, and with each day that passed, Polk felt more strongly than ever that Trist's terms were too generous to Mexico. Under the influence of the aggressive expansionists in his cabinet, the president had concluded that the ideal location for a boundary would fall somewhere along the twenty-sixth parallel, running directly west from Matamoros below the southern tip of Texas at the Rio Grande, including at least a portion of Baja California. This would have given the United States another 187,000 square miles, or about a third more of Mexico than in the terms of the treaty he had delivered to Nicholas Trist. On January 2, Polk informed his cabinet that at the very least, "we might accede to a cession of New Mexico, the two Californias, and the passage across the Isthmus of Tehuantepec, paying for them a much less sum than Mr. Trist had been authorized to offer, and that we should in addition secure the port of Tampico."[1]

But Polk had no idea what was happening in Mexico. "Neither General Scott nor Trist has written a line to the Government by the train that left Mexico on the 13th of January," he fumed in his diary in early February. "There is a conspiracy" between Scott and Trist, he was sure, "to put the government at defiance and make a treaty of some sort." Had Polk known

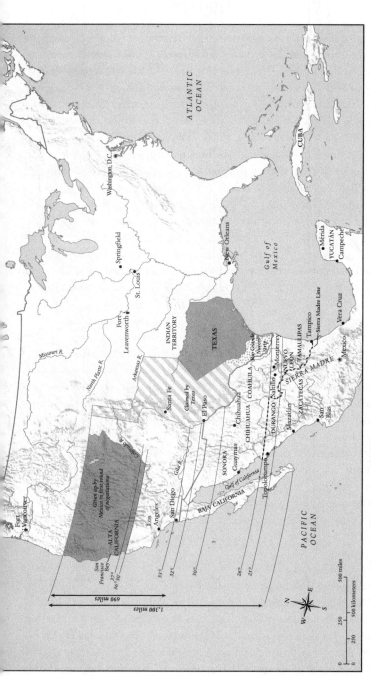

ANNEXING MEXICO This map illustrates potential annexations contemplated by the Polk administration in the fall of 1847 as well as the limited territorial cession initially offered by Mexican negotiators. Some Democratic expansionists hoped to take all of Mexico as spoils of war. Many Whigs, including Henry Clay, argued against taking any territory.

the true condition of matters in the Mexican capital, he would not have been reassured. In the final weeks of January, wealthy Mexican supporters of American annexation offered General Scott $1.25 million to accept the presidency of Mexico and oversee the annexation of the country to the United States. Mexican annexationists invited other American officers, including Ulysses S. Grant, to meetings to discuss the issue. At the end of January, Manuel Zamorg, a major in the Mexican national guard, warned a member of the Mexican legation in Paris about the "lamentable" condition "into which our beloved country is drifting. Mexico is beginning to be erased for the catalogue of nations," he wrote. "The Yankees are already in possession of two thirds of the country. . . . [A]ll the elements of a prompt and complete dissolution exist." Britain's minister to the United States wrote back to London that "there is a growing conviction in the minds of the people" that all of Mexico would be annexed.[2]

Scott had no interest in becoming president of Mexico, nor did he want to see Mexico annexed to the United States. Grant wanted nothing more than to go home. However they might feel about the people of Mexico or prospects for annexation, the soldiers, to a man, wanted the war over. "I hope there may be peace," one soldier wrote home to his family in New Orleans in February, "for I have not a hostile feeling against these Mexicanos tho' I . . . believe they prove treacherous more than any people I know." War had lost its appeal. Looking around at "some of the sad effects of war in the wasted forms of soldiers & others with loss of arms &c," this soldier wondered, "how much misery and distress is caused in the beautiful world of ours by sin."[3]

Scott understood the political divisions that were making it difficult for Mexicans to agree on a treaty, but the fact was that any day an officer might arrive from the United States with orders to physically remove Nicholas Trist from army headquarters. Clearly there was no more time for negotiation. Unless a treaty was signed immediately, Scott threatened, he would march his troops into the countryside and resume warfare against the Mexican people.

Provisional president Manuel de la Peña y Peña, recognizing the imminent danger to the continued existence of Mexico, gave his permission to the Mexican commissioners to sign a treaty of peace with Trist. His decision, the commissioners were told, was based on a number of factors, including "the extreme scantiness of resources, . . . the probability that the United States may prove every day more exacting in their demands," and the "duty" of the government "to put an end to the calamities from which the country is suffering and of checking the projects of annexation to North America."[4]

Trist and his Mexican counterparts met in the town of Guadalupe Hidalgo. The location was no accident. Guadalupe Hidalgo was considered by the people of Mexico "the most sacred" spot "on earth, as being the scene of the miraculous appearance of the Virgin for the purpose of declaring that Mexico was taken under Her protection."[5] Mexico, all the commissioners realized, had never been more in need of protection than at that moment.

On February 2, 1848, three Mexican commissioners and one recalled American signed their names to a treaty of peace in the "sanctuary" of the cathedral in Guadalupe Hidalgo. It was a solemn moment. Just before he picked up his pen, one of the men turned to Trist and said, "This must be a proud moment for you; no less proud for you than it is humiliating for us." Trist replied, "We are making *peace*, let that be our only thought." But he admitted to his family, "Could those Mexicans have seen into my heart at that moment, they would have known that my feeling of shame as an American was far stronger than theirs could be as Mexicans." Trist had felt shame throughout the negotiations, but particularly "at moments when I felt it necessary to *insist* upon things that they were averse to. Had my course at such moments been governed by my conscience as a man, and my sense of justice as an individual American, I should have *yielded* in every instance." But Trist knew full well that his vindictive president would find any opportunity to reject a treaty he had negotiated against orders, both out of anger at his betrayal and from the belief that a future treaty would bring more of Mexico into American hands.[6]

Trist did not yield. The terms of the Treaty of Guadalupe Hidalgo aligned closely with those Polk had specified in his original document, with the exception of the fact that Mexico kept Baja California. Trist was even savvy enough to authorize a U.S. payment of only fifteen million dollars in exchange for 525,000 square miles of Mexican land, when Polk had specified a maximum of twenty million. The United States agreed to recognize Mexican land grants and property rights, to provide a route to citizenship for those Mexican residents of the annexed territories who remained in what was now the United States, and to restrain raiding by Indian tribes over the border into Mexico, although none of these three promises would be fully met by the United States. Mexico relinquished all claims to Texas and recognized the Rio Grande as the border between Mexico and the United States.

It was not the most generous treaty Trist could have negotiated, but it was perhaps the most generous the president would accept. He hoped Polk would accept it. But Trist had no sense of what would happen, either to the treaty or to him. That his career in Washington was over was clear. The day before he put his signature on the document, he wrote his wife, Virginia, "I will live on bread and water before I will again hold office of any kind."[7] He had no idea how close to the mark this prediction would be. But he knew with absolute certainty that he had done the right thing, both for Mexico and for the United States. His "conscience as a man" was clear.

James Freaner, the New Orleans correspondent who had advised Trist to continue negotiating the treaty after his recall, rushed the treaty to Washington in just seventeen days, a record for any war correspondence. He arrived at James Buchanan's Washington home after dark, looking every bit like a person who hadn't bathed or slept in days. Buchanan immediately brought the treaty to the White House, and at 9:00 p.m. on February 19 began reading it out loud to an incredulous president. They discussed it together, and then Buchanan returned home.

Polk was left alone with the treaty of peace that he had so long wished for but was unsure he could accept. He stayed up late into the night reading it over. He was keenly aware of the country's war fatigue. Nothing he did or said seemed to diminish it. Though Democrats would not stop calling for the annexation of all of Mexico, he knew full well that the antiwar movement was in the ascendancy. "Mr. Trist had acted very badly," he wrote in his diary before going to bed, "but notwithstanding this, if on further examination the Treaty is one that can be accepted, it should not be rejected on account of his bad conduct."[8]

After lengthy and animated cabinet discussions the next day, Polk concluded that he had to accept Trist's treaty. He didn't want to accept it, and Buchanan and Walker insisted he reject it and demand more land from Mexico. "If the treaty was now to be made," he fumed, "I should demand more territory, perhaps to make the Sierra Madre the line." Sonora, Chihuahua, and Coahuila were relatively unpopulated, and legendary for their mineral wealth. The acquisition of that territory would also ensure good land for a southern transcontinental railroad route, an objective fervently desired by the businessmen of the South. The coastal territory of Baja California offered access to both the Pacific Ocean and the Gulf of California. It didn't take a visionary to see that this land could be valuable to the United States, and that the United States would make good use of it.[9]

But given the hostility of Congress, Polk felt he had little choice but to submit the treaty to the Senate for ratification. Because were he to reject Trist's treaty, what would be the "consequences"? "A majority of one branch of Congress is opposed to my administration; they have falsely charged that the war was brought on and is continued by me with a view to the conquest of Mexico," Polk wrote. "If I were now to reject a treaty made upon my own terms . . . the probability is that Congress would not grant either men or money to prosecute the war . . . and I might . . . lose the two Provinces of New Mexico and Upper California, which were ceded to the United States by this treaty."[10]

Trist's treaty was far from perfect, but it was the best option open to him. At least it guaranteed the acquisition of California. Polk had entered office intent on bringing California into the Union. Trist's treaty ensured that America's destiny on the Pacific would be fulfilled. Polk's destiny, as the agent of American empire, was also fulfilled. At noon on February 21, the president called his cabinet together and announced his decision to submit the Treaty of Guadalupe Hidalgo to the Senate for ratification. When James Buchanan tried to talk him out of it, insisting on the need for a greater territorial cession, Polk chastised him, reminding the presidential hopeful that at the start of the war Buchanan had been opposed to taking any territory from Mexico at all. Polk's mind was made up; the last thing he needed now was politically motivated antagonism in his own cabinet. "No candidate for the Presidency ought ever to remain in the Cabinet," he sighed to his diary later that night.[11]

News of the treaty swept through Washington. Before seeing so much as a draft, congressmen were passing judgment on it. Many agreed with Buchanan that the terms were far too lenient to Mexico. A large number of Whigs adopted the opposite view, that any territorial cession was too much. And members of both parties asked whether it was right to consider a treaty negotiated by a recalled commissioner.

But the same day Polk submitted the Treaty of Guadalupe Hidalgo to the Senate, John Quincy Adams collapsed in his seat in the House of Representatives in a paralytic stroke. He was just about to cast his final antiwar vote, against a resolution of thanks to army officers in Mexico. Discussion of the treaty abruptly ceased; balls and dinners in honor of George Washington's birthday were canceled. Adams regained consciousness long enough to ask for Henry Clay. Weeping, Clay was brought to his side and clasped his hand. Two days later, on February 23, 1848, the great antislavery voice died.

Polk raised black crepe over the front door of the White House and ordered all government business suspended for two days. And as he sat down to write in his diary at the end of another long day, he thought about his place in history. "The first seven Presidents are all now dead," he wrote in his characteristically unsentimental manner. "The ninth President is also dead. Mr. Van Buren who was the eighth President and Mr. Tyler . . . are the only two of my predecessors who now survive." But this brush with mortality did nothing to ease his hatred of Nicholas Trist. After reading some of the "arrogant, highly exceptional, & . . . insulting" dispatches sent by Trist with the treaty, Polk finally sent an order for the diplomat to be bodily removed from the headquarters of the army in Mexico and escorted to Veracruz.[12]

Abraham Lincoln was also thinking about mortality. After witnessing Adams's collapse in the House, he learned he was to be a pallbearer in the elaborate state funeral. He, along with other congressional Whigs, escorted Adams's remains to "the place designated for interment." Only a few days later, while gloomy letters from Illinois about his "Spotty" reputation back home were arriving by mail, Lincoln cast his first antislavery vote as a congressman. He voted in support of the Wilmot Proviso banning slavery from all territory gained from Mexico, which was once again being introduced by northerners despite the fact that it had no chance of passing in the southern-controlled Senate. The proviso had twice been approved in the House since it was initially introduced by David Wilmot, and twice it had been defeated in the Senate.[13]

Lincoln had always been quiet about slavery. During his congressional campaign, he had avoided any mention of the topic. No more. After several meetings with his housemate Joshua Giddings, Lincoln began preparing resolutions to abolish slavery in Washington, D.C. The freshman congressman from Illinois and the abolitionist worked together on a gradual emancipation bill, which offered compensation to slave owners for their property. Joshua Giddings praised the bill. In 1860 he reminded abolitionists that Lincoln had "cast aside the shackles of his party and took his stand . . . laboring in the cause of humanity" with the bill. But in the end Lincoln did not introduce it to Congress. He delivered speeches alongside abolitionist congressional Whigs. The old economic questions that used to inspire him up until now took a backseat to issues of liberty and freedom.[14]

And he could take pride in the role he played in ending the war. Whatever reservations senators on both sides of the aisle held about the Treaty of Guadalupe Hidalgo were muted in the solemn days following John Quincy Adams's funeral. After revising articles in the treaty that would recognize Spanish and Mexican land grants, and modifying the language about citizenship, the treaty overwhelmingly passed the Senate on March 10. And on May 19, almost exactly two years after the U.S. Congress had first assented to Polk's war bill, Mexico's Congress ratified the revised treaty. San Francisco was alive with rumors of gold in the California hills that spring, but as so often was the case in the course of the war, limited communication made all the difference. Mexico City didn't receive news about the astounding find at Sutter's Mill until three months after signing ownership of its El Dorado over to the United States.

Polk got California, but it was the antiwar movement that conquered a peace. The American public had turned against the war for a number of reasons, not all of which were admirable. Many were motivated by racism, unwilling to offer citizenship to the people of Mexico. The year 1848 marked the first time that the fear of incorporating supposedly "inferior races" into the United States limited the nation's territorial expansion. Racism would continue to shape anti-imperialism for the rest of the century, most notably when the Senate rejected President Ulysses S. Grant's treaty to annex the Dominican Republic in 1870 on racial grounds.[15] Others opposed annexing Mexican territory because they feared the increasing power of slaveholders. Some simply concluded that Mexican land wasn't worth the sacrifice of American blood and money.

But had Nicholas Trist not concluded that justice required him to disobey his president and negotiate a lenient peace treaty with Mexico, no Treaty of Guadalupe Hidalgo would have emerged in 1848. Had Clay not spoken out in Lexington, popular meetings supporting his resolutions would not have bloomed, and congressmen would have restrained their rhetoric. Lincoln might not have opposed the war at all. Had journalists and soldiers lacked the courage to report atrocities, clerics such as Albert Hale might never have preached against the iniquity of the war, and the public would not have understood the true cost of the conflict. Had the people of Massachusetts not protested the war as immoral, the residents of other states would not have known that sustained opposition was both possible and patriotic.

Although Polk never mentioned Lincoln or his attacks directly, the cumulative effect of national antiwar agitation generally, and congressional antiwar agitation in particular, was to limit both the duration of the war and Polk's demands for Mexican territory. Lincoln's Spot Resolutions were his signature position in the Thirtieth Congress. Had he chosen to focus on tariffs during the first months of his congressional term, would Polk have felt the same degree of assault from Congress? It is impossible to know for sure, but at the very least Lincoln could conclude that his stance against the war had contributed to Polk's decision to accept the Treaty of Guadalupe Hidalgo. Charles Averill's fictional Mexican ranchero attempted to kidnap

Nicholas Trist in order to prevent an ignominious peace for Mexico, but the man Illinois Democrats labeled the "Ranchero Spotty" may well have helped Trist accomplish his mission.

Nicholas Trist returned from Mexico to face the enduring contempt of James Polk. The president might sign the treaty, but he would give Trist no credit for it. He fired the "impudent and unqualified scoundrel" and withheld the pay he had earned during his stay in Mexico.[16] Polk did everything in his power to prevent Trist from receiving either credit for his success or future employment. And he carried his hatred of Trist to his grave.

No one came to Trist's aid, and he proved unsuited "both by taste and qualification" to "the *rough roll and tumble* contests of professional calling." In desperate need of funds, he spent the next twenty years battling poverty, renting out rooms in his house, and toiling as paymaster for a railroad company. But he never apologized for his actions in Mexico. In 1848 Trist proudly told the House of Representatives, "If I am to have a fault, I would rather speak too harshly, and thrust forth truth unwisely, than to have played the hypocrite and held truth in."[17]

In 1861 Winfield Scott appealed to the Lincoln administration to appoint Trist revenue collector of Philadelphia, but his petition was ignored. Perhaps Trist was too much of a Democrat for employment in a Republican administration. Or perhaps Lincoln viewed Trist as simply another job seeker, with Scott's recommendation lacking the weight of one by a Jefferson or Jackson. After all, the two men never knew each other, despite their shared labor in the creation of America's first national antiwar movement.

It wasn't until Trist's seventieth birthday, in 1870, that Congress finally granted the diplomat the back pay he was owed for his service in Mexico, with interest. It was no member of Trist's beloved Democratic Party who took up his cause, but the Massachusetts antiwar agitator Charles Sumner, the man willing to jettison a lifelong friendship with Robert Winthrop over his war vote. With the sectional issues raised by the U.S.-Mexican War "resolved" through the Civil War, both northerners and southerners found it at last possible to acknowledge the service of Nicholas Trist. President Ulysses S. Grant appointed Trist postmaster of Alexandria, Virginia. Finally, Trist got the posting he had dreamed of, and he spent four happy years there before his death in 1874.

Henry Clay helped to crystallize antiwar sentiment throughout the northern half of the country and to provide a practical outlet for opposition to the war with his call to action. The Lexington resolutions became

Nicholas P. Trist, 1855–65. Polk never forgave Trist for disobeying his orders. Exiled from the State Department, Trist spent the following two decades in poverty. Library of Congress Prints and Photographs Division.

the Whig platform on the war and were proudly reprinted in the 1848 *Whig Almanac*. Clay had taken a clear gamble with his courageous speech, but at a cost to his career. It was his willingness to jeopardize his political base in the South that made his words so compelling in the North, and enabled Whigs, Free-Soil Party members, and disaffected northern Democrats to rally around the Lexington resolutions. "It may be that Mr. Clay has uttered the truth too boldly for popularity at the moment," a correspondent to the *Milwaukee Sentinel and Gazette* suggested. "But succeeding years will increase the conviction that a truer or bolder man never stood forward to enlighten and guide his countrymen, even against their will."[18] Although this speech more than any other mobilized the national antiwar movement, it also, in a sense, made Henry Clay the second martyr to the war in his own family.

For Henry Clay would not win the presidential nomination in 1848.

It was his Lexington speech that killed his candidacy. One longtime "sincere friend" of Abraham Lincoln's, the *Tazewell* (Illinois) *Whig* editor Anson G. Henry, wrote Lincoln not long after he heard about the speech.

Henry believed that the territorial position Clay had staked out would be fatal to the Whig Party. He admitted to Lincoln that he felt "a very great anxiety to know what course you design taking in relation to the Mexican War. I hope you will not feel disposed to go with Mr. Clay against all Territory." He predicted that "that speech of Mr Clay will beat us as a party for years to come, unless we can unite upon 'Old Zach.' "[19]

In fact, Anson Henry's concern about the electability of antiwar Whigs was shared by Lincoln. As much as Lincoln admired Henry Clay, he agreed that the Sage of Ashland's courageous Lexington speech doomed him as a candidate. He voted against a "no territory" resolution in early January when one appeared before Congress.[20]

And so, even while attacking Polk on the floor of Congress, Abraham Lincoln began to work for Zachary Taylor's election. As the lone Whig from Illinois in Congress, he was in a unique position to shape Taylor's candidacy. In notes he prepared in January 1848 for a speech to be delivered by the presidential candidate and war hero, Lincoln suggested that Taylor tell his audience: "As to the Mexican war, I still think the defensive line policy the best to terminate it—In a final treaty of peace, we shall probably be under a sort of necessity of taking some teritory; but it is my desire that we shall not acquire any extending so far South as to enlarge and agrivate the distracting question of slavery—Should I come into the presidency before these questions shall be settled, I should act in relation to them in accordance with the views here expressed."[21] One of Clay's most adoring supporters, a man who devoted his congressional term to reiterating many of the things he had heard in Lexington on a rainy afternoon, turned against Clay in 1848.

The Whigs had their second and final victory in a presidential election that year, as in 1840, with a war hero at the head of the ticket. Southerners mistakenly supposed that General Taylor, a Louisiana slaveholder, would protect their interests. But when it came time for California to enter the Union, Taylor supported the Wilmot Proviso, leading infuriated southerners to threaten secession unless Mexican Cession lands were opened up to slavery.

Henry Clay, unelectable nationally, returned to the Senate in 1849. The following year, Clay introduced the Compromise of 1850. His omnibus bill failed to receive a majority, but once again his powers of persuasion proved crucial in saving the nation. Illinois Democrat Stephen A. Douglas engineered the separate passage of all the bills contained in Clay's original proposal. It brought California into the Union as a free state, finally resolved Texas's lingering boundary claims over New Mexico, and temporarily

Henry Clay, ca. 1850. Portrait by Mathew Brady. Clay as he appeared the year of his final great compromise. Library of Congress Prints and Photographs Division.

averted disunion. Mississippi senator Henry Foote, who drew a pistol on Thomas Hart Benton during the heated debate in 1850, later wrote, "Had there been one such man in the Congress of the United States as Henry Clay in 1860–61, there would, I feel sure, have been no Civil War."[22] Clay died less than two years after the passage of the 1850 compromise.

Polk left the presidential office in the hands of the Whig general he had inadvertently made famous. As he slowly returned to Nashville with Sarah, he thought about similar trips he had made in the past. He reminisced about the trip with Jackson at the close of his remarkable presidency, when Old Hickory told Sarah she would one day be First Lady. And of course he remembered the trip north to Washington at the start of his own term. Now things had come full circle. He was the president returning home after his own remarkably successful term in office. He had lived up to Jackson's example and fulfilled Old Hickory's mission. The couple was feted in every town along the route, just as Jackson had been. But James found he had just a fraction of his old energy. They all wanted him to speak, and he "felt it was right to do so." But Sarah cut his addresses short; she couldn't shake the "feeling" that James's "life was at stake."[23]

The trip nearly killed him. Sarah never forgot how much "this triumphal progress" weakened her husband. By the time they reached their new home in Nashville, Polk Place, his condition was obvious to everyone. The Nashville *Union* wrote that at his reception, "the feebleness of the late President was apparent," and "the most intense anxiety for his health has pervaded the city."[24]

Three months later, Polk was dead. Few doubted that he had worked himself to death. And yet during his single brilliant term, he accomplished a feat that earlier presidents would have considered impossible. With the help of his wife, Sarah, he masterminded, provoked, and successfully prosecuted a war that turned the United States into a world power. To James and Sarah Polk, the war was not an unjust conflict, an unethical clash; it was a patriotic mission. Sarah dismissed the protests just as her husband had done. "Of course there were some opposed," she told a Nashville reporter, "there is always somebody opposed to everything." But until the end of her life she maintained that the acquisition of Texas, California, and New Mexico were "among the most important events in the history of this country."[25] With his conscience clear, James K. Polk, on his deathbed, asked to be baptized. Distancing himself from Sarah for one of the few times in his life, he joined not her Presbyterian Church but that of the Methodists.

Though three men of conscience had sacrificed careers to oppose him, had even managed to bring a "wicked war" to a close, it was Polk who was triumphant. Mexico lost half its territory. Gone were the provinces of Alta California, Nuevo Mexico, and parts of Tamaulipas, Coahuila, and Sonora. That land became California, Nevada, and Utah, and parts of Arizona, New Mexico, Oklahoma, Kansas, Colorado, and Texas. In total more than 12,500 U.S. soldiers perished, as well as at least 25,000 Mexicans. It was the crowning moment for Manifest Destiny and fed the dreams of those Americans who believed the United States should take even more territory by force, dreams that had their realization in the Spanish-American War of 1898.[26]

But Polk's war didn't merely change the country's face. It set a number of precedents that would shape the future of American diplomacy and warfare. His was the first American war against a neighboring republic, the first started with a presidential lie, and the first that a large number of American people felt guilty about.

Beyond these firsts, the U.S.-Mexican War had an explicit catastrophic impact: it fractured the delicate sectional balance within the United States. Ralph Waldo Emerson famously predicted in 1846 that the United States would defeat Mexico but that "Mexico will poison us." The poison took effect immediately. When once it had been understood where it was legal to own slaves and where it was not, that stability was now disturbed. News of gold at Sutter's Mill brought a hundred thousand people to California in a little more than a year. In 1848 and again in early 1849, James K. Polk appealed to Congress to grant California territorial status, but the issue of slavery made it impossible for representatives to reach an agreement. Southerners had already brought their slaves to California, but the majority of settlers were adamantly opposed to slavery. Southerners refused to accept that they and their slaves would be banned from the Mexican lands they had shed so much blood for. Northerners were equally adamant that their sacrifice translate into "free soil" where they and their children could work free from association with slavery. Victory in Mexico spurred expansionists in both sections of the country to push for more land, in Hawaii, Central America, the Yucatán, and particularly Cuba, further exacerbating sectional tensions. The stage was set for secession. It was an argument that could not be settled with words.[27]

The war raised fundamental questions, questions that proved too painful to answer at the time. After dismantling a neighboring republic for the sole purpose of aggrandizement, could the United States any longer make claims to altruism in international affairs? After Polk provoked a war and then lied to Congress about it, could presidents be trusted to behave honestly in matters of life and death? After annexing Mexico's northwest, could the United States still contrast its acts with the imperialist oppression of its then-nemesis, Britain? Why had it been so easy to manipulate the American public to support a war as contrary to American principles as this one? How could the opposition party so readily surrender its objections as the Whigs did in 1846?

The conflict Polk engineered became the transformative event of the era. It not only changed the nation but also created a new generation of leaders, for good and for ill. In the military, Robert E. Lee, Ulysses S. Grant, Stonewall Jackson, George Meade, and Jefferson Davis all first experienced military command in Mexico. It was there that they learned the basis of the strategy and tactics that dominated the Civil War. Polk's war also catapulted the officers Zachary Taylor and Franklin Pierce into presidencies for which they were woefully ill equipped.

Then there was the congressman from Illinois.

In 1848 a Democrat won election to Congress from the Seventh Congressional District. The seat held by Hardin, Baker, and Lincoln was no longer safe for the Whigs. Many blamed Lincoln's antiwar activism for the loss. Lincoln returned home in 1849 and did not run again for Congress. But he had learned something that might now be called Lincolnesque: the necessity of melding political and ethical considerations. As he protested the war and condemned slavery, he was not embracing a simple politics of morality, though it must often have seemed to his few supporters that his sense of decency was mangling his ambition. In fact, he was learning to avoid false dichotomies between morality and hard political decisions. The war showed him how to make ambition, ethics, and politics work in concert. He helped to bring the war to a close, and then helped elect a war hero from his own party to the presidency.[28]

But he never forgot Henry Clay. When Clay died in Washington in 1852, Lincoln delivered a eulogy at the Springfield statehouse. Most of Clay's eulogists praised his genius for compromise. Lincoln did not. He focused instead on Clay's "devotion to human liberty." Lincoln's portrait of Clay was of a man who sacrificed for what was right. "The long enduring spell with which the souls of men were bound to him, is a miracle," Lincoln proclaimed.[29] Taking a stand against the U.S.-Mexican War helped make Clay great. Taking a similar stand made Lincoln a better politician, and perhaps also a better person.

Ten years later, when he ran for the Senate, the people of Illinois had not forgotten what he'd said about the war. Despite the fact that Lincoln was careful while in Congress to always vote for supplies for the troops, his words haunted him politically for the rest of his life. During their famed 1858 senatorial campaign debates, Stephen A. Douglas reminded the Illinois public that "whilst in Congress" Lincoln "distinguished himself by his opposition to the Mexican War, taking the side of the common enemy against his own country; and when he returned home he found that the indignation of the people followed him everywhere, and he was again submerged or obliged to retire into private life, forgotten by his former friends." The editor of the *Chicago Tribune* wrote a confidential letter to Lincoln afterward, warning the candidate that Douglas's charges were "calculated to do mischief" among potential Republican voters. "Tens of thousands of our party are old Democrats, and you know their sentiments on this Mexican War supply question."[30]

Again in 1860, Lincoln's opponents revisited the legend of the Ranchero Spotty, accusing him of aiding and abetting the enemy in 1848. The charges did not fall on dull ears, as questions about Lincoln's patriotism and actions at that time remained unresolved among voters of all educational levels. One "undisided yet . . . honest man" wrote Republican candidate Lincoln in 1860 to ask two questions. "The first is this did you vote against sending provisions to the soldiers when they was in mexico . . . the second is this did you refuse to vote A bill of thanks to the soldiers that fought in mexico did you say that you would not vote A bill of thanks to the soldiers without they would add this amendment to it. that it was an injust war."[31]

A New York iron merchant also hoped for clarification before casting his vote in 1860. On business stationery featuring an attractive representation of his spacious iron dealership, William H. Wilson queried Lincoln, "Will you be kind enough to say if you *did* or *did not* while you were in congress vote against supplies to the american army while on the Battle fields of Mexico. The charge has been brought forward by your opponents and *I* have as often charged it to be a *falsehood* and although opposed to betting I as a last resort have agreed to back *my* opinion that such was not the fact."[32]

Lincoln won in 1860, of course. And while America's unjust war of imperial desire shoved the nation into the most horrible of national fractures, yet at the same it time helped create the leader who was able to reunite the states. It was Lincoln who would prove the greatest man of his generation, not Polk, Clay, Trist, or his once unstoppable rival, John Hardin. The Battle of Buena Vista and its pantheon of heroes had faded from memory by the time Abraham Lincoln lost his life in the service of his country eighteen years later.

Lineage

THE NATION FORGOT about Colonel John Hardin, but his children did not. In 1851 their mother married Reuben Hyde Walworth, the last chancellor of New York State and a widower twenty-four years her senior. The Chancellor, as he was universally known, moved the Hardin family into his mansion in Saratoga, New York. In an attempt to emulate their father's military glory, both of the Hardin boys fought in the Civil War. Martin became a brigadier general in the Union Army, while Lemuel joined a band of Confederate raiders in border-state Kentucky and later fled to Canada. Both men sustained serious injuries in the conflict.

Ellen Hardin gained greater fame than either of her brothers, though some of it was decidedly unwanted. At age twenty, just a year after her mother's wedding, she married her stepbrother, Mansfield Walworth. They had six children in quick succession, and Mansfield found success as an author of lowbrow popular fiction. On the surface, the family was attractive and prosperous, but Mansfield proved emotionally unstable and physically abused his wife. Ellen left him. After he threatened her life in 1873, their eldest son, Frank, shot him to death in a New York hotel room. The "uncommonly shocking murder" in such an elite family became a media sensation, with reporters avidly following the resulting trial. Frank was convicted of parricide. Intent on overturning his conviction, Ellen put herself through law school at New York University, a singularly rare thing for a woman to do in the 1870s. More remarkably, she managed to secure Frank's release from prison in 1877 on the grounds of legal insanity.[1]

Left to support a large family, Ellen practiced law for a period of time, but she felt increasingly drawn to her childhood love of history—a passion she attributed to her father's influence. She recounted how her father would read history to her when she was a girl, "and he accompanied the reading by explanations of the geography and government of the nations named." He had encouraged her interest. "When I asked for something to read," she recalled, "I was sent to 'Plutarch's Lives' which became like a long continued fairy story to my young imagination."[2]

As Ellen grew older she discovered that America's history was just as compelling as Europe's. It was all around her in upstate New York, and she set out to document and commemorate it. In the years after the Civil War, she took the lead in preserving Saratoga's Revolutionary War battlefields. Her interests in historic preservation took a national turn when she spearheaded a campaign in 1876 for funds to renovate George Washington's home at Mount Vernon. Suddenly, Ellen Hardin Walworth was a figure of importance in her own right, and found herself invited to the same sort of social events in Washington, D.C., that her father, as a freshman congressman, had attended thirty years earlier. She corresponded with the wives of Presidents Harrison, McKinley, and Wilson, and was one of the first people to propose the establishment of the U.S. National Archives, in a speech at the World's Columbian Expedition in Chicago.

Ellen began to write, and found she was good at it. Her husband found success as a novelist, but she gravitated toward fact. A skilled amateur geologist, she was one of the first women to publish a paper in the *Proceedings of the American Association for the Advancement of Science*. But above all else it was the history of the early United States that she enjoyed chronicling. She wrote the visitor's guide to the Saratoga battlefields, a rousing history of the Saratoga Campaign, and the official history of the Saratoga Monument Association. She began publishing historical articles, edited a journal, and became a prolific author on topics related to the Revolutionary War.

Despite the formative influence of the U.S.-Mexican War on her life, Ellen wrote just a single article on the 1847 conflict, a lengthy and technical military analysis of the Battle of Buena Vista that she published in 1874. Her narrative of the conflict was long on praise for the Whigs, including her father, who overcame their political scruples to volunteer, and short on analysis of the larger implications of the conflict. She condemned Taylor's management of the battle and suggested that had the army built breastworks the night before the battle, many lives would have been saved.[3] And then she returned to writing about the Revolution.

It is telling that Ellen Hardin Walworth devoted her later life to promoting the memory of the Revolutionary War, rather than the U.S. war with Mexico. In Mexico, *la invasion norteamericana* exerted a powerful force in the political realignment of the late nineteenth century, the creation of a centralized state, and the forging of a common Mexican identity. But the half-life of the war north of the border region was remarkably short. In the decades after the Civil War, the 1847 conflict faded from memory. Most Americans, including Ellen, preferred to think about it as little as possible. One of Polk's supporters assured the president in 1846 that over time his actions would be vindicated. "History will be . . . ready with her sentence of condemnation" for those who opposed the president and his war, the Democratic stalwart predicted, just as the opponents of the War of 1812 were later demonized. "It cannot be doubted that in a few years, fewer than elapsed after the war of 1812, those now assailing you for the war with Mexico and the principles on which it is waged, will be as anxious to throw oblivion over their conduct as were those who denounced Mr. Madison for the war against England."[4]

But Polk's supporters were wrong. It was antiwar forces that ultimately proved victorious in the battle over the memory of the 1847 war. In 1879 former president Ulysses S. Grant told a journalist, "I do not think there was ever a more wicked war than that waged by the United States on Mexico. I thought so at the time, when I was a youngster, only I had not moral courage enough to resign." At the end of his life he elaborated on his feelings. The U.S.-Mexican War was "one of the most unjust ever waged by a stronger against a weaker nation," he wrote in his memoirs. The Civil War, he declared, was "our punishment" for that "transgression."[5]

By the late nineteenth century, Grant's views had become mainstream. The Republican Party, born from the collapse of the Whig Party in the 1850s, adopted the Whig view of the war as its own and dominated national politics through the second half of the century. Republicans asserted that the 1847 war was wicked, wrong, and a blot on the nation's proud military history. Ellen Hardin wasn't the only American to much prefer the Revolution. Far better to focus on a war that all Americans could agree was right and just, a war for principle, rather than the fatal and destructive war for empire that tore the nation apart. Better to return, at least in memory, to a period when Americans were united against an oppressor.

After a life full of tragedy and drama, Ellen Hardin found meaning in the past, in the sacrifices of soldiers who died before she was born. She cultivated a patriotism grounded in her links to that past, and as she looked around at the inequality and social unrest of the late nineteenth century, she became increasingly convinced that such historically grounded patriotism not only had been good for her personally but also could help uplift the nation as a whole. She believed that the knowledge of what their "forefathers and mothers . . . sacrificed for home and country" might allow Americans "to comprehend the price of the legacy left, and to realize that if we hold this magnificent inheritance . . . we must keep the camp fires of loyalty alive, that there shall be no wavering of devotion to the principles they planted, her institutions must be kept pure, her laws just, her government upright."[6]

On Columbus Day in 1890, Ellen and three like-minded women met together in the parlor of the Strathmore Arms Hotel in Washington, D.C. Their goal was to found a women's organization devoted to the promotion of historic memory and American patriotism. They vowed to work together to "perpetuate the memory and spirit of the men and women who achieved American Independence," and to "cherish, maintain, and extend the institutions of American freedom, to foster true patriotism and love of country, and to aid in securing for mankind all the blessings of liberty." They imagined chapters of their "patriotic and national Society" in towns and cities of every state in the Union. Thinking big, they invited Sarah Polk to join their board of directors as an honorary vice president. The eighty-seven-year-old former First Lady, still dressed in black forty years after the death of her husband and still living in Polk Place, the Nashville home she and James had shared for just three months, happily accepted the invitation. Mrs. James K. Polk entirely endorsed the patriotic mission of the group, which was so close to her own. Who had been more instrumental in securing "the blessings of liberty" for mankind than she and James? Had her own husband not given his life for this very cause?[7]

The vice presidency of the organization Ellen Hardin founded was one of the last honors in Sarah's long life. Less than a year later she died at home, and was buried next to James on the Polk Place grounds.

As for Ellen, she never forgot her father, but she had trouble finding a lesson in his sacrifice. She could summarize his career in a single sentence: "He was a member of Congress from Illinois, was opposed to the annexation of Texas, but when war was declared against Mexico he raised a regiment, was in the battles of Gen'l Taylor's Division, and lost his life in the battle of Buena Vista." But what did it mean? She contemplated writing his biography and even conducted research for the project. But she set it aside and returned to writing about the war of 1776.[8]

*Ellen Hardin Walworth, 1899. As director general
of the Women's National War Relief Association,
John Hardin's daughter directed the outfitting of an
ambulance ship and yellow fever hospital during the
Spanish-American War while promoting the expansion
of the Daughters of the American Revolution overseas.*
Women's National War Relief Association, *The Women's
National War Relief Association* (New York: Printed by order
of the Board of Directors, 1899), vii.

Although she was truly a daughter of the U.S.-Mexican War, she and her
colleagues named their new organization the Daughters of the American
Revolution. Ellen provided the society with its first motto, *Amor patriae,*
Latin for "love of country," with *patriae,* or "country," derived from *pater,* or
"father"—love of the fatherland. The sole requirement for membership was
"proven lineal descent" from a patriot of the American Revolution, something she, Sarah Polk, and the other organizers all shared.[9]

As she proudly documented in her application for admission as a charter
member of the DAR on December 16, 1890, Ellen Hardin had as a patriotic
forefather John Hardin. This was not the John Hardin who was a colonel in

the U.S.-Mexican War, and for whom a county seat in Illinois was named, but her great-grandfather John Hardin, a colonel in Wayne's campaign, a lieutenant in Morgan's rifle corps, and the recipient of public thanks from General Gates for his "distinguished services" at the Battle of Saratoga. "When the first call for troops was made to resist Great Britain John Hardin began recruiting," she proudly stated. "He was in the march through Canada and in every engagement and movement of the Rifle Corps until 1779."[10]

She looked back to the John Hardin for whom Hardin County in Kentucky, Hardin County in Ohio, and Hardin County in Illinois were named, a man whom Ellen never knew but had no problem imagining and describing. But hers was a selective history. She recounted how "in 1792 he was sent from Kentucky by special order of General Washington, through General Wilkinson, on a mission of peace to the Indians of Northern Ohio, and was massacred by them." But she left out of the story John Hardin's long history of violence against Indians. She never mentioned his assaults on Indian villages from Virginia to Indiana, despite the fame those acts gained him among both white and Indian people during his life. She said nothing about his troubled history with the Shawnee who killed him. And she certainly never mentioned the slave who was murdered by his side.[11]

The Daughters of the American Revolution was founded in the fervent belief that awareness about America's first patriots would lead Americans to live up to "the principles they planted." But John Hardin's history with slaves and Indians was not the legacy Ellen cared to transmit. Western expansion had always come at a cost to someone. In her nostalgic remembrance, however, the patriots of the Revolutionary War were guiltless of the sins not just of their fathers but of *her* father. Theirs was a war for freedom, not oppression.

Through the Daughters of the American Revolution, Ellen elevated her bond with the original American John Hardin over that with her father. She created an organization that to this day asserts the special status of those whose blood is drawn from warriors of the country's war for independence, rather than war for empire. "From these Colonial struggles," the DAR asserted, "will come an American manhood that will build a structure for liberty to endure forever." Ellen ignored the many similarities between the two John Hardins, two men who never missed an opportunity to fight, who were among the first to raise troops to face the enemy, who both were colonels in the U.S. Army and generals in their state militia, who both were killed in the name of Manifest Destiny while accompanied by unacknowledged and unfree African American servants. Both men were dead before the age of thirty-nine. Ellen may never have considered the extent to which the Revolution, the Indian wars that killed the original John Hardin, and the war with Mexico that killed her father were linked. Nor did she publicly recognize the manner in which slavery and Indian killing became part of the structure that was passed down through the generations. She believed that "American manhood" would be born from Colonial struggles. Certainly, this was true in the case of her own family.[12]

Her organization was successful beyond anyone's expectations. One thousand women joined in the first year. By 1901 there were DAR chapters in every state, as well as in two conquests of the recent Spanish-American War, the territories of Puerto Rico and the Philippines. From her post as director general of the Women's National War Relief Association (another association she helped found), Ellen was in a superb position to both provide comfort to America's soldiers fighting against Spain and advance the DAR in the country's new colonial possessions. By 1906 there were more than 50,000 dues-paying members of the Daughters of the American Revolution. In 2011 there were 165,000 members. More than 850,000 American women have joined the DAR since the organization's inception.

The U.S.-Mexican War is one of the few American wars not commemorated in Washington, D.C. There is no monument to the 1847 conflict in the nation's capital, not even a statue. But the National Society of the Daughters of the American Revolution, with almost three thousand chapters in all fifty states and eleven foreign countries, lays claim to an imposing marble edifice just two blocks from the White House. The sprawling Beaux Arts structure, as large as a city block, contains not only administrative offices but also D.C.'s biggest concert hall, a charming historical museum, a series of rooms furnished with period antiques (some of which belonged to the Walworth family), and one of the largest genealogical libraries in the nation.

The cool, high-ceilinged library, free and open to the public, is an oasis of calm just off the busy Washington Mall. Potted plants soak up the ample light pouring through intricately etched skylights, and flags of the fifty states wave softly in an air-conditioned breeze. The chandeliers are primarily decorative. It is an excellent place to think about lineage, and patrons make the most of it. Those who aren't playing with their phones or making use of the computer terminals are poring over genealogical materials at long mahogany tables.

Gazing down over all of them is a life-sized portrait labeled "Ellen Hardin Walworth. Founder, Daughters of the American Revolution." Ellen looks regal in a dress of black velvet and cream lace with three-quarter-length sleeves. The outfit perfectly matches the silver highlights in her thick, dark hair. The bodice of her gown is clasped with a heavy gold DAR brooch closely resembling a military medal, and the portrait painter has painstakingly printed the word *founder* in the center of the brooch so that it can be read from several feet away. Ellen gazes up from the book she holds in her lap, her posture erect. She has been caught in the act of reading. Or perhaps she was reading out loud, telling a story about sacrifice, inheritance, and American history.

Acknowledgments

I HAVE ACCRUED a tremendous number of debts in the process of researching and writing this book. Any scholar hoping to say something new about Henry Clay, James K. Polk, Abraham Lincoln, or the war between the United States and Mexico is forced to contend with a daunting historiography on each of these topics. This book was only possible because generations of remarkable scholars sorted through letters, edited papers, and gracefully synthesized existing scholarship to make sense of these men and the war that drew them together. My reliance on the work of Jean H. Baker, K. Jack Bauer, Albert Jeremiah Beveridge, Gabor Boritt, Eric Foner, William E. Gienapp, David and Jeanne Heidler, Daniel Walker Howe, Frederick Merk, Mark E. Neely Jr., Merrill Peterson, Robert Remini, Joel Silbey, and particularly Charles Sellers will be obvious to readers familiar with their classic works.

My debt to the institutions and individuals who facilitated my research is no less acute, and easier to narrate. The John Simon Guggenheim Foundation, American Philosophical Society, Gilder Lehrman Foundation, Huntington Library, and, at Penn State, the Institute for the Arts and Humanities and Richards Civil War Era Center each provided financial support for this project. Librarians and archivists at the Abraham Lincoln Presidential Library, Amon Carter Museum of American Art, Ashland: The Henry Clay Estate, Bancroft Library, British Library, Chicago History Museum, Daughters of the American Revolution Library, Historical Society of Pennsylvania, Huntington Library, James K. Polk Memorial Association, Library of Congress, Louisiana State University Special Collections, Massachusetts Historical Society, Monticello, New-York Historical Society, Ohio Historical Society, Santa Barbara Mission Archives, and Wisconsin Historical Society were enormously helpful, as was the staff of the Penn State University libraries, particularly Eric Novotny. Agnes Hamberger at the Saratoga Springs History Museum deserves special thanks not only for her extensive assistance with research but also for her unflagging support of this project. Former Jacksonville, Illinois, mayor Ron Tendick generously shared his research on the Hardin family. Anne Brinton slogged through microfilm on my behalf, Alexandria Lockett and William Cossen helped with copyediting and proofreading, and Peter Van Lidth de Jeude provided translations of German accounts of the war.

I am also in the debt of colleagues who generously provided their time and knowledge to making this study better. Kevin Adams, John Belohlavek, Andrew Burstein, Andrew Cayton, Brian DeLay, Richard Doyle, Daniel Walker Howe, Nancy Isenberg, Alexis McCrossen, Mark E. Neely Jr., Carol Reardon, and Andrés Reséndez each read and commented on a draft of this manuscript. Sean Trainor managed to complete a detailed line edit of the initial draft by lamplight while camping. Their suggestions, corrections, criticism, and support have vastly improved this book and saved me the embarrassment of a great number of errors. Remaining errors are of course my own.

My wonderful colleagues and students at Penn State University have helped me refine my arguments, as have audiences at lectures and conferences over the previous eight years. Discussions about this project with William Blair, Gregg Cantrell, Patricia Cline Cohen, Robert Devens, Jonathan Earle, Gary Gallagher, Kristin Hoganson, Walter Johnson, Anthony E. Kaye, Robert E. May, Chandra Manning, Francesca Morgan, Anne C. Rose, Naoko Shibusawa, Michael Vorenberg, Ronald and Mary Zboray, and Andrew Zimmerman have been particularly useful. Mark Neely's knowledge of all things Lincoln has been a much-appreciated resource from the earliest stage of this project. The Society for Historians of the Early American Republic has proven a wonderfully nurturing environment for thinking through the history of this most crucial era.

My brothers, Mike and Ken Greenberg, have shaped my approach to the war over years of discussions about U.S.-Mexico relations. My parents, Kenneth and Jane Lee Greenberg, have long nurtured my interest in history. They always hoped I would write a book that people might actually read. Jessica Greenberg has been a tireless booster of my work. Daily e-mails with Alexis McCrossen have proven a crucial source of analysis, inspiration, and support. Rich Doyle, always eager to toss ideas back and forth, kept me focused on the big picture. It is an honor to publish this book with Knopf. My editor, Andrew Miller, and editorial assistants Andrew Carlson and Mark Chiusano have been a pleasure to work with. Without the encouragement of my indomitable book agents, Sydelle Kramer and Susan Rabiner, this book would never have been written. They know how much they have shaped this project.

Finally, my greatest thanks go to my family, Rich, Jackson, and Violet Doyle. Without their love and support I would be nowhere. They have put up with my obsessive discussion of the Hardin family, out-of-town research trips, and general book-related distraction for too many years. I offer them the dedication of this book knowing full well the gesture is nothing compared to the debt I owe each of them.

Notes

AHSDN Archivo Histórico de la Secretaría de la Defensa de la Nación, Mexico City

ALP Abraham Lincoln Papers, Library of Congress

CG U.S. Congress, *Congressional Globe*

CW *Collected Works of Abraham Lincoln*, ed. Roy P. Balser et al. (New Brunswick, NJ: Rutgers University Press, 1953)

DC *Diplomatic Correspondence of the United States, Inter-American Affairs, 1831–1860*, ed. William R. Manning, 8 vols. (Washington, DC: Carnegie Endowment for International Peace, 1938)

DNI *Daily National Intelligencer*, Washington, DC

HFP Hardin Family Papers, Chicago History Museum

HSP Historical Society of Pennsylvania

LC Library of Congress

NYH *New York Herald*

NYHS New-York Historical Society

MHS Massachusetts Historical Society

PHC *The Papers of Henry Clay*, ed. James F. Hopkins, Mary W. M. Hargreaves, et al., 11 vols. (Lexington: University of Kentucky Press, 1959–92)

PPBL Palmerston Papers, Vol. CXXXI, Manuscripts Division, British Library

UNC University of North Carolina

WFA Walworth Family Archive, Saratoga Springs History Museum

INTRODUCTION

1. Comprehensive histories of the war with an emphasis on the military experience include K. Jack Bauer, *The Mexican War: 1846–1848* (New York: Macmillan, 1974), John D. Eisenhower, *So Far from God: The U.S. War with Mexico, 1846–1848* (Norman: University of Oklahoma Press. 2000), and David A. Clary, *Eagles and Empire: The United States, Mexico, and the Struggle for a Continent* (New York: Bantam, 2009). Clary's volume is notable for its coverage of Mexico's military history. On the Army of the West, see Winston Groom, *Kearny's March: The Epic Creation of the American West, 1846–1847* (New York: Knopf, 2011).

2. On Mexico's experiences in the war, see Jesús Velasco Márquez, *La Guerra del '47 y la*

opinión pública (1845–1848) (New York: Cambridge University Press, 2005). Also Clary, *Eagles and Empire;* Irving W. Levinson, *Wars Within War: Mexican Guerrillas, Domestic Elites, and the United States of America, 1846–1848* (Fort Worth, TX: TCU Press, 2005); Timothy J. Henderson, *A Glorious Defeat: Mexico and Its War with the United States* (New York: Hill and Wang, 2007), and particularly on the context for war, Andrés Reséndez, *Changing National Identities on the Frontier: Texas and New Mexico, 1800–1850* (New York: Cambridge University Press, 2005).

3. The best (and only) biographical study of John J. Hardin is Nancy L. Cox, "A Life of John Hardin of Illinois, 1810–1847" (M.A. thesis, Miami University, 1964). Portions of Hardin's life have also been explored by Richard Lawrence Miller, *Lincoln and His World: Prairie Politician* (Mechanicsburg, PA: Stackpole Books, 2008); and to a lesser degree by Geoffrey O'Brien, *The Fall of the House of Walworth: A Tale of Madness and Murder in Gilded Age America* (New York: Henry Holt, 2010).

4. The majority of scholars who have written about Trist's career have followed the lead of Democratic critics in the 1840s who condemned the diplomat's behavior and belittled his abilities. See, for example, Jack Nortrup, "Nicholas Trist's Mission to Mexico: A Reinterpretation," *Southwestern Historical Quarterly* 71, no. 3 (1968): 321–46; David M. Pletcher, *The Diplomacy of Annexation: Texas, Oregon, and the Mexican War* (Columbia: University of Missouri Press, 1975), 501. Two important exceptions are Dean B. Mahin, *Olive Branch and Sword: The United States and Mexico, 1845–1848* (Jefferson, NC: McFarland, 1997), and Wallace Ohrt, *Defiant Peacemaker: Nicholas Trist in the Mexican War* (College Station: Texas A&M Press, 1997).

5. See Robert W. Merry's *A Country of Vast Designs: James K. Polk, the Mexican War and the Conquest of the American Continent* (New York: Simon & Schuster, 2009) for a positive portrait that acknowledges Polk's deceit and vindictive actions. Charles Sellers's unparalleled two-volume biography of Polk, *James K. Polk: Jacksonian* and *James K. Polk: Continentalist* (Princeton, NJ: Princeton University Press, 1957, 1966), is vastly less sympathetic than Merry's. William Dusinberre's *Slavemaster President: The Double Career of James K. Polk* (New York: Oxford University Press, 2007) offers a highly critical assessment.

6. See, for example, David S. Heidler and Jeanne T. Heidler, *Henry Clay: The Essential American* (New York: Random House, 2010); Maurice Baxter, *Henry Clay and the American System* (Lexington: University Press of Kentucky, 1995); Clement Eaton, *Henry Clay and the Art of American Politics* (Boston: Little, Brown, 1957).

7. See, for example, Robert V. Remini's *Henry Clay: Statesman for the Union* (New York: Norton, 1991).

8. Donald W. Riddle, *Congressman Abraham Lincoln* (Urbana: University of Illinois Press, 1957), 4.

9. Don E. Fehrenbacher, *Prelude to Greatness: Lincoln in the 1850s* (Stanford, CA: Stanford University Press, 1962), 1. See also Mark E. Neely Jr., "Lincoln and the Mexican War: An Argument by Analogy," *Civil War History* 24 (Mar. 1978): 5–24, and Gabor S. Boritt, "A Question of Political Suicide? Lincoln's Opposition to the Mexican War," *Journal of the Illinois State Historical Society* 67 (Feb. 1974): 79–100.

10. Scholars have argued that "the opposition to the War of 1812 outmatched any antiwar sentiment that has since followed," based on the divided congressional response to the initial June 1812 war bill. But the response of Congress to a call for war does not reflect the evolving stance of Americans over the course of a war. The antiwar movement in 1812 was passionate but largely limited to New England. It never took on a grassroots character, and shrank rather than grew over time. While antiwar activists in 1812 had a positive impact on the growth of free speech in America, and formed

America's first national peace societies, their views were far less diffuse than those of antiwar activists in 1847. Congressional representatives, particularly in 1846, were more circumspect than those in 1812 because opposition to the war in 1812 led to the demise of the Federalist Party. See Rachel Hope Cleves, *The Reign of Terror in America: Visions of Violence from Anti-Jacobinism to Antislavery* (New York: Cambridge University Press, 2009), 153–93, quote on 156. Also Donald R. Hickey, *The War of 1812: A Forgotten Conflict* (Urbana: University of Illinois Press, 1989); Valarie H. Ziegler, *The Advocates of Peace in Antebellum America* (Bloomington: University of Indiana Press, 1992); Richard Buel, *America on the Brink: How the Political Struggle over the War of 1812 Almost Destroyed the Young Republic* (New York: Palgrave Macmillan, 2006).

11. William Jay, *A Review of the Causes and Consequences of the Mexican War* (Boston: American Peace Society, 1853); Justin Smith, *The War with Mexico*, 2 vols. (New York: Macmillan, 1919).

12. John H. Schroeder, *Mr. Polk's War: American Opposition and Dissent, 1846–1848* (Madison: University of Wisconsin Press, 1973), 162.

13. Robert W. Johannsen, *To the Halls of the Montezumas: The Mexican War in the American Imagination* (New York: Oxford University Press, 1985), 279. Two recent studies have given more attention to the antiwar movement: see Daniel Walker Howe, *What Hath God Wrought: The Transformation of America, 1815–1845* (New York: Oxford University Press, 2007), 768–69, and Paul Foos, *A Short, Offhand, Killing Affair: Soldiers and Social Conflict During the Mexican-American War* (Chapel Hill: University of North Carolina Press, 2002), 48–49, 65–67.

14. Robert Ryal Miller, *Shamrock and Sword: The Saint Patrick's Battalion in the U.S.-Mexican War* (Norman: University of Oklahoma Press, 1989), 174. Americans have always held conflicted feelings about military service, and desertion rates from both wartime and peacetime armies were high throughout the nineteenth century. On military service and desertion, see Edward M. Coffman, *The Old Army: A Portrait of the American Army in Peacetime, 1784–1898* (New York: Oxford University Press, 1986); John Phillips Resch, *Suffering Soldiers: Revolutionary War Veterans, Moral Sentiment, and Political Culture in the Early Republic* (Amherst: University of Massachusetts Press, 1999); Kevin Adams, *Class and Race in the Frontier Army: Military Life in the West, 1870–1890* (Norman: University of Oklahoma Press, 2009). Adams attributes high U.S. Army desertion rates to an understanding of citizenship as contractual. The notion that citizens could voluntarily choose their allegiances, they believed, also afforded them the flexibility to leave service when they pleased.

15. Both figures are disputed. No one counted Mexican casualties, and there are over a thousand missing U.S. soldiers, likely killed by irregular forces, who have not factored into the 10 percent figure. According to the Department of Defense, 13,283 Americans died in the war with Mexico, which would indicate a mortality rate of 17 percent. Even the most conservative estimate of American casualties indicates that this war was far more deadly than all but the Civil War, thirteen years later. Clifton D. Bryant, *The Handbook of Death and Dying* (Thousand Oaks, CA: Sage, 2003), 1:545; Clary, *Eagles and Empire*, 131, 412; Levinson, *Wars Within War*, 123–24.

16. Pletcher, *Diplomacy of Annexation*, 609–10.

CHAPTER I. VALENTINE'S DAY

1. Leigh Eric Schmidt, "The Fashioning of a Modern Holiday: St. Valentine's Day, 1840–1870," *Winterthur Portfolio* 28, no. 4 (Winter 1993): 239; "Valentine's Day," *Southern*

Patriot (Charleston, SC), Feb. 15, 1844; thirty thousand figure, "St. Valentine's Day," Baltimore *Sun*, Feb. 19, 1844.

2. Schmidt, "Fashioning of a Modern Holiday," 214; "Valentine's Day," *Boston Daily Evening Transcript*, Feb. 20, 1844.

3. Frankfort (KY) *Commonwealth*, May 7, 1844, quote in Robert Vincent Remini, *Henry Clay: Statesman for the Union* (New York: Norton, 1991), 642.

4. "Mr. Clay's Speech," *Niles' Weekly Register*, Mar. 3, 1832, 11.

5. Madeleine McDowell, "Recollections of Henry Clay," *Century Magazine*, May 1895, 768; Gustave Koerner, *Memoirs of Gustave Koerner, 1809–1896*, ed. Thomas J. McCormack (Cedar Rapids, IA: Torch Press, 1909), 1:349.

6. John S. Littell, *The Clay Minstrel, or National Songster*, 2nd ed. (New York: Greeley and McElrath, 1844), 261; Octavia Walton LeVert, "A Tribute to Henry Clay," in Edwin Anderson Alderman, Joel Chandler Harris, and Charles William Kent, eds., *Library of Southern Literature* (New Orleans: Martin and Hoyt, 1907), 7:32–37.

7. Remini, *Henry Clay*, xi; Joseph M. Rogers, *The True Henry Clay* (Philadelphia: J. B. Lippincott, 1904), 250.

8. "Valentine's Day," *Southern Patriot* (Charleston, SC), Feb. 15, 1844. The news of Texas appeared in "Late and Important from Texas," New Orleans *Daily Picayune*, Feb. 14, 1844.

9. Henry Clay to John J. Crittenden, Feb. 15, 1844, *PHC*, 10:6–7.

10. San Filipe de Austin *Telegraph and Texas Register*, Oct. 17, 1835, quote in Quintard Taylor, *In Search of the Racial Frontier: African Americans in the American West, 1528–1990* (New York: Norton, 1998), 42. See also Daniel Walker Howe, *What Hath God Wrought: The Transformation of America, 1815–1845* (New York: Oxford University Press, 2007), 661–71; Gregg Cantrell, *Stephen F. Austin: Empresario of Texas* (New Haven, CT: Yale University Press, 1999), 344–45.

11. Benjamin Lundy ("Citizen of the United States"), *The War in Texas; A Review of Facts and Circumstances, Showing That This Contest Is a Crusade Against Mexico, Set on Foot and Supported by Slaveholders, Land Speculators, & c. in Order to Re-establish, Extend, and Perpetuate the System of Slavery and the Slave Trade*, 2nd ed. (Philadelphia: Merrihew and Gunn, 1837), prefatory note.

12. Quote in Otis A. Singletary, *The Mexican War* (Chicago: University of Chicago Press, 1960), 15–16.

13. Paul Lack, "Slavery and the Texas Revolution," *Southwestern Historical Quarterly* 89 (1985): 181–202.

14. "Treaties of Velasco," *Handbook of Texas Online*, Texas State Historical Association, www.tshaonline.org/handbook/online/articles/mgt05.

15. "Speech of Patrick Collins," *Ohio Statesman* (Columbus, OH), Jan. 26, 1844.

16. "Annexation of Texas," *Albany Evening Journal*, May 11, 1843.

17. "Salvation of the Union," in Edward P. Crapol, *John Tyler: The Accidental President* (Chapel Hill: University of North Carolina Press, 2006), 202.

18. Murphy to Jones, Feb. 14, 1844, in Sen. Doc., 28th Cong., 1st sess. (ser. 435), no. 349, 4–6.

19. Quote from "The Annexation of Texas," *North American* (Philadelphia), Nov. 24, 1843; see also "Annexation of Texas," Charleston *Southern Patriot*, Nov. 20, 1843; "Annexation of Texas," *Republican Farmer* (Bridgeport, CT), Nov. 21, 1843.

20. Henry Clay letter to Leverett Saltonstall, Lexington, Dec. 4, 1843, *PHC*, 9:896.

21. See "Election Correspondence," *Emancipator* (New York), Dec. 12, 1843; no title, *Daily Atlas*, Dec. 26, 1843.

22. Henry Clay to Leverett Saltonstall, Lexington, Dec. 4, 1843, *PHC*, 9:896; Henry Clay to John J. Crittenden, Lexington, Dec. 5, 1843, *PHC*, 9:897–98.

23. "Annexation of Texas," *Emancipator and Free American* (New York), Dec. 28, 1843; "Texas," *Emancipator* (New York), Jan. 25, 1844.

24. A. P. Upshur, "Letter of A. P. Upshur to J. C. Calhoun," *William and Mary Quarterly* 16, no. 4 (Oct. 1936): 555–57, quote on 557.

25. "Annexation of Texas," *Emancipator and Free American* (New York), Dec. 28, 1843.

26. Invitation to "Hon. Mr. Hardin & Lady," WFA.

27. "Extraordinary Intelligence from Washington!" *New York Herald*, Mar. 1, 1844.

28. Hardin to David A. Smith, Mar. 1, 1844, HFP, Box 14:3.

29. "Most Awful and Most Lamentable Catastrophe!" *DNI*, Feb. 29, 1844; Crapol, *John Tyler*, 208–9; John Tyler, "The Dead of the Cabinet," in Lyon Tyler, *The Letters and Times of the Tylers* (Richmond, VA: Whittet and Shepperson, 1885), 2:389–92.

30. John Tyler to Mary Jones Tyler, Washington, DC, Mar. 4, 1844, in Tyler, *Life and Times of the Tylers*, 2:289.

31. Henry Clay to Lucretia Hart Clay, Mobile, AL, Mar. 2, 1844, *PHC*, 10:8.

32. Letter to Henry Clay from "Many of your fellow citizens," Charleston, SC, ca. Apr. 4, 1844, *PHC*, 10:17.

33. *Daily Picayune* (New Orleans), Apr. 6, 1844.

34. Henry Clay to John J. Crittenden, Savannah, GA, Mar. 24, 1844, *PHC*, 10:14.

35. *DNI*, Apr. 27, 1844; Glyndon G. Van Deusen, *The Life of Henry Clay* (Boston: Little, Brown, 1937), 365.

36. Clay to John Crittenden, Norfolk, VA, Apr. 21, 1844, *PHC*, 10:48.

37. Daniel Feller, "A Brother in Arms: Benjamin Tappan and the Antislavery Democracy," *Journal of American History* 88, no. 1 (2001): 66.

38. "The Presidential Question—Troubles of the Democracy!" *NYH*, May 9, 1844; M. Van Buren to Hon. W. H. Hammet, Lindenwold, Apr. 20, 1844, *Macon Georgia Telegraph*, May 14, 1844.

39. John C. Calhoun to Richard Pakenham, Apr. 27, 1844, in Meriwether et al., *Papers of Calhoun*, 18:273–78.

40. A. P. Upshur, "Letter of A. P. Upshur to J. C. Calhoun," 556–57.

41. Jun. 10, 1844, *CG*, 28th Cong., 1st sess., 653.

42. Letter from "Franklin," Washington, DC, Apr. 29, 1844, published in Philadelphia *Public Ledger*, Apr. 30, 1844.

43. Philip Hone, *Diary of Philip Hone, 1828–1851* (New York: Dodd, Mead, 1889), 2:219–20.

44. John Hardin to Sarah Hardin, May 3, 1844, HFP, Box 15:11.

45. "The Whig Procession," Baltimore *Sun*, May 3, 1844.

46. "The Following Account of the Whig Assemblage at Baltimore," *Berkshire County Whig*, May 9, 1844; "Baltimore Whig Convention," *NYH*, May 1, 1844.

47. "The Grand Whig Nomination at Last," *NYH*, May 3, 1844; Hone, *Diary of Philip Hone*, 2:217–18.

48. Henry Clay to John M. Berrien et al., Washington, DC, May 2, 1844, *PHC*, 10:52; Henry Clay to Thurlow Weed, Washington, DC, May 6, 1844, *PHC*, 10:54.

49. Letter from "Franklin," Washington, DC, Apr. 29, 1844, published in the Philadelphia *Public Ledger;* Apr. 30, 1844.

50. Henry Clay to Thurlow Weed, Washington, DC, May 6, 1844, *PHC*, 10:54; "The Next Presidency—Mr. Clay's Prospects," *NYH*, May 17, 1844.

51. Quote in Remini, *Henry Clay*, 646.

52. Francis Blair quote in Charles Sellers, *James K. Polk, Continentalist* (Princeton, NJ: Princeton University Press, 1966), 68–69.

CHAPTER 2. "WHO IS JAMES K. POLK?"

1. Andrew Jackson. *The Papers of Andrew Jackson*, ed. Daniel Feller, Harold D. Moser, Laura-Eve Moss, and Thomas Coens (Knoxville: University of Tennessee Press, 2007), 7:42.

2. On the Jackson "image," see Andrew Burstein, *The Passions of Andrew Jackson* (New York: Knopf, 2003), 207–40.

3. Quote in Michael A. Lofarro, "David Crockett," *Tennessee Encyclopedia of History and Culture*, ed. Caroll Van West (Nashville: Tennessee Historical Society, 1998), 219.

4. Robert W. Ikard, "Surgical Operation on James K. Polk by Ephraim McDowell or the Search for Polk's Gallstone," *Tennessee Historical Quarterly* 43, no. 3 (1984): 121–31. Ikard argues that the surgery most likely left Polk impotent.

5. Rhetoric quote in George H. Hickman, *The Life and Public Services of the Hon. James Knox Polk: With a Compendium of His Speeches on Various Public Measures, Also a Sketch of the Life of the Hon. George Mifflin Dallas* (Baltimore: N. Hickman, 1844), 8; Adams quote, John Quincy Adams, *Memoirs of John Quincy Adams*, ed. Charles Francis Adams (New York: AMS Press, 1970), 9:64.

6. Anson and Fanny Nelson, *Memorials of Sarah Childress Polk* (New York: Anson D. F. Randolph, 1892), 68.

7. Ibid., 68, 94.

8. Ibid., 16.

9. Ibid., 50.

10. Samuel H. Laughlin to J. K. Polk, May 30, 1835, *Correspondence of James K. Polk*, ed. Herbert Weaver and Wayne Cutler et al., 11 vols. (Knoxville: University of Tennessee Press, 1969–2009), 3:209; Catherine Allgor, *Parlor Politics: In Which the Ladies of Washington Help Build a City and a Government* (Charlottesville: University of Virginia Press, 2000).

11. Quote in Charles Sellers, *James K. Polk, Continentalist, 1843–1846* (Princeton, NJ: Princeton University Press, 1966), 2:71–72.

12. On Polk's slave owning, see William Dusinberre, *Slavemaster President: The Double Career of James K. Polk* (New York: Oxford University Press, 2007).

13. Adams, *Memoirs*, 4:531; Thomas R. Hietala, *Manifest Design: Anxious Aggrandizement in Late Jacksonian America* (Ithaca, NY: Cornell University Press, 1985), 30–31 n. 41.

14. "Col. Polk's Letter," *Southern Patriot* (Charleston, SC), May 9, 1844; James K. Polk, "Letters of James K. Polk to Cave Johnson, 1833–1848," *Tennessee Historical Magazine* 1 (Sep. 1915): 209–56, quote on 240.

15. Letter from "Franklin," Washington, DC, Apr. 29, 1844, published in the Philadelphia *Public Ledger*, Apr. 30, 1844.

16. Sellers, *James K. Polk, Continentalist*, 71; Polk, "Letters of James K. Polk to Cave Johnson, 1833–1848," 240–41.

17. Polk, "Letters of James K. Polk to Cave Johnson, 1833–1848," 240.

18. On the appeal of Manifest Destiny, see Amy S. Greenberg, *Manifest Destiny and American Territorial Expansion: A Brief History with Documents* (Boston: Bedford/St. Martin's, 2012). For a historiographical overview of the economic and social changes of the era, see Daniel Walker Howe, *What Hath God Wrought: The Transformation of America, 1815–1848* (New York: Oxford University Press, 2007), 856–78.

19. Quote in "The Two Baltimore Conventions," *Daily Atlas*, May 30, 1844; "Democratic National Convention," Baltimore *Sun*, May 28, 1844.

20. "Texas—The Prospect," *Liberator*, May 24, 1844.

21. Quote in Sellers, *James K. Polk, Continentalist*, 91.
22. Robert Seager II, *And Tyler Too: A Biography of John and Julia Gardiner Tyler* (New York: McGraw-Hill, 1963), 228; "The Two Baltimore Conventions," *Daily Atlas*, May 30, 1844.
23. "Correspondence of the Express, Baltimore, May 27, Night," *Cleveland Herald*, Jun. 1, 1844; "The Baltimore Loco Foco Convention," *Daily Atlas*, May 31, 1844.
24. "The Baltimore Loco Foco Convention," *Daily Atlas*, May 31, 1844; "Democratic Meeting in Baltimore," *North American and Daily Advertiser* (Philadelphia), May 30, 1844.
25. "Democratic Meeting in Baltimore," *North American and Daily Advertiser* (Philadelphia), May 30, 1844.
26. Hickman, *Life and Public Services*, 26; Ben Perley Poore, *Perley's Reminiscences of Sixty Years in the National Metropolis* (Tecumseh, MI: A. W. Mills, 1886), 321.
27. For a more flattering portrait of Dallas, see John M. Belohlavek, *George Mifflin Dallas: Jacksonian Patrician* (State College: Pennsylvania State University Press, 1977).
28. "The Responses to the Nomination of Mr. Polk," *Easton* (MD) *Gazette*, Jun. 8, 1844; "The Loco Foco Candidates," *Daily Atlas*, Jun. 4, 1844; Benton quote in Glyndon G. Van Deusen, *The Life of Henry Clay* (Boston: Little, Brown, 1937), 367.
29. Henry Clay letter to Willie P. Mangum, Lexington, Jun. 7, 1844, *PHC*, 10:66; "The 'Democratic Nomination,' " *DNI*, May 30, 1844.
30. "The Loco Foco Candidates," *Daily Atlas*, Jun. 4, 1844; "Washington Correspondence," (Philadelphia) *North American and Daily Advertiser*, May 31, 1844; Philip Hone, *Diary of Philip Hone*, 2:224; "The Responses to the Nomination of Mr. Polk," *Easton* (MD) *Gazette*, Jun. 8, 1844.
31. "The Democratic Nomination at Last," *NYH*, May 31, 1844.
32. "The 'Democratic Nomination,' " *DNI*, May 30, 1844.
33. Washington *Standard* quote in "The Responses to the Nomination of Mr. Polk," *Easton* (MD) *Gazette*, Jun. 8, 1844.
34. "The Democratic Nomination at Last," *NYH*, May 31, 1844.
35. "The 'Democratic Nomination,' " *DNI*, May 30, 1844; Washington *Standard* quote in "The Responses to the Nomination of Mr. Polk," *Easton* (MD) *Gazette*, Jun. 8, 1844.
36. Wendy Moonan, "Antiques: A Gothic Tale of a Bedstead Fit for a President," *New York Times*, Nov. 3, 2000.
37. Henry Clay letter to Willie P. Mangum, Lexington, Jun. 7, 1844, *PHC*, 10:66; "The Democratic Nomination at Last," *NYH*, May 31, 1844. Issue 152.

CHAPTER 3. THE UPSET

1. Harriet Martineau, *Retrospect of Western Travel* (New York: Charles Lohman, 1838), 1:174.
2. Henry Alexander Wise, *Seven Decades of the Union: The Humanities and Materialism* (Philadelphia: Lippincott, 1876), 171. David S. and Jeanne T. Heidler refute the veracity of this story, which was widely reprinted by the late nineteenth century. See *Henry Clay: The Essential American* (New York: Random House, 2010), 310.
3. "Warn the Committee!" American Antiquarian Society, 1844; Henry Clay to John M. Clayton, Blue Licks, Aug. 22, 1844, *PHC*, 10:102.
4. "The Democratic Nominations," *Barre* (MA) *Gazette*, Jun. 14, 1844; Anton and Fanny Nelson, *Memorials of Sarah Childress Polk* (New York: Anson D. F. Randolph, 1892), 96, 43–44.
5. Nelson, *Memorials of Sarah Childress Polk*, 49.

6. George H. Hickman, *The Life and Public Services of the Hon. James Knox Polk: With a Compendium of His Speeches on Various Public Measures, Also a Sketch of the Life of the Hon. George Mifflin Dallas* (Baltimore: N. Hickman, 1844), 4, 6; "The Democratic Nominations," *Barre* (MA) *Gazette*, Jun. 14, 1844.

7. Enos Cobb, "Eulogy on Polk and Dallas," Burlington, VT, 1844, AAS 14254, American Broadsides.

8. Andrew Jackson, *Correspondence*, 6:275; quote in Augustus C. Buell, *History of Andrew Jackson, Pioneer, Patriot, Soldier, Politician, President* (New York: Charles Scribner, 1904), 2:384.

9. Edwin Erle Sparks, ed., *The Lincoln-Douglas Debates* (Dansville, NY: F. A. Owen, 1918), 32.

10. Fragment on Government, Abraham Lincoln, *CW*, 2:220–21.

11. Douglas L. Wilson and Rodney O. Davis, eds., *Herndon's Informants: Letters, Interviews, and Statements About Abraham Lincoln* (Urbana: University of Illinois Press, 1989); 372, 390, 18. Many thanks to Mark E. Neely Jr. for bringing this to my attention.

12. Communication to the people of Sangamo County, Mar. 9, 1832, *CW*, 1:9; William H. Herndon and Jesse W. Welk, *Abraham Lincoln: The True Story of a Great Life* (New York: Appleton, 1892), 90, 95.

13. Quote in Albert Jeremiah Beveridge, *Lincoln, 1809–1865* (New York: Houghton Mifflin, 1927), 1:309.

14. Harriett Chapman quote in William E. Gienapp, *Abraham Lincoln and Civil War America, A Biography* (New York: Oxford University Press, 2002), 37; Jean H. Baker, *Mary Todd Lincoln* (New York: Norton, 1987), 133.

15. Quote in Baker, *Mary Todd Lincoln*, 133.

16. Eric Foner, *The Fiery Trial: Abraham Lincoln and American Slavery* (New York: Norton, 2010), 77.

17. Abraham Lincoln, *Lincoln Day by Day: A Chronology, 1809–1865*, ed. Earl Schenck Miers (Washington, DC: Lincoln Sesquicentennial Commission, 1960), 1:227, 2:229.

18. Abraham Lincoln to Williamson Durley, Oct. 3, 1845, *CW*, 1:347–48.

19. Lincoln to Richard S. Thomas, Springfield, IL, Feb. 14, 1843, *CW*, 1:307.

20. Quote in Herndon, *Lincoln*, 254.

21. Mansfield Tracy Walworth, "Colonel John Hardin," *Historical Magazine and Notes and Queries Concerning the Antiquities*, 2nd ser., 5 (1869): 237, 235; Ellen Hardin Walworth, "Charter Member, Application for Membership #5," Dec. 1890, Manuscript Collection. Daughters of the American Revolution Library, Centennial Hall, Washington, DC; Mary S. Lockwood, *Lineage Book of the Charter Members of the Daughters of the American Revolution* (Harrisburg, PA: Harrisburg Publishing, 1895), 1:2–3.

22. Robert Ralston Jones, *Fort Washington at Cincinnati, Ohio* (Cincinnati: Society of Colonial Wars in the State of Ohio, 1902), 28; Andrew R. L. Cayton, *Frontier Indiana* (Bloomington: Indiana University Press, 1996), 149–56.

23. Walworth, "Colonel John Hardin," 237.

24. Abraham Lincoln to Jesse W. Fell [with enclosure by Lincoln], Dec. 20, 1859, ALP.

25. Beveridge, *Lincoln*, 1:180; Gustave Koerner, *Memoirs of Gustave Koerner, 1809–1896*, ed. Thomas J. McCormack (Cedar Rapids, IA: Torch Press, 1909), 1:499.

26. Beveridge, *Lincoln*, 1:306; William Henry Milburn, *The Lance, Cross and Canoe; The Flatboat, Rifle and Plough in the Valley of the Mississippi* (New York: N. D. Thompson, 1892), 672.

27. Lincoln to Speed, Mar. 24, 1843, *CW*, 1:201.

28. John J. Brown to John J. Hardin, Nov. 8, 1844, Danville, IL, HFP, Box 15:3.

29. Quotes from Alexander Anderson in Michael A. Morrison, *Slavery and the American West: The Eclipse of Manifest Destiny and the Coming of the Civil War* (Chapel Hill: University of North Carolina Press, 1997), 31.

30. James E. Winston, "The Annexation of Texas and the Mississippi Democrats," *Southwestern Historical Review* 25, no. 1 (1921): 5; Koerner, *Memoirs of Gustave Koerner,* 1:488; Morrison, *Slavery and the American West,* 31.

31. Fred Anderson and Andrew Cayton, *The Dominion of War: Empire and Liberty in North America, 1500–2000* (New York: Penguin, 2005), 248–59.

32. On Mexican development, see Philip L. Russell, *The History of Mexico from Pre-Conquest to Present* (New York: Routledge, 2010), 161–64, 182–83.

33. David A. Clary, *Eagles and Empire: The United States, Mexico, and the Struggle for a Continent* (New York: Bantam, 2009), 24; Brian DeLay, *War of a Thousand Deserts: Indian Raids and the U.S.-Mexican War* (New Haven, CT: Yale University Press, 2009).

34. "The Great War Meeting," *New York Herald,* Jan. 30, 1848; on Americanizing cultural forces in northern Mexico, see Andrés Reséndez, *Changing National Identities on the Frontier: Texas and New Mexico, 1800–1850* (New York: Cambridge University Press, 1995).

35. James K. Polk, "Letters of James K. Polk to Cave Johnson, 1833–1848," *Tennessee Historical Magazine* 1 (Sep. 1915): 209–56, quote on 245.

36. "Mr. Clay's Last Texas Letter," *Pittsfield* (MA) *Sun,* Sep. 19, 1844.

37. Ibid.; "Electors of Michigan!" (1844), American Broadsides and Ephemera, ser. 1, no. 14258.

38. "Workingman's Song #2," in John S. Littell, *The Clay Minstrel, or National Songster,* 2nd ed. (New York: Greeley and McElrath, 1844), 339.

39. "Gallant Harry, the Song of the Clay Club of Germantown," in Littell, *The Clay Minstrel,* 158; Ronald J. Zboray and Mary Saracino Zboray, *Voices Without Votes: Women and Politics in Antebellum New England* (Durham: University of New Hampshire Press, 2010), 135; Nathan Sargent, *Public Men and Events, from the Commencement of Mr. Monroe's Administration, in 1817, to the Close of Mr. Fillmore's Administration in 1853* (Philadelphia: J. B. Lippincott, 1875), 2:246; on female partisanship, see Elizabeth R. Varon, *We Mean to Be Counted: White Women and Politics in Antebellum Virginia* (Chapel Hill: University of North Carolina Press, 1998).

40. David S. Heidler and Jeanne T. Heidler, *Henry Clay: The Essential American* (New York: Random House, 2010), 424–25.

41. John Hickey, *The Democratic Lute, and Minstrel: Comprising a Great Number of Patriotic, Sentimental, and Comic Political Songs and Duetts: Entirely Original* (Philadelphia: H. B. Pierson, 1844), 5.

42. Whether the Liberty Party vote was responsible for Clay's loss has been the subject of ample debate. Most Liberty Party members in New York were Whigs who had voluntarily left the party in large part because they disagreed with the positions of men like Clay. To suggest they would have voted for Clay had there been no Liberty Party ignores the fact that there was one. See, for example, Lee Benson, *The Concept of Jacksonian Democracy: New York as a Test Case* (New York: Atheneum, 1969), 133–36; Vernon L. Volpe, "The Liberty Party and Polk's Election, 1844," *Historian* 23 (Jan. 1991): 697. For a counterargument, see Daniel Walker Howe, *The Political Culture of the American Whigs* (Chicago: University of Chicago Press, 1979), 144.

43. Mrs. Robert S. Todd to Mary Todd Lincoln, quoted in Glyndon G. Van Deusen, *The Life of Henry Clay* (Boston: Little, Brown, 1937), 376.

44. Nelson, *Memorials of Sarah Childress Polk,* 76–77.

45. Ibid., 77; Blacksmith Harry to Polk, Nov. 28, 1844, in James K. Polk Papers, LC.
46. Jackson to W. B. Lewis, Feb. 4, 1845, quoted in Sellers, *Polk, Continentalist*, 184.
47. Andrew Jackson Jr. to A. O. P. Nicholson, Jun. 17, 1845, quote in Jon Meacham, *American Lion: Andrew Jackson in the White House* (New York: Random House, 2008), 304; Remini, *Clay*, 1 n. 1.
48. James D. Richardson, ed., *A Compilation of the Messages and Papers of the Presidents* (Washington: GPO, 1901), 4:373–82; Sellers, *Polk, Continentalist*, 209.
49. Raleigh letter quotes, *DNI*, Apr. 27, 1844.

CHAPTER 4. SPEAKING CANNON FIRE

1. Waddy Thompson to Daniel Webster, Apr. 11, 1843, *DC*, 8:544; David A. Clary, *Eagles and Empire: The United States, Mexico, and the Struggle for a Continent* (New York: Bantam, 2009), 55; *El Mosquito Mexicano*, Dec. 16, 1842, quote in George Brack, *Mexico Views Manifest Destiny, 1821–1846: An Essay on the Origins of the Mexican War* (Albuquerque: University of New Mexico Press, 1975), 103.
2. Lieutenant Charles Wilkes, *Narrative of the United States Exploring Expedition During the Years 1838, 1839, 1840, 1841, 1842* (Philadelphia: Lea and Blanchard, 1845), 5:171.
3. Elizabeth Fries Lumis Ellet, *The Court Circles of the Republic* (Philadelphia, 1872), 381, quote in Charles Sellers, *James K. Polk, Continentalist, 1843–1846* (Princeton, NJ: Princeton University Press, 1966), 2:163; Martin Van Buren to Polk, Jan. 18, 1845, Polk Papers, LC.
4. James K. Polk, "Letters of James K. Polk to Cave Johnson, 1833–1848," *Tennessee Historial Magazine* 1 (Sep. 1915): 254.
5. Gideon Wells quote in Richard R. Stenberg, "President Polk and California: Additional Documents," *Pacific Historical Review* 10 (1941): 217–19, quotes on 219.
6. Senator Dix quote in Sellers, *Polk, Continentalist*, 218.
7. Gideon Wells quote in Stenberg, "President Polk and California," 219.
8. James K. Polk, *Diary of a President: James K. Polk*, ed. Milo Quaife, 4 vols. (Columbia, TN: James K. Polk Memorial Association, 2005), 4:350; see also Paul H. Bergeron, *The Presidency of James K. Polk* (Lawrence: University of Kansas Press, 1987), 23–49.
9. *Correspondence of James K. Polk*, ed. Herbert Weaver and Wayne Cutler et al., 11 vols. (Knoxville: University of Tennessee Press, 1969–2009), 7:355–56; Anton and Fanny Nelson, *Memorials of Sarah Childress Polk* (New York: Anson D. F. Randolph, 1892), 52.
10. Quote in Sellers, *Polk, Continentalist*, 308; Nelson, *Memorials of Sarah Childress Polk*, 54.
11. Nelson, *Memorials of Sarah Childress Polk*, 94.
12. John Robert Irelan, *The Republic, or the History of the United States of America* (Chicago: Fairbanks and Palmer, 1888), 11:675; Nelson, *Memorials of Sarah Childress Polk*, 81.
13. Nelson, *Memorials of Sarah Childress Polk*, 93.
14. Ibid., 79–80.
15. Ibid., 112.
16. Irelan, *Republic*, 675.
17. Ibid.; John Reed Bumgarner, *Sarah Childress Polk: A Biography of the Remarkable First Lady* (Jefferson, NC: McFarland and Co, 1997), 59; Nelson, *Memorials of Sarah Childress Polk*, 51–52.
18. Quote in Ronald J. Zboray and Mary Saracino Zboray, *Voices Without Votes: Women and Politics in Antebellum New England* (Durham: University of New Hampshire Press, 2010), 146–47.

19. Stenberg, "President Polk and California," 219; Sellers, *Polk: Continentalist*, 213.

20. George E. Ellis, *Letters upon the Annexation of Texas. Addressed to Hon. John Quincy Adams* (Boston: White, Lewis, and Potter, 1845), 47, 6, 23.

21. *El Defensor de las Leyes* (Mexico City), Mar. 26, 1845; *El Siglo Diez y Nueve*, Nov. 31, 1845; both quotes in Brack, *Mexico Views Manifest Destiny*, 141, 143.

22. Comunicación circular que el Exmo. Sr. Don Manuel Peña y Peña estendió en el año de 1845, como ministro de relaciones, sobre la cuestión de paz o Guerra, según el estado que guardaba en aquella época (Querétero, Nov. 27, 1845), quote in Brack, *Mexico Views Manifest Destiny*, 161; Buchanan to Slidell, Nov. 10, 1845, *DC*, 8:172–82.

23. Louis Martin Sears, *John Slidell* (Durham, NC: Duke University Press, 1925), 45; John Slidell to James Buchanan, New Orleans, Sep. 25, 1845, in *Works of James Buchanan*, ed. John Bassett Moore (Philadelphia: J. B. Lippincott, 1909), 6:264.

24. Stenberg, "President Polk and California," 218.

25. Ibid. For a stronger statement on Polk's duplicity, see Glenn W. Price, *Origins of the War with Mexico: the Polk-Stockton Intrigue* (Austin: University of Texas Press, 1967).

26. Buchanan to Slidell, Mar. 12, 1846, Executive Document, 29th Cong., 1st sess., 1845–46, Number 196, 56.

27. Ibid.; Slidell to Polk, Mexico, Dec. 29, 1845, *Correspondence of James K. Polk*, 10:449.

28. "Henry Clay and Ashland," *Cleveland Daily Herald*, May 31, 1845.

29. Heidler, *Henry Clay*, 397; "Henry Clay and Ashland," *Cleveland Daily Herald*, May 31, 1845; "The Shades of Ashland," *Cleveland Daily Herald*, Sep. 5, 1843.

30. "The Shades of Ashland," *Cleveland Daily Herald*, Sep. 5, 1843; "Henry Clay and Ashland," *Cleveland Daily Herald*, May 31, 1845; Koerner, *Memoirs of Gustave Koerner*, 1:350.

31. "Henry Clay and Ashland," *Cleveland Daily Herald*, May 31, 1845.

32. Madeleine McDowell, "Recollections of Henry Clay," *Century Magazine*, May 1895, 765–70, quotes on 768.

33. Clay to Mary Bayard, Lexington, Feb. 4, 1845, *PHC*, 10:197; Clay to Mary Bayard, Lexington, May 7, 1846, *PHC*, 10:267.

34. H. Clay and Richard L. Troutman, "The Emancipation of Slaves by Henry Clay," *Journal of Negro History* 40, no. 2 (Apr. 1955): 179–81.

35. Glyndon G. Van Deusen, *The Life of Henry Clay* (Boston: Little, Brown, 1937), 379–80.

36. Tilford to Clay, Feb. 17, 1845, *PHC*, 10:200.

37. Henry Clay to Henry Clay Jr., Mar. 29, 1830, *PHC*, 8:185; Henry Clay to Henry Clay Jr., Apr. 2, 1827, *PHC*, 6:385; Henry Clay Jr., Diary, 1840–41, University of Kentucky Special Collections.

38. Van Deusen, *Life of Henry Clay*, 233.

39. Clay to Henry Clay Jr. Lexington, Apr. 8, 1845, *PHC*, 10:215.

40. Polk, *Diary*, 1:85.

41. Ibid.

42. William L. Marcy to Zachary Taylor, Jan. 13, 1846, in *Messages of the President of the United States with the Correspondence, Therewith Communicated, Between the Secretary of War and Other Officers of the Government, on the Subject of the Mexican War*, House Executive Documents, 30th Cong. 1st sess., no. 60 (Washington, DC: Wendell and Van Benthuysen, 1848), 89–90.

43. Slidell to Buchanan, Jalapa, Mar. 18, 1846, Executive Document, 29th Cong., 1st sess., 1845–1846, no. 196, 57.

44. On Anglophobia, see Sam W. Haynes, *Unfinished Revolution: The Early American Republic in a British World* (Charlottesville: University of Virginia Press, 2010).

45. Robert Charles Winthrop, *A Memoir of Robert C. Winthrop* (Boston: Little, Brown, 1897),

39–40; information on King John in Charles H. Shattuck, *Shakespeare on the American Stage: From the Hallams to Edwin Booth* (Washington, DC: Folger Shakespeare Library, 1976), 69.

46. William H. Herndon and Jesse W. Welk, *Abraham Lincoln: The True Story of a Great Life* (New York: Appleton, 1892), 256; John Boyle to John J. Hardin, Tremont, IL, Nov. 27, 1844, HFP, Box 15:4; George T. Davis to Hardin, Nov. 24, 1844, HFP, Box 15:4.

47. Isaac Arnold, *The Life of Abraham Lincoln* (Chicago: Jansen, McClurg, 1885), 82–83; Jean H. Baker, *Mary Todd Lincoln, A Biography* (New York: Norton, 1987), 112–13.

48. Herndon, *Lincoln*, 257; Lincoln to Hardin, Springfield, May 21, 1844, *CW*, 1:336. See also Lincoln to Hardin, Springfield, Dec. 17, 1844, *CW*, 1:342–43.

49. Hardin to David A. Smith, Mar. 1, 1844, HFP, Box 14:3.

50. Nancy L. Cox, "A Life of John Hardin of Illinois, 1810–1847" (M.A. thesis, Miami University, 1964), 82–98, quote on 88.

51. John J. Hardin, *Speech of Mr. J. J. Hardin, of Illinois Reviewing the Principles of James K. Polk and the Leaders of Modern Democracy* (Washington, DC: J. and G. S. Gideon, 1844), 3.

52. John J. Hardin to David A. Smith, Jul. 12, 1844, HFP, Box 15:3; John Hardin to Ellen Hardin, Dec. 1, 1843, WFA.

53. John J. Hardin to Sarah Hardin, May 26, 1844, HFP, 15:2; *Sangamo Journal*, May 3 and 10, 1844.

54. *Sangamo Journal*, Jun. 12, 1845.

55. Ellen Hardin Walworth, "Charter Member, Application for Membership #5," Dec. 1890, Manuscript Collection. Daughters of the American Revolution Library, Centennial Hall, Washington, DC. See also Frederick Gerhard, *Illinois as It Is* (Chicago: Keen and Lee, 1857), 118–19.

56. Lincoln to Benjamin F. James, Springfield, Jan. 14, 1846, *CW*, 1:353–54; Lincoln to Boal, Jan. 7, 1846, *CW*, 1:352–53; Cox, "Hardin," 113.

57. Quote in Beveridge, *Lincoln*, 1:372; Lincoln to Hardin, Springfield, Jan. 19, 1846, *CW*, 1:356–57.

58. Quote in Beveridge, *Lincoln*, 1:373–74.

59. Quote in Herndon, *Lincoln*, 95.

60. *Sangamo Journal*, Jun. 12, 1845.

61. Hardin to Major Dunlap, Feb. 5, 1846, HFP, Box 16.

62. *Sangamo Journal*, Apr. 23, 1846, quoted in Beveridge, *Lincoln*, 1:375–76.

CHAPTER 5. "THE MISCHIEF IS DONE"

1. Nicholas Trist letter, May 4, 1833, quote in James Parton, *Life of Andrew Jackson* (New York: Mason Brothers, 1860), 3:605.

2. Elizabeth Trist to Nicholas Trist, Feb. 9, 1820, Trist Papers, UNC, Folder 19.

3. Nicholas Trist to Andrew Jackson Donelson, Feb. 10, 1830, Trist Papers, LC.

4. James K. Polk, *Diary of a President: James K. Polk*, ed. Milo Quaife, 4 vols. (Columbia, TN: James K. Polk Memorial Association, 2005), 4:261; n.d., Trist Papers, LC, Reel 6.

5. Polk, *Diary*, 4:261.

6. N.d., Trist Papers, LC, Reel 6.

7. Polk, *Diary*, 1:354.

8. Anson and Fanny Nelson, *Memorials of Sarah Childress Polk* (New York: Anson D. F. Randolph, 1892), 99.

9. New Orleans *Delta* and New Orleans *Bulletin*, quoted in "Mexican Affairs," *South Caro-

lina Temperance Advocate and Register of Agriculture and General Literature (Columbia, SC), Apr. 23, 1846.

10. Nelson, *Memorials of Sarah Childress Polk*, 103.

11. Walt Whitman, *Brooklyn Daily Eagle*, May 11, 1846.

12. Robert C. Winthrop, *A Memoir of Robert C. Winthrop* (Boston: Little, Brown, 1897), 40; "Affairs with Mexico," *Daily Sentinel and Gazette* (Milwaukee, WI), Apr. 29, 1846.

13. Polk, *Diary*, 1:354.

14. Stephen A. Douglas to Hardin, May 2, 1846, *Letters of Stephen A. Douglas*, ed. Robert Johannsen (Urbana: University of Illinois Pess, 1961), 137, 138 n. 1.

15. Ethan Allen Hitchcock, *Fifty Years in Camp and Field*, ed. W. A. Croffut (New York: Putnam, 1909), 200; on the Seminole War, see Edward M. Coffman, *The Old Army: A Portrait of the American Army in Peacetime, 1784–1898* (New York: Oxford University Press, 1986), 49–52.

16. Hitchcock, *Fifty Years in Camp and Field*, 198.

17. K. Jack Bauer, *Zachary Taylor: Soldier, Planter, Statesman of the Old Southwest* (Baton Rouge: Louisiana State University Press, 1985), 117–18; William L. Marcy to Zachary Taylor, Oct. 16, 1845, in *Messages of the President of the United States . . . on the Subject of the Mexican War*, House Executive Documents, 30th Cong., 1st sess., no. 60 (Washington, DC: Wendell and Van Benthuysen, 1848), 89–90.

18. K. Jack Bauer, *The Mexican War: 1846–1848* (New York: Macmillan, 1974), 34.

19. Marcy to Taylor, Jan. 13, 1846. *Messages of the President . . . on the Subject of the Mexican War*, 91; Hitchcock, *Fifty Years in Camp and Field*, 200.

20. Bauer, *Mexican War*, 26; Grant to Julia Dent, Mar. 3, 1846, *Papers of Ulysses S. Grant*, ed. John Y. Simon (Carbondale: Southern Illinois University Press, 1967), 1:74–75; *Messages of the President . . . on the Subject of the Mexican War*, 119–20; Will discussed in Bauer, *Zachary Taylor*, 125 n. 47.

21. Frederick Law Olmsted, *A Journey Through Texas, or a Saddle-Trip on the Southwestern Frontier*, ed. Witold Rybczynski (Lincoln: University of Nebraska Press, 2004), 314; Ephraim Kirby Smith, *To Mexico with Scott: Letters of E. Kirby Smith to His Wife* (Cambridge, MA: Harvard University Press, 1919), 28; Otto Engelmann, ed., "The Second Illinois in the Mexican War: Mexican War Letters of Adolph Engelmann, 1846–1847," *Journal of the Illinois State Historical Society* 26, no. 4 (Jan. 1934): 357–452, quote on 388–89.

22. Hitchcock, *Fifty Years in Camp and Field*, 213.

23. Robert Ryal Miller, *Shamrock and Sword: The Saint Patrick's Batallion in the U.S.-Mexican War* (Norman: University of Oklahoma Press, 1989), 17.

24. Desertion cited in "Our relations with Mexico," Philadelphia *North American*, May 11, 1846; Singletary, *Mexican War*, 12.

25. Polk, *Diary*, 1:375–76.

26. Ibid., 1:382.

27. Ibid.

28. "War with Mexico," *Mississippian*, Apr. 15, 1846; Walt Whitman, *Brooklyn Daily Eagle*, May 11, 1846; Polk, *Diary*, 1:384.

29. Polk, *Diary*, 1:389–90.

30. Ibid., 1:390.

31. James D. Richardson, ed., *A Compilation of the Messages and Papers of the Presidents* (Washington, DC, 1901), 4:442–43.

32. *CG*, 29th Cong., 1st session, 1846, 794.

33. *New York Tribune*, quote in "The Army of Occupation," *Liberator*, May 1, 1846; Charleston Mercury, quoted in *DNI*, May 11, 1846.

34. Adams to Richard Rush, May 20, 1818, in John Quincy Adams, *The Writings of John Quincy Adams*, ed. Worthington Chauncey Ford (New York: Macmillan, 1916), 6:322.

35. John Quincy Adams, *Memoirs of John Quincy Adams*, ed. Charles Francis Adams (New York: AMS Press, 1970), 12:255–66; Robert Winthrop to "my dear Clifford," May 15, 1846, Winthrop Family Papers, MHS, Boston, Reel 24.

36. Robert Winthrop to "my dear Clifford," May 15, 1846, Winthrop Family Papers, MHS.

37. Ibid.; "War with Mexico Declared," *Cleveland Herald*, May 18, 1846, see also *DNI*, May 13, 1846, *Scioto Gazette* (Chillicothe, OH), May 21, 1846.

38. Robert Winthrop to "my dear Clifford," May 15, 1846, Winthrop Family Papers, MHS; "War with Mexico Declared," *Cleveland Herald*, May 18, 1846. See also *DNI*, May 13, 1846; *Scioto Gazette* (Chillicothe, OH), May 21, 1846.

39. Clifford to Winthrop, May 18, 1846. Winthrop Family Papers, MHS.

40. Polk, *Diary*, 1:391–92.

41. Ibid., 1:393.

42. *CG*, 29th Cong., 1st sess., 1846, 786; Calhoun to Henry W. Conner, May 15, 1846, in *Papers of John C. Calhoun*, ed. John Caldwell Calhoun, Robert Lee Meriwether, Clyde Norman Wilson, William Edwin Hemphill, and Shirley Bright Cook (Columbia: University of South Carolina Press, 1996), 111; quoted in Sellers, *Polk, Continentalist*, 418.

43. Calhoun to Henry W. Conner, May 15, 1846, in *Papers of John C. Calhoun*, 111.

44. "The War with Mexico—New Troops in the Field," New Orleans *Tropic*, quoted in the *Mississippi Free Trader and Natchez Gazette*, May 14, 1846.

45. Polk, *Diary*, 1:393.

46. Ibid., 1:397–98.

47. Ibid., 1:399.

48. James K. Polk to William H. Polk, Jul. 14, 1846, *Correspondence of James K. Polk*, ed. Herbert Weaver and Wayne Cutler et al., 11 vols. (Knoxville: University of Tennessee Press, 1969–2009), 11:245–46.

CHAPTER 6. A TAME, SPIRITLESS FELLOW

1. Abraham Lincoln, *CW*, 1:408, 416; Gabor Boritt, *Lincoln and the Economics of the American Dream* (Memphis: Memphis State University, 1978), 109–10.

2. Illinois *State Register*, Jul. 17, 1846.

3. John McHenry to John Hardin, May 12, 1846, HFP, Box 16.

4. Ibid.

5. Illinois *State Register*, May 29, 1845; "General Orders," *Sangamo Journal*, May 28, 1846; Geo. Davis to Hardin, Alton, May 30, 1846, HFP, Box 16; Nancy L. Cox, "A Life of John Hardin of Illinois, 1810–1847" (M.A. thesis, Miami University, 1964), 169.

6. David Logan to Hardin, May 23, 1846, HFP, Box 16; Thomas Ford to "Dear General," Springfield, May 18, 1846, HFP, Box 16.

7. H. L. Cooley to Hardin, May 24, 1846, Steamer *LaClede*, Miss. River, HFP, Box 16; "General Orders," *Sangamo Journal*, May 28, 1846.

8. "Let It Be Well Done," *Sangamo Journal*, Jun. 4, 1846; Illinois *State Register*, Dec. 27, 1844; E. H. Merryman to John Hardin, Springfield, May 22, 1846, HFP, Box 16.

9. Samuel Bigger McCartney, "Illinois in the Mexican War" (M.A. thesis, Northwestern University, 1939), 29.

10. James Davis to Hardin, May 29, 1846, HFP, Box 16.

11. Letter from Charles Francis Adams, *Boston Whig*, Jun. 2, 1846; letter to "My Dear

Whipple, Jun. 19, 1846," *Liberator*, Aug. 21, 1846; see, for example, *CG*, 29th Cong., 2d sess., 204, 213, 245; 30th Cong., 1st sess., 62, 135,349.

12. Eric Foner, *The Fiery Trial: Abraham Lincoln and American Slavery* (New York: Norton, 2010), 22; Willard L. King, *Lincoln's Manager, David Davis* (Cambridge, MA: Harvard University Press, 1960), 54.

13. Illinois *State Register*, Jul. 3, 1846; Albert Jeremiah Beveridge, *Lincoln, 1809–1865* (New York: Houghton Mifflin, 1927), 1:377.

14. Abraham Lincoln, *CW*, 3:512.

15. King, *Lincoln's Manager*, 54.

16. David A. Smith to John Hardin, Jul. 10, 1846, Jacksonville, HFP, Box 16.

17. Abraham Lincoln to David Smith, Dec. 3, 1847, *CW*, 1:416.

18. For a firsthand account of the difficulties facing the army, see Manuel Balbontín, *La invasion Americana 1846 á 1848: Apunetes del subteniente de artillería Manuel Balbontín* (Mexico City: Tip. De Gonzalo Esteva, 1883).

19. Otis A. Singletary, *The Mexican War* (Chicago: University of Chicago Press, 1960), 32.

20. Calvin Benjamin to Issac Tracy, Metamoras, Mexico, Mar. 29, 1846, Calvin Benjamin Papers, LC.

21. "Late and Important from Mexico," *Floridian* (Tallahassee), Aug. 1, 1846.

22. "The Fields of Palo Alto," *Cleveland Herald*, Jun. 2, 1846; John H. McHenry to Hardin, Washington, DC, May 26, 1846, HFP, Box 16; "The Heroes of 'Palo Alto' and 'Resaca De La Palmas,'" *Raleigh Register, and North-Carolina Gazette*, Jul. 7, 1846; "Glorious News of Our Army," *Sangamo Journal*, May 28, 1846; see also "Glorious News of Our Army," *Baltimore Sun*, May 19, 1846; "Glorious Victory!!" *South Carolina Temperance Advocate and Register of Agriculture and General Literature* (Columbia, SC), Aug. 27, 1846.

23. "Letter from the Field of Battle," Milwaukee *Daily Sentinel and Gazette*, Jun. 1, 1846; "Old Rough and Ready," *North American* (Philadelphia), Jun. 17, 1846; meeting reported in *Sangamo Journal*, Jul. 9, 1846.

24. Polk, *Diary*, 1:444; "Santa Fe Taken, Without the Firing of a Gun!" *Daily Atlas*, Sep. 9, 1846.

25. "Highly Important News," *Polynesian* (Honolulu), Aug. 8, 1846; see also "Reported Taking of California," *North American* (Philadelphia), Aug. 19, 1846.

26. A. Lopez and Leva et al. before the Judge of First Instance, Rancho San Julian, Aug. 28, 1846 (doc. 530), Delfina de la Guerra Collection, Santa Barbara Mission Archives. See also Albert Camarillo, *Chicanos in a Changing Society: From Mexican Pueblos to American Barrios in Santa Barbara and Southern California, 1848–1930* (Cambridge, MA: Harvard University Press, 1979), 6–10; Louise Pubols, *The Father of All: The de la Guerra Family, Power, and Patriarchy in Mexican California* (Berkeley: University of California Press, 2009), 256–88.

27. Robert F. Stockton to James K. Polk, Ciudad de los Angeles, Aug. 26, 1846, *Correspondence of James K. Polk*, ed. Herbert Weaver and Wayne Cutler et al., 11 vols. (Knoxville: University of Tennessee Press, 1969–2009), 10:293–94.

28. New Orleans *Picayune*, Apr. 13, 1847, quoted in Thomas William Reilly, "American Reporters and the Mexican War 1846–1848" (Ph.D diss., University of Minnesota, 1975), 1:21.

29. "Response to the Call of the Governor," *Sangamo Journal*, Jun. 4, 1846.

30. William H. Herndon and Jesse W. Weik, *Abraham Lincoln: The True Story of a Great Life* (New York: Appleton, 1892), 258–59.

31. Clay to Horace Greeley, New York City, Jun. 23, 1846, PHC, 10:274.

32. Henry Clay to Octavia Walton LeVert, Mobile, AL, Jun. 25, 1846, PHC, 10:274.

33. Henry Clay to Francis Lieber, Aug. 20, 1846, *PHC*, 10:278; Henry Clay to Dr. George McClellan, Lexington, Sep. 24, 1846, *PHC*, 10:280; Dr. George McClellan to Henry Clay, Philadelphia, Sep. 17, 1846, *PHC*, 10:279; Henry Clay to Dr. George McClellan, Lexington, Sep. 24, 1846, *PHC*, 10:280.

34. Henry Clay to Octavia Walton LeVert, Lexington, Nov. 6, 1846, *PHC*, 10:284; Henry Clay Jr. to Henry Clay, Camp at Agua Nueva, Feb. 12, 1847, *PHC*, 10:306; details on drunkenness, Damon Eubank, *The Response of Kentucky to the Mexican War, 1846–1848* (Lewiston, NY: Edwin Mellen Press, 2004), 42.

35. Ramón Alcaraz et al., *The Other Side: Or, Notes for the History of the War Between Mexico and the United States*, trans. Albert C. Ramsey (New York: John Wiley, 1850), 80.

36. James K. Polk, *Diary of a President: James K. Polk*, ed. Milo Quaife, 4 vols. (Columbia, TN: James K. Polk Memorial Association, 2005), 2:181, 184.

37. Ibid., 1:496.

38. "The Spirit of the Country," Philadelphia *North American*, May 25, 1846.

39. "Monterey Mexico, Oct. 20, 1846" and letter from "Point Isabel, Nov. 1, 1846," both in "Later from the Army," Augusta *Chronicle*, Nov. 20, 1846.

40. "Relief of the Sick Soldiers," Alexandria *Gazette*, Oct. 30, 1846; letter from "H," Balize (LA), Nov. 14, 1846, in "Later from the Army," Augusta *Chronicle*, Nov. 20, 1846; King, *Lincoln's Manager*, 54–55.

41. Paul Foos, *A Short, Offhand, Killing Affair: Soldiers and Social Conflict During the Mexican-American War* (Chapel Hill: University of North Carolina Press, 2002), 22–23, 85. On unskilled labor options, see Seth Rockman, *Scraping By: Wage Labor, Slavery, and Survival in Early Baltimore* (Baltimore: Johns Hopkins University Press, 2008).

42. James M. McCaffrey, *Army of Manifest Destiny: The American Soldier in the Mexican War, 1846–1848* (New York: New York University Press, 1992), 119–20, quote on 120; Foos, *A Short, Offhand, Killing Affair*, 32–33. On firefighting and professionalization, Amy Greenberg, *Cause for Alarm: The Volunteer Fire Department in the Nineteenth-Century City* (Princeton, NJ: Princeton University Press, 1998).

43. Ulysses S. Grant, *Memoirs and Selected Letters: Personal Memoirs of U. S. Grant; Selected Letters, 1839–1865* (New York: Literary Classics of the United States, 1990), 918; on atrocity, see Foos, *A Short, Offhand, Killing Affair*, 113–37.

44. James Buckner Barry, *Buck Barry: Texas Ranger and Frontiersman*, ed. James K. Greer (Lincoln: University of Nebraska Press, 1978), 40.

45. "From Mexico," New Orleans *Picayune*, Oct. 6, 1847, quoted in *DNI*, Oct. 17, 1846; Philip Norbourne Barbour, *Journals of the Late Brevet Major Philip Norbourne Barbour and His Wife Isabella Hopkins Barbour: Written During the War with Mexico—1846*, ed. Rhoda van Bibber Tanner Doubleday (New York: G. P. Putnam's Sons, 1936), 95; "From the Charleston *Mercury*: Affairs at Monterey, Monterey (Mexico)," Oct. 11, 1846, in *Niles' National Register*, Nov. 21, 1846; F. L. Gifford to Bunkhead, May 20, 1846, Palmerston Papers, British Library, VI:37.

46. "From the Charleston *Mercury*: Affairs at Monterey, Monterey (Mexico)," Oct. 11, 1846, in *Niles' National Register*, Nov. 21, 1846; George Meade, *The Life and Letters of General George Gordon Meade* (New York: Charles Scribner's Sons, 1913), 1:147.

47. "From Monterey," correspondence of the New Orleans *Delta*, Dec. 1, 1846, in *DNI*, Jan. 1, 1847; Frank A. Hardy to Horace Hardy, Oct. 23, 1846, Frank Hardy letters, Ohio Historical Society.

48. "From Monterey," correspondence of the New Orleans *Delta*, Dec. 1, 1846, in *DNI*, Jan. 1, 1847.

49. Zachary Taylor, *Letters of Zachary Taylor from the Battlefield of the Mexican War*, ed. Wil-

liam H. Swanson (Rochester, NY: Genesee Press, 1908), 22, 24; Winfield Scott, *Memoirs of Lieutenant-General Scott* (New York: Sheldon, 1864), 2:392; Scott to Marcy, Jan. 16, 1847, quoted in Mark E. Neely Jr., *The Civil War and the Limits of Destruction* (Cambridge, MA: Harvard University Press, 2007), 9; Francis Baylies, *A Narrative of Major General Wool's Campaign in Mexico: In the Years 1846, 1847 & 1848* (Albany: Little, 1851), 57.

50. "The Spirit of the Country," Philadelphia *North American*, May 25, 1846.
51. Abraham Lincoln to Joshua Speed, Oct. 22, 1846, *CW*, 1:391.
52. Ellen Hardin Walworth, "The Battle of Buena Vista," *American Monthly Magazine* IV (Jan. 1894): 128; Samuel Bigger McCartney, "Illinois in the Mexican War" (M.A. thesis, Northwestern University, 1939), 32.
53. John Hardin to Sarah Hardin, Aug. 3, 1846, La Vaca, Texas, HFP, Box 17:2.

CHAPTER 7. BUENA VISTA

1. John Hardin letter to "My dear sister" (Margaret McKee), San Antonio, TX, Sep. 27, 1846, HFP, Box 17.
2. John Hardin to Sarah Hardin, Aug. 3, 1846, La Vaca, TX, HFP, Box 17.
3. Hardin to Sarah, Jul. 23, 1846, steamer *Missouri*, "Within 40 Miles of New Orleans" HFP, Box 17:2; John Hardin letter to Dear Smith, San Antonio, Sep. 30, 1846, HFP, Box 17; John Hardin to Sarah Hardin, Aug. 29, 1846, Camp Crockett, 3 miles from San Antonio, HFP, Box 17; "Flare up Among the Illinois Volunteers," *Daily Atlas*, Aug. 14, 1846; *Milwaukee Sentinel*, Aug. 14, 1846. Report originally published in New Orleans (unnamed paper) and St. Louis *Republican*.
4. John Hardin letter to Dear Smith, San Antonio, Sep. 30, 1846, HFP, Box 17; Zachary Taylor to R. C. Wood, Camargo, Mexico, Aug. 11, 1846, in *Letters of Zachary Taylor from the Battlefield of the Mexican War*, ed. William H. Swanson (Rochester, NY: Genesee Press, 1908), 38.
5. Ellen Hardin to John Hardin, Jacksonville, Aug. 1846, HFP, Box 17; John Hardin letter to Dear Smith, San Antonio, Sep. 30, 1846, HFP, Box 17.
6. Samuel Bigger McCartney,"Illinois in the Mexican War" (M.A. thesis, Northwestern University, 1939), 41.
7. Grant to Julia Dent, Jul. 6, 1845, in *Papers of Ulysses S. Grant*, ed. John Y. Simon (Carbondale: Southern Illinois University Press, 1967), 1:49; Robert Hunter to Sarah Jane Hunter, Apr. 21, 1846. Robert and Sarah Jane Hunter Letters, 1846–1847, LSU Special Collections; Robert E. May, "Invisible Men: Blacks and the U.S. Army in the Mexican War," in Darlene Clark Hine, ed., *A Question of Manhood: A Reader in U.S. Black Men's History and Masculinity* (Bloomington: Indiana University Press, 1999), 473–85.
8. William Cooper Nell, *The Colored Patriots of the American Revolution: With Sketches of Several Distinguished Colored Persons* (Boston: Robert F. Wallcut, 1855), 391.
9. James Bearden to Henry E. Dummer, Apr. 10, 1847, Jacksonville, IL, Abraham Lincoln Presidential Library, Manuscripts Collection; John T. Stuart to John J. Hardin, Aug. 30, 1833, HFP, Box 11.
10. Paul Finkelman, "Evading the Ordinance: The Persistence of Bondage in Indiana and Illinois," *Journal of the Early Republic* 9 (Spring 1989): 35–48.
11. Richard Lawrence Miller, *Lincoln and His World: Prairie Politician* (Mechanicsburg, PA: Stackpole Books, 2008), 1:194; Finkelman, "Evading the Ordinance."
12. "Illinois a Slaveholding State," *Liberator*, Mar. 31, 1854.
13. Jean H. Baker, *Mary Todd Lincoln* (New York: Norton, 1987), 105–8.

14. Philip Nourbourne Barbour, *Journals of the Late Brevet Major Philip Norbourne Barbour and His Wife Martha Isabella Hopkins Barbour: Written During the War with Mexico—1846,* ed. Rhoda van Bibber Tanner Doubleday (New York: G. P. Putnam's Sons, 1936), 28; May, "Invisible Men," 473; Robert Ryal Miller, *Shamrock and Sword: The Saint Patrick's Batallion in the U.S.-Mexican War* (Norman: University of Oklahoma Press, 1989), 31.

15. John Hardin, "Memorandums of Travel in Texas and Mexico with the Army of Chihuahua in the Summer and Autumn of 1846," 10–12, 14, HFP, Box 17:2; Brian DeLay, *War of a Thousand Deserts: Indian Raids and the U.S.-Mexican War* (New Haven, CT: Yale University Press, 2009).

16. John Hardin, "Memorandums of Travel in Texas and Mexico with the Army of Chihuahua in the Summer and Autumn of 1846," Oct. 16, 25, 27, HFP, Box 17:2.

17. Zachary Taylor to R. C. Wood, Agua Nueva, Mexico, Feb. 9, 1847, *Letters of Zachary Taylor,* 85.

18. James K. Polk, *Diary of a President: James K. Polk,* ed. Milo Quaife, 4 vols. (Columbia, TN: James K. Polk Memorial Association, 2005), 1:417–18.

19. Letter from Henry Clay Jr. to Henry Clay, Feb. 12, 1847, *PHC,* 10:306.

20. Henry Clay to Octavia LeVert, New Orleans, Dec. 19, 1846, *PHC,* 10:299; Henry Clay to John Pendleton Kennedy, New Orleans, Dec. 27, 1846, *PHC,* 10:301.

21. "Toast at the Dinner of the New England Society of Louisiana," *PHC,* 10:300.

22. "Mr. Clay," *Mississippian,* Jan. 14, 1847; Lowell *Journal* and Worcester *Spy* quoted in "Beating Their Idol," *Emancipator,* Feb. 17, 1847.

23. "Mexican War," Vermont *Gazette,* Jan. 19, 1847. See also New Orleans *Picayune,* Dec. 23, 1846; Augusta *Chronicle,* Dec. 30, 1846; Baltimore *Sun,* Jan. 4, 1847; New Hampshire *Gazette,* Dec. 14, 1847; Philadelphia *North American,* Jan. 4, 1847; *Cleveland Herald,* Jan. 7, 1847; Lowell *Journal* and Worcester *Spy* quoted in "Beating Their Idol," *Emancipator,* Feb. 17, 1847.

24. Thomas D. Tennery, *The Mexican War Diary of Thomas D. Tennary,* ed. D. E. Livingston-Little (Norman: University of Oklahoma Press, 1970), 66.

25. Quote in Felice Flanery Lewis, *Trailing Clouds of Glory: Zachary Taylor's Mexican War Campaign and His Emerging Civil War Leaders* (Tuscaloosa: University of Alabama Press, 2010), 173.

26. Samuel E. Chamberlain, *My Confession: Recollections of a Rogue,* ed. William H. Goetzmann (Austin: Texas State Historical Association, 1996), 119.

27. Fred Anderson and Andrew Cayton, *The Dominion of War: Empire and Liberty in North America, 1500–2000* (New York: Penguin, 2005), 261–62.

28. Quote ibid., 271. On Santa Anna, see Will Fowler, *Santa Anna of Mexico* (Lincoln: University of Nebraska Press, 2007).

29. Thomas Hart Benton, *Thirty Years' View; or, A History of the Working of the American Government for Thirty Years, from 1820–1850.* (New York: D. Appleton, 1873), 2:680.

30. James K. Polk to William H. Haywood Jr., Oct. 10, 1846, *Correspondence of James K. Polk,* ed. Herbert Weaver and Wayne Cutler et al., 11 vols. (Knoxville: University of Tennessee Press, 1969–2009), 11:349.

31. James K. Polk to William H. Polk, Oct. 2, 1846, *Correspondence of James K. Polk,* 11:349.

32. Letter from Henry Clay Jr. to Henry Clay, Feb. 12, 1847, *PHC,* 10:307.

33. John Hardin letter to "dear wife," Parras, Mexico, Dec. 7, 1846, HFP, Box 17:3.

34. John Hardin letter to Smith, Parras, Mexico, Dec. 10, 1846, HFP, Box 17:3.

35. "Quarrel between Gen. Wool and Col. Hardin," Trenton *State Gazette,* Jan. 29, 1847.

36. Letter from Henry Clay Jr. to Henry Clay, Feb. 12, 1847, *PHC,* 10:305; report of inebriation, Frankfort (KY) *Commonwealth,* Nov. 17, 1846.

37. John Hardin letter to Smith, Parras, Mexico, Dec. 10, 1846, HFP, Box 17:3; Archibald

Yell to James K. Polk, Monclov, Mexico, Nov. 5, 1846, *Correspondence of James K. Polk*, 11:385; Lewis, *Trailing Clouds of Glory*, 173.

38. Zachary Taylor to R. C. Wood, Monterrey, Mexico, Nov. 26, 1846, *Letters of Zachary Taylor*, 71; Zachary Taylor to R. C. Wood, Matamoras, Mexico, Jun. 21, 1846, *Letters of Zachary Taylor*, 13–14.

39. John Hardin, "Memorandums of Travel in Texas and Mexico with the Army of Chihuahua in the Summer and Autumn of 1846," 40–42, Oct. 23, 1846, HFP, Box 17:2.

40. John Hardin letter to Smith, Parras, Mexico, Dec. 10, 1846, HFP, Box 17:3; John Hardin letter to "Dear Henry" [Capt. John Henry], Parras, Mexico, Dec. 16, 1846, HFP, Box 17:3.

41. John Hardin letter to "Dear Henry" [Capt. John Henry], Parras, Mexico, Dec. 16, 1846, HFP, Box 17:3.

42. "In our Remarks," *Genius of Liberty* (Veracruz), Oct. 5, 1847; "Pleasures of Soldiering," *Richmond Enquirer* cited in *Niles' National Register* 71 (Sep. 26, 1846): 55.

43. "In our Remarks," *Genius of Liberty* (Veracruz), Oct. 5, 1847; Zachary Taylor to R. C. Wood, Monterrey, Mexico, Dec. 10, 1846, *Letters of Zachary Taylor*, 75. See also the letters of Alexander Somerville Wotherspoon to Louisa Kuhn, Wotherspoon Family Papers, LC.

44. Diary of William H. Daniel, 1846–47, Manuscript Department, Filson Club, Louisville, KY, 34, 44, quote in Richard V. Salisbury, "Kentuckians at the Battle of Buena Vista," *Filson Club Historical Quarterly* 61, no. 1 (Jan. 1987): 34–53, quote on 36.

45. Ellen Hardin Walworth, "Mrs. Ellen Hardin Walworth," *American Monthly Magazine* (Jul. 1893): 43.

46. Ellen Hardin Walworth, "Earliest Recollections," undated manuscript, WFA.

47. John Hardin to Ellen Hardin, Washington City, Dec. 1, 1843, WFA.

48. John Hardin to Ellen Hardin, Encantada, Mexico, 12 miles south of Saltillo, Jan. 3, 1847, HFP, Box 17:3.

49. Sarah Hardin to John Hardin, Lang Syne, Dec. 20, 1846 (from Princeton, MS), HFP, Box 17:3; information on Abram Smith plantation and slaves based on 1850 Census from Kent T. Dollar, *Soldiers of the Cross: Confederate Soldier-Christians and the Impact of the War on their Faith* (Macon, GA: Mercer University Press, 2005), 20.

50. Sarah Hardin to John Hardin, Lang Syne, Dec. 15, 1846, HFP, Box 17:3.

51. John Hardin to Sarah Hardin, Encantada, Mexico, Feb. 7, 1847, HFP, Box 17:3.

52. Transcript of John Hardin letter to Stephan Douglas, Feb. 4, 1847, HFP, Box 17:3.

53. John Hardin to Ellen Hardin, Jan., 31, 1847, HFP, Box 17:3.

54. John Hardin to Sarah Hardin, Agua Nuevo, Feb. 21, 1847, transcript, WFP.

55. John Palmer diary, Dec. 27, 1846, Huntington Library.

56. Samuel Chamberlain, *My Confession: Recollections of a Rogue*, ed. William H. Goetzmann (Austin: Texas State Historical Association, 1996), 133–34.

57. Manuscript by Lyman Guinnip to Senator Richard Yates (n.d.), 1–2, HFP, Box 17:2.

58. Chamberlain, *My Confession*, 157; *Ottawa Free Trader*, Apr. 16, 1847, quoted in McCartney, "Illinois in the Mexican War," 45; Guinnip manuscript, 2, HPF, Box 17:2.

59. Guinnip manuscript, 3–4, HPF, Box 17:2.

60. "Buena Vista," *DNI*, Apr. 7, 1847.

61. Guinnip manuscript, 5, HPF, Box 17:2.

62. Dr. John Upsher Lafon to R. J. Jackson, Feb. 24, 1847, Manuscript Collection, Kentucky Historical Society, Frankfort, quote in Richard V. Salisbury, "Kentuckians at the Battle of Buena Vista," *Filson Club Historical Quarterly* 61, no. 1 (Jan. 1987): 34–53, quote on 51; McCartney, "Illinois in the Mexican War," 49.

63. David A. Clary, *Eagles and Empire: The United States, Mexico, and the Struggle for a Continent* (New York: Bantam, 2009), 280.

64. "New York Gossip," New Orleans *Picayune*, Apr. 13, 1847.
65. John Frost, *The Life of Major-General Zachary Taylor* (New York, 1847), 335; "Honor to the Hero," *Brooklyn Daily Eagle*, Apr. 3, 1847; "Dying Moments of Lieut. Col. Henry Clay Jr.," *Union Magazine of Literature and Art* I (Jul. 1847): 44.

CHAPTER 8. INSCRUTABLE PROVIDENCE

1. Henry Clay to Mary Mentelle Clay, Feb. 8, 1847, *PHC*, 10:304; Henry Clay to Lucretia Clay, Mar. 13, 1847, *PHC*, 10:313.
2. Henry Clay to Mary S. Bayard, Apr. 16, 1847, *PHC*, 10:321.
3. Cary H. Fry to Henry Clay, Mar. 22, 1847, *PHC*, 10:314; Joseph Morgan Rogers, *The True Henry Clay* (Philadelphia: J. B. Lippincott, 1904), 151.
4. Henry Clay to William N. Mercer, Apr. 1, 1847, *PHC*, 10:315; Carl Schurz, *Henry Clay* (New York: F. Ungar, 1968), 2:288.
5. Henry Clay to William N. Mercer, Apr. 13, 1847, *PHC*, 10:320.
6. "Buena Vista," *DNI*, Apr. 7, 1847.
7. Henry Clay to John M. Clayton, Apr. 16, 1847, *PHC*, 10:322.
8. "Dying Moments of Lieut. Col. Henry Clay Jr.," *Union Magazine of Literature and Art* I (Jul. 1847): 44; "Resolutions of the Democratic Whig Young Men's General Committee of the City of New York," Apr. 8, 1847, *PHC*, 10:317.
9. Albert Pike, "Buena Vista," in Burton Egbert Stevenson, ed., *Poems of American History* (Boston: Houghton Mifflin, 1908), 366.
10. Horace Hoskins Houghton, *Poems* (Galena, IL: H. H. Houghton, 1878), 44.
11. "Buena Vista," *DNI*, Apr. 7, 1847.
12. Zachary Taylor to Henry Clay, Mar. 1, 1847, *PHC*, 10:312.
13. *DNI*, Jan. 28, 1848; Henry Clay letter to H. R. Robinson, New York City, Dec. 24, 1847, *PHC*, 10:392.
14. Rebecca Frick to Henry Clay, Danville, PA, May 1847, *PHC*, 10:327.
15. "On the 5th inst," New Orleans *Delta*, Apr. 14, 1847.
16. Martin Van Buren to Henry Clay, "Lindenwald," near Kinderhook, NY, Aug. 17, 1847, *PHC*, 10:346.
17. Henry Clay to Robert Morris, May 6, 1847, *PHC*, 10:328; James H. Otey to Henry Clay, "Mercer Hall," Columbia, TN, Jul. 9, 1847, *PHC*, 10:338.
18. "From Ashland, Ky.," *National Aegis*, Jul. 28, 1847.
19. Henry Clay to Mary S. Bayard, White Sulphur Springs, VA, Aug. 7, 1847, *PHC*, 10:344; "Funeral Ceremonies in Kentucky," New Hampshire *Gazette*, Aug. 3, 1847; Henry Clay to J. D. G. Quirk, Lexington, KY, Jul. 16, 1847, *PHC*, 10:340. See also Quirk to Clay, Jun. 29, 1847, *PHC*, 10:337.
20. "Calhoun—Clay—Webster—Benton," from the Massachusetts *Quarterly Review*, reprinted in *Liberator*, Jan. 7, 1848. On the same theme, see "The Progress of Christian Civilization," *Emancipator*, May 12, 1847.
21. William Henry Perrin, J. H. Battle, and G. C. Kniffin, *Kentucky: A History of the State*, 7th ed. (Louisville, KY: F. A. Battey, 1887), 347–48.
22. Thomas D. Tennery, *The Mexican War Diary of Thomas D. Tennary*, ed. D. E. Livingston-Little (Norman: University of Oklahoma Press, 1970), 72.
23. "Col. Hardin; Veracruz," Cleveland *Plain Dealer*, May 11, 1847.
24. Theodore McGinnis letter to William Beal, Feb. 23, 1847, Emma Beal Stott Genealogical Items, Wisconsin Historical Society.

25. Turner Crooker letter to "dear Mother," Apr. 3, 1847, Crooker Family Letters, Wisconsin Historical Society; John Kreitzer Journal, Mar. 29, 1847, HSP.

26. Turner Crooker letter to "dear Mother," Apr. 3, 1847, Crooker Family Letters, Wisconsin Historical Society; Ethan Allen Hitchcock, *Fifty Years in Camp and Field*, ed. W. A. Crofut (New York: Putnam, 2009), 248; "Surrender of Vera Cruz," New Orleans *Delta*, Apr. 11, 1847; statistics in K. Jack Bauer, *The Mexican War: 1846–1848* (New York: Macmillan, 1974), 252.

27. Carlos María de Bustamante, *El Nuevo bernal díaz del castillo* (Mexico City: Imprenta de Vicente García Torres, 1847), 2:154-55; Hitchcock, *Fifty Years in Camp and Field*, 248; Bauer, *The Mexican War*, 252; Irving W. Levinson, *Wars Within War: Mexican Guerrillas, Domestic Elites, and the United States of America, 1846–1848* (Fort Worth, TX: TCU Press, 2005), 31.

28. *Princeton* citation in "John of York," "Army Correspondence," Philadelphia *North American*, Apr. 17, 1847.

29. New Orleans *Picayune*, Apr. 9, 1847, quote in "The Surrender of Vera Cruz," *DNI*, Apr. 17, 1847; "John of York," "Army Correspondence," Philadelphia *North American*, Apr. 17, 1847; "Surrender of Vera Cruz," New Orleans *Delta*, Apr. 11, 1847.

30. Thomas William Reilly, "American Reporters and the Mexican War 1846–1848" (Ph.D. diss., University of Minnesota, 1975), 256; Paul Foos, *A Short, Offhand, Killing Affair: Soldiers and Social Conflict During the Mexican-American War* (Chapel Hill: University of North Carolina Press, 2002), 125; "John of York," "Army Correspondence," Philadelphia *North American*, Apr. 17, 1847.

31. James K. Polk, *Diary of a President: James K. Polk*, ed. Milo Quaife, 4 vols. (Columbia, TN: James K. Polk Memorial Association, 2005), 2:360; Eugene Irving McCormac, *James K. Polk, a Political Biography* (Berkeley: University of California Press, 1922), 327; Polk to William Childress, Jan. 12, 1846, *Correspondence of James K. Polk*, ed. Herbert Weaver and Wayne Cutler et al., 11 vols. (Knoxville: University of Tennessee Press, 1969–2009), 11:17.

32. John F. H. Claiborne, *Life and Correspondence of John A. Quitman* (New York: Harper and Bros., 1860), 1:237; Polk, *Diary*, 2:74, 456.

33. Polk, *Diary*, 2:465.

34. Ibid., 2:466; Andrew Jackson to Nicholas Trist, Sep. 16, 1835, Trist Papers, LC.

35. Elizabeth Trist to Nicholas Trist, Feb. 9, 1820. Trist Papers, UNC.

36. Nicholas Trist quote in Dean B. Mahin, *Olive Branch and Sword: The United States and Mexico, 1845–1848* (Jefferson, NC: McFarland, 1997), 89; James Buchanan to Nicholas Trist, Apr. 15, 1847, *DC*, 8:205.

37. Nicholas Trist to General Scott, Jan. 12, 1861, UNC, Box 6.

38. Gideon Wells quote in Richard R. Stenberg, "President Polk and California: Additional Documents," *Pacific Historical Review* 10 (1941): 217–19, quotes on 219; Nicholas Trist to General Scott, Jan. 12, 1861, UNC, Box 6.

39. Nicholas Trist to General Scott, Jan. 12, 1861, UNC, Box 6.

CHAPTER 9. NEEDLESS, WICKED, AND WRONG

1. Ellen Hardin Walworth, "Mrs. Ellen Hardin Walworth," *American Monthly Magazine*, Jul. 1893, 45.

2. Tom Reilly, *War with Mexico! America's Reporters Cover the Battlefront*, ed. Manley Witten (Lawrence: University of Kansas Press, 2010), 98; Dean B. Mahin, *Olive Branch and Sword: The United States and Mexico, 1845–1848* (Jefferson, NC: McFarland, 1997), 45.

3. Reilly, *War with Mexico!*, 99.

4. "Mrs. Hardin," Peoria *Register*, quoted in *Emancipator*, May 5, 1847; quote in "Col. J. J. Hardin," Fayetteville *Observer*, Apr. 20, 1847; "The Late Col. Hardin," *Daily Atlas*, Apr. 21, 1847.

5. *Obsequies of Col. John J. Hardin at Jacksonville, Illinois, Jul. 14, 1847* (Jacksonville, IL: Morgan Journal, 1847), 2; "Glorious News from the Army!," St. Louis *Republican*, quoted in the *Sangamo Journal*, Apr. 1, 1847; "Death of Gen. J. J. Hardin," St. Louis *Republican*, quote in the *Sangamo Journal*, Apr. 1, 1847.

6. Joseph Gillespie to Smith, Apr. 9, 1847, HFP, Box 17; William B. Warren to Sarah Hardin, Saltillo Mexico, Feb. 24, 1847, HFP Box 17; Sarah Hardin to Myra Hardin, n.d., HFP, Box 17.

7. "Resolutions Adopted at John J. Hardin Memorial Meeting," Apr. 5, 1847, *CW*, 1:392–93.

8. Joseph Gillespie, quoted in Frank J. Heinl, "Jacksonville and Morgan County: An Historical Review," *Journal of the Illinois State Historical Society* 18, no. 1 (Apr. 1925): 11; Gustave Koerner, *Memoirs of Gustave Koerner, 1809–1896*, ed. Thomas J. McCormack (Cedar Rapids, IA: Torch Press, 1909), 499; "Correspondence of the *Phoenix*," *Vermont Phoenix*, Jul. 1, 1847; David Davis to Judge Walker, Jun. 25, 1847, HFP, Box 17.

9. John Hardin to Sarah Hardin, Encantada, Mexico, Feb. 7, 1847, HFP, Box 17:3.

10. G. S. Boritt, *Lincoln and the Economics of the American Dream* (Memphis: Memphis State University Press, 1978), 129.

11. "Great 'Rough and Ready' Meeting," *Milwaukee Sentinel*, Apr. 22, 1847; "Buena Vista," *DNI*, Apr. 7, 1847.

12. "Col. Hardin," Maine *Cultivator* and Hallowell *Gazette*, Jun. 19, 1847; "Western Intelligence," Baltimore *Sun*, Jun. 17, 1847; The Late Col. J. J. Hardin, from the N. O. *Picayune*," *Albany Evening Journal*, Jun. 30, 1847; Mansfield Tracy Walworth, "Colonel John Hardin," *Historical Magazine and Notes and Queries Concerning the Antiquities*, 2nd ser., 5 (1869): 236.

13. "Honors to the Heroic Dead," *Philadelphia Inquirer*, Jul. 28, 1847.

14. Robert E. May, "Invisible Men: Blacks and the U.S. Army in the Mexican War," in Darlene Clark Hine, ed., *A Question of Manhood: A Reader in U.S. Black Men's History and Masculinity* (Bloomington: Indiana University Press, 1999), 473–85.

15. "Col. Hardin," *Milwaukee Sentinel*, Apr. 17, 1847.

16. "Reception of the Illinois Volunteers in St. Louis," Arkansas *Weekly Gazette*, Jul. 29, 1847.

17. "The Honored Dead," St. Louis *New Era*, quoted in the *Sangamo Journal*, Jul. 23, 1847.

18. "Funeral of General Hardin," *Sangamo Journal*, Jul. 20, 1847; Harry E. Pratt, ed., *Illinois as Lincoln Knew It: A Boston Reporter's Record of a Trip in 1847* (Springfield, IL: Abraham Lincoln Association, 1938), 40.

19. "Correspondence of the *Phoenix*," *Vermont Phoenix*, Jul. 1, 1847; Ellen Hardin Walworth, "To the Christian Herald," Jan. 25, 1905, manuscript, WFA, 1.

20. Ellen Hardin Walworth, "Mrs. Ellen Hardin Walworth," *American Monthly Magazine*, Jul. 1893, 42–49, quote on 44.

21. Illinois Constitutional Convention, *Constitution of the State of Illinois* (Springfield, IL: Lanphier and Walker, 1847), 38, 37; Eric Foner, *The Fiery Trial: Abraham Lincoln and American Slavery* (New York: Norton, 2010), 31.

22. Foner, *The Fiery Trial*, 25.

23. "The Convention," *Sangamo Journal*, Jul. 9, 1847; *Obsequies of Col. John J. Hardin*, 7.

24. Pratt, *Illinois as Lincoln Knew It*, 33–34.

25. *Obsequies of Col. John J. Hardin*, 22–24, 2; Ellen Hardin Walworth, "To the Christian Herald," Jan. 25, 1905, WFA, 7.

26. *Obsequies of Col. John J. Hardin*, 12–13.
27. Ibid., 12–13, 15–16. On restrained manhood and martial manhood, see Amy S. Greenberg, *Manifest Manhood and the Antebellum American Empire* (New York: Cambridge University Press, 2005).
28. Charles M. Eames, *Historic Morgan and Classic Jacksonville* (Jacksonville, IL: Daily Journal Steam Job Printing Office, 1885), 100; letter from "Western Farmer" in the *National Era*, Aug. 5, 1847.
29. *Obsequies of Col. John J. Hardin*, 8–9.
30. Ibid., 13.
31. "Funeral of General Hardin," *Sangamo Journal*, Jul. 20, 1847.
32. Pratt, *Illinois as Lincoln Knew It*, 42.
33. Letter from "Western Farmer" in the *National Era*, Aug. 5, 1847.
34. Pratt, *Illinois as Lincoln Knew It*, 42.
35. Davis to Walker, Dec. 6, 1846, quote in Willard R. King, *Lincoln's Manager, David Davis* (Cambridge, MA: Harvard University Press, 1960), 55; Chicago *Western Citizen*, Feb. 16, 1847, quote in Paul Foos, *A Short, Offhand, Killing Affair: Soldiers and Social Conflict During the Mexican-American War* (Chapel Hill: University of North Carolina Press, 2002), 49.
36. Letter from "Western Farmer" in the *National Era*, Aug. 5, 1847; Pratt, *Illinois as Lincoln Knew It*, 28.
37. Pratt, *Illinois as Lincoln Knew It*, 43.
38. Albert Hale, *Two Discourses on the Subject of the War Between the U. States and Mexico* (Springfield, IL: *Sangamo Journal*, 1847), 13.
39. *History of Sangamon County, Illinois: Together with Sketches of Its Cities* (Chicago: Interstate, 1881), 671.
40. Hale, *Two Discourses on the Subject of the War*, 3.
41. Quote in Hale, *Two Discourses on the Subject of the War*, 3; *Sangamo Journal*, Jul. 20, 1847.
42. "John of York," "Letters from the Army," Philadelphia *North American*, May 4, 1847.
43. *Ashtabula (OH) Sentinel*, May 3, 1847; New Orleans *Picayune*, Jan. 27, 1847.
44. Rachel Hope Cleves, *The Reign of Terror in America: Visions of Violence from Anti-Jacobinism to Antislavery* (New York: Cambridge University Press, 2009), 161–68.
45. Jeffrey L. Pasley, *"The Tyranny of Printers": Newspaper Politics in the Early American Republic* (Charlottesville: University of Virginia Press, 2001), 244–47; Cleves, *Reign of Terror*, 168–70.
46. "John of York," "Letters from the Army," Philadelphia *North American*, May 4, 1847.
47. "Direful Vengeance," *Milwaukee Sentinel*, Apr. 23, 1847. For reporting see, for example, *Milwaukee Sentinel*, Apr. 23, 1847; San Augustine *Red Lander*, Apr. 24, 1847.
48. "Direful Vengeance," *Milwaukee Sentinel*, Apr. 23, 1847; "John of York," "Letters from the Army," Philadelphia *North American*, May 4, 1847.
49. "Special Correspondence of the *Picayune*," New Orleans *Picayune*, Nov. 10, 1847; Thomas William Reilly, "American Reporters and the Mexican War 1846–1848" (Ph.D. diss., University of Minnesota, 1975), 301–2.
50. "Special correspondence of the *Picayune*," New Orleans *Picayune*, May 13, 1847; Reilly, "American Reporters and the Mexican War 1846–1848," 302; New Orleans *Picayune*, Nov. 27, 1847; "A Heavy Retribution," *American Flag* (Matamoros, Mexico), May 5, 1847. See also "Atrocities," *Flag of Freedom* (Puebla, Mexico), Nov. 24, 1847.
51. *CG*, appendix, 29th Cong., 2d sess., Feb. 11, 1847, 216–17.
52. James D. Richardson, ed., *A Compilation of the Messages and Papers of the Presidents* (Washington, DC: GPO, 1901), 5:2321–56; Massachusetts—General Court—House of

Representatives, "Documents Relating to the U.S.-Mexican War," House Number 200: Commonwealth of Massachusetts, Apr. 22, 1847, 4–8, NYHS.

53. Henry David Thoreau, *Walden and Civil Disobedience*, ed. Jonathan Levin (New York: Barnes and Noble Books, 2003), 265.

54. See Jonathan H. Earle, *Jacksonian Antislavery and the Politics of Free Soil, 1824–1854* (Chapel Hill: University of North Carolina Press, 2003).

55. "A Captain of the Volunteers," *Alta California: Embracing Notices of the Climate, Soil, and Agricultural Products of Northern Mexico and The Pacific Seaboard: Also a History of the Military and Naval Operations of the United States Directed Against the Territories of Northern Mexico, in the Year 1846–47* (Philadelphia: H. Packer, 1847), 53, 61.

56. Walt Whitman, "Shall We Fight It Out?" *Brooklyn Daily Eagle*, May 11, 1846; Walt Whitman, "American Workingmen, Versus Slavery," *Brooklyn Daily Eagle*, Sep. 1, 1847.

57. Wm. Vanderbeek, "General Taylor's Quick Step" (New York, 1846), in "Music for the Nation: American Sheet Music, 1820–1860," Library of Congress, Music Division; G. N. Allen, *Incidents and Sufferings in the Mexican War, with Accounts of Hardships Endured* (Boston: 1847); "Soon to Close! Donnavan's Grand Serial of Panorama of Mexico!," Boston, 1848, American Broadsides and Ephemera.

58. North Carolina *Newbernian*, quote in "Spirit of the Free Press," Kennebec (ME) *Journal*, Jun. 1, 1847; John Sherman to W. T. Sherman, May 2, 1847, in *The Sherman Letters*, ed. Rachel Sherman Thorndike (New York, 1894), 38–39; *CG*, 30th Cong., 1st sess., Feb. 29, 1848, 402–3. See the indices to the House and Senate Journals for the 29th and 30th Congresses for a complete list of petitions.

59. Jane Grey Swisshelm, *Half a Century* (Chicago: Jansen, McClurg, 1880), 95–96.

60. Rebecca Gratz to Ann, Jul. 22, 1847, in *Letters of Rebecca Gratz*, ed. David Philipson (Philadelphia: Jewish Publication Society of American, 1929), 341–42; Rebecca Frick to Henry Clay, Danville, PA, May 1847, *PHC*, 10:327; Annie B. Roach diary, Lamb Family Papers, Massachusetts Historical Society; Moses Smith letter to Melinda Powers, Feb. 12, 1847, Louisiana State University Special Collections.

61. "The War," *Berkshire County Whig*, May 20, 1847; Emily Huse letter to Mrs. Olive Washburn, Sep. 1847, Manuscripts, Wisconsin Historical Society.

62. Taylor to Robert Wood, camp near Monterrey, Mexico, Nov. 2, 1847, Taylor, *Letters*, 148.

CHAPTER 10. WAR MEASURES

1. James K. Polk, *Diary of a President: James K. Polk*, ed. Milo Quaife, 4 vols. (Columbia, TN: James K. Polk Memorial Association, 2005), 2:492.

2. Manuel Zamorg to Andrew Osuguera, Apr. 30, 1847, Zamorg Papers, NYHS.

3. Turner Crooker letter to "dear Mother," Apr. 27, 1847, Crooker Family Letters, Wisconsin Historical Society; "Cerro Gordo," *Boletín de Noticias* (Mexico City), May 1, 1847.

4. "Another Glorious Victory! Battle of Cerro Gordo," New Orleans *Delta*, May 1, 1847; John Kreitzer Journal, Apr. 19, 1847, HSP.

5. "Cerro Gordo," *Boletín de Noticias* (Mexico City), May 1, 1847. On Mexico's embrace of guerrilla forces after Cerro Gordo, see "Expedición de patentes, para organización de guerrillas de la Guardia Nacional, de acuerdo con el Reglamento de 28 de abril de 1847," Folder XI/481.3/2586, AHSDN. See also Folders XI/481.3/2579, XI/481.3/2580, AHSDN.

6. Otto Zirckel, *Tagebuch geschrieben während der nordamerikanisch-mexikanischen Campagne in den Jahren 1847 und 1848 auf beiden Operationslinien* (Halle: H. W. Schmidt, 1849), 1–3, translation by Peter van Lidth de Jeude; Paul Foos, *A Short, Offhand, Killing Affair:*

Soldiers and Social Conflict During the Mexican-American War (Chapel Hill: University of North Carolina Press, 2002), 22.

7. Harry E. Pratt, ed., *Illinois as Lincoln Knew It: A Boston Reporter's Record of a Trip in 1847* (Springfield, IL: Abraham Lincoln Association, 1938), 45; Michael Feldberg, *The Turbulent Era: Riot and Disorder in Jacksonian America* (New York: Oxford University Press, 1980), 7–13.

8. "Catholic Irish, Frenchmen, and German of the Invading Army!" Huatusco, Jun. 6, 1847, George Cadwalader Papers—436, Folder #8, HSP, "El president de la república Mexicana a las tropas que vienen enganchadas en el ejército de los Estados Unidos de Norte América," Aug. 14, 1847, Folder XI/481.3/2613, AHSDN.

9. John Kreitzer Journal, Apr. 21, 1847. HSP; John Jacob Oswandel, *Notes of the Mexican War* (Philadelphia: N.p., 1885), 145.

10. Carl von Grone, *Briefe über Nord-Amerika und Mexiko und den zwischen beiden gerührten krieg* (Braunschweig: Druck von G. Westermann, 1850), 62–63. Translation by Peter van Lidth de Jeude.

11. "Col P. M. Butler," *Raleigh Register, and North-Carolina Gazette*, Jun. 4, 1847.

12. Oswandel, *Notes of the Mexican War*, 206; "John of York," "Letters from the Army, Camp Near Jalapa, 30 April," Philadelphia *North American*, May 28, 1847; six Illinois soldiers: John Kreitzer Journal, May 2, 1847, HSP.

13. "Our Army Correspondence, Jun. 11, 1847," *North American and United States Gazette*, Dec. 10, 1847.

14. Winfield Scott, *Memoirs of Lieutenant-General Scott* (New York: Sheldon, 1864), 2:579.

15. Ibid.; Nicholas Trist to Virginia Trist, May 21, 1847, LC Trist Papers, Reel 2.

16. Winfield Scott to Nicholas Trist, May 29, 1847, LC Trist Papers, Reel 2; Nicholas Trist to Virginia Trist, May 15, 1847, LC Trist Papers, Reel 2; Scott to Marcy, Jun. 4, 1847, Executive Documents, Senate, 30th Cong., 1st sess., 1847, #29, 7:130.

17. Polk, *Diary*, 3:57–59.

18. Quote in Otis A. Singletary, *The Mexican War* (Chicago: University of Chicago Press, 1960), 84.

19. George Turnbull Moore Davis, *Autobiography of the Late Col. Geo. T. M. Davis: Captain and Aid-de-camp Scott's Army of Invasion* (New York: Jenkins and McCowan, 1891), 290, 192; quote in Singletary, *Mexican War*, 83.

20. Davis, *Autobiography of the Late Col. Geo. T. M. Davis*, 228; Robert Ryal Miller, *Shamrock and Sword: The Saint Patrick's Batallion in the U.S.-Mexican War* (Norman: University of Oklahoma Press, 1989), 104.

21. Quote in Singletary, *Mexican War*, 94.

22. K. Jack Bauer, *The Mexican War: 1846–1848* (New York: Macmillan, 1974), 308–11.

23. Quotes in Guillermo Prieto, *Memorias de mis tiempos* (Paris: Librería de la Vda. de C. Bouret, 1906), 423, translation by the author; Miller, *Shamrock and Sword*, 105; Bauer, *Mexican War*, 308–11.

24. Prieto, *Memorias de mis tiempos*, 417–19, translation by the author.

25. Ignacio de Mora y Villamil to Zachary Taylor, San Luis Potosi, May 10, 1847, House Ex. Doc. 60, 30th Cong, 1st sess., 1139–41.

26. David A. Clary, *Eagles and Empire: The United States, Mexico, and the Struggle for a Continent* (New York: Bantam, 2009), 379–80; Tom Reilly, *War with Mexico! America's Reporters Cover the Battlefront*, ed. Manley Witten (Lawrence: University of Kansas Press, 2010), 152.

27. Scott to Marcy, Jul. 25, 1847, Executive Documents, Senate, 30th Cong., 1st sess., 1847, #29, 7:135; Scott, *Memoirs*, 2:579; Nicholas Trist to James Buchanan, Jul. 23, 1847, Trist Papers, LC, Reel 8.

28. Nicholas Trist to Virginia Trist, Oct. 18, 1847, Trist Papers, LC.

29. Palmerston, Oct. 29, 1847, PPBL, 14; "The Great War Meeting," *NYH,* Jan. 30, 1848; *NYH,* Oct. 8, 1847. See also Amy Greenberg, *Manifest Manhood and the Antebellum American Empire* (New York: Cambridge University Press, 2005), 22.

30. Ben Perley Poore, *Perley's Reminiscences of Sixty Years in the National Metropolis* (Tecumseh, MI: A. W. Mills, 1886), 1:329-30.

CHAPTER II. DUTY AND JUSTICE

1. James K. Polk, *Diary of a President: James K. Polk,* ed. Milo Quaife, 4 vols. (Columbia, TN: James K. Polk Memorial Association, 2005), 3:468.

2. Ibid., 3:483, 468.

3. Ibid., 3:483.

4. J. A. Smith to Virginia Trist, Jun. 2, 1847, Louisville. Trist Papers UNC, Folder 137; H. B. Trist to Virginia Trist, Jul. 31, 1847, Bowdon, Trist Papers, UNC, Folder 137.

5. H. B. Trist to Virginia Trist, Jul. 31, 1847, Bowdon, Trist Papers, UNC, Folder 137; "Policy of the American Government," *Daily American Star* (Mexico City), Nov. 17, 1847; Charles Averill, *The Mexican Ranchero; or, The Maid of the Chapparal: A Romance of the Mexican War* (Boston: F. Gleason, 1847); Martha A. Clough, *Zuleika: or the Castilian Captive* (Boston: F. Gleason, 1849), 102.

6. Background on novel in Sacvan Bercovitch, ed., *The Cambridge History of American Literature* (Cambridge: Cambridge University Press, 1995), 2:162; Jaime Javier Rodríguez, *The Literatures of the U.S.-Mexican War: Narrative, Time, and Identity* (Austin: University of Texas, 2010), 29-32; Shelley Streeby, *American Sensations: Class, Empire and the Production of Popular Culture* (Berkeley: University of California Press, 2002), 105-23.

7. "The Great War Meeting," *NYH,* Jan. 30, 1848; Philadelphia *Public Ledger,* Dec. 11, 1847.

8. John M. Brannan, letter to his brother Benjamin F. Brannan (Frank) from the City of Mexico, Oct. 24, 1847, Miscellaneous Brannan, J. M. Papers, NYHS.

9. Averill, *The Mexican Ranchero,* 45.

10. Ibid., 45-46.

11. Ibid., 100.

12. Polk, *Diary,* 3:76-77.

13. Ibid., 3:200; Buchanan to Nicholas Trist, Oct. 25, 1847, Trist Papers, LC.

14. Polk, *Diary,* 3:199, 267.

15. Ibid., 3:163.

16. Ibid., 3:256, 10, 91.

17. Ibid., 3:91, 26.

18. Anson and Fanny Nelson, *Memorials of Sarah Childress Polk* (New York: Anson D. F. Randolph, 1892), 115-16.

19. Polk, *Diary,* 3:184.

20. Ibid., 3:185, 186.

21. Taylor Adjutant General, Oct. 15, 1846, House Executive Document 60, 29th Cong., 1st sess., 353; John Frost, *Pictorial History of Mexico and the Mexican War* (Philadelphia, 1871), 339; Polk, *Diary,* 3:229, 226. For support of the Sierra Madre Line among American soldiers, see "Mexico and the United States," *Free American* (Veracruz), Dec. 10, 1847.

22. "Dinner to Gen. Scott at Sandusky," *DNI,* Oct. 15, 1852; Scott to Santa Anna, Aug. 21, 1847, Manning, *DC,* 8:922.

23. Ulysses Grant to Julia Dent, Jan. 9, 1848, Tacabaya, Mexico, *Memoirs and Selected Letters:*

Personal Memoirs of U. S. Grant; Selected Letters 1839–1865 (New York: Literary Classics of the United States, 1990), 928; letter from C. B. Ogburn to Issac Golden, Misc. Mss. Ogburn, C. B. Camp in Saltillo, Mexico, Dec. 19, 1847, NYHS.

24. New Orleans *Picayune*, Dec. 19, 1847; New Orleans *Crescent*, Apr. 22, 1848; "Massacre of Mexican Citizens!" New Orleans *Picayune*, reprinted in the Albany *Journal*, Mar. 16, 1848.

25. Virginia Trist to Tuckerman, Aug. 23, 1863 (filed with Jul. 8 enclosure), Trist Papers, UNC, Folder 225.

26. Ulysses Grant to Julia, Jan. 9, 1848, Tacabaya, Mexico, *Memoirs and Selected Letters*, 928; John M. Brannan to his brother Benjamin F. Brannan (Frank) from the City of Mexico, Oct. 24, 1847, Miscellaneous Brannan, J. M. Papers, NYHS.

27. Quote in Ellen Hardin Walworth, "To the Christian Herald," Jan. 25, 1905, manuscript, WFA, 2; J. Winston Coleman Jr., *Stage-Coach Days in the Bluegrass* (Lexington: University Press of Kentucky, 1995), 137.

28. Quote in Donald W. Riddle, *Congressman Abraham Lincoln* (Urbana: University of Illinois Press, 1957), 13.

29. David S. Heidler and Jeanne T. Heidler, *Henry Clay: The Essential American* (New York: Random House, 2010), 42.

30. Ibid., xx.

31. Dennis Hanks to Herndon, Mar. 12, 1866, quoted in William H. Townsend, *Lincoln and His Wife's Home Town* (Indianapolis: Bobbs Merrill, 1929), 89.

32. Nathan Sargent, *Public Men and Events, from the Commencement of Mr. Monroe's Administration, in 1817, to the Close of Mr. Fillmore's Administration in 1853* (Philadelphia: J. B. Lippincott, 1875), 2:34.

33. Abraham Lincoln, "To Henry Clay," Aug. 29, 1842, *CW*, 1:297.

34. Massachusetts House of Representatives, "Documents Relating to the U.S.-Mexican War," House Doc. 200, Commonwealth of Massachusetts, Apr. 22, 1847, NYHS.

35. Henry Clay to John M. Clayton, Apr. 17, 1847, *PHC*, 10:322; Clay to Richard Henry Wilde, Apr. 10, 1847, *PHC*, 10:319; Speech to Delegations of Citizens from New York City, Trenton, New Haven and Philadelphia, Cape May, N.J, Aug. 20, 1847, *PHC*, 10:347.

36. Henry Clay Jr. to Henry Clay, Feb. 12, 1847, *PHC*, 10:306. Most scholars examining Clay's later career have assumed that he was actively pursuing the Whig presidential nomination in 1848, and delivered his Lexington address in order to strengthen his position in the North. "His Lexington speech was the all but formal launch of his campaign for the nomination" (Heidler, *Henry Clay*, 427). Clay, however, was adamant that he was not seeking the presidency, particularly after the backlash against his speech in the South.

37. "The Gathering at Lexington," *Hudson River Chronicle*, Nov. 16, 1847; "New York, Monday, Nov. 15," *Milwaukee Sentinel and Gazette*, Dec. 1, 1847.

38. "Mr. Clay at Lexington," Baltimore *Sun*, Nov. 18, 1847.

39. Clay, *Speeches of Clay*, 367–69.

40. "Mr. Clay's Lexington Speech," *Whig Almanac*, 1848: 19–28.

41. "New York, Monday, Nov. 15," *Milwaukee Sentinel and Gazette*, Dec. 1, 1847.

42. "Mr. Clay's Speech and Resolutions," *Daily Atlas*, Nov. 17, 1847; "New York, Monday, Nov. 15," *Milwaukee Sentinel and Gazette*, Dec. 1, 1847; "Clay's Pronunciamiento," *New Hampshire Patriot and State Gazette*, Nov. 18. 1847.

43. "New York, Monday, Nov. 15," *Milwaukee Sentinel and Gazette*, Dec. 1, 1847.

44. "Mould the Clay," *Liberator* (Boston), Feb. 18, 1848.

45. "The Whig Policy, as Viewed by Our Army in Mexico," *Washington Union*, quoted

in the (Bridgeport, CT) *Republican Farmer*, Dec. 7, 1847; "Voice from Tennessee," (Augusta, ME) *Age*, Dec. 10, 1847; Merrill D. Peterson, *The Great Triumvirate: Webster, Clay, and Calhoun* (New York: Oxford University Press 1987), 435; "Henry Clay," *North American* (Mexico City), Jan. 25, 1848.

46. Michael F. Holt, *The Rise and Fall of the American Whig Party* (New York: Oxford University Press, 1999), 281; "Mr. Clay," Georgia *Telegraph*, Dec. 7, 1847.

47. "Meetings in Favor of the War," *North American* (Mexico City), Jan. 26, 1848; Compton to Palmerston, Nov. 28, 1847, PPBL, 82; see "Progress of the Lexington Movement," Richmond *Enquirer*, Dec. 3, 1847, for details on scope of meetings. Also "A Response," *Emancipator*, Dec. 8, 1847.

48. "Important from Mexico!" *Daily Atlas*, Dec. 22, 1847; "The Clay Whigs of New York City," *National Era*, Dec. 30, 1847; "The Philadelphia Papers," *Daily Atlas*, Dec. 8, 1847; "Great Anti-War Meeting in Philadelphia," *Daily Atlas*, Dec. 9, 1847; "A Voice from Philadelphia," *DNI*, Dec. 9, 1847.

49. "The Whigs of Trenton," *DNI*, Nov. 27, 1847; "Anti-War Meeting," *DNI*, Dec. 2, 1847; "The Anti-War Meeting," *Cleveland Herald*, Feb. 23, 1848; George Turnbull Moore Davis, *Autobiography of the Late Col. Geo. T. M. Davis: Captain and Aid-de-Camp, Scott's Army of Invasion* (New York: Jenkins and McCowan, 1891), 295; "Great Anti-War Meeting in Philadelphia," *Daily Atlas*, Dec. 9, 1847.

50. "Great Anti-War Meeting in Philadelphia," *Daily Atlas*, Dec. 9, 1847.

51. William Herndon quoted in Gabor S. Boritt, *Lincoln and the Economics of the American Dream* (Memphis, Memphis State University Press, 1978), 137.

52. "Policy of the American Government," *Daily American Star* (Mexico City), Nov. 17, 1847; Virginia Trist to Tuckerman, Aug. 23, 1863 (filed with Jul. 8 enclosure), Trist Papers, UNC, Folder 225. On soldier behavior, see letters of Maria Wilkins to Lieutenant William D. Wilkins, Dec. 13, 1847, April 29, 1848, William D. Wilkins Papers, LC.

53. Nicholas Trist to Edward Thornton, Jul. 15, 1847, Trist Papers, LC; pro-annexation articles from central Mexico, see "Annexation," *Flag of Freedom* (Puebla, Mexico), Nov. 24, 1847; *El Norte Americano* (Mexico City), Nov. 5 and 30, 1847; "Policy of the American Government," *Daily American Star* (Mexico City), Nov. 17, 1847.

54. Nicholas Trist to Thornton, Dec. 4, 1847, *DC*, 8:985; Winfield Scott, *Memoirs of Lieutenant-General Scott* (New York: Sheldon, 1864), 2:576; Thornton to Nicholas Trist, Nov. 22, 1847, Trist Papers, LC; Nicholas Trist 1848 manuscript, Trist Papers, UNC.

55. Nicholas Trist to S. M. Felton, Apr. 5, 1847, Trist Papers, LC; Nicholas Trist to Buchanan, Dec. 6, 1847, DC, 8:888; Nicholas Trist to Buchanan, Dec. 4, 1847, *DC*, 8:987; Compton to Palmerston, Nov. 28, 1847, PPBL, 82.

56. Polk, *Diary*, 3:252; Virginia Trist to Tuckerman, Aug. 23, 1863 (filed with Jul. 8 enclosure), Trist Papers, UNC, Folder 225.

57. Polk, *Diary*, 3:301.

58. Lincoln, *CW*, 4:184; Lincoln, "To William H. Herndon, Dec. 13, 1847," *CW*, 1:420.

CHAPTER 12. TO CONQUER A PEACE

1. Giddings to L. W. Giddings, May 10, 1846, Giddings Papers, Ohio Historical Society.

2. *CG*, 29th Cong., 1st sess., Appendix, 643–44.

3. Sumner to Winthrop, Boston, Aug. 5, 1846, Winthrop Family Papers, MHS.

4. Winthrop to Sumner, Aug. 7, 1846, Winthrop Family Papers, MHS; Sumner to Winthrop, Boston, Aug. 10, 1846, Winthrop Family Papers, MHS.

5. Winthrop to Mrs. Gardner, Feb. 2, 1847; Winthrop to Appleton, Feb. 5, 1847; Winthrop to Mrs. Gardner, Washington, DC, Jun. 18, 1846, all Winthrop Family Papers, MHS.

6. James D. Richardson, ed., *A Compilation of the Messages and Papers of the Presidents* (Washington, DC: GPO, 1901), 4:533–49.

7. Francis Baylies, *A Narrative of Major General Wool's Campaign in Mexico: In the Years 1846, 1847 & 1848* (Albany: Little, 1851), 5; David A. Clary, *Eagles and Empire: The United States, Mexico, and the Struggle for a Continent* (New York: Bantam, 2009), 324 (quote), 284, 339.

8. Quote in John H. Schroeder, *Mr. Polk's War: American Opposition and Dissent, 1846–1848* (Madison: University of Wisconsin Press, 1973), 69–70.

9. Georgetown (SC) *Winyah Observer*, Oct. 13, 1847, Nov. 3, 1847, quote in Ernest McPherson Lander Jr., *Reluctant Imperialists: Calhoun, The South Carolinians, and the Mexican War* (Baton Rouge: Louisiana State University Press, 1980), 151–52.

10. Abraham Lincoln, Dec. 22, 1847 (Printed Resolution and Preamble on Mexican War: "Spot Resolutions"), ALP. Available online at http://memory.loc.gov/ammem/alhtml/alhome.html.

11. *CG*, 30th Cong., 1st sess., 95.

12. William H. Herndon and Jesse W. Weik, *Abraham Lincoln: The True Story of a Great Life* (New York: Appleton, 1892), 266.

13. Lincoln, *CW*, 1:446–47.

14. Abraham Lincoln to Congress, Jan. 12, 1848 (revised draft prepared for publication), ALP.

15. Quoted in Albert Jeremiah Beveridge, *Abraham Lincoln, 1809–1858* (New York: Houghton Mifflin, 1927), 1:430.

16. *DNI*, Jan. 20, 1848.

17. "Boston *Daily Atlas*, Speech of Mr. Lincoln, of Illinois, on the Reference of the President's Message." Jan. 27, 1848, Brattleboro (VT) *Semi-Weekly Eagle*, Feb. 4, 1848. The *Arkansas Weekly Gazette* offered the preamble and resolutions of his speech in full: "The War with Mexico," Jan. 13, 1848.

18. "Editorial Correspondence," *Daily Atlas*, Jan. 15, 1848. Slight variations of this report appeared in New London (CT) *Morning News*, Jan. 25, 1848; Alexandria (VA) *Gazette*, Feb. 8, 1848; Trenton (NJ) *State Gazette*, Feb. 4, 1848; and the *People's Advocate and New London (CT) County Republican*, Jan. 26, 1848. Most quoted him as saying that "Military Glory is a rainbow, which rises in the heavens and dazzles with its luster; but it comes forth from *clouds of desolated cities and showers of human blood.*" *Southern Patriot*, Feb. 11, 1848, described Lincoln and left out any discussion of his speech.

19. *Baltimore Patriot* quoted in Rockford (IL) *Forum*, Jan. 19, 1848.

20. "By Magnetic Telegraph," *Daily Atlas*, Jan. 13, 1847; see also "Congress," *Raleigh Register, and North-Carolina Gazette*, Jan. 19, 1848; Augusta (ME) *Chronicle*, Dec. 28, 1848; Augusta (ME) *Age*, Dec. 31, 1848; Keene (NH) *Sentinel*, Dec. 30, 1847; Easton (MD) *Gazette*, Jan. 22, 1848; *Wachusetts Star*, Jan. 18, 1848; Litchfield (CT) *Republican*, Dec. 30, 1847; *National Aegis*, Jan. 19, 1848; *Emancipator*, Jan. 19, 1848; *Richmond Enquirer*, Jan. 14, 1848; New Bedford (MA) *Mercury*, Jan. 14, 1848; New Orleans *Picayune*, Jan. 2 and Jan. 20, 1848; *Philadelphia Inquirer*, Dec. 23, 1847; Bennington (VT) *Gazette*, Jan. 19, 1848.

21. *Missouri Republican* quoted in the *Illinois Journal*, Feb. 3, 1848.

22. " 'Spotty' Lincoln, of Illinois," *Illinois Globe*, quoted in the *Daily Ohio Statesman*, Feb. 3, 1848.

23. "Benedict Arnold" and "Ranchero Spotty" in Illinois *State Register*, Mar. 10, 1848; "Died" in the Peoria *Press*, quote in the Illinois *State Register*, Feb. 25, 1848; David Herbert Donald, *Lincoln* (New York, 1995), 125; see Gabor S. Boritt, "A Question of Political

Suicide? Lincoln's Opposition to the Mexican War," *Journal of the Illinois State Historical Society* 67 (Feb. 1974): 87, for a complete list of citations.

24. Newton Curtis, *The Hunted Chief: or Female Ranchero* (New York, 1847), 3; Polk quote in Richardson, *Compilation of the Messages and Papers of the Presidents*, 4:473; on the impact of guerrilla activity on U.S. forces, see Irving W. Levinson, *Wars Within War: Mexican Guerrillas, Domestic Elites, and the United States of America, 1846–1848* (Fort Worth, TX: TCU Press, 2005).

25. Herndon, *Abraham Lincoln*, 269–70.

26. Ibid.; Lincoln to Herndon, Feb. 2, 1848, in Lincoln, *CW*, 1:448; *CG*, Appendix, 30th Cong., 1st sess., 161.

27. *CG*, Appendix, 30th Cong., 1st sess., 163.

28. Lincoln, *CW*, 1:515.

29. Lincoln to Herndon, Feb. 2, 1848, in Lincoln, *CW*, 1:448.

CHAPTER 13. A CLEAR CONSCIENCE

1. James K. Polk, *Diary of a President: James K. Polk*, ed. Milo Quaife, 4 vols. (Columbia, TN: James K. Polk Memorial Association, 2005), 3:277.

2. Ibid., 3:329; letters from Manuel G. Zamorg, major of the National Guard of Veracruz, to Andrew Osuguera, Mexican Legation at Paris, Jan. 31, 1847, Zamorg Papers, NYHS; Compton to Palmerston, Jan. 27, 1848, PPBL, 130.

3. G. Loomis to "Charity," New Orleans, Feb. 23, 1848, LSU Special Collections.

4. George Lockhart Rives, *The United States and Mexico, 1821–1848* (New York: Charles Scribner's Sons, 1913), 2:612.

5. Nicholas Trist to Buchanan, Feb. 2, 1848 *DC*, 8:1059.

6. Virginia Trist to Tuckerman, Aug. 23, 1863 (filed with Jul. 8 enclosure), Trist Papers, UNC, Folder 225.

7. Nicholas Trist to Virginia Trist, Feb. 1, 1848. Trist Papers, LC.

8. Polk, *Diary*, 3:345.

9. Ibid., 3:348. The leading scholar of the All Mexico Movement concluded that Trist's treaty "seems to have been an essential factor in preventing the absorption of Mexico." John D. P. Fuller, *The Movement for the Acquisition of All Mexico, 1846–1848* (Baltimore: Johns Hopkins University Press, 1936), 93.

10. Polk, *Diary*, 3:348.

11. Ibid., 3:350.

12. Ibid., 3:356–57.

13. "Mr. Adams, His Funeral," *NYH*, Feb. 26, 1848.

14. Joshua Giddings quote in Eric Foner, *The Fiery Trial: Abraham Lincoln and American Slavery* (New York: Norton, 2010), 58.

15. On racism and expansion, see Eric T. L. Lott, *Race over Empire: Racism and U.S. Imperialism, 1865–1900* (Chapel Hill: University of North Carolina Press, 2004); Paul Kramer, *The Blood of Government: Race, Empire, the United States, and the Philippines* (Chapel Hill: University of North Carolina Press, 2006).

16. Polk, *Diary*, 3:358.

17. George W. Randolph to Virginia Trist, Mar. 9, 1848, Charlottesville, VA, Trist Family Papers, UNC; *CG*, 30th Cong., 1st sess., 1058.

18. "New York, Monday, Nov. 15," *Milwaukee Sentinel and Gazette*, Dec. 1, 1847.

19. Anson G. Henry to Abraham Lincoln, Dec. 29, 1847, ALP.

20. Mark E. Neely, "War and Partisanship: What Lincoln Learned from James K. Polk," *Journal of the Illinois State Historical Society (1908–1984)* 74, no. 3 (Autumn 1981): 199–216.

21. Abraham Lincoln, [Jan.?] 1848 (Notes on What Zachary Taylor Should Say), ALP.

22. Henry S. Foote, *Casket of Reminiscences* (Washington, DC: Chronicle, 1874), 30. For an alternative view of Clay's role in 1850, see Holman Hamilton, "Democratic Senate Leadership and the Compromise of 1850," *Mississippi Valley Historical Review* 41, no. 3 (Dec. 1954): 403–18.

23. Anson and Fanny Nelson, *Memorials of Sarah Childress Polk* (New York: Anson D. F. Randolph, 1892), 136.

24. Nashville *Union*, Apr. 3, 1849; Nelson, *Memorials of Sarah Childress Polk*, 136, 137.

25. Nelson, *Memorials of Sarah Childress Polk*, 199.

26. Clifford D. Bryant, *The Handbook of Death and Dying* (Thousand Oaks, CA: Sage, 2003), 1:545; David A. Clary, *Eagles and Empire: The United States, Mexico, and the Struggle for a Continent* (New York: Bantam, 2009), 131, 412.

27. Ralph Waldo Emerson, *Miscellaneous Notebooks of Ralph Waldo Emerson (1843–1847)*, ed. Ralph Orth and Alfred Ferguson (Cambridge, MA: Harvard University Press, 1971), 9:430–31.

28. Illinois *State Register*, Jun. 23, 1848.

29. Lincoln, *CW*, 2:124.

30. "First Joint Debate, Ottawa, Aug. 21, 1858," *The Lincoln-Douglas Debates of 1858*, ed. Robert W. Johannsen (New York: Oxford University Press, 1965), 42; Joseph Medill to Abraham Lincoln, Jun. 23, 1858 (Senate), ALP.

31. William Honselman to Abraham Lincoln, Oct. 21, 1860, ALP.

32. William H. Wilson to Abraham Lincoln, Oct. 29, 1860, ALP.

EPILOGUE. LINEAGE

1. George Templeton Strong, *The Diary of George Templeton Strong*, ed. Allen Nevins (New York: Macmillan, 1952), 483.

2. Ellen Hardin Walworth, "To the Christian Herald," Jan. 25, 1905, unpublished manuscript, WFP.

3. Ellen Hardin Walworth, "The Battle of Buena Vista," *American Monthly Magazine* IV (Jan. 1894): 124–62.

4. Richard Rush to James K. Polk, Dec. 13, 1846, *Correspondence of James K. Polk*, ed. Herbert Weaver and Wayne Cutler et al., 11 vols. (Knoxville: University of Tennessee Press, 1969–2009), 11:418.

5. John Russell Young, *Around the World with General Grant* (New York: American News, 1879), 2:447–48; Ulysses S. Grant, *Memoirs and Selected Letters: Personal Memoirs of U. S. Grant; Selected Letters, 1839–1865* (New York: Literary Classics of the United States, 1990), 42.

6. Mary S. Lockwood, *Lineage Book of the Charter Members of the Daughters of the American Revolution* (Harrisburg, PA: Harrisburg Publishing, 1895), 1:x.

7. Ibid., 1:xiii.

8. Ellen Hardin Walworth, "Charter Member, Application for Membership #5," Dec. 1890, Manuscript Collection. Daughters of the American Revolution Library, Centennial Hall, Washington, DC.

9. *Report of the Daughters of the American Revolution, 1890–1897*, Senate Doc. 164, 55th Cong., 3rd sess. (Washington, DC: GPO, 1899), 7.

10. Ellen Hardin Walworth, "Charter Member, Application for Membership #5," Dec. 1890, Manuscript Collection. Daughters of the American Revolution Library, Centennial Hall, Washington, DC.

11. Ibid.

12. Lockwood, *Lineage Book,* 1:x.

Bibliography

UNPUBLISHED DOCUMENTS AND MANUSCRIPTS

Abraham Lincoln Presidential Library

James Bearden, letter to Henry E. Dummer, Apr. 10, 1847.

American Antiquarian Society

Anonymous. "Warn the Committee!" 1844.
Cobb, Enos. "Eulogy on Polk and Dallas." Burlington, VT, 1844.

American Broadsides and Ephemera

Anonymous. "Electors of Michigan!" 1844. Series 1, no. 14258.
Anonymous. "Soon to Close! Donnavan's Grand Serial of Panorama of Mexico!" Boston, 1848. Series 1, no. 7208.

Archivo Histórico de la Secretaría de la Defensa de la Nación, Mexico City

Folder XI/481.3.

British Library

Palmerston Papers.

Chicago History Museum

Hardin Family Papers.

Daughters of the American Revolution Library, Centennial Hall, Washington, DC

Ellen Hardin Walworth, "Charter Member, Application for Membership #5." December 1890. Manuscript collection.

Historical Society of Pennsylvania

George Cadwalader Papers.
John Kreitzer Journal, 1846–48.

Huntington Library, San Marino, CA

John Palmer Diary.

Library of Congress, Manuscript Division

Calvin Benjamin Papers.
Abraham Lincoln Papers. Available online at http://memory.loc.gov/ammem/alhtml/
    alhome.html.
James K. Polk Papers, microfilm.
Nicholas P. Trist Papers, microfilm.
William D. Wilkins Papers.
Wotherspoon Family Papers.

Library of Congress, Music Division

Wm. Vanderbeek, "General Taylor's Quick Step." New York, 1846. In "Music for the Nation:
    American Sheet Music, 1820–1860."

Louisiana State University Special Collections

Robert and Sarah Jane Hunter Letters, 1846–47.
G. Loomis letter, 1848.
Moses Smith letter, Feb. 12, 1847.

Massachusetts Historical Society

Winthrop Family Papers, microfilm.
Annie B. Roach diary, Lamb Family Papers.

New-York Historical Society

John M. Brannan Papers.
Massachusetts—General Court—House of Representatives, "Documents Relating to the
    U.S.-Mexican War."
Misc. Mss., C. B. Ogburn.
Manuel G. Zamorg Papers.

Ohio Historical Society

Philemon B. Ewing Papers.
Giddings Papers, microfilm.
Frank A. Hardy Letters.

Santa Barbara Mission Archives

Delfina de la Guerra Collection.

Saratoga Springs History Museum

Walworth Family Archives.

Southern Historical Collection, University of North Carolina Library

Nicholas P. Trist Papers, microfilm.

University of Kentucky Special Collections

Henry Clay Jr. diary, 1840–41, microfilm.

Wisconsin Historical Society

Crooker Family Letters.
Emma Beal Stott Genealogical Items.
Emily Huse letter to Mrs. Olive Washburn, September 1847.

NEWSPAPERS

Age (Augusta, ME)
Albany Evening Journal (New York)
Alexandria Gazette (Virginia)
American Flag (Matamoros, Mexico)
Arkansas Weekly Gazette (Little Rock)
Ashtabula Sentinel (Ohio)
Augusta Chronicle (Georgia)
Baltimore *Sun* (Maryland)
Barre Gazette (Massachusetts)
Berkshire County Whig (Massachusetts)
Boletín de Noticias (Mexico City)
Boston Daily Evening Transcript
Brattleboro Weekly Eagle (Vermont)
Brooklyn Daily Eagle
Cleveland Herald (Ohio)
U.S. Congress, *Congressional Globe*
Daily American Star (Mexico City)
Daily Atlas (Boston)
Daily Sentinel and Gazette (Milwaukee, WI)
Daily National Intelligencer (Washington, DC)
Easton *Gazette* (Maryland)
Emancipator (New York)
Emancipator and Free American (New York)
Flag of Freedom (Puebla, Mexico)
Floridian (Tallahassee)
Frankfort *Commonwealth* (Kentucky)
Free American (Veracruz)
Genius of Liberty (Veracruz)
Hudson River Chronicle (Sing Sing, NY)
Illinois Journal (Springfield)

Illinois *State Register* (Springfield)
Kennebec Journal (Maine)
Liberator (Boston)
Litchfield Republican (Connecticut)
Macon Georgia Telegraph
Maine Cultivator and Hallowell Gazette
Mercury (New Bedford, MA)
Milwaukee Sentinel
Mississippi Free Trader and Natchez Gazette
Mississippian
Morning News (New London, CT)
Nashville Union
National Aegis (Worcester, MA)
New Hampshire Gazette (Portsmouth)
New Hampshire Patriot (Concord)
New Orleans Crescent
New Orleans *Picayune*
New Orleans *Delta*
National Era (Washington, DC)
New York Herald
New York Times
New York Tribune
Niles' Register (Baltimore)
El Norte Americano (Mexico City)
North American (Mexico City)
North American (Philadelphia)
North American and Daily Advertiser (Philadelphia)
North American and United States Gazette (Philadelphia)
Observer (Fayetteville, AR)
Ohio Statesman (Columbus)
People's Advocate and New London County Republican (Connecticut)
Peoria Press (Illinois)
Philadelphia Inquirer
Pittsfield Sun (Massachusetts)
Polynesian (Honolulu)
Public Ledger (Philadelphia)
Raleigh Register, and North-Carolina Gazette
Red Lander (San Augustine, TX)
Republican Farmer (Bridgeport, CT)
Richmond Enquirer (Virginia)
Rockford Forum (Illinois)
Sangamo Journal (Illinois)
Scioto Gazette (Chillicothe, OH)
Sentinel (Keene, NH)
South Carolina Temperance Advocate and Register of Agriculture and General Literature
Southern Patriot (Charleston, SC)
St. Louis Republican
Trenton State Gazette (New Jersey)
Union (Washington, DC)
Vermont Gazette (Bennington)

Vermont Phoenix (Brattleboro)
Wachusetts Star (Massachusetts)
Winyah Observer (Georgetown, SC)

BOOKS

Adams, John Quincy. *Memoirs of John Quincy Adams.* Vol. 12. Ed. Charles Francis Adams. New York, AMS Press, 1970.

Adams, Kevin. *Class and Race in the Frontier Army: Military Life in the West, 1870–1890.* Norman: University of Oklahoma Press, 2009.

Album Pintoresco de la República Méxicana. Mexico: Hallase en la estamperia de Julio Michaud y Thomas, ca. 1848–50.

Alcaraz, Ramón, et al. *The Other Side: or, Notes for the History of the War Between Mexico and the United States.* Trans. Albert C. Ramsey. New York: John Wiley, 1850.

Allen, G. N. *Incidents and Sufferings in the Mexican War, with Accounts of Hardships Endured.* Boston: Lieut. G. N. Allen, 1847.

Allgor, Catherine. *Parlor Politics: In Which the Ladies of Washington Help Build a City and a Government.* Charlottesville: University of Virginia Press, 2000.

Anderson, Fred, and Andrew Cayton. *The Dominion of War: Empire and Liberty in North America, 1500–2000.* New York: Penguin, 2005.

Arnold, Isaac. *The Life of Abraham Lincoln.* Chicago: Jansen, McClurg, 1885.

Averill, Charles. *The Mexican Ranchero; or, The Maid of the Chapparal.* Boston: F. Gleason, 1847.

Baker, Jean H. *Mary Todd Lincoln.* New York: Norton, 1987.

Balbontín, Manuel. *La invasion Americana 1846 á 1848: Apunetes del subteniente de artillería Manuel Balbontín.* Mexico City: Tip. De Gonzalo Esteva, 1883.

Barbour, Philip Norbourne. *Journals of the Late Brevet Major Philip Norbourne Barbour and His Wife Martha Isabella Hopkins Barbour: Written During the War with Mexico—1846.* Ed. Rhoda van Bibber Tanner Doubleday. New York: G. P. Putnam's Sons, 1936.

Barry, James Buckner. *Buck Barry: Texas Ranger and Frontiersman.* Ed. James K. Greer. Lincoln: University of Nebraska Press, 1978.

Bauer, K. Jack. *The Mexican War: 1846–1848.* New York: Macmillan, 1974.

———. *Zachary Taylor: Soldier, Planter, Statesman of the Old Southwest.* Baton Rouge: Louisiana State University Press, 1985.

Baxter, Maurice. *Henry Clay and the American System.* Lexington: University Press of Kentucky, 1995.

Baylies, Francis. *A Narrative of Major General Wool's Campaign in Mexico: In the Years 1846, 1847 & 1848.* Albany: Little, 1851.

Belohlavek, John M. *George Mifflin Dallas: Jacksonian Patrician.* State College: Pennsylvania State University Press, 1977.

Benson, Lee. *The Concept of Jacksonian Democracy: New York as a Test Case.* New York: Atheneum, 1969.

Benton, Thomas Hart. *Thirty Years' View; or, A History of the Working of the American Government for Thirty Years, from 1820–1850.* Vol. 2. New York: D. Appleton, 1873.

Bercovitch, Sacvan, ed. *The Cambridge History of American Literature.* Vol. 2. Cambridge: Cambridge University Press. 1995.

Bergeron, Paul H. *The Presidency of James K. Polk.* Lawrence: University of Kansas Press, 1987.

Beveridge, Albert Jeremiah. *Abraham Lincoln, 1809–1865.* Vol. 1. New York: Houghton Mifflin, 1927.

Boritt, G. S. *Lincoln and the Economics of the American Dream*. Memphis: Memphis State University Press, 1978.

Brack, George. *Mexico Views Manifest Destiny, 1821–1846: An Essay on the Origins of the Mexican War*. Albuquerque: University of New Mexico Press. 1975.

Bryant, Clifton D. *The Handbook of Death and Dying*. Vol. 1. Thousand Oaks, CA: Sage, 2003.

Buchanan, James. *Works of James Buchanan*. Ed. John Bassett Moore. Philadelphia: J. B. Lippincott, 1909.

Buel, Richard. *America on the Brink: How the Political Struggle over the War of 1812 Almost Destroyed the Young Republic*. New York: Palgrave Macmillan, 2006.

Buell, Augustus C. *History of Andrew Jackson, Pioneer, Patriot, Soldier, Politician, President*. New York: Charles Scribner, 1904.

Bumgarner, John Reed. *Sarah Childress Polk: A Biography of the Remarkable First Lady*. Jefferson, NC: McFarland, 1997.

Burstein, Andrew. *The Passions of Andrew Jackson*. New York: Knopf, 2003.

Bustamante, Carlos María de. *El Nuevo bernal díaz del Castillo*. Mexico City: Imprenta de Vicente García Torres, 1847.

Calhoun, John Caldwell. *Papers of John C. Calhoun*. Ed. Robert Lee Meriwether, Clyde Norman Wilson, William Edwin Hemphill, and Shirley Bright Cook. Columbia: University of South Carolina Press, 1996.

Camarillo, Albert. *Chicanos in a Changing Society: From Mexican Pueblos to American Barrios in Santa Barbara and Southern California, 1848–1930*. Cambridge, MA: Harvard University Press, 1979.

Cantrell, Gregg. *Stephen F. Austin: Empresario of Texas*. New Haven, CT: Yale University Press, 2001.

A Captain of the Volunteers. *Alta California: Embracing Notices of the Climate, Soil, and Agricultural Products of Northern Mexico and the Pacific Seaboard: Also a History of the Military and Naval Operations of the United States Directed Against the Territories of Northern Mexico, in the Year 1846–47*. Philadelphia: H. Packer, 1847.

Cayton, Andrew R. L. *Frontier Indiana*. Bloomington: Indiana University Press, 1996.

Chamberlain, Samuel E. *My Confession: Recollections of a Rogue*. Ed. William H. Goetzmann. Austin: Texas State Historical Association, 1996.

Chance, Joseph E. *Jefferson Davis's Mexican War Regiment*. Jackson: University of Mississippi Press, 1991.

Claiborne, John F. H. *Life and Correspondence of John A. Quitman*. 2 vols. New York: Harper and Bros., 1860.

Clary, David A. *Eagles and Empire: The United States, Mexico, and the Struggle for a Continent*. New York: Bantam, 2009.

Clay, Henry. *The Papers of Henry Clay*. Ed. James F. Hopkins, Mary W. M. Hargreaves, et al. 11 vols. Lexington: University Press of Kentucky, 1959–92.

Cleves, Rachel Hope. *The Reign of Terror in America: Visions of Violence from Anti-Jacobinism to Antislavery*. New York: Cambridge University Press, 2009.

Clough, Martha A. *Zuleika: or the Castilian Captive*. Boston: F. Gleason, 1849.

Coffman, Edward M. *The Old Army: A Portrait of the American Army in Pecetime, 1784–1898*. New York: Oxford University Press, 1986.

Coleman, J. Winston, Jr. *Stage-Coach Days in the Bluegrass*. Lexington: University Press of Kentucky, 1995.

Crapol, Edward P. *John Tyler: The Accidental President*. Chapel Hill: University of North Carolina Press, 2006.

Curtis, Newton. *The Hunted Chief: or Female Ranchero: A Tale of the Mexican War*. New York: W. F. Burgess, 1847.

Davis, George Turnbull Moore. *Autobiography of the Late Col. Geo. T. M. Davis: Captain and Aid-de-Camp Scott's Army of Invasion*. New York: Jenkins and McCowan, 1891.

DeLay, Brian. *War of a Thousand Deserts: Indian Raids and the U.S.-Mexican War*. New Haven, CT: Yale University Press, 2008.

Dollar, Kent T. *Soldiers of the Cross: Confederate Soldier-Christians and the Impact of the War on Their Faith*. Macon, GA: Mercer University Press, 2005.

Donald, David Herbert. *Lincoln*. New York: Simon & Schuster, 1995.

Douglas, Stephen A. *Letters of Stephen A. Douglas*. Ed. Robert Johannsen. Urbana: University of Illinois Press, 1961.

Dusinberre, William. *Slavemaster President: The Double Career of James K. Polk*. New York: Oxford University Press, 2007.

Eames, Charles M. *Historic Morgan and Classic Jacksonville*. Jacksonville, IL: Daily Journal Steam Job Printing Office, 1885.

Earle, Jonathan H. *Jacksonian Antislavery and the Politics of Free Soil, 1824–1854*. Chapel Hill: University of North Carolina Press, 2003.

Eaton, Clement. *Henry Clay and the Art of American Politics*. Boston: Little, Brown, 1957.

Eisenhower, John D. *So Far from God: The U.S. War with Mexico, 1846–1848*. Norman: University of Oklahoma Press, 2000.

Ellet, Elizabeth Fries Lumis. *The Court Circles of the Republic*. Philadelphia: Philadelphia Publishing, 1872.

Ellis, George E. *Letters upon the Annexation of Texas. Addressed to Hon. John Quincy Adams*. Boston: White, Lewis, and Potter, 1845.

Emerson, Ralph Waldo. *Miscellaneous Notebooks of Ralph Waldo Emerson*. Vol. 9. Ed. Ralph Orth and Alfred Ferguson. Cambridge, MA: Harvard University Press, 1971.

Eubank, Damon. *The Response of Kentucky to the Mexican War, 1846–1848*. Lewiston, NY: Edwin Mellen Press, 2004.

Fehrenbacher, Don E. *Prelude to Greatness: Lincoln in the 1850s*. Palo Alto, CA: Stanford University Press, 1962.

Feldberg, Michael. *The Turbulent Era: Riot and Disorder in Jacksonian America*. New York: Oxford University Press, 1980.

Foner, Eric. *The Fiery Trial: Abraham Lincoln and American Slavery*. New York: Norton, 2010.

Foos, Paul. *A Short, Offhand, Killing Affair: Soldiers and Social Conflict During the Mexican-American War*. Chapel Hill: University of North Carolina Press, 2002.

Foote, Henry S. *Casket of Reminiscences*. Washington, DC: Chronicle, 1874.

Fowler, Will. *Santa Anna of Mexico*. Lincoln: University of Nebraska Press, 2007.

Frost, John. *The Life of Major-General Zachary Taylor*. New York: G. S. Appleton, 1847.

———. *Pictorial History of Mexico and the Mexican War: Comprising an Account of the Ancient Aztec Empire, the Conquest by Cortes, Mexico Under the Spaniards, the Mexican Revolution, the Republic, the Texan War, and the Recent War with the United States*. Philadelphia: Charles De Silver, 1871.

Fuller, John D. P. *The Movement for the Acquisition of All Mexico, 1846–1848*. Baltimore: Johns Hopkins University Press, 1936.

Gerhard, Frederick. *Illinois as It Is*. Chicago: Keen and Lee, 1857.

Gienapp, William E. *Abraham Lincoln and Civil War America, A Biography*. New York: Oxford University Press, 2002.

Grant, Ulysses S. *Memoirs and Selected Letters: Personal Memoirs of U.S. Grant; Selected Letters 1839–1865*. New York: Literary Classics of the United States, 1990.

———. *Papers of Ulysses S. Grant*. Ed. John Y. Simon. Carbondale: Southern Illinois University Press, 1967.

Gratz, Rebecca. *Letters of Rebecca Gratz*. Ed. David Philipson. Philadelphia: Jewish Publication Society of America, 1929.

Greenberg, Amy S. *Cause for Alarm: The Volunteer Fire Department in the Nineteenth Century*. Princeton, NJ: Princeton University Press, 1998.

———. *Manifest Destiny and American Territorial Expansion: A Brief History with Documents*. Boston: Bedford/St. Martin's, 2012.

———. *Manifest Manhood and the Antebellum American Empire*. New York: Cambridge University Press, 2005.

Groom, Winston. *Kearny's March: The Epic Creation of the American West, 1846–1847*. New York: Knopf, 2011.

Hale, Albert. *Two Discourses on the Subject of the War Between the U. States and Mexico*. Springfield, IL: *Sangamo Journal*, 1847.

Hall, Claude H. *Abel Parker Upshur*. Madison: State Historical Society of Wisconsin, 1964.

Handbook of Texas Online. Texas State Historical Association. Available at www.tshaonline.org.

Hardin, John J. *Speech of Mr. J. J. Hardin, of Illinois Reviewing the Principles of James K. Polk and the Leaders of Modern Democracy*. Washington, DC: J. and G. S. Gideon, 1844.

Haynes, Sam W. *James K. Polk and the Expansionist Impulse*. New York: Longman, 2002.

———. *Unfinished Revolution: The Early American Republic in a British World*. Charlottesville: University of Virginia Press, 2010.

Heidler, David S., and Jeanne T. Heidler. *Henry Clay: The Essential American*. New York: Random House, 2010.

Henderson, Timothy J. *A Glorious Defeat: Mexico and Its War with the United States*. New York: Hill and Wang, 2007.

Henshaw, John C. *Recollections of the War with Mexico*. Ed. Gary F. Kurutz. Columbia: University of Missouri Press, 2008.

Herndon, William H., and Jesse W. Weik. *Abraham Lincoln: The True Story of a Great Life*. New York: Appleton, 1892.

Hickey, Donald R. *The War of 1812: A Forgotten Conflict*. Urbana: University of Illinois Press, 1989.

Hickey, John. *The Democratic Lute, and Minstrel: Comprising a Great Number of Patriotic, Sentimental, and Comic Political Songs and Duetts: Entirely Original*. Philadelphia: H. B. Pierson, 1844.

Hickman, George H. *The Life and Public Services of the Hon. James Knox Polk: With a Compendium of His Speeches on Various Public Measures, Also a Sketch of the Life of the Hon. George Mifflin Dallas*. Baltimore: N. Hickman, 1844.

Hietala, Thomas R. *Manifest Design: Anxious Aggrandizement in Late Jacksonian America*. Ithaca, NY: Cornell University Press, 1985.

History of Sangamon County, Illinois: Together with Sketches of Its Cities, Villages, and Townships. Chicago: Interstate, 1881.

Hitchcock, Ethan Allen. *Fifty Years in Camp and Field*. Ed. W. A. Croffut. New York: Putnam, 1909.

Hone, Philip. *Diary of Philip Hone, 1828–1851*. Vol. 2. New York: Dodd, Mead, 1889.

Howe, Daniel Walker. *The Political Culture of the American Whigs*. Chicago: University of Chicago Press, 1979.

———. *What Hath God Wrought: The Transformation of America, 1815–1845*. New York: Oxford University Press, 2007.

Ignatiev, Noel. *How the Irish Became White*. New York: Routledge, 1996.

Illinois Constitutional Convention. *Constitution of the State of Illinois*. Springfield: Lanphier and Walker, 1847.

Irelan, John Robert. *The Republic, or the History of the United States of America.* Chicago: Fairbanks and Palmer, 1888.

Jackson, Andrew. *Correspondence of Andrew Jackson.* Vols. 1–7. Ed. John Spencer Bassett and David Maydole Matteson. Washington, DC: Carnegie Institute, 1926–35.

———. *The Papers of Andrew Jackson.* Vol. 7. Ed. Daniel Feller, Harold D. Moser, Laura-Eve Moss, and Thomas Coens. Knoxville: University of Tennessee Press, 2007.

Johannsen, Robert W., ed. *The Lincoln-Douglas Debates of 1858.* New York: Oxford University Press, 1965.

Jones, Robert Ralston. *Fort Washington at Cincinnati, Ohio.* Cincinnati: Society of Colonial Wars in the State of Ohio, 1902.

Kane, John K. *Autobiography of the Honorable John K. Kane, 1795–1858.* Philadelphia: College Offset Press, 1949.

King, Willard L. *Lincoln's Manager, David Davis.* Cambridge, MA: Harvard University Press, 1960.

Koerner, Gustave. *Memoirs of Gustave Koerner, 1809–1896.* Ed. Thomas J. McCormack. Cedar Rapids, IA: Torch Press, 1909.

Kramer, Paul. *The Blood of Government: Race, Empire, the United States, and the Philippines.* Chapel Hill: University of North Carolina Press, 2006.

Lander, Ernest McPherson Jr. *Reluctant Imperialists: Calhoun, the South Carolinians, and the Mexican War.* Baton Rouge: Louisiana State University Press, 1980.

Levinson, Irving W. *Wars Within War: Mexican Guerrillas, Domestic Elites, and the United States of America, 1846–1848.* Fort Worth, TX: TCU Press, 2005.

Lewis, Felice Flanery. *Trailing Clouds of Glory: Zachary Taylor's Mexican War Campaign and His Emerging Civil War Leaders.* Tuscaloosa: University of Alabama Press, 2010.

Lincoln, Abraham. *Collected Works of Abraham Lincoln.* Ed. Roy P. Balser et al. New Brunswick, NJ: Rutgers University Press.

Littell, John S. *The Clay Minstrel, or National Songster.* 2nd ed. New York: Greeley and McElrath, 1844.

Lockwood, Mary S. *Lineage Book of the Charter Members of the Daughters of the American Revolution.* Vol. 1. Harrisburg, PA: Harrisburg Publishing, 1895.

Love, Eric T. L. *Race over Empire: Racism and U.S. Imperialism, 1865–1900.* Chapel Hill: University of North Carolina Press, 2004.

Lundy, Benjamin [Citizen of the United States]. *The War in Texas; A Review of Facts and Circumstances, Showing That This Contest Is a Crusade Against Mexico, Set on Foot by Slaveholders, Land Speculators, & c. in Order to Re-establish, Extend, and Perpetuate the System of Slavery and the Slave Trade.* 2nd ed. Philadelphia: Merrihew and Gunn, 1837.

Mahin, Dean B. *Olive Branch and Sword: The United States and Mexico, 1845–1848.* Jefferson, NC: McFarland, 1997.

Manning, William R., ed. *Diplomatic Correspondence of the United States, Inter-American Affairs, 1831–1860.* 8 vols. Washington, DC: Carnegie Endowment for International Peace, 1938.

Márquez, Jesús Velasco. *La Guerra del '47 y la opinión pública (1845–1848).* New York: Cambridge University Press, [1975] 2005.

Martineau, Harriet. *Retrospect of Western Travel.* New York: Charles Lohman, 1838.

McCaffrey, James M. *Army of Manifest Destiny: The American Soldier in the Mexican War, 1846–1848.* New York: New York University Press, 1992.

McCormac, Eugene Irving. *James K. Polk, a Political Biography.* Berkeley: University of California Press, 1922.

McPherson, James M. *Battle Cry of Freedom: The Civil War Era.* New York. Oxford University Press, 1988.

Meacham, Jon. *American Lion: Andrew Jackson in the White House.* New York: Random House, 2008.

Merry, Robert W. *A Country of Vast Designs: James K. Polk, the Mexican War and the Conquest of the American Continent.* New York: Simon & Schuster, 2009.

Messages of the President of the United States, Therewith Communicated, Between the Secretary of War and Other Officers of the Government, on the Subject of the Mexican War. House Executive Documents, 30th Cong. 1st sess., no. 60. Washington: Wendell and Van Benthuysen, 1848.

Miers, Earl Schenck, ed. *Lincoln Day by Day: A Chronology, 1809–1865.* Washington, DC: Lincoln Sesquicentennial Commission, 1960.

Milburn, William Henry. *The Lance, Cross and Canoe; The Flatboat, Rifle and Plough in the Valley of the Mississippi.* New York: N. D. Thompson, 1892.

Miller, Richard Lawrence. *Lincoln and His World: Prairie Politician.* Mechanicsburg, PA: Stackpole Books, 2008.

Miller, Robert Ryal. *Shamrock and Sword: The Saint Patrick's Battalion in the U.S.-Mexican War.* Norman: University of Oklahoma Press, 1989.

Morrison, Michael A. *Slavery and the American West: The Eclipse of Manifest Destiny and the Coming of the Civil War.* Chapel Hill: University of North Carolina Press, 1997.

Murphy to Jones, Feb. 14, 1844. Senate Documents. 28th Congress, 1st sess. (ser. 435), no. 349.

Neely, Mark E., Jr. *The Civil War and the Limits of Destruction.* Cambridge, MA: Harvard University Press, 2007.

Nell, William Cooper. *The Colored Patriots of the American Revolution: With Sketches of Several Distinguished Colored Persons.* Boston: Robert F. Wallcut, 1855.

Nelson, Anson, and Fanny Nelson. *Memorials of Sarah Childress Polk.* New York: Anson D. F. Randolph, 1892.

O'Brien, Geoffrey. *The Fall of the House of Walworth: A Tale of Madness and Murder in Gilded Age America.* New York: Henry Holt, 2010.

Obsequies of Col. John J. Hardin at Jacksonville, Illinois, Jul. 14, 1847. Jacksonville, IL: Morgan Journal, 1847.

Ohrt, Wallace. *Defiant Peacemaker: Nicholas Trist in the Mexican War.* College Station: Texas A&M Press, 1997.

Olmsted, Frederick Law. *A Journey Through Texas, or a Saddle-Trip on the Southwestern Frontier.* Ed. Witold Rybczynski. Lincoln: University of Nebraska Press, 2004.

Oswandel, John Jacob. *Notes of the Mexican War, 1846–47–48.* Philadelphia: N.p., 1885.

Parton, James. *Life of Andrew Jackson.* New York: Mason Brothers, 1860.

Pasley, Jeffrey L. *"The Tyranny of Printers": Newspaper Politics in the Early American Republic.* Charlottesville: University of Virginia Press, 2001.

Perrin, William Henry, J. H. Battle, and G. C. Kniffin. *Kentucky: A History of the State.* 7th ed. Louisville, KY: F. A. Battey, 1887.

Peterson, Merrill D. *The Great Triumvirate: Webster, Clay, and Calhoun.* New York: Oxford University Press 1987

Peyton, Jesse E. *Reminiscences of the Past.* Philadelphia: J. B. Lippincott, 1895.

Philipson, David. *Letters of Rebecca Gratz.* Philadelphia: Jewish Publication Society of America, 1929.

Pletcher, David M. *The Diplomacy of Annexation: Texas, Oregon, and the Mexican War.* Columbia: University of Missouri Press, 1975.

Polk, James K. *Correspondence of James K. Polk.* Ed. Herbert Weaver and Wayne Cutler et al. 11 vols. Knoxville: University of Tennessee Press, 1969–2009.

———. *Diary of a President: James K. Polk*. Ed. Milo Quaife. 4 vols. Columbia, TN: James K. Polk Memorial Association, 2005.

Poore, Ben Perley. *Perley's Reminiscences of Sixty Years in the National Metropolis*. Tecumseh, MI: A. W. Mills, 1886.

Pratt, Harry E., ed. *Illinois as Lincoln Knew It: A Boston Reporter's Record of a Trip in 1847*. Springfield, IL: Abraham Lincoln Association, 1938.

Price, Glenn W. *Origins of the War with Mexico: The Polk-Stockton Intrigue*. Austin: University of Texas Press, 1967.

Prieto, Guillermo. *Memorias de mis tiempos*. Paris: Librería de la Vda. de C. Bouret, 1906.

Pubols, Louise. *The Father of All: The de la Guerra Family, Power, and Patriarchy in Mexican California*. Berkeley: University of California Press, 2009.

Reid, Samuel C. *The Scouting Expeditions of McCulloch's Texas Rangers*. Freeport, NY: Books for Libraries Press, [1847] 1970.

Reilly, Tom. *War with Mexico! America's Reporters Cover the Battlefront*. Ed. Manley Witten. Lawrence: University of Kansas Press., 2010.

Remini, Robert Vincent. *Henry Clay: Statesman for the Union*. New York: Norton, 1991.

———. *John Quincy Adams*. New York: Henry Holt, 2002.

Report of the Daughters of the American Revolution, 1890–1897. Senate Doc. 164, 55th Congress, 3rd sess. Washington, DC: GPO, 1899.

Reséndez, Andrés. *Changing National Identities on the Frontier: Texas and New Mexico, 1800–1850*. New York: Cambridge University Press, 1995.

Resch, John Phillips. *Suffering Soldiers: Revolutionary War Veterans, Moral Sentiment, and Political Culture in the Early Republic*. Amherst: University of Massachusetts Press, 1999.

Richardson, James D., ed. *A Compilation of the Messages and Papers of the Presidents*. Washington, DC: GPO, 1901.

Riddle, Donald W. *Congressman Abraham Lincoln*. Urbana: University of Illinois Press, 1957.

Rives, George Lockhart. *The United States and Mexico, 1821–1848*. New York: Charles Scribner's Sons, 1913.

Robertson, John Blout. *Reminiscences of a Campaign in Mexico: By a Member of the Blood-First*. Nashville: John York, 1949.

Rockman, Seth. *Scraping By: Wage Labor, Slavery, and Survival in Early Baltimore*. Baltimore: Johns Hopkins University Press, 2008.

Rodríguez, Jaime Javier. *The Literatures of the U.S.-Mexican War: Narrative, Time, and Identity*. Austin: University of Texas Press, 2010.

Rogers, Joseph M. *The True Henry Clay*. Philadelphia: J. B. Lippincott, 1904.

Russell, Philip L. *The History of Mexico from Pre-Conquest to Present*. New York: Routledge, 2010.

Sandweiss, Martha A., Rick Stewart, and Ben W. Huseman. *Eyewitness to War: Prints and Daguerreotypes of the Mexican War, 1846–1848*. Fort Worth, TX: Amon Carter Museum, 1989.

Sargent, Nathan. *Public Men and Events, from the Commencement of Mr. Monroe's Administration, in 1817, to the Close of Mr. Fillmore's Administration in 1853*. Vol. 2. Philadelphia: J. P. Lippincott, 1875.

Schroeder, John H. *Mr. Polk's War: American Opposition and Dissent, 1846–1848*. Madison: University of Wisconsin Press, 1973.

Scott, Winfield. *Memoirs of Lieutenant-General Scott*. Vol. 2. New York: Sheldon, 1864.

Seager, Robert II. *And Tyler Too: A Biography of John and Julia Gardiner Tyler*. New York: McGraw-Hill, 1963.

Sears, Louis Martin. *John Slidell*. Durham, NC: Duke University Press, 1925.

Sellers, Charles. *James K. Polk: Continentalist, 1843–1846*. Vol. 2. Princeton, NJ: Princeton University Press, 1966.

———. *James K. Polk: Jacksonian, 1795–1843*. Vol. 1. Princeton, NJ: Princeton University Press, 1957.

Shattuck, Charles H. *Shakespeare on the American Stage: From the Hallams to Edwin Booth*. Washington, DC: Folger Shakespeare Library, 1976.

Singletary, Otis A. *The Mexican War*. Chicago: University of Chicago Press, 1960.

Smith, Ephraim Kirby. *To Mexico with Scott: Letters of Captain E. Kirby Smith to His Wife*. Cambridge, MA: Harvard University Press, 1917.

Sparks, Edwin Erle, ed. *The Lincoln-Douglas Debates*. Dansville, NY: F. A. Owen, 1918.

Streeby, Shelley. *American Sensations: Class, Empire, and the Production of Popular Culture*. Berkeley: University of California Press, 2002.

Strong, George Templeton. *The Diary of George Templeton Strong*. Ed. Allen Nevins. New York: Macmillan, 1952.

Swisshelm, Jane Grey. *Half a Century*. Chicago: Jansen, McClurg, 1880.

Taylor, Quintard. *In Search of the Racial Frontier: African Americans in the American West, 1528–1990*. New York: Norton, 1998.

Taylor, Zachary. *Letters of Zachary Taylor from the Battlefield of the Mexican War*. Ed. William H. Swanson. Rochester, NY: Genesee Press, 1908.

Tennery, Thomas D. *The Mexican War Diary of Thomas D. Tennary*. Ed. D. E. Livingston-Little. Norman: University of Oklahoma Press, 1970.

Thoreau, Henry David. *Walden and Civil Disobedience*. Ed. Jonathan Levin. New York: Barnes and Noble Books, 2003.

Thorndike, Rachel Sherman, ed. *The Sherman Letters*. New York: Charles Scribner's Sons, 1894.

Thorpe, Thomas Bangs. *Our Army at Monterey*. Philadelphia: Cary and Hart, 1847.

Townsend, William H. *Lincoln and His Wife's Home Town*. Indianapolis: Bobbs Merrill, 1929.

U.S. Department of Veterans Affairs. Office of Public Affairs. *America's Wars Fact Sheet*. Washington, DC: GPO, 2007.

Van Deusen, Glyndon G. *The Life of Henry Clay*. Boston: Little, Brown, 1937.

Varon, Elizabeth R. *We Mean to Be Counted: White Women and Politics in Antebellum Virginia*. Chapel Hill: University of North Carolina Press, 1998.

von Grone, Carl. *Briefe über Nord-Amerika und Mexiko und den zwischen beiden gerührten krieg*. Braunschweig: Druck von G. Westermann, 1850.

Wilkes, Lieutenant Charles. *Narrative of the United States Exploring Expedition During the Years 1838, 1839, 1840, 1841, 1842*. Vol. 5. Philadelphia: Lea and Blanchard, 1845.

Wilson, Douglas L., and Rodney O. Davis, eds. *Herndon's Informants: Letters, Interviews, and Statements About Abraham Lincoln*. Urbana: University of Illinois Press, 1989.

Winthrop, Robert C. Jr. *A Memoir of Robert C. Winthrop*. Boston: Little, Brown, 1897.

Wise, Henry Alexander. *Seven Decades of the Union: The Humanities and Materialism*. Philadelphia: Lippincott, 1876.

Young, John Russell. *Around the World with General Grant*. New York: American News Company, 1879.

Zboray, Ronald J., and Mary Saracino Zboray. *Voices Without Votes: Women and Politics in Antebellum New England*. Durham: University of New Hampshire Press, 2010.

Ziegler, Valarie, H. *The Advocates of Peace in Antebellum America*. Bloomington: Indiana University Press, 1992.

Zirckel, Otto. *Tagebuch geschrieben während der nordamerikanisch-mexikanischen Campagne in den Jahren 1847 und 1848 auf beiden Operationslinien*. Halle: H. W. Schmidt, 1849.

DISSERTATIONS AND THESES

Cox, Nancy L. "A Life of John Hardin of Illinois, 1810–1847." M.A. thesis. Miami University, Oxford, OH, 1964.

Johnson, Tyler V. " 'That Spirit of Chivalry': Tennessee and Indiana Volunteers in the Mexican War." M.A. thesis. University of Tennessee at Knoxville, 2003.

McCartney, Samuel Bigger. "Illinois in the Mexican War." M.A. thesis. Northwestern University, Evanston, IL, 1939.

Reilly, Thomas William. "American Reporters and the Mexican War 1846–1848." 2 vols. Ph.D. dissertation. University of Minnesota, 1975.

Yoder, Randy L. "Rackensackers and Rangers: Brutality in the Conquest of Northern Mexico, 1846–1848." M.A. thesis. Oklahoma State University, 2006.

JOURNAL ARTICLES

Boritt, Gabor S. "A Question of Political Suicide? Lincoln's Opposition to the Mexican War." *Journal of the Illinois State Historical Society* 67 (Feb. 1974): 79–100.

Clay, H., and Richard L. Troutman. "The Emancipation of Slaves by Henry Clay." *Journal of Negro History* 40, no. 2 (Apr. 1955): 179–81.

Feller, Daniel. "A Brother in Arms: Benjamin Tappan and the Antislavery Democracy." *Journal of American History* 88, no. 1 (2001): 48–74.

Finkelman, Paul. "Evading the Ordinance: The Persistence of Bondage in Indiana and Illinois." *Journal of the Early Republic* 9 (Spring 1989): 35–48.

Hamilton, Holman. "Democratic Senate Leadership and the Compromise of 1850." *Mississippi Valley Historical Review* 41, no. 3 (Dec. 1954): 403–18.

Heinl, Frank J. "Jacksonville and Morgan County: An Historical Review." *Journal of the Illinois State Historical Society* 18, no. 1 (Apr. 1925): 5–38.

Hospodor, Gregory S. " 'Bound by All the Ties of Honor': Southern Honor, the Mississippians, and the Mexican War." *Journal of Mississippi History* 61 (Spring 1999): 1–28.

Ikard, Robert W. "Surgical Operation on James K. Polk by Ephraim McDowell or the Search for Polk's Gallstone." *Tennessee Historical Quarterly* 43, no. 3 (1984): 121–31.

Johnson, Tyler V. " 'To Take up Arms Against Brethren of the Same Faith': Lower Midwestern Catholic Volunteers in the Mexican-American War." *Armed Forces and Society* 32, no. 4 (Jul. 2006).

Kirkland, Caroline, ed. "Dying Moments of Lieut. Col. Henry Clay Jr." *Union Magazine of Literature and Art* I (Jul. 1847): 44.

Lack, Paul. "Slavery and the Texas Revolution." *Southwestern Historical Quarterly* 89 (1985): 181–202.

McDowell, Madeleine. "Recollections of Henry Clay." *Century Magazine*, May 1895, 765–70.

Merk, Frederick. "Dissent in the Mexican War." *Proceedings of the Massachusetts Historical Society*, 3rd ser., 81 (1969): 120–36.

Neely, Mark E., Jr. "Lincoln and the Mexican War: An Argument by Analogy." *Civil War History* 24 (Mar. 1978): 5–24.

———. "War and Partisanship: What Lincoln Learned from James K. Polk." *Journal of the Illinois State Historical Society* 74, no. 3 (Aug. 1981): 199–216.

Nortrup, Jack. "Nicholas Trist's Mission to Mexico: A Reinterpretation." *Southwestern Historical Quarterly* 71, no. 3 (1968): 321–46.

Pinheiro, John C. "Extending the Light and Blessings of Our Purer Faith: Anti-Catholic Sentiment Among American Soldiers in the U.S.-Mexican War." *Journal of Popular Culture* 35 (Oct. 2001): 129–52.

Polk, James K. "Letters of James K. Polk to Cave Johnson, 1833–1848." *Tennessee Historical Magazine* 1 (Sep. 1915): 209–56.

Schmidt, Leigh Eric. "The Fashioning of a Modern Holiday: St. Valentine's Day, 1840–1870." *Winterthur Portfolio* 28, no. 4 (Winter 1993): 209–45.

Sioussat, St. George. "The Mexican War Letter of Col. William Bowen Campbell, of Tennessee. Written to Governor David Campbell, of Virginia, 1846–1847." *Tennessee Historical Magazine* 1 (Mar. 1915): 129–67.

Stenberg, Richard R. "President Polk and California: Additional Documents." *Pacific Historical Review* 10 (1941): 217–19.

Upshur, A. P. "Letter of A. P. Upshur to J. C. Calhoun." *William and Mary Quarterly*, 2nd ser., 16, no. 4 (Oct. 1936): 554–57.

Volpe, Vernon L. "The Liberty Party and Polk's Election, 1844." *Historian* 23 (Jan. 1991): 691–710.

Walworth, Ellen Hardin. "The Battle of Buena Vista." *American Monthly Magazine* IV (Jan. 1894): 124–62.

———. "Mrs. Ellen Hardin Walworth." *American Monthly Magazine* III (Jul. 1893): 42–49.

Walworth, Mansfield Tracy. "Colonel John Hardin." *Historical Magazine and Notes and Queries Concerning the Antiquities*, 2nd ser., 5 (1869): 233–37.

Winston, James E. "The Annexation of Texas and the Mississippi Democrats." *Southwestern Historical Review* 25, no. 1 (1921): 1–25.

ARTICLES IN BOOKS

Boucher, Chauncey S., and Robert P. Brooks, eds. "Correspondence Addressed to John C. Calhoun 1837–1849." In *Annual Report of the American Historical Association for the Year 1919*. Washington, DC: GPO, 1930.

LeVert, Octavia Walton. "A Tribute to Henry Clay." In Edwin Anderson Alderman, Joel Chandler Harris, and Charles William Kent, eds., *Library of Southern Literature*. New Orleans: Martin and Hoyt, 1907.

Lofarro, Michael A. "David Crockett." In Caroll Van West, ed., *The Tennessee Encyclopedia of History and Culture*. Nashville: Tennessee Historical Society, 1998.

May, Robert E. "Invisible Men: Blacks and the U.S. Army in the Mexican War." In Darlene Clark Hine, ed., *A Question of Manhood: A Reader in U.S. Black Men's History and Masculinity*. Bloomington: Indiana University Press, 1999.

Tyler, John. "The Dead of the Cabinet." In Lyon Tyler, ed., *The Letters and Times of the Tylers*. Richmond: Whittet and Shepperson, 1885.

Index

Page numbers in *italics* refer to illustrations.